JUDGING BERTHA WILSON:
LAW AS LARGE AS LIFE

PATRONS OF THE SOCIETY

The Osgoode Society is supported by a grant from
The Law Foundation of Ontario

THE LAW
FOUNDATION
OF ONTARIO

The Society also thanks The Law Society of Upper Canada
for its continuing support.

JUDGING BERTHA WILSON

Law as Large as Life

ELLEN ANDERSON

Published for The Osgoode Society for Canadian Legal History by

University of Toronto Press

Toronto Buffalo London

Printed in Canada

ISBN 0–8020–3648–1

Printed on acid-free paper

Portrait of the Honourable Bertha Wilson, 1999, by Mary Lennox Hourd. Oil on canvas, 114.38 cm × 94 cm. Commissioned by Osler, Hoskin & Harcourt and donated to the Supreme Court of Canada. By permission of Osler, Hoskin & Harcourt.

National Library of Canada Cataloguing in Publication Data

Anderson, Ellen Mary
Judging Bertha Wilson : law as large as life

(Osgoode Society for Canadian Legal History series)
Includes bibliographical references and index.
ISBN 0-8020-3648-1

1. Wilson, Bertha   2. Canada – Supreme Court – Biography.
3. Women judges – Canada – Biography.   I. Osgoode Society for
Canadian Legal History.   II. Title.   III. Series.

KE8248.W54A54 2001   347.71′035′092   C2001-901095-8

University of Toronto Press acknowledges the financial assistance to its publishing program of the Canada Council for the Arts and the Ontario Arts Council.

University of Toronto Press acknowledges the financial support for its publishing activities of the Government of Canada through the Book Publishing Industry Development Program (BPIDP).

Contents

Contents vii

PART THREE
Life after Judging

Foreword

THE OSGOODE SOCIETY

As a book about the first woman to be appointed to the Ontario Court of Appeal and to the Supreme Court of Canada, this biography of Bertha Wilson will have an inherent interest to many readers. Its importance also derives in large measure from the fact that she joined the Supreme Court at that critical moment when the Charter was entrenched and, as Ellen Anderson demonstrates, she played a large role in setting the course for Charter interpretation.

To those who appreciate good biography, much of the interest in this book derives from Ellen Anderson's account of the early life in Scotland of Bertha and her husband John, a Presbyterian minister, of their decision to migrate to Canada, and then, some time later, of Bertha Wilson's decision to study law as a mature student and of its impact on her mind and spirit. For those interested in gender relationships, both within the intimacy of the family and in the practice of law in a large Toronto law firm, this book must hold a special appeal, and it offers not a few surprises.

Ellen Anderson, who practises law in Stroud, Ontario, makes no secret of the fact that she is an admirer of Bertha Wilson, and some may feel that her closeness to her subject creates difficulties. But what has been gained in the research and writing of this biography from the closeness and mutual confidence between Ellen Anderson and Bertha and John Wilson has been enormous, and the reader benefits on almost every page.

The Osgoode Society wishes to thank most warmly both the author and her subject; we also thank Osler, Hoskin & Harcourt for assisting financially in bringing the manuscript to publication, and Diane Mew for her constructive and painstaking work as editor.

The purpose of The Osgoode Society for Canadian Legal History is to encourage research and writing in the history of Canadian law. The Society, which was incorporated in 1979 and is registered as a charity, was founded at the initiative of the Honourable R. Roy McMurtry, a former attorney general for Ontario, now Chief Justice of Ontario, and officials of the Law Society of Upper Canada. Its efforts to stimulate the study of legal history in Canada include a research support program, a graduate student research assistance program, and work in the fields of oral history and legal archives. The Society publishes volumes of interest to the Society's members that contribute to legal-historical scholarship in Canada, including studies of the courts, the judiciary and the legal profession, biographies, collections of documents, studies in criminology and penology, accounts of significant trials, and work in the social and economic history of the law.

Current directors of The Osgoode Society for Canadian Legal History are Robert Armstrong, Jane Banfield, Kenneth Binks, Brian Bucknall, Archie Campbell, Kirby Chown, J. Douglas Ewart, Martin Friedland, Elizabeth Goldberg, John Honsberger, Vern Krishna, Virginia MacLean, Wendy Matheson, Roy McMurtry, Brendan O'Brien, Peter Oliver, Paul Reinhardt, Joel Richler, James Spence, Richard Tinsley, and David Young.

The annual report and information about membership may be obtained by writing: The Osgoode Society for Canadian Legal History, Osgoode Hall, 130 Queen Street West, Toronto, Ontario. M5H 2N6. Telephone: 416-947-3321. E-mail: mmacfarl@lsuc.on.ca.

R. Roy McMurtry
President

Peter N. Oliver
Editor-in-Chief

Foreword

by Bertha Wilson

When Ellen Anderson suggested I might write a foreword to this biography my thoughts naturally turned to Robert Burns:

> O wad some Pow'r the giftie gie us
> To see oursels as others see us!

For it is often through another's eye that we really and truly see ourselves. I have been most fortunate in the choice of the artist who painted my portrait and the author who wrote this book, and I am deeply indebted to them.

Dr Anderson has been an indefatigable researcher and commentator. Like any good teacher, she is the grand expositor and her acute distillation of legal technicalities can be readily understood by the interested reader. As a skilled analyst she has successfully prodded my memory to unearth incidents and circumstances long since forgotten and has laid bare a story that has sometimes surprised even myself. She has assumed my identity so totally as to become in effect a philosophical alter ego and the resulting picture is like a mirror before which I can echo, 'Yes, that's me.'

But I must acknowledge that whatever I have achieved has unquestionably been with the support and cooperation of others. No man or woman is an island: we are all inextricably bound together by an invisible thread and our life and work is fundamentally the product of a communal effort.

18 March 2001
Ottawa

Preface

'Will Women Judges Really Make a Difference?'[1] This was the mildly inquiring and characteristically modest title of a speech delivered by Bertha Wilson in 1990 in the dead of winter at Osgoode Hall Law School. Wilson had agreed to survey current literature on the particular perspectives women might bring to the role of judging and to consider these perspectives in relation to the traditional requirement that judges be both independent and impartial. The tone of the speech was informal but the scholarship thorough and careful. For neither the first nor the last time in her remarkable career of public service, however, Wilson managed to set off a firestorm of controversy.

Within less than a week REAL Women tried to have Wilson discredited and removed from the Supreme Court, laying a complaint before the Canadian Judicial Council. Merely questioning whether it is ever feasible to achieve judicial neutrality, the group charged, was in itself enough to reveal Wilson to be a feminist judge who had violated her own judicial oath of impartiality and was accordingly incapacitated from the execution of her judicial duties.

Perhaps this was one time Wilson could have anticipated some of that reaction. Even before the lecture Wilson had received the pointed suggestion that she revise her title and call her speech 'Women Judges *Will Really* Make a Difference.' The occasion was the fourth annual Barbara Betcherman Memorial Lecture[2] and the organizers at York would have preferred a more confident assertion of the importance and even the necessity that more women judges be appointed.

What better candidate to carry their banner? Bertha Wilson was the first woman judge appointed to any appellate court in Canada and the first woman appointed to the Supreme Court of Canada. But confrontation has never been Wilson's style and despite the labels attached to her judgments and to her scholarly writings by other commentators, she declines to identify herself as a feminist.

The speech as delivered began on an ironic and somewhat self-deprecating note:

> When I was appointed to the Supreme Court of Canada in the Spring of 1982, a great many women from all across the country telephoned, cabled or wrote to me rejoicing in my appointment. 'Now,' they said, 'we are represented on Canada's highest court. This is the beginning of a new era for women.' So why was *I* not rejoicing? Why did *I* not share the tremendous confidence of these women?
>
> First came the realization that no one could live up to the expectations of my well-wishers. I had the sense of being doomed to failure, not because of any excess of humility on my part or any desire to shirk the responsibility of the office, but because I knew from hard experience that the law does not work that way. Change in the law comes slowly and incrementally; that is its nature. It responds to changes in society; it seldom initiates them. And while I was prepared – and, indeed, as a woman judge, anxious – to respond to these changes, I wondered to what extent I would be constrained in my attempts to do so by the nature of judicial office itself.[3]

It is a poignant introduction which can serve to preface a number of the themes we will explore in this examination of Bertha Wilson's life in the law. Many of these themes are rooted in her early childhood experience in Scotland before her emigration to Canada in 1949. Others are traceable to her immersion, both through her exposure to academic studies of philosophy and through a more unconscious process of acculturation, in the doctrines of the Scottish Enlightenment. Equally prominent is the influence of the Church of Scotland ethos that infused her early years and persists to the present in a profound religious reverence which is no longer necessarily or exclusively Christian.

Wilson's recognition of the multiplicity of sources which bear on the evolution of the law is typical of the multiplicity and flexibility of the approaches she herself generally brought to the process of writing judgments. That the common law develops incrementally out of a dynamic and shifting relationship between legislation and social consensus is another theme which persists in Wilson's judgments and scholarly writings.

Postmodernism is a concept notoriously resistant to definition. If this multiplicity and blurring of boundaries is also characteristic of postmodernisms more generally, and if Wilson can be characterized as a postmodern judge, then we will see that her postmodernism is a distinctively principled and moral one. Wilson judgments may incorporate aspects of feminist theory from time to time but not by repudiating traditional modernist tools of legal analysis. During her years on the bench Wilson also supported procedural reforms which permitted the court to take judicial notice of a broader variety of legal facts, to hear from a broader variety of legal subjects, and to accord deference to a broader variety of adjudicative tribunals as she deemed it necessary to do justice.

Wilson has routinely been accused of judicial activism, but her record shows that she respects law's incremental development, frustratingly slow though it may be. And although she was fearless in speaking out when she felt it necessary, she did not seek out confrontation for its own sake. In a 1983 speech she had delivered in Winnipeg on the topic of sexual equality, she had explained why neither legislatures nor judicial activists are able to impose change in social consensus:

> The main impediment to the implementation of sexual equality provisions is prevailing social attitudes. You can legislate equality all you want, but you cannot make people think it and live it, particularly if they have been conditioned through inherited tradition and their own life experience to the concept of inequality. Indeed, the first step, I believe, is to appreciate the common humanity of men and women. We are human beings first and foremost, and only secondarily male and female.[4]

It reads more like apology or perhaps apologia rather than any clearly identifiable variety of feminism. Nevertheless that 1983 speech had been sufficient to provoke the first complaint by REAL Women calling for her removal from the bench.

Bora Laskin was then still chief justice and Bertha Wilson was summoned to his office where he requested a copy of the speech for his review. The interview was daunting. Laskin subsequently conferred with Mr Justice Brian Dickson who had been present when Bertha Wilson gave the speech in Winnipeg. Dickson considered that the probable cause for complaint was the impassioned manner in which Wilson had delivered her speech rather than the speech's content, which he agreed was inoffensive enough. But Wilson had felt keenly that the implied rebuke was a black mark on her record. Despite Dickson's support and Laskin's decision not to investigate any further, she worried about whether she had violated the appropriate constraints of judicial office, a hot issue at the time.

And seven years later that REAL Women incident must have been on her mind again. This time, as if to forestall criticism, Wilson's delivery was notably low key, even dry, but as a pre-emptive strategy for cooling reaction it did not work. The response of her audience was overwhelmingly enthusiastic; yet in spite of that favourable reaction, her own antennae were functioning well. The fresh complaint by REAL Women could not have come as a complete surprise. It was a relief, of course, when this complaint was also swiftly dismissed by the Canadian Judicial Council. However, the experience again was not a pleasant one.

In December of 1990 Wilson stepped down from the Supreme Court, a full seven years before the mandatory retirement age of seventy-five. Although REAL Women spokesperson Gwendolyn Landolt ungraciously and publicly rejoiced in Wilson's early departure from the court, Wilson denies that REAL Women had anything to do with her decision to leave. There were a number of other projects which she was interested in pursuing, including an ambitious and controversial study on gender equality in the legal profession undertaken for the Canadian Bar Association and an even more ambitious, complex, and demanding six-year stint on the Royal Commission for Aboriginal Peoples.

It is now possible to sketch out a preliminary answer to that 1990 question, 'Will Women Judges Really Make a Difference?,' answering with a slightly revised version of the title preferred by the York lecture organizers back in 1990. There can be no question whatsoever that this particular woman judge really *did* make a difference. But how can the full extent of Wilson's contributions be measured, given their multiplicity and variety and the reality that so many of them still remain to be realized?

We know, because of the incremental nature of the common law Wilson values so greatly, that Canadian jurisprudence will continue to evolve based on the precedents found in her judgments. Modifications of mainstream modernist Canadian legal culture are being ushered in which make legal education and the practice of law more compatible with diverse approaches to law, thanks in part to Wilson's post-judicial projects. There is reason for optimism about the increasing diversity of backgrounds from which Canadian judges at all levels are being appointed – a diversity reflective of the increasingly postmodern society Canada has become. There is already evidence that judges are reweaving some of the alternative strands into the development of the common law that Wilson provided through her diverging concurrences and dissenting judgments.

Wilson's lifetime encompasses a period of unprecedented change in Canadian political and legal history. Her Supreme Court career began at the same time as the patriation of the constitution and entrenchment of the Charter of Rights and Freedoms. Simultaneously, Wilson has helped to create a shifting Canadian consensus about justice, about fairness, and about reciprocal rights and responsibilities.

The question is how and why she was able to achieve this stance of principled flexibility. Judging is a human activity we all engage in all of the time; if we cannot resist judging this judge, it may be most appropriate to turn to Wilson herself for some preliminary advice on how to go about it. On a number of occasions, Wilson said that before judging, it is necessary to enter into the very skin of the person to be judged, and to make his or her experience part of your own. This, she knew, is not an easy task.

During the course of her career on the bench and immediately afterwards, Wilson's personal reticence and her recognition of judicial decorum meant that she consented only very rarely to be interviewed for publication; she herself wrote or spoke sparingly about her own experience. But entering into the skin of someone else's experience is made immeasurably easier when the attempt is met with a reciprocal response, as it has been here. Freed finally from all constraints of public office, Bertha Wilson has been remarkably warm and generous in sharing her life story for the purposes of this biography.

Acknowledgments

If it takes a village to raise a child, the birth of this biography also required the assistance of many people who consented to be interviewed and who shared with me their anecdotes, speculations, thoughts, emotions, photographs, and documents.

First and foremost among these have been Madame Justice Bertha Wilson herself and her husband, the Reverend John Wilson. They had read my LL.B. study of the Wilson judgments and published writings and agreed to meet with me informally for the first time on 5 May 1997 at the University of Ottawa office assigned to Wilson as scholar-in-residence upon her retirement from the Supreme Court.

After that first interview Bertha Wilson consented to a series of interviews to be carried out on behalf of the Osgoode Society for Canadian Legal History as part of its ongoing oral history project. It was not possible to schedule these immediately but we were in quite frequent contact over the next eighteen months. There were numerous telephone conversations, letters, and faxes and from time to time the Wilsons sent along parcels of additional unpublished materials. Unless otherwise noted, the photos in this book appear courtesy of the Wilsons.

The formal taped interviews took place over four days in August 1998 and continued for another four days in May 1999. John Wilson helped me to root through the Wilsons' personal memorabilia in their apartment lockers and then consented to a taped interview himself.

When these primary interviews were completed, the Wilsons went to endless trouble to help me set up interviews with relatives, friends, and former colleagues in Scotland, Ottawa, Toronto, Halifax, and Vancouver. The Osgoode Society generously funded my travel expenses throughout Canada for the primary interviews and for the adjunct interviews; a list of these adjunct interviews is provided at the end of the biography. Transcripts of those interviews for which the subjects consented to be taped were expertly prepared for the Society by its executive assistant, Marilyn MacFarlane.

Many persons and institutions assisted me in obtaining access to written documentation relating to Bertha Wilson's life and career; again, a list of archival sources and the people who manage them has been provided.

I gratefully acknowledge the support of the Canadian Bar Association, which by awarding me its Viscount Bennett Fellowship in 1999–2000 enabled me to enrol in the doctoral program at the Faculty of Law, University of Toronto. Professor Brian Langille, the associate dean of the graduate programs at the Faculty of Law, was welcoming and helpful; executive assistant Julia Hall ensured that I was kept informed of all requirements and provided a friendly face within the faculty. A very much larger version of this biography, entitled 'Bertha Wilson: Postmodern Judge in a Postmodern Time,' was submitted as the thesis for that doctorate.

University of Toronto Faculty of Law and History Professor Jim Phillips supervised both my original LL.B. study of the Wilson jurisprudence and my LL.M. thesis, which explored the historic import of Scottish Enlightenment common-sense philosophies into Canadian universities and their effects on Canadian law and culture. Professor Phillips, who had himself served as one of Wilson's Supreme Court clerks in 1987–8, arranged for me to carry out the Osgoode Society interviews with Madame Justice Wilson and he supervised the doctoral thesis on which this published biography is based. He has been a constant source of help and advice, piloting this project through academic and publication hurdles for eight years. From time to time, he has sportingly permitted me to outdrive him on the golf course.

University Professor Linda Hutcheon, of the Department of English and the Centre for Comparative Literature, had admitted me to her graduate class in postmodern theory in 1994–5 and then helped supervise my LL.B.-directed research paper in 1995–6. It was my great good luck that once again she was willing to help me out by serving on my doctoral committee; Linda Hutcheon is one of the most widely published experts on postmodern theory in the world, and also the most generous and kind of friends. Professors Phillips and Hutcheon were joined by University Professor Martin Friedland of the Faculty of Law who brought his expertise in criminal law and his extensive experience in legal publishing to bear on this project. All three of them provided timely and helpful criticism of the thesis as it was researched and written during 1999–2000.

Peter Oliver, editor-in-chief for the Osgoode Society, tried hard to quell his profound reservations about those aspects of the postmodern analytical framework which persisted in a diminished form from thesis into book and provided guidance throughout the publication process. There were helpful suggestions provided by several anonymous readers who wrote reports for the Osgoode Society manuscript review process; any errors which remain are, of course, my responsibility. Osler, Hoskin & Harcourt, the Toronto law firm where Bertha Wilson worked for seventeen years to establish a unique research practice, made funds available which enabled the Society to hire an expert editor, Diane Mew. I am particularly grateful for her help in shrinking the exhaustive end-noting and case analysis of the original thesis into more manageable book length.

My law firm, Gibson & Adams in Stroud, Ontario, provided unlimited use of its space and office equipment. George Gibson, my husband's partner in the practice of law, has been extraordinarily patient with my research and writing and has never objected to my usurpation of a spare office to store the vast collection of 'Berthiana' documentation I accumulated. I am also grateful for the kindness of the close-knit team of legal assistants who work at Gibson & Adams: Kelly Campbell, Barbara Jeffels, Silvia Mills, Tonya Reive, Julie Rhodes, and Donna Young.

Once I had began to write the biography in September 1999, the Wilsons read drafts chapter by chapter, offered annotations and new anecdotes, referred me to new sources of materials, read the entire manuscript through a second time before it was submitted as the thesis for my doctorate, and remained attentive and helpful throughout the pre-publication process. It has been a pleasure to have had the opportunity of working with such extraordinary people; their companionable marriage is so clearly the foundation of all their achievements and it is an inspiration to everyone who has had the good fortune of knowing them.

My own husband, Michael Adams, began encouraging me to go to law school from the time of our marriage in 1979. Other commitments intervened, including the birth of our children – Emily in 1984 and David in 1987; but finally I was able to enrol in an LL.B. at University of Toronto in 1993. Mike assumed most of the childcare while I commuted from Barrie. Then in 1997 he encouraged me to take on the LL.M. at the same time as bar admissions. After only one year of practice it was he who willingly agreed that I should apply for the doctorate. Mike made me the gift of the trip to Scotland in celebration of our twentieth wedding anniversary in August 1999 so that we could see Kirkcaldy and Aberdeen and Macduff and (not incidentally) so the two of us could play all of the golf courses young Bertha had walked with her father and her two brothers. This work could not have been accomplished without Mike's affectionate enthusiasm and unwavering support.

PART ONE

The Preparatory Years:
Life before the Bench

1

Growing Up:
Daughter, Sister, and Student

We are in the Wilsons' apartment in the leafy Ottawa district of Lindenlea in early August of 1998. Light streams in through the windows overlooking the Gatineau Hills to the north and the city landscape to the south. There are balconies on either side with red geraniums and petunias and a pair of Japanese bronze cranes.

Bertha Wilson has greeted me at the elevator with a warm embrace as if I am an old friend. There is some stiffness in her gait (she is almost seventy-five) but her cheeks have an eager pink flush and her blue eyes are affectionate. She leads me down the hall to their two-floor penthouse suite, inquiring after my drive from Barrie with that gentle charm mentioned by everyone who knows her, concerned to put me at ease.

Bertha had read the initial study of her jurisprudence and academic writings I completed in 1996. There have been frequent phone conversations with Bertha or John Wilson since then and a number of letters. I have met them once before, in May of 1997 at Bertha's University of Ottawa office, for a lengthy, exploratory conversation. Today, at home, she is dressed less formally. But her long-sleeved tunic blouse is buttoned to the neck above her white trousers and comfortable shoes and her auburn hair in its signature chin-length blunt cut is immaculately set with a high wave over her forehead.

We have been trying for eighteen months to schedule a series of taped interviews about her life and work for a biography for the Osgoode Society. She has also given me permission to use the material and she knows how eager I am to get started. Bertha looks eager, too, but also apprehensive. It is difficult for so private a person to talk about her own history and she has told me she is a little worried that she may not remember as much as she would want to about the legal arguments themselves. She is also worried about how appropriate it is to talk about her judgments for publication. I know that, having made the commitment to the Osgoode Society, the Wilson sense of duty and obligation will not let her rest until the job has been done. But it is also my hope that the experience can be an enjoyable one for her and give her an opportunity to reflect and reconsider and to set the record straight where she wants to do so.

Before we start, Bertha wants to show me around their new place. The summer of 1997 was spent moving across the street from the white stucco house they had bought in 1982 and the move was something of an ordeal, sorting through a lifetime's books and writings and deciding what had to be discarded. There have been periods of ill health, some of them quite serious, with considerable pain from time to time. Now both the Wilsons are feeling settled and, on this particular day, well. John Wilson's study is straight ahead across the hall, with French doors and generous shelving laden mostly with books of philosophy, both classical and contemporary, and a colour photograph portrait of Bertha Wilson in her red Supreme Court robes on the wall. John is cordial and welcoming, wearing comfortable loose clothing and a polished circular stone pendant around his neck which looks to be of aboriginal craftsmanship.

Bertha's own study, to the left, is meticulously neat, with a desk looking out onto the balcony, filing cabinets, mostly legal texts on her shelves, and framed pictures of the children born to her Supreme Court clerks. She shows me their bedroom with its brilliant blue bedspreads and a series of jewel-toned prints on a medieval stained-glass French theme.

Upstairs is a kitchen and dining room on the left and an enormous living room on the right with a fireplace and more shelves, this time filled with books on art and literature and history and a considerable collection of large framed oil paintings – two nudes, some landscapes, and a few still lifes. There is a cabinet record player next to the hearth, a glowing multicoloured Oriental carpet on the floor, a coffee table. Bertha invites me to sit on a cream iris brocade sofa and I get the recording equipment organized.

She herself prefers a more upright pink and gold striped damask chair. I pull it forward a little closer to the microphone on the table. She leans forward, her shoulders rounded, swinging her glasses by one arm, trembling slightly. Before I can hit the record button, she begins to speak.

FAMILY LIFE

Bertha Wilson was born on 18 September 1923 in Kirkcaldy, Scotland, to Archibald and Christina Noble Wernham, the youngest of three children and their only daughter.[1] Kirkcaldy, an industrial town on the north shore of the Firth of Forth almost directly across from Edinburgh, was in the 1920s best known for its malodorous linoleum factory. But Bertha's father was one social rung up from a factory worker. He worked as a commercial traveller in stationery, travelling around Scotland by bus and train to service his various accounts. As a consequence he was not home much during the week.

Archibald Wernham's family had for several generations owned a stationery business in Peterhead, a coastal town in northeast Scotland. It was sufficiently prosperous to afford them upper middle-class status and a substantial home with servants. But Archibald's parents saw no need to educate him past the age of eleven, when he was withdrawn from school and set to work as a delivery boy in the family firm. He served as a soldier during the First World War and met his wife Christina, who was a nurse at a hospital in Elgin. She came from a simple evangelical fishing family in Fraserburgh and had herself left school at the age of twelve. The class difference was such that the marriage did not meet with the approval of the Wernham family. Christina was left very much on her own to cope with her first baby, also named Archibald Garden Wernham, while her new husband returned to war. This experience embittered her and estranged her from the Wernhams, but it created a strong bond between young Archie and his mother which lasted throughout their lives.

After the war Wernham decided to leave the family firm and find employment elsewhere, although in the same line of work. Bertha remembers her father as a gentle and devout man who was meticulously careful about the organization of his accounts for his employer. Her mother was the family disciplinarian. She may have had little patience with organized religion but she expected her high moral standards to be met; she was also fiercely ambitious for her children.

The family settled in Kirkcaldy, now including another son, James, who was born three years before Bertha. Their flat on Hendry Road, in a row of identical two-storey buildings set back well from the road, was on a public or council housing estate. An arch in the centre of the block led out back to a common fenced garden where Wilson can remember playing with her two older brothers. The whole area was new at the time, although Bertha does not believe that her family were the first residents of their particular dwelling.

No one in Kirkcaldy then or now took much notice that the town was also the birthplace of the Scottish Enlightenment philosopher and economist, Adam Smith. It is interesting, however, that in the year of Wilson's birth a public works project of a type Smith would surely have approved had just been completed along the sea coast at Kirkcaldy. Construction of a massive esplanade provided employment and a source of income to fishermen and factory hands out of work because of a downturn in the economy.

The Wernham family moved to Aberdeen when Bertha was only three, so not surprisingly she has relatively few memories of Kirkcaldy. Pictures of the young family show Mr Wernham as a large man with a mild, sweet expression. His wife is very much the unsmiling and respectable young matron who takes her responsibilities seriously; all three children are brushed and polished and look beautifully cared for, but her tenderness towards them is revealed in the gesture of her hand or the angle of her head. There is a photograph of young Bertha in front of the Hendry Road house with her brothers, scowling a little and wearing rather voluminous handknitted leggings. This was known in the family as the 'baby dumpling' picture and Bertha was regularly teased about her plumpness; she does recall her trips up to the granite shop on the corner and her fondness for the sweeties that could be purchased there.

Her clearest recollection, probably filled in by stories her mother told her in later years, was that the Kirkcaldy school around the corner from Hendry Road was simply not good enough for the Wernham children. Archie had been identified early by his teachers as a remarkably gifted student. The Wernhams, denied much formal schooling themselves, subscribed wholeheartedly to the democratic Scottish ideology that individuals could raise themselves up by their bootstraps through hard work and education. By the time Archie was eight, his parents had enrolled him at Robert Gordon's College in Aberdeen.

Archibald Wernham found a new job selling stationery. The family moved to a new bungalow in Cheyne Road and Bertha lived there with her family for the next eighteen years. Christina Wernham missed Kirkcaldy and their new home was named 'Raith' after the Kirkcaldy football team, the Raith Rovers. She grew rambler roses on the side walls and her rose bushes out in front were her pride and joy. At the back was a modest vegetable garden and a strawberry patch.

Across the street from the new house there was a farm for the first several years with horses grazing in the fields. Bertha became very fond of Jackie, the young boy who lived at the farm. He was just a little older than she. A vigorous courtship was carried on primarily through competition; the two children loved to race their hoops (called 'girds' in Scotland) down Cheyne Road. One day, when he noticed that Bertha had lost her special gird stick, Jackie gallantly threw her a new one. She failed to catch it; a protruding nail neither of them had noticed struck her face and blood immediately gushed out. She could not see anything.

The young lad knew that he had to take responsibility even if he got into trouble. He led her by the hand to her mother as fast as they could go. Mrs Wernham was horrified at the sight of her little girl drenched in blood; she was sure that her daughter had lost an eye and felt guilty that she had permitted her daughter to play with such a rough and tumble boy. The doctor was called to the house – no light matter in that era, when you paid for a visit.

When the blood was cleaned away, her mother was relieved that the nail had just missed Bertha's eye, although it did leave a nasty wound at the inner right corner. The farmer and his wife both came round to apologize for their son's part in the accident; nevertheless, from then on the children of the neighbourhood were not encouraged to gather and play freely, either inside or even outside in the street in front of the house.

There was a heavy mortgage on the new house and Archie's school fees imposed an additional financial burden on the family. Private school for the other two was impossible, so Jim and Bertha were both enrolled in the primary school up the street and then later at Aberdeen Central Secondary School. Beretha would later recall life at home in those days.

It was quite a small bungalow, it had a kitchen and a scullery, two bedrooms and a parlour, and the parlour was Archie's. That is where he studied. He was quite young at the time. That was his, that was his spot, and he was a real classic student, he just did nothing but study, neither Jim nor I were like that, we weren't inclined that way, but he was. And it used to be really, I found it embarrassing, but my mother would say to me, 'These kids are making far too much noise out on the street, Archie can't study with that racket going on, go out and tell them to tone it down.' And I used to go out and say that my brother is trying to study, you are making too much noise. I think they thought I was nuts. And probably this wasn't much appreciated, I am quite sure. Because you know at that time it was roller skating and everything and it was a nice private street with just these bungalows. But I often think of that now. How everything centred around this person. And, of course, it paid off because he turned out to be very brilliant and did awfully well.

Mrs Wernham had to take in summer visitors to help make ends meet. The visitors got the front bedroom and were served their meals in the parlour, with young Bertha acting as maid, relishing whatever tips came her way. At first all three children slept in the back bedroom with the parents in an unfinished loft upstairs; later the boys were moved upstairs, but the Wernham family could never afford to have dormers installed and rooms finished on the second floor as many of their neighbours did.

Life continued to be a struggle financially even after Archibald Wernham became a partner in the Aberdeen stationery business. The purchase of any new piece of furniture was cause for celebration and Bertha can remember the acquiring of each item, including chandeliers for the parlour. But even as the house was furnished and became increasingly respectable, attaining the middle-class standards so important in that era, the Wernhams rarely invited people to visit. Christina did not make friends easily, and the house was never one where adult acquaintances felt comfortable casually dropping in for afternoon tea or cards in the evening.

CHURCH AND SCHOOL

The house was close to the university, St Machar's Cathedral, and the local golf course, all important institutions for the Wernhams. Jim and Archie regularly played golf with their father at King's Links, and sometimes Bertha tagged along. The boys became good enough to caddy for pocket money in the summer at the golf course in Cruden Bay where their maternal grandmother lived. Bertha loved her summers there and grew to know intimately its spectacularly beautiful landscape with its rolling sand dunes and its yellow broom and purple heather.

It was Jim, Bertha, and their father who attended regularly at St Machar's Cathedral, just west of the house. Archie did not attend. He refused to participate in any religious activities on the grounds that he was an atheist and that religious faith was quite incompatible with reason. He did not hesitate to express his derogatory attitude towards people who were devout, even including his own father.

Mrs Wernham also preferred to stay home; she had had her fill of organized religion as a girl growing up in Fraserburgh. According to Bertha,

> She used to tell me how she was made to go to church and Sunday School, practically lived in the church on Sundays. And in her home you weren't allowed to do work or do anything on the Sabbath. The women

polished and cleaned the men's shoes and got them ready for church on Sunday, but this had to be done on Saturday night. And all the cooking and baking had to be done on Saturday, because you didn't do anything like this on Sunday. And even when I was a teenager and we used to go out to my Granny's for holidays, the only thing you were allowed to read on Sunday was the Bible. And my aunt used to get a magazine, which was the favourite magazine in Scotland, called the Peoples' Friend, and it came out every week and it had love stories and all sorts of things, and my aunt used to read this, and I used to read this. But whenever any of the relatives came to the door, the Peoples' Friend was out of my hand and the Bible in it. It was really ludicrous.

Mrs Wernham was devout in her own way and in any event she recognized her duty. Once her husband had been appointed an elder of St Machar's, she began to assist with church events, as was expected of all the elders' wives.

The young Bertha had taken church attendance pretty much for granted. She thought little about the meaning of religion until one day, sitting next to her father at St Machar's, she became aware of the intensity of his devotions and was awed by the passion underlying his beliefs. Wilson has a deep affection for her father, whom she remembers as 'a gentle and kindly soul, the sort of person who would do anything for anybody.'

Bertha's strongest recollection of her primary school years in Aberdeen dates from the first day when her mother walked her up the street and introduced her to her formidable infant teacher. She seemed to the little girl a rather tough lady as she swooped down Cheyne Road on her motorcycle and parked it in the schoolyard, where it was a subject of great interest to all the school children. The public school years provided adequate preparation for Aberdeen Central Secondary but were unremarkable in themselves. Wilson characterizes herself as a late bloomer, with none of the early intellectual fervour of her elder brother or even the solid accomplishments of her brother Jim.

Archie had distinguished himself at Robert Gordon's. He won a scholarship to the University of Aberdeen where he studied classics and then to Balliol College, Oxford, where he studied classical philosophy. He taught both classics and moral philosophy in Edinburgh and at St Andrews before his return to Aberdeen University in 1960 and subsequent appointment as dean of the Faculty of Arts. As an academic, the publication of Spinoza's *Political Works* in 1958 (which Archie had translated and edited) was his greatest achievement. He channelled his life so narrowly and intellectually that he never understood others at all well; 'his people thing,' Bertha says, 'was very poor.'

Were the sacrifices made by the Wernham family to pay private school fees for Archie, who was considered by all of them to be a bit of a genius, justified in the end? Jim Wernham seems to have done just as well or perhaps even better out of his public school experience in Aberdeen. He followed Archie to the university two blocks south of Cheyne Road where he studied modern philosophy. He won a scholarship to Cambridge where he added studies in theology and then another scholarship to the New York Seminary where he contemplated for a time becoming a clergyman. Instead, he taught philosophy, first at the University of Toronto, and later at Carleton University in Ottawa. He established a reputation as a wonderful teacher, beloved by his students and noted for engaging with them in the intense debate characteristic of a genuinely democratic approach to intellectual activity. Bertha says that in Ottawa she still meets people for whom her greatest claim to fame is that she is the sister of Jim Wernham, the very best teacher they ever had.

Relatively few of Bertha's public school classmates finished high school and joined her at the University of Aberdeen. Most of the children who went to public school with her could not afford university or had parents who simply did not think in terms of higher education. It was most unusual for a lower middle-class family such as the Wernhams to have three children attending university. And although the Wernhams were extremely proud of their children's accomplishments (and even astonished by them) Mrs Wernham found the kind of vigorous debate and philosophical speculation in which they engaged around the family table somewhat fruitless and annoying.

Bertha did have one close friend from Aberdeen Central who went on to university with her and subsequently to teachers' college. Bertha Wernham and Clara Greig were almost inseparable between the ages of thirteen and twenty-one. Clara spent a good deal of time at the Wilson home on Cheyne Road, warmly welcomed by Mrs Wernham, who approved of her daughter's friendship with this clever and ambitious young girl.

According to Clara Greig Cheetham,[2] admission to Aberdeen Central was granted only after prospective twelve-year-old entrants completed competitive entrance examinations. The headmaster, Dr John (Jock)

Robertson, 'was a very hard taskmaster, interested only in academic excellence.' Punctilious attention to grammar, spelling, and punctuation was of the utmost importance. And interestingly enough, girls and boys were equally pressed to excel. Jock Robertson was also concerned that the girls did not take time away from their serious studies of English, mathematics, French, Latin, botany, zoology, art, history, and geography to pursue the traditional courses in cooking or sewing. This seems likely to have been less a matter of equality of the sexes, however, than protection of his own reputation for academic rigour; when one young female graduate was granted admission to the faculty of medicine at the University of Aberdeen, Robertson remarked that no doubt her enrolment was the reason he had seen workmen engaged in extending the cemetery!

Bertha Wilson states frankly that she did not cut the grade as far as Jock Robertson was concerned. In order to gain admission to the University of Aberdeen a high school student had to sit examinations and achieve 'highers' in at least three advanced courses. The headmaster refused to permit her to try for these highers on the grounds that he did not believe she was capable of passing the three exams. He would not consent to her tainting the record of his school by attempting three highers and achieving only two. The only alternate route was to sit the university's own entrance exams. As Wilson tells the story:

> When he went through the classroom and indicated what we were going to be allowed to sit for, I was told I was just going to be allowed to sit for two highers and I complained and said, 'I must sit for three highers because my parents want me to go to the university and I can't go to university with two highers.' And he said, 'Well, if you want to go to university, I am not going to let you sit more than two highers, but you can sit the university's own exams for entrance and try to get enough highers to get in with adding what you got there to what you got here.' So I said okay. So I went home and I told my mother, she was of course as mad as a wet hen, and she said, 'You are going to sit five highers at the university's own exams' and I did and I got them.'

Mrs Wernham was determined. She was accustomed to running the household and, especially after her experience with her young husband during the war, she considered life a pretty grim task. People had to fight to secure a respectable position. Bertha, who would have been just as happy to leave high school and get a job working in a sweet shop, was not allowed to take the easy way out.

Was Jock Robertson pleased and congratulatory about the surprisingly stellar achievement of this student whom he considered to be solidly average, at best? Not at all; his authority to decide who should go on to university had been usurped and he was furious. Young Bertha was caught in the middle, compelled to continue with school although she herself says that she would never have gone on but for her mother's insistence that she get an education as good as her brothers'.

UNIVERSITY STUDIES: WAR AND ROMANCE

The Second World War had begun in September 1939, the month Bertha turned sixteen, when she was still at school:

> Being a student during the years of war was a fairly serious business and our extra-curricular activities were all connected with the war effort, firewatching, observer corps and home guard. After a night's bombing raid – for which there was no such thing in those days as psychological counselling – we were expected to be at class on time. A missing name at roll call usually indicated injury or something worse. We knew our way of life was threatened and our environment became a kind of practical laboratory. I majored in history and philosophy but the study of British history or Plato's ideal state took on a special meaning, and against the backdrop of the war the discussion of political ideals and social values was far more than an academic exercise. It was a time which sharpened the natural idealism of someone in her late teens and early 20s and made a profound impression on one's outlook and thinking.[3]

Aberdeen did not see much bombing during the war, but it was subjected to unpredictable 'last chance' raids by the German airforce. If frustrated by anti-aircraft fire in their raids on British cities, the German planes would unload their bombs over Aberdeen and similar populated areas before heading across the sea back home.

Most of us can recall our first realization that our parents are not demi-gods but mere mortals, full of human fears. For Bertha Wilson that moment came lying beside her father in an air raid shelter as the bombs came rattling down above her and her family. She thought that the earth was moving:

The thing I will never forget was the shaking of the mattress that was in the air raid shelter and this trembling and I said 'This is really shaking' and my father said, 'No, it is me.' He said, 'I can't stop shaking.' And that made such an impression on me as a teenager because my father was absolutely fearless, to me, he was rock solid and the very idea that he could be frightened has always stayed with me because I thought, I couldn't believe it. Your father didn't get frightened.

It was very difficult for her to comprehend that despite the religious faith which grounded his fearlessness he too was shaking with terror and unable to sleep.

It was at the end of the first few months of war that Jim first brought John Wilson home. The two had struck up a friendship at the university, where they both took classes in philosophy. John Wilson was himself a brilliant student, the top graduate of Banff Academy in both English and classics, but he was from a farming family near the village of Ordiquhill which had little sympathy with his academic pursuits. At Christmas of 1939 he preferred to stay in Aberdeen rather than return home for the holiday. Jim Wernham and John Wilson enjoyed collaborating on their philosophy papers; both of them had come to the special attention of Professor John Laird, the Hume expert at Aberdeen, and they had an assignment to be completed before returning to class in January. For John, the study of moral philosophy was preliminary to the career he had mapped out. He already knew that on completion of his masters degree he would be continuing his studies in theology to become ordained as a minister in the Church of Scotland.

John's first visit to Cheyne Road was through the kitchen where some major redecorating was under way. Bertha recalls:

Jim had not sort of adverted to the fact that we were having our kitchen painted and the painter was me, of course. So here I am slopping on the green paint onto our kitchen when John steps in through the back door ... So that was how we met. And I guess we sort of hit it off, although my mother did not view this burgeoning relationship with any great enthusiasm. She had other ideas. She didn't like the idea that I might end up as a minister's wife.

They did indeed hit it off. According to Clara Greig, Bertha was a bonnie lass. Certainly John Wilson was not at all deceived by her painter's disguise. Within a few days, he asked her out. John remembers standing in line for over two hours to obtain theatre tickets to a production he knew Bertha wanted to see and then inquiring with elaborate casualness, 'I just happen to have these, would you like to go?' This subterfuge did not fool Archie, who overheard it, for even a second.

But for Bertha's parents, John Wilson's financial situation and future prospects were not his only drawback. Although as a potential divinity student he would have probably been entitled to a military deferment in any event, John also chose to present himself very publicly as a pacifist. Archie would soon enlist with the Royal Artillery in London and of course both Mr and Mrs Wernham had done their duty during the First World War; pacifism was a stance they could not admire. Furthermore, they both rejected John's left-wing political views and considered him to be a bad influence on their daughter. It was a point of pride with lower middle class people like Archibald and Christina Wernham to dissociate themselves from socialist trade unions, which were for the workers, and to assert their own potential to climb higher up the social ladder through education and hard work by supporting the conservative politics espoused by their social betters.

And what did Bertha's schoolmates think of the romance? 'The Divines,' as divinity students were sardonically known among the young women on campus, were generally considered a stuffy lot and not in much demand as potential husbands. John Wilson seemed a little older than the average student. He was not a tall man and already balding. His politics may not have been conservative but his clothing was; he wore an old-fashioned navy overcoat and thick laced shoes with toe caps. Moreover, he was exceptionally strait-laced even for a Divine and resented by those companions who considered him to be riding herd on Bertha's other university friendships. Clara Greig Cheetham remembers one such incident:

> Every forenoon in King's College Chapel at 11 a.m. there was a ten minute prayer session which students could attend between classes. However, a competing attraction was staged daily in the Pavilion when students indulged in 'Coffee and Chat.' One day, when Bertha and I had joined some of our classmates for refreshments, John appeared at the door. He had apparently been expecting to meet Bertha somewhere to go to the chapel and she had kept him waiting, for he accused her of 'indulging in a lot of female nonsense and adolescent ballyhoo' instead of keeping her *rendez vous* with him. The rest of us were suitably chastened!

But regardless of her friends' reactions, Bertha remained loyal to John and indifferent to the admiring glances which came her way from other would-be escorts. From her perspective, undoubtedly, John was merely reminding her where her priorities lay.

The two of them regularly attended at Student Christian Movement meetings and retreats. More than fifty years later, Bertha was to remember an image introduced to her by a speaker at one of these SCM retreats: the notion that 'God' functions conceptually like a picture frame, with the picture within that frame varying from individual to individual at various times. The multiplicity of the image and the freshness and intimacy generated by that multiplicity is what seems to have appealed to her.[4]

Despite her reluctance to attend university, Bertha did well enough. She and John both completed the course, and neither of them had to resit any of their examinations. This was quite an achievement, since the examinations set by the University of Aberdeen in the 1940s were formidable indeed. Neither of them, however, obtained any honours; these distinctions were awarded sparingly.

Bertha studied Latin, considered by her to be largely a waste of time; comparative psychology at both general and advanced levels, which she particularly enjoyed because of the stimulating and progressive Professor Rex Knight; multiple courses in English, French, and history; and logic and moral philosophy, again at both general and advanced levels, benefiting from the excellent relationships already established by her brothers with Professor Laird and Professor Ferguson, who was another distinguished member of the faculty. Aberdeen University at that period was steeped in Scottish Enlightenment philosophy, especially in the 'common sense' variant most compatible with religious faith,[5] but this was for the Wernhams and for John Wilson probably as much a matter of nationalistic pride and unconscious ideology as a focus for deliberate academic scrutiny.[6]

Although Bertha Wilson insists that she experienced no great intellectual awakening before Dalhousie Law School, nevertheless in a speech which she delivered on the Scottish Enlightenment many years later she did recount her enduring memory of John Laird lecturing on David Hume, who was in her opinion the main luminary of that eighteenth-century apogee of Scottish culture. Laird, she says, had a greater influence on her and her family than anyone else at Aberdeen and he seems to have embodied the mild and somewhat bemused personality for which Hume himself was so well known. Clara Cheetham recalls Laird lecturing in a trance and wandering around the campus as the quintessential absent-minded professor.

Hume's attack on linear concepts of causation, based on his cheerful observations of the randomness of contingency, necessarily entailed his acceptance of the provisionality of truth and of human identity itself. Like Archie Wernham, but with less intellectual disdain, Hume was a religious sceptic, as his observations of the provisionality of truth logically required him to be. And he did not abandon his agnosticism even on his death bed.

Wilson recalls that Laird's lectures on Humean contingency and scepticism inspired many Aberdonians to take their philosophy studies off campus for practical billiard hall experiments of their own. Bertha and John's own less recreational application of Hume would soon enough be required in their struggles with complex moral issues at their first parish. At a deeper level there is in both Wilsons an unmistakeably Humean optimism about the contingency and happenstance of the events of their own lives, which co-exists paradoxically with their equally persistent and rigorous Protestant ethic. Individuals are required to take responsibility for their own achievements through planning and hard work.

It was also at Aberdeen that Bertha was introduced to the works of Lord Monboddo and Lord Kames, whom she considers 'pioneers in a field which would now be called sociology.'[7] Monboddo and Kames were both interested in expanding the study of law to take into account scientific information gleaned from a variety of contemporary academic disciplines, a stance which Wilson herself was to advocate through her support of intervenor groups and her expansion of judicial notice to include sociological and psychological evidence.

John Wilson completed his masters degree in 1942 and was awarded the BD in 1945. He was an excellent student, winning the Martin Prize for Christian Evidence in his final year. This was the most distinguished honour in Divinity at Aberdeen and John had been determined to obtain it, even though to do so required the laborious memorization of two thick tomes of philosophical theology and then the explication of their contents in a gruelling examination.

John was both devout and ambitious to excel, but a large part of the attraction of the Martin Prize was the £100 attached to the award. This was a considerable sum in those days; John's first year's salary as a minister was just £400. With the prize money in hand, John set off to a jewellery shop and spent every penny on an engagement ring for Bertha –

two matched and exceptionally beautiful diamonds in a simple gold setting.

Bertha also finished her MA in 1944 and went off to Teachers' Training College that fall. Her mother had grudgingly agreed to the marriage if John was successful in obtaining a parish after graduation. But since she did not consider this very likely, she insisted that Bertha obtain her teaching qualification as a fallback position. And Bertha leaped over this hurdle conscientiously, preparing her practice teaching lessons for the two afternoons each week the student teachers were assigned to city classrooms. There was also a great emphasis at teachers' college on setting a good example at all times in the classroom, especially a good moral example, which was to be communicated through strict control of the student teacher's deportment. The student teacher was expected to show due deference for the college lecturers as well as for senior teachers in the schools where they performed their practice lessons, rising when they came into the staff room. But Bertha had no desire to become a teacher. Two years of successful classroom inspections after graduation from teachers' college would have been required to obtain the permanent teaching qualification; to her mother's keen disappointment, Bertha did not complete these steps.

John had had no difficulty in obtaining work as assistant at St Nicholas West Church in Aberdeen immediately after his graduation, but this was not sufficient to meet Mrs Wernham's condition. Moreover, it was not a position which suited him. On the assistant fell the chore of providing hatch and dispatch services for everyone in the parish, whether devout or not; he organized five funerals in his first week alone. Even worse, the incumbent minister was as displeased with John's politics as were Bertha's parents.

However, within less than a year John had successfully applied to be minister of Doune parish church in Macduff, a compact eighteenth-century fishing village high on the Hill of Doune across the River Deveron from Banff. He was not quite twenty-six and the appointment of such a young minister was unprecedented. But he was coming home to his native heath, as he phrased it, and he knew exactly 'how these people ticked inside and out, which was a great advantage.'

Mrs Wernham could mount no further opposition. Bertha was of age, and John obviously needed a wife to assist in his new ministry. The whole of Cheyne Road attended the 14 December wedding in King's College Chapel with John's stepsister, Isabel, and Jim's future wife, Rosemary, as bridesmaids and both Wernham brothers as groomsmen.

Wartime rationing was still in effect. When at the reception afterwards John congratulated himself on obtaining a wife without spending any coupons, Mr Wernham jovially pointed out that dressing Bertha had taken all the clothing coupons he had. The wedding photograph shows John, very dapper indeed, beaming joyously. Bertha is elegant in a classic satin draped bodice and diaphanous veil with a pearl tiara in her hair but a somewhat stony expression. Considerable diplomacy had been required to persuade her mother to attend the ceremony at all, although it was also obvious to the proper Mrs Wernham that to refuse would have been a scandal within their tightly-connected neighbourhood as well as deeply wounding to her daughter.

2

The Clergyman's Wife

The countryside south of Macduff in early August is a patchwork stitched by stone walls. Across the road, sheep graze with angora goats in green pastures and fields of pale golden barley ripen in the sun. A distant row of beech trees is silhouetted against the sky. The door of the granite farmhouse stands hospitably open.

Her voice on the telephone is polite but distinctly disappointed. The elderly lady had received a message about the Wilsons from her minister, the Reverend David Randall, and ever since had been sitting impatiently beside her phone. But it was not my call she was anticipating and when I identify myself, it is clearly a considerable let-down.

'I thought John Wilson was coming to see me,' she says. Almost eighty and a little hard of hearing, she had been in John's class at Banff Academy and remembers very well his cleverness and his kindness from his student days. She recalls how overjoyed she had been when he returned as the minister of Doune Church in January 1946. 'He was a fine minister and everyone loved him,' she tells me. 'He started up a youth group I went to and he was very good friends with my husband,' she goes on.

I listen patiently for several minutes and when there is a pause ask gently whether she also remembers Bertha Wilson. 'Oh, no, no, no,' the tone is a little impatient now. 'She was from Aberdeen.' And the unspoken suggestion is that Bertha Wilson might just as well have been from another planet.

MACDUFF: AN EDUCATION FOR LIVING

Fifty years ago Macduff was an insular community, like many another Scottish coastal fishing village. Within the Church of Scotland in that era, it was expected that the minister's wife would participate fully but unobtrusively in the life of the parish. Whatever she contributed would be taken for granted, attributed to her husband, and not particularly memorable. The church at Macduff, built in 1805 on the highest point of the Hill of Doune, still dominates the shoreline. When the Wilsons arrived, it functioned as the primary social institution in the town, providing not just spiritual sustenance but support for all forms of moral and physical welfare, from education to entertainment. Bertha Wilson accepted that she would be vital to her husband's success. She also realized very soon that, although the scope of her tasks was infinite and her labour unpaid, her work for the most part would also be unheralded; this concerned her not at all.

But before either of the Wilsons could get to work at Macduff in 1945 the first order of business was John's ordination as the new minister. Even though there was a flu epidemic in the area at the time, an unprecedented crowd was in attendance at Doune Church. There was a full service of worship before the ordination ceremony itself, followed by a lengthy exhortation in which the Reverend Wilson was directed to make good use of his talents and his congregation was directed to support him. The illness of one local minister did mean that a sermon which had also been scheduled was dispensed with.[1]

One cannot help but suspect, however, that the opportunity of seeing the new Mrs John Wilson at the social meeting afterwards in the church hall was in itself a considerable attraction. Refreshments were provided by the Women's Guild and members of all the congregations in town seem to have attended. There was a variety of musical entertainment and monologues to follow, but John's charm and warmth were quite obviously the highlight of the occasion.

In his thanks for the church's ordination gift of his pulpit robes he stressed his family connection with Banffshire. He mentioned the pride Macduffers had even then in the reputation their town enjoyed as a holiday resort – with the careful proviso that he and his bride were there not for a holiday but 'a spot of real hard work' – and he asserted his confident expectation of the congregation's support.

The following evening, John Wilson preached his first sermon. Perhaps it was that day he discovered the smooth texture of the velvet-

covered pulpit, which he would rub lovingly when a particular inspiration struck him. The length of the church runs east to west parallel to
the coast, which has the effect of arranging the congregation in broad
and shallow ranks closer than is customary to the altar. The walls are
white, the interior serene, and the minister's back is to the sea. Behind
Reverend Wilson on either side were the beautiful stained-glass
windows installed after the First World War. On the right of the pulpit
in jewelled blues and reds is the Children's Window, a highly praised
work of art that had been displayed at the Royal Academy in London
before its installation in Macduff.[2] John was to make programming
for children the highlight of his ministry and he initiated the tradition
of the children's homily, usually based on a nursery rhyme or familiar
children's story, the aspect of the Sunday service which Bertha thought
he did best.[3]

Meanwhile, Bertha's immediate task was to get settled in their new
house. This was not easy. The manse was a draughty Victorian mansion
almost a mile out of town, built of pebble dash and granite and sur-
rounded by rather gloomy trees. There were ten huge rooms, including
five bedrooms, none of them cozy, maid's quarters adjacent to the
kitchen with bells to summon the maid – but, of course, no maid to
respond. On the positive side, there was indoor plumbing, fine stained
glass around the front entrance, and holly bushes for no-cost Christmas
decorations.

A railway line ran at the bottom of the garden across the River
Deveron to Banff. Glebe lands surrounding the manse in the Howe (or
valley) of Gellymill were rented out to neighbouring farmers as a source
of church revenues. The house had been gifted to the church by the Earl
of Fife, but only for as long as the house continued to be used for church
purposes. Funds for the updating and maintenance of the manse in the
lean postwar years were in short supply.

Cheyne Road may have been crowded, but in Aberdeen the Wernhams had had all the modern conveniences, including electricity and
central heating and a proper stove. At the manse in Doune, Bertha had
to learn to cook over an open fire in pots suspended from hooks. Laun-
dry had to be scrubbed with a brush in the scullery tub and carpets
had to be brushed by hand. It took hours each week to fill lamps with
paraffin, trim their wicks and polish their glass chimneys just to light
the small area of the house the Wilsons occupied, and even so the
house was dark inside.[4] Obtaining groceries meant negotiating with
John for the use of their single bicycle (an over-size man's model which

certain members of the congregation believed completely inappropriate for Bertha's use in any event) and then pedalling up and down hill into town.

To save on these arduous treks, she decided to keep chickens, which were housed across the road in the stone stables belonging to the church property. John gave each of the chickens a name, which tended to diminish their eligibility for the pot. The local fishermen could be relied upon to bring regular supplies of fish to the house and the miller came by with extra sacks of oatmeal. John and Bertha also acquired a striped cat which they named Satan because, as John explains it, 'sin is always shades of grey.' Satan was joined by a small and notably glossy cocker spaniel, Lorna Doune.

When they arrived at Macduff the house was completely unfurnished. It was a source of some pain that Bertha's mother, still angry about the wedding, almost never visited her daughter and son-in-law in Macduff; Bertha's brothers and father and Clara Greig were all regular visitors, and of course John's family was close by. But Mrs Wernham, who had the satisfaction of seeing her prophecy that life as a minister's wife would involve considerable drudgery and poverty amply fulfilled, nevertheless did assist in obtaining furniture. She visited various auction houses when estates were sold up and helped the young couple obtain the minimum pieces that they needed.

Of course the Wilsons were expected to entertain from time to time and parishioners frequently came to the house for pastoral counselling. The main floor at least had to look respectable. The 'flying carpet,' their one and only, was lifted and moved from room to room depending on whether the prospective visitor was coming for counselling in John's study or for tea in the morning room. Given that the fireplace in John's study smoked badly, the morning room was the preferred location, but the Wilsons burned peat in all of the fireplaces because of the postwar coal shortage. During their entire time in Macduff the second storey of the manse remained largely empty and unheated; but it provided excellent storage for apples and pears which were spread out over the floors and slowly used up all winter long.

Bertha and John did not have the luxury of waiting until their home was in order before plunging into the life of the town. Before the Wilsons' arrival, there had been a withdrawal from public life and from the life of the church, particularly by the young people of the town, which was disturbing. Bertha immediately put her teacher's training to good use. She and John began right away to develop a range of new activities for the youngest children, the teenagers, and the young adults and married couples of the community. Not all of these activities were 'churchy' by any means.

There was, of course, the Women's Guild and the Women's Missionary Society, Girl Guides, Boy Scouts, Sunday School and always the sermons to prepare. John devoted a great deal of time and attention to the church music, relying on his talented and experienced organist, a Mr McNeil, for all kinds of advice and assistance, in the belief that hearty singing would encourage church attendance. There was a Nursing Association, which Bertha chaired. It provided a weekly clinic with a local doctor in attendance to weigh babies and diagnose ailments of mothers and infants. Bertha provided tea and cookies for those awaiting attention and sharing in the local gossip. She was also active in the Lifeboat Guild, a ladies' auxiliary which raised funds for sea rescue equipment that was absolutely indispensable in a fishing town.

Together the Wilsons set up two youth clubs. One was pragmatically intended to fill in gaps in the formal education then offered in the school. Students were graduating without knowing how to open a bank account, so a bank manager was brought in to the youth club to speak to them. If they were to be guided to grow up as good citizens they needed to know more about their relationship with the police, so a local bobby was invited to another meeting. Teenage girls, eying the glamorous and well-educated Mrs Wilson from the big city of Aberdeen, were naturally curious about the latest trends in hair styling and makeup; lessons were arranged.

The second club was meant for young working singles and couples who were encouraged to engage in a number of activities. Some joined the badminton league which met in the parish hall over on Market Street. The church elders and their wives were all invited to dinner in turn at the manse. Extremely important to church fundraising were the social events – the teas, bazaars, sales of work, and especially the whist drives, which always involved an elaborate supper organized in turns by two or three of the couples in the congregation.

All of this built the life of the community and increased church attendance dramatically. The Wilsons were astonishingly successful in their first parish:

All the roads led from ground-level, water level, up to the church and I will never forget it, I always loved to watch on Sunday, the people streaming up all of these roads, coming to the services, and they couldn't believe it themselves. The people, themselves, couldn't believe that it was actually happening.

A news article dating from Easter of 1946 and headlined 'Where They Queue for Communion,' pointed out that attendance figures had soared since the previous January when the Wilsons had arrived in Macduff. John and Bertha loved their work, even though they were busy every day of the week and had no time whatsoever for holidays other than (for Bertha) two weeks at Guide camp in the summer.

The Wilsons were, in turn, well loved, especially John. He is remembered racing the Sunday School children through the streets to the church hall and sledging with them down the snow-covered hill behind the church towards the sea. Scottish country dance music was very popular at that time and there was a radio broadcast everyone listened to Monday nights, generally with their windows wide open. John Wilson was seen on several Monday nights dancing all the way down Gellymill Street to the church. And he was so much in demand for his performances at Robbie Burns suppers, where he would bring down the house with his jokes in broad dialect, that one member of the congregation became his unofficial booker. It was a great pleasure to hear this scholarly, sensitive man speaking just like the simplest farmer – the very background from which he came. 'Get oot amon' my neeps ye toon's daert – it's nae fit ye eat, it's fit ye connach an' blad' was the punch line to one of his most requested routines.[5] Certainly no one thought of him as a stuffy Divine. And yet, above all, Wilson is remembered as a truly charismatic, profoundly spiritual preacher.

CONSCIENCE AND COMPROMISE

Unfortunately, there was also a darker side to life in Macduff, a side which called upon all of the wisdom Bertha and John could muster. These experiences drew to the fullest extent possible on their training in moral philosophy and psychology:

> It was a hectic life and a hard one. But I think it was there that I started to get some insight into how people tick. I became intimately involved with the drama of the daily lives of these people, their joys and their sorrows and, at sea, their terrible tragedies. I realized despite the many years spent on my formal education in school, at university and at teacher training college, how little of life I knew. I discovered how complicated people are,

how lonely proud people are, how dependent on the rest of us old people are. It was the beginning of my education for living.[6]

At Macduff, Bertha Wilson encountered for the first time what she unabashedly characterizes as human evil. She describes these experiences with quite natural reticence, but they troubled both her and John greatly. In football-mad Scotland, for example, it was controversial for John to raise in his sermons the issue of football pools and the social problems created by gambling; it was even more controversial to propose a public discussion afterwards. The same article lauding the increased attendance figures at Easter service reports that the new minister intended to do just that. The anonymous reporter sounds an ominous warning note: 'There are those who do not entirely agree with his policy, but all admire him for his sincerity.' A change in social consensus could not be imposed too quickly and moral challenge was not welcome if it hit too close to home. The gregarious young minister was not invited to inquire into what his parishioners still considered to be a private moral realm outside the proper reach of the church.

When the parishioners were themselves the victims of evil or malevolence, the Wilsons reacted with sympathetic indignation. However, they reluctantly learned to temper this indignation with a realistic assessment of their capacity to effect reform in a closed and highly stratified society where many of the worst offenders considered themselves the social betters of their minister and his wife. Despite her substantial education, Bertha was quite diffident about confronting members of the landed gentry or the wealthy merchant class. In the postwar period, rationing still cut across class lines and imposed a certain equality of scarcity, but the social hierarchy was nicely observed. She was very conscious of how inappropriate it was for the minister's wife to say anything which could be construed as political. She and John voted for the Labour party but kept it quiet. They knew full well that most of their parishioners, whether well-to-do or less so, supported the Conservatives and identified their interests with those of the British aristocracy who came to Scotland to hunt or fish. John had the training in theology and the ordination which he felt entitled him and even obligated him to speak out, regardless of the social position of the person whose behaviour was in question. However, he too came quite quickly to realize that speaking out on behalf of disadvantaged parishioners might only cause them greater difficulties.

What was absolutely incomprehensible to both the Wilsons was the failure of some local shopkeepers, including elders in their church, to integrate the ethical values they purported to uphold with their actual business practices. It was shocking to discover that their devout grocer purchased one grade of butter in a single large block and then subdivided it, selling off half as superior quality for a premium price and the rest as the ordinary butter it was. A young shop girl who worked at the local draper's shop had a similar story to tell. This merchant instructed his assistant to put out on a sales rack a mixture of quality garments, genuinely marked down from their real value, interspersed with cheaper goods brought in solely for the purposes of the sale with misleading sale tickets indicating they too had been marked down. The shop girl wanted to know if it was her Christian duty to disclose this dishonesty to her friends who came to the store and selected an inferior garment believing themselves to be obtaining a bargain. She knew if she did so she might very well lose her job which she relied upon to support her aged mother.

These troubled souls had no option but to sacrifice their own integrity. John Wilson spent hours counselling them, acknowledging the necessity of compromise, and looking for theological justification of that compromise which would still afford them some comfort and dignity. There was little more the minister could do except preach a series of sermons on the subject of business ethics. And this was tricky because the sermons had to be pointed enough to be effective but not so pointed that he betrayed pastoral confidences or jeopardized jobs. It was also important not to alienate those pillars of the church who supported it financially and who frequently had other good qualities to commend them.

However necessary it might have been to counsel compromise to those parishioners who realistically had no alternatives, the idealistic young minister and his wife were not in good conscience able to tolerate compromise of their own principles. They had education and no dependants; their circumstances were not such that they had to be boxed in. And despite John's best efforts, he had to admit that his sermons did not seem to be creating much reform within the local shops. He began to wonder if it might be possible to use his pastoral skills more directly; so fascinated was he by the ethical challenges facing business that he even began to think he might prefer to leave the traditional ministry.

By 1949 Bertha and John felt that they had accomplished all they could in Macduff; at many levels they had been outstandingly successful and yet they were always conscious that their moral and social philosophy was fundamentally dissonant with the values of the community they were attempting to serve. With Bertha's support, John applied for a position as a sort of corporate chaplain with a London firm manufacturing various kinds of food products. He did not get the job; however, both the Wilsons sustained their interest in the integration of Adam Smith-style ethics and economics throughout their careers and found many later opportunities to put it to practical use.

The experience of being turned down was useful, however, because it made John realize just how much he wanted a change. Jim Wernham had sent back glowing reports from Canada. The Canadian economy was booming in the postwar era; because of its many Scottish immigrants, Canada had evolved a society that had sustained many of the cultural values already familiar to the Wilsons, while at the same time avoiding those repugnant rigidities of class structure so deeply rooted in the United Kingdom. With a little surplus wealth there seemed to be more people in Canada who shared the Wilsons' socialist stances. John came to the conclusion that if he could find a ministry in Canada, these differences would make his work within the church more satisfying or at least that immigration to Canada might serve as one incremental step towards the change he was seeking. At any rate, it was worth a try.

ON THE BOUNDARY: IMMIGRATION TO CANADA

John had seen an advertisement in a church paper that a congregation in Renfrew not far from Ottawa, was seeking a Scottish minister for its new Presbyterian church. He applied and received news early on a Sunday, as he and Bertha were getting ready for a Boy Scout/Girl Guide church parade, that there were hundreds of signatures on the 'call' for him to come to Canada. Although they postponed active discussion to get on with the chores of the day, by nightfall they both realized that the decision had been made: they wanted to go.

The problem was, of course, that they had no money to pay their fares. But for the donations of fish and oatmeal, they would have had a very difficult time indeed surviving on the small stipend their congregation had been able to pay them. But they also had no money to ship their furniture and that turned out to be the solution to their problem. The two of them began to speculate about what they could get for the various pieces acquired by Mrs Wernham at the auction houses. A sale was organized, a huge crowd showed up, and they ended up making far more money than their furnishings were worth simply because everyone wanted to own something which had belonged to the popular young minister. Bertha and John sailed on the *Aquitania* at the end of August 1949. The newspaper account of their departure concludes simply, 'Mr and Mrs Wilson will be greatly missed in Macduff.' Sadly, Lorne Doune and Satan had to be left behind. The Wilsons were never to acquire any other pets.

When they left, Bertha's extraordinary contribution was recognized. One of the church elders said to the two of them, 'We may find another John Wilson, but we will never find another Bertha Wilson.' Was he hurt by this assessment, Bertha asked him somewhat anxiously. She need not have been worried; John had always understood how unusual her abilities were and fully appreciated all she had done. He laughed and agreed.

What was it like, arriving in Halifax and then setting out by train to their new home in Renfrew? The Wilsons had not anticipated how very much like greenhorns they would feel; the experience, especially for Bertha, was unexpectedly disorienting. In some ways, Canada was more Scottish than the country they had left behind;[7] in others it was utterly new and strange.

The ten-day voyage on a converted troop ship had been pretty uncomfortable, with the women's quarters separated from the men's. And on disembarkation, some of the Wilsons' most innocent questions received puzzling replies, establishing that their fundamental assumptions were all awry in this strange new land. John asked a porter on the train what time it was and was asked in turn, 'What time do you want?' The Wilsons had never before experienced the shifting time zones which are a part of life in this vast country. Shortly the train began to get cooler and the Wilsons assumed that they were climbing into the mountains; what fools they felt when the porter introduced them for the first time to air conditioning.

Jim Wernham, his wife Rosemary, and their small son Christopher were living in Toronto where Jim was teaching in the University of Toronto philosophy department, but they were unable to meet the new arrivals; and in fact, despite the fondness between brother and sister, the Wernham family style tended to be one of sturdy independence.[8] The Presbyterian minister from Arnprior and his wife greeted the Wilsons at the train station and took them in to their manse for a week of acclimatization, touring them through Algonquin Park. The Wilsons' photograph album records how awestruck they were by Canada's wilderness and wildlife, but at least the deer were friendly and came right up to the car to be fed out of their hands.

The Renfrew congregation was not unfriendly, but there was no role there for a minister's wife – or at least, not the kind of role Bertha had been accustomed to fulfil. Some parishioners of that era remember her as 'very shy but competent and always willing to give assistance'; others recall her as outgoing and more actively involved in church activities.[9] However, it is clear that there were no leadership functions reserved for her at the Ladies' Aid or the Women's Missionary Society or the Sunday School; in the annual reports for Renfrew Presbyterian Church Bertha's name is not anywhere in evidence except to record her dutiful contributions to the church collection plate.

But the absence of a place in the community was more literal than that; there was not even a home for the young couple to move into. The beautiful new church had been completed, as advertised, and there were plans in the works for an equally beautiful manse of matching Ottawa Valley stone, but funds were not yet available. In the meantime, the Wilsons were installed for the first year in temporary manse lodgings furnished by the church members right down to the pots and pans in the kitchen and the pictures on the wall, some of which were not much to the Wilsons' taste, but nevertheless a source of merriment and mischief: 'We used to have fun when we had visitors coming to the manse who had contributed these pictures. We had to rush down to the basement and gather the ones they had donated and hang them before they arrived.'

When these lodgings were sold and converted into the Cochrane Anderson Funeral Home with the new manse still not built, the Reverend Wilson and his wife were moved into a property on the outskirts of town which had been willed to an unmarried male parishioner who required housekeeping services. This was a job Bertha was permitted to undertake since it saved on expenditures for the minister's room and board otherwise payable by their thrifty congregation.

The cornerstone was not laid for the manse until October of 1950 and constructions costs were budgeted in excess of $18,000, a fabulous sum for the time. All church members and groups were being urged to raise funds; for example, the Sunday School had taken on the task of raising the $200 required for the new manse chimney. Given that she would benefit the most when the new house was completed, the minister's wife could quite reasonably be pressed to do her part as well. Ironically, even after they had finally moved in, there was still no real place for the minister's wife in this showplace. It was taken for granted that Bertha would hold continuous open house at the convenience of all those who had assisted with the financing of the manse together with anyone else who just wanted to have a look.

The new minister had been inducted on 13 September 1949 with what seemed to be the sumptuous salary of just over $2,000. John quickly found his feet in the familiar rhythms of parish life, and the differences he experienced were, on the whole, positive ones signalling the more egalitarian society he had 'left Scotland to find. It is true John tried unsuccessfully to arrange for an ecumenical Remembrance Day service which was simply not on in sectarian small town Ontario at mid-century. But his innovation of a Christmas Eve service was well received. Choir practice and sermon writing and public speaking engagements soon filled his calendar and John's charming manner was very popular, with much less offence taken in Renfrew than in Macduff against his socialist leanings. John was soon able to afford his first car, a spiffy little Ford Prefect, which added a great deal to his pleasure in his new job.

For one of the first and only times in her life, Bertha was left with time on her hands. If there was not much of a role for her as a minister's wife in Canada – this was not the tradition – if she even felt as if she were letting down the side a little, nevertheless she was certainly not going to sit at home moping. Curling with the ladies of all denominations in town nicely occupied many winter afternoons and Bertha's team was soon quite successful, travelling to tournaments all around Renfrew. Photographs show Bertha in her short fur-topped boots and jaunty cap throwing a rock, sweeping, and then posed with her broom at a sunny outdoor curling rink, her eyes fairly sparkling with pleasure.

This subversive initiative at a little ecumenicity of her own may have raised a few eyebrows but there were no real objections. Nevertheless, Bertha never forgot what it felt like to be a new immigrant and she has spoken movingly about the experience: 'An immigrant is someone who lives always on the boundary between two worlds. She has, in a manner of speaking, been born twice; and this personal duality colours and shapes all her thoughts and actions.'[10] The result is a sense that one is never really at home in either place, belonging in both but in neither; and Wilson believes that this is a quintessential state of mind experienced by all immigrants. Wilson never lost her distinctive Aberdeen accent yet she is aware that she is only what she calls an audible minority immigrant, not a member of a visible minority for whom the immigrant experience is usually much tougher.

Why did John Wilson, who was happy and content enough, not simply opt to stay on in Renfrew? Even in Macduff he had begun to think about moving out of the traditional ministry; in November of 1949, within months of their arrival in Renfrew, he had already met the man who would help him chart a new course.

A small bronze war memorial was to be unveiled in the church in honour of those who had served in the Second World War. In Aberdeen, John Wilson had taken a very public stance on pacifism; he had not served. Accordingly, he invited his congregation to find a guest speaker who could more appropriately conduct the service of dedication. They chose the Chaplain of the Fleet for the Royal Canadian Navy stationed in Ottawa, the Reverend Ernie Foote, who happened to be a Presbyterian and who also happened to have a summer cottage not far from Renfrew. Foote and John Wilson struck up a warm friendship; many visits followed with Foote dropping in on the Wilsons when he was heading to his cottage for the weekend. In late 1951, shortly after they had moved into the new manse, it was Foote who recruited John to serve as a naval chaplain in the Korean War. In the end Wilson served a six-year hitch.

This was, on John's part, a deliberate act of expiation, not so much for past sins but for past omissions. He had come to believe that there remained outstanding a duty of military service from the Second World War which he had not fulfilled. When he had reached that realization, he acted fast.

By Easter of 1952, basic training completed at Stadacona, he had flown to Tokyo and was already in active service in Korea on the destroyer HMCS *Cayuga*, stationed overseas without leave for the next twelve months. To his own astonishment and delight, this avowed socialist and pacifist discovered that military life and hierarchy and uniforms suited him very well. He enjoyed the tight, cohesive community of life at sea. He relished the strangeness of being the only high-nosed, round-eyed foreigner on a Tokyo street, shopping for an opal ring to send home to Bertha. He loved bunking down in a swinging hammock, sailing through the dark night of the Indian Ocean with phosphorescent flying fish flashing past the deck, or discovering after the fact in Ceylon that the 'filet mignon' he had just eaten was elephant's foot. John missed his wife – they wrote to each other often – but the world was opening up for him and he had confidence that she too was coping well on her own.

OTTAWA ON HER OWN

John Wilson had had to be replaced as minister of Renfrew Presbyterian Church and both John and Bertha agreed that once he had left Bertha should not stay on in the town. Barely moved in, she packed up and left the glorious new manse to make way for the incoming pastor. Before he had left, John helped her move their belongings into a rented duplex in the French-Catholic working-class district of eastend Ottawa, on Emond Street. But for the first time in her life Bertha Wilson needed to find a paying job to support herself and getting one proved more difficult than either of them would have guessed. Although she was perfectly willing to work in a shop, she was told that with her university background she was overqualified and would likely make the other staff uncomfortable. On the other hand, requalifying to teach school would have taken almost a year and that made no sense whatsoever.

There was an anxious period of searching and then, luckily, Bertha noticed a newspaper advertisement seeking a receptionist for two dentists. This was encouraging because it listed all the job requirements. She was confident that she could answer the phone, make the appointments, and keep the accounts; she was worried only about developing x-rays, and the dentists – a Dr Hudson and a Dr Beach – realized in the initial interview what a find she was. They quickly reassured her that keeping the darkroom door shut was not beyond her capabilities.

Bertha prepared plaster animals to hand out to the children, read them stories in the waiting room, and comforted fearful adults as necessary with her characteristic competence (dentistry was frequently a painful business in that era). Not only did she take pleasure in getting her first pay cheque earned entirely from her own labours; she also had the reward of putting to work some of her pastoral skills which had been lying fallow since Macduff.

One incident which involved considerable time and effort concerned a single patient who believed herself to be pregnant. This was a scandalous matter in the 1950s; it could destroy a woman's future marriageability and was generally hushed up at all costs, most often through the expediency of an extended visit to a convenient aunt in a distant city followed by a closed adoption. However, this young lady was determined to follow the more unusual route of obtaining an abortion as soon as possible in order to avoid any possibility of detection even by her own family. Bertha was called upon for consultation and ultimately for celebration when the pregnancy turned out to be a false alarm. For the first time in her life she had come to grips with her own moral beliefs about abortion, having seen the torture the woman went through in reaching such a decision. Bertha found herself totally unable to condemn the woman for the choice she would have made.

Both dentists were interested in religious issues, one active in the United Church and the other in the Moral Rearmament movement, and they enjoyed lively discussions with their remarkably well-educated receptionist. From time to time in her role as naval chaplain's wife she had the sad duty of making calls to the parents of those sailors who had died while under John Wilson's pastoral care in Korea. But life for this young career woman was by no means all work and moral anguishing and intellectual discussion. With her characteristic zest for a new adventure, Bertha soon developed a circle of friends who were neither school chums nor parishioners and she began to have a wonderful time.

Knox Presbyterian Church in downtown Ottawa was around the corner from her new office on Metcalfe Street. She had a great admiration for its progressive minister, the Reverend Colin Miller, attending the early morning service he had established for business people and becoming active as stage manager in Knox's amateur theatrical group. But she often went to Sunday services at the Catholic church in Vanier, polishing up her university French and Latin in the process; in fact, the priest did not even realize that Bertha was not of his faith until he visited her home and noticed a picture of John in clerical garb sitting on a table.

Wilson realized in retrospect that her year on her own in Ottawa had been a watershed experience:

> The separation was rough and I was often very lonely but in a strange way it felt good to be doing something by myself. What I had done before, and done very happily, was through my marriage to a minister. The satisfaction I had was subtly different; it was direct and not derivative. I was my own centre of reference now. I had to look to my own resources only and it was a revelation and a joy to discover that I had them. I developed a new sense of confidence in myself and was intensely proud of every new hurdle that I crossed. I know that this first experience on my own was a necessary prelude to my career in law.[11]

John was sailing home to Halifax and Bertha's year in exile was at an end with only one more adventure to come. The Reverend Foote had been keeping an eye on her, introducing her to various navy people in Ottawa and regularly including her in navy parties. It was he who vetoed Bertha's plan to drive alone through Quebec to Halifax in the unreliable old Prefect, and insisted that she travel for safety with another navy chaplain.

The car did break down on a lonely country road, the chaplain leaped out and raised the hood, and Bertha was left at the wheel, panicking as she watched his head being jerked lower and lower as his long silk scarf became more and more entangled in the engine. When she managed to get the ignition turned off, her companion was too embarrassed to deal with the question of obtaining accommodation for the night with no village or inn in sight. Bertha's refurbished French was put to good use in explaining to the inhabitants of the nearest farmhouse that she was not the wife of *this* chaplain and that the two of them would want separate rooms if at all possible.

The four-cylinder Prefect, it turned out, was operating on only one cylinder, but Bertha and her borrowed chaplain were able to get it all the way to Halifax, arriving a few days before John returned on the *Nootka*. His first question was, 'Are you still driving that old thing?' She explained that supporting herself on her salary as the dentists' receptionist did not stretch to the purchase of a new vehicle. Nevertheless, the Prefect was patched up and functioned very well all the way to Florida, where John and Bertha enjoyed a well-earned holiday getting to know each other all over again. The next phase of their lives was about to begin.

3

Diligence at Dalhousie

It is May 1999 and not a particularly hot day, but we have a hot and dusty job ahead of us. John Wilson is dressed in khaki shorts and a golf shirt.

We meet at the elevators of the apartment building in Ottawa and head down. Awaiting us are two large basement storage lockers crammed with all the memorabilia that the Wilsons could not bear to part with and also could not accommodate in their apartment in 1997 at the time of their move.

The material is housed in two lockers. John has a grocery cart ready to load items which look as if they might be useful to me into my car. Bertha Wilson is resting after the morning's interview session, the sixth time we have met. Behind a wooden slatted door of the first locker are stacks of cardboard boxes, taped and labelled. Framed pictures and photographs and diplomas are carefully wrapped in tissue paper; we open a few, cautiously, but leave most of these alone. Academic hoods and hats from the twenty-nine honourary degrees bestowed on Bertha Wilson have been neatly folded away. There are boxes of academic speeches and journal article offprints, sermons, more philosophy and legal texts, and several filing cabinets mostly filled with printed background materials for the Aboriginal Royal Commission and the Gender Equality study. And there is a variety of containers full of newspaper clippings. John Wilson had assigned himself the role of scanning the press and compiling articles he thought should come to Bertha's attention: criticisms or praise of judgments which had already been released, sociological information that might be useful to her for cases she was working on, reactions to the post-judicial studies.

How lucky it was for me they kept all they did. We set to sorting it out, work-

ing together in an easy rhythm. In his eightieth year, John works with unflagging enthusiasm and good humour, sensing my excitement and sharing the memories particular items evoke for him. And at some point during the course of this labour he has become John, insisting that we drop the 'Mr Wilson' permanently.

One envelope in particular catches John's attention. It contains clippings and photographs from the Dalhousie Law School days and he wants to look at these documents a little more closely.

John Wilson, a complex and accomplished person in his own right, has been utterly central to everything Bertha Wilson has achieved since they first met. It is not possible to begin to understand her story without speaking to him, but their relationship is also an intensely private one. Always friendly and helpful, he has also been understandably reluctant to speak for the record.

You see, that is another example of how fortuitous things were, we found ourselves in Halifax across the street from the law school, although when Bertha was thinking about returning to university, she did a year's work for a doctor and a dentist in Halifax and then she decided to take some courses at Dalhousie, and I remember very clearly thinking, what would she do, continue her philosophy or do fine art or whatever. I remember being quite surprised when I said, 'Well, what did you do?' And she said, 'I joined the law school.' And by Christmas of that year, Ellen, the bug had bitten her ... that mysterious thing in law, whatever it was, just was the spark that ignited the brain.

SOPPING IT UP: THE LAW STUDENT AS SPONGE

The Wilsons' little basement apartment at 82 Oxford Street in Halifax consisted of only two main rooms, with low ceilings and exposed pipes. But neither of the Wilsons is very tall. They painted the pipes brightly and used them for drying their clothes. A more persistent drawback was the apartment's unfortunate tendency to flood during rainstorms. John would rush out with his shovel; by digging trench around the doorway; he was usually successful in diverting the deluge. On the positive side, they were on good terms with their landlords. The Echts had left behind positions of some social status to come to Canada as refugees from a pogrom in the Polish area of Danzig not knowing a word of English. John sympathized with Mr Echt's frustration when he could not find the word he needed to express his thoughts.

If the ceilings were low, the rent was also low enough that they could live on John's income from the navy. Bertha spent the better part of another year working in Halifax again as a receptionist, this time to brother Doctors Leonard and Howard Goldberg. She saved up her pay cheques for university tuition, although she still had no clear idea of what she intended to study.

While she waited and worked and thought through her future direction, Wilson also came to appreciate how uncannily familiar her new home was. Nova Scotia is, of course, very Scottish in its culture; even the architecture and the geography of the city encompassed elements that echoed with her past. Halifax's civic buildings are typically of dressed stone; its tall houses of random granite or clapboard with third-floor triple-bay dormer windows line the steep streets which plunge towards the sea. From the apartment she could hear trains down the hill west of Oxford Street about the same distance away as the railway track at the manse in Macduff. Although Bertha had given up the game, there was even a seaside golf course close by along the North West Arm.

By the end of the year, she had made up her mind. Tuition money in hand, she walked to Dalhousie University and petitioned for entry to its law school. It is widely known that Bertha Wilson loved her three years at Dalhousie and that she did very well there, once she managed to get in. But Dean Horace Read had not been at all keen to admit her.

There were five other women students in Bertha's class so her gender was not entirely the problem.[1] At thirty-one, she was considerably older than the average student, but her mature student status was not really the issue either; there were at least two other older students who were more readily admitted in 1954. John Charters was leaving a career as a naval officer, and Lilias Toward, who had held the position of Atlantic Regional Secretary of the Community Planning Association of Canada before enrolling in law school, was a wealthy widow from Cape Breton already then old enough to have a son at the University of New Brunswick.

What disturbed Dean Read was his fear that Mrs Wilson might lack commitment to the rigours of the program. In fairness, she gave him some reason for reaching this assessment. First of all, Wilson had told Read during her entrance interview that she had no intention whatsoever of practising law upon graduation. She wanted primarily to study law as an extension of her liberal education begun at Aberdeen. And even worse, she had quite frankly disclosed that she was at loose ends. John was stationed on rotation at the three naval bases around Halifax, working mostly with the young recruits and providing them with religious education; there was not even a residual role for a chaplain's wife under these circumstances. It is true that the law school's location was conveniently close to the Wilsons' apartment; however, Bertha made it clear to Dean Read that, convenience aside, she knew Dalhousie was particularly celebrated for its law faculty.

None of this seemed to Dean Read sufficient to permit her to take up a space in his classroom. His reply, immortalized in Bertha Wilson's own writings, was memorable: '"Have you any appreciation," he asked, "of how tough a course the law is? This is not something you can do in your spare time. We have no room here for dilettantes. Why don't you just go home and take up crocheting?"'[2] But there was no policy of restriction on admission to Dalhousie Law School in the early 1950s for students who had completed an undergraduate degree, although the failure rate out of first year was quite high. Horace Read was not able to dissuade Bertha from enrolling at Dal and in fact it soon became apparent that here was an exceptionally diligent student who was certainly no dilettante.

At Aberdeen, Bertha had completed her courses conscientiously but without much academic enthusiasm. Dalhousie Law School, on the contrary, was from the first day an experience that changed her whole way of thinking. Although valuing her previous education in logic and moral philosophy and history, Bertha regreted that she did not study law earlier rather than spending her time on general arts courses and teachers' training college.

Bertha was a little shy when she arrived at Dalhousie to attend her first class. It was a good thing that another older woman was in sight:

'She looked in and saw the air blue with smoke and the place filled with young men,' Lilias Toward, then 44, and a first year law student herself, remember[ed]. 'She was about to close the door and leave when she saw me. Because I was so much older than the other students, I guess she thought I was a professor. But when I didn't go to the lectern, she didn't go and slipped into the front row beside me.'[3]

And once settled in, she knew that law was her thing and she 'sopped it up like a sponge.' There were a few courses – especially the more mathematically based studies – where she had to grit her teeth and plough her way through with sheer determination; mortgages and taxation and law office accounting were not great favourites. But in general, the quality of instruction at Dalhousie was high and Bertha thrived on anything with a philosophical foundation.

CLASSROOM AND CURRICULUM

The students who survived literally moved up during their three years at law school. In the basement across the hall from the first-year classroom there was a common room, but the women were not welcome there. On the main floor the second-year classroom was to the right and the faculty offices to the left of the entrance. Third-year students sat around the reading tables in the chapel-like Dunn Library on the top floor. And for Wilson, who approached her studies in law with an almost religious devotion, this was one of the most pleasant spaces on campus. From time to time she acted as librarian, welcoming the opportunity to assist students who had run into thorny research problems to find the books which they needed.

The first-year criminal law instructor, Judge Pottier, was something of a dandy whose immaculate attire and jewelled stick pins distracted the ladies from his dissertations on *mens rea* and the burden of proof. Wilson performed competently enough, but criminal law was not of particular interest to her at that time. Interestingly enough, a good deal of John's work at the naval base involved acting as quasi-defence counsel for sailors who were up before their superior officers on disciplinary charges. It was during this period that he shared with Bertha his realization that every mother considers her son, no matter what he has done, to be a good boy at heart. If he got into trouble, he was the unfortunate victim of circumstances which had compelled him (but surely only temporarily) into reprehensible behaviour.

Contracts, taught in first year by Dean Read himself, addressed the concepts of condition precedent, condition subsequent, parol evidence, and the doctrines of frustration, misrepresentation, and mistake, all fundamental to Wilson's subsequent career. Read had been reluctant to admit her but he was fair-minded. He read aloud in class an answer from Bertha's first Christmas exam paper, distinguishing between a 'true offer' and a 'mere puff' advertisement for a sewing machine, to illustrate the correct approach to the problem. Bertha was thrilled when Read added the comment, 'I think I'll make a lawyer of you yet.'

Professor Lorne Clarke taught second-year corporate law from a formidably thick syllabus. Bertha remembers him as a confident and cheerful instructor who carried on his classes with great good humour and flair. Professor Meagher's second- and third-year classes in civil procedure seemed to focus primarily on the swearing of oaths but Bertha was to develop an intense interest and expertise in the procedural aspects of law: intervention, leave to appeal, and particularly the procedural ramifications of the Charter.

Maritime shipping law was a required course at Dalhousie, illustrated by Professor Meagher with model boats in a bucket. John Wilson claims (perhaps apocryphally) that Bertha acquired her own flotilla to work out additional problems relating to ships meeting, crossing, and passing in the bathtub at home. And on the morning of one examination the little apartment at 82 Oxford was entirely awash in its own thoroughly unpleasant sea. This time it was not just the regular flooding after a rainstorm. The sewers had backed up into the toilet, bathtub, and sinks and out onto the floor. Bertha, uncharacteristically, burst into tears.

John packed her off to school, called the naval base at Stadacona and told his superior that he had a domestic crisis on his hands. Fortifying himself internally with the better part of a bottle of naval rum, he draped their single rug over the ceiling pipes, stripped down to his shorts and began swabbing the floors with the strongest disinfectant he could find. By the time Bertha returned everything was shipshape again, although the legs on their bed had lost about six inches of their varnish.

The first- and second-year property law courses were a major focus of interest for Bertha Wilson. This was partly because she found Professor Graham Murray such a sweetheart, but also because he offered a thorough grounding in the fundamental principles of property law. But Murray was far from dogmatic or definitive in his approach. A somewhat gangly, horse-faced man, he was more interested in conceptual subtleties than in black letter law and encouraged his students to consider conflicting interpretations of the case law on the syllabus. When asked a question, Murray was famous for replying, 'Well, I don't know, what do you think?'[4]

His classes, which he would hold outdoors if the weather was fine, tended to be entertaining and informal. Murray illustrated the concepts of possession and ownership with intriguing problems of swarming bees, escaping fish, and a discovered cache of jewels all related back to the Roman law distinction between dominion over and interests in property. Wilson was familiar with the concept of a limited interest in property from her Macduff days in the manse; she would find herself still drawing on Professor Murray's teachings during her work in aboriginal concepts of property as stewardship over shared resources – concepts that have a remarkable similarity to classical notions of dominion.

Professor William R. Lederman taught the first-year course in torts which evoked in Bertha an ambivalent response. Dalhousie had been a much earlier convert than University of Toronto to the case book method of studying law and in later years Bertha Wilson was to urge law students to consider it an essential part of their training in legal analysis to read the cases in their case books rather than resort to canned briefs.[5] There is no question that Wilson found torts conceptually interesting and the method of teaching it generally appropriate. However, she considered the case book approach to be too much of a good thing. The torts course suffered from the excessive number of cases (some 187) with which Dalhousie students were expected to be familiar for the examination.

And the minute Bertha arrived home from the torts exam she discovered a disaster: she had been so preoccupied with all the case law that she had tucked her paper inside her briefcase instead of submitting it to the invigilator. After all her hard work she was sure that this meant she would fail. Her heart began to pound in a panic and she raced as fast as she could to Lederman's office on the first floor of the Law School building.

'Professor Lederman,' she burst out, 'I've got my examination right here, will you still accept it? I forgot to hand it in.'

'Of course, Mrs Wilson,' he replied mildly and without any hesitation, 'I haven't even begun to look at them yet.'

Professor Lederman's trusting and kindly response meant everything to the anxious student and she never forgot it. However, when her paper had been marked she was disappointed in the grade and went again to speak to him. He handed the exam to her and had her read aloud her answer to a question involving a hockey player who had deliberately hit another player during the game with his stick. She had taken for granted rather than specifying that this act constituted the tort of assault, Lederman explained; to get a higher grade, it would have been necessary to set out the basic reasoning step by step from the beginning, document the reasoning at each stage, and only then to deal with the more technical points. Wilson, who as a mature student may have been a little rusty in her exam-writing technique but who had a thorough grounding in logic from Aberdeen, was grateful. She had no further difficulties with the 'fact situation' testing typical of law school.[6]

She came into her own in Lederman's second-year class in constitutional law. Lederman was the first Canadian constitutional scholar to stress that the courts should engage in balancing the overlapping powers of federal and provincial jurisdictions; he reasoned that the ambiguity and the incompleteness of the British North America Act of 1867, born out of a rather tenuous political compromise, required such balancing as an alternative to rigid statutory analysis. More generally, the words of a statute, in Lederman's opinion, could become meaningful only when they were 'related to the cultural, social and economic realities of the society for which they were and are intended.'[7]

Professor Lederman was also the instructor in third-year jurisprudence, which Wilson thoroughly enjoyed. Lederman intended this course to be 'fully integrative,' providing an overview of the legal system which included consideration of analytic logic, social utility and the value systems of the various theories of justice. He wanted to induce his students to 'rise above the particulars' of the other subjects they were required to study and he had each student prepare an essay on a particular jurisprudential subject.[8] It is easy to imagine how much Wilson would enjoy this opportunity to approach law on a philosophical footing.

She was to hear from Lederman occasionally during her days on the bench if a judgment particularly won his approval. After he left Dalhousie to become dean at Queen's University Law School, Wilson could always be persuaded to travel down from Toronto or Ottawa to Kingston to speak to his students. When Lederman died in 1992, she prepared a speech for the symposium held at Queen's in his honour.

Wilson considers Lederman to have contributed the most to her intellectual development while she was at Dalhousie and singles him out as the professor who had the most enduring influence on her subsequent judicial career. He was for her the ideal teacher; although naturally shy and reserved, his wry humour bridged the gap between professor and students. Dedicated, brilliant, and demanding of himself, he accepted that those of his students who were interested in a life outside law school were nevertheless likely to make significant contributions later on to the profession and their communities. For students such as Bertha Wilson who did want to make their studies their focus, Lederman was willing to acknowledge their intellectual discipline and to respond with kindly criticism which inspired even greater effort.

SOCIAL LIFE AND STUDY GROUP

The taste for social life which Bertha had discovered in Ottawa continued in Halifax but with a new focus on law. The younger students met for Friday afternoon beer sessions; Bertha Wilson did not participate in these although she certainly did not express any disapproval of those who did.[9] The Wilsons often attended St David's Presbyterian Church for Sunday service, joining enthusiastically in the lusty rendition of the psalms by the congregation. But Bertha was not a local; despite the link between her own Scots origins and the pervasive Scottishness of Nova Scotia, she was not enmeshed in the web of cultural and blood connections which formed Nova Scotian society and she did not share fully in the middle-class ethos of most of her classmates.

The legal community in Nova Scotia in the 1950s tended to be very tightly knit. Many of the law students at Dalhousie already knew each other; a number of them had fathers or uncles who had graduated from Dalhousie and practised law in Halifax or in the outlying communities of Nova Scotia.[10] For the most part, students could be confident that on graduation, jobs awaited them close to home in family firms. Failing a course or even a complete year was not necessarily disastrous; Bertha's classmate, Pat Harris, recalls a certain student with a lawyer father who repeated first year three times before passing. As a result, and although the curriculum demanded that law students work reasonably hard, they seem to have done so without particular stress. There was time for a robust social life, regular weekend parties, and high jinks; on one occasion, for example, the other women students in Bertha's year disguised themselves in oilskins and sou'westers to go drinking with the men at a local fishermen's tavern where females were not permitted.

For the majority of students it mattered less to get top grades than to establish the cordial relationships with their future colleagues which would stand them in good stead over a lifetime of practice.[11] They were aiming for Barrington Street, not Bay Street, and for a comfortable and respectable life of professional and community service rather than a focus on amassing personal wealth. For those students who were ambitious, whether academically or financially or both, there was a tacit understanding that it did not do to be too overt about it.

There also tended to be close interrelationships between the professional bar and the legal academics on faculty. Over the decades Dalhousie has traditionally relied upon 'downtowners,' its own graduate practitioners, to provide guest lectures and to teach short courses.[12] And among its professional academics a disproportionate percentage of Dalhousie graduates have returned to the faculty as tenured professors, often after a graduate degree in law from Harvard or elsewhere south of the border.

Purdy Crawford, himself a native Nova Scotian two years ahead of Bertha Wilson at Dal, was one notable exception. A legend at Dalhousie for his stellar intellect, he leavened that reputation with his notable bonhomie and his generosity in holding impromptu tutorials on the library steps to help other students experiencing difficulties. Wilson met him at Dal but came to know him much better during practice at Osler, Hoskin & Harcourt in Toronto; at that time, however, he was not one of her closest friends, being primarily focused on mounting his way up the law firm ladder.

What set apart the members of Bertha's closest circle at law school was their intense focus on their studies, which served to propel them to the top of the class. Bertha, Lilias Toward, and John Charters were joined for a time by David Fraser and more permanently by Ron Pugsley and Matt Epstein. As Pugsley describes it, membership in the group was by invitation. During the first few weeks of class he had sat in the front row and asked a great number of questions. Lilias was obviously impressed by his abilities and she asked him if he would be interested in getting together to review cases and concepts on a regular basis with a few other students. 'How often do you have in mind and who else is going to be involved?' Ron asked. 'So far, it's just me and Bertha and we want to meet every Friday night,' Lilias replied.

This created a bit of a problem. Ron had a steady girlfriend; Friday night was frat party night and she had the reasonable expectation that the two of them would go out together instead of spending the night alone while Ron met with a couple of other women. But Ron explained the situation to her, got her agreement to let him try it for a few weeks and then realized how valuable the sessions were to him. Very shortly, the group had expanded to include the other men.

At first they rotated among the various students' homes, but most of them lived at home with their parents or in tiny apartments like Bertha's and hosting the gatherings caused too much disruption. Within a few months they had decided on Lilias Toward's beautiful waterfront house at 36 Rockcliffe Street as their permanent meeting place. Lilias was generous with her hospitality, but these were not social occasions by any means. The group members brought their week's notes with them. They reviewed every difficult case. They dug out old examinations and individual students were assigned responsibility for preparing model answers to be read aloud. They dissected everything they had been taught, taking nothing for granted and even preparing discussion topics for the next week's classes. Their law professors made them think and thinking made them question. Wilson was aware that this intense questioning meant that the group could be something of a nuisance for the rest of the class.[13]

There was a sense among the other students in their year that some of the members of the group had forgotten how to have fun and were raising the standard of expected achievement. Worse, they tended to control the classroom discussion in accordance with the directions their own studies had taken them. If one student in the group faltered in responding to a question or if the answer to a question prepared by the group was not satisfactory then another student might stand up and continue the discussion. For some of the more easy-going professors it could be an intimidating experience to be confronted by this extremely well-prepared group.

John Charters, who was married with two small children, had made a considerable financial sacrifice to attend law school. He quite frankly admitted that he intended to become prosperous through the practice of law. With all the self-confidence born of his successful career in the navy prior to law school, he could be unpleasantly aggressive in his questioning and openly critical of those instructors whom he considered did not meet his standards. He was determined to get his money's worth out of his tuition.

On one occasion, for example, he wanted Professor Graham Murray to provide him with the definitive explanation of the archaic and mysterious law of perpetuities. Professor Murray rested his head in his hands, sighed and replied with his characteristic diffidence, 'I don't think I'll ever understand it myself.' This was not the kind of answer which Charters considered at all acceptable. He muttered audibly about Murray's fuzzy thinking and Murray in turn was heard to complain more discreetly in faculty meetings about the group's tactics. Even twenty-five years later, Murray remembered Wilson's study group. 'I've never seen anything like it before or since,'[14] he recalled, and not with pleasure.

By all accounts, Bertha never participated in Charters's style of in-class intimidation. Professor Lorne Clarke recalls that she was exceptionally well prepared and that her comments and questions were right on point. However, she was invariably low key and even gracious in her manner. Always conscious of her working-class origins, Wilson's new-found academic intensity had affinities with the Calvinist ideology of the democratic intellect through which the individual could raise herself up through her own efforts; what ambition she had was more social than financial.

Her primary drive, however, was her fervent interest in the theoretical underpinnings of law. For the first time she was finding academic study exciting in itself. It might not have looked like it to the young and single law students who quite understandably devoted as much time as possible to dating and beer drinking, but Bertha was having fun. She had finally caught the fever which had infected her brothers and her husband at Aberdeen. The more abstract and philosophical the speculation engaged in by the legal scholars on faculty at Dalhousie, the more she enjoyed it.

What made it all the more enjoyable to her was that, unlike the vigorous debates around the table at Cheyne Road which had so exasperated her mother, legal theory illuminated issues which had direct application to life. She could see principled solutions to the pragmatic problems facing the parishioners she had counselled as a minister's wife. Her classroom contributions to legal analysis are remembered as always strongly characterized by 'a concern for what she felt was right, what was honourable.'[15] Her growing recognition of the power of law's pragmatic application meant that Bertha Wilson had come to the realization that she was after all going to want to practise law after graduation in some way or another.

Within the group there was a certain amount of internal rivalry which Wilson considered fair game. When Charters told her that he was going to win top marks in jurisprudence and in constitutional law, Wilson let him know she would be challenging him for both these honours and did so successfully. In their graduating year, she as plaintiff and Charters as defendant shared the Smith Shield for legal argument, mooting a contracts case before three judges. But it was Charters, who worked so hard at law school without apparently enjoying it much or continuing in practice for very long after graduation, who won the gold medal.

Wilson may not have graduated top of her class[16] but in Clarke's opinion she exhibited the most scholarly curiosity of all the students in her year and was often well ahead of her classmates in the probing quality of the comments and questions which she contributed. And among this keen and competitive group, Bertha in her trademark black sweaters was always noted for her kindness in lending her notes or consoling the lovelorn as much as for the acuity of her legal analysis.[17] Although older, female, a little prim, not native to Nova Scotia, and much more studious than the average student, she is nevertheless remembered as having fitted in beautifully. Her own well-tested marriage offered her a stability and security many of the younger students lacked.

It was because she was confident of John's support (he did all the cooking and shopping, she did the cleaning) that she was able to focus wholeheartedly on her studies. Wilson herself insists that what she learned by talking about law from her fellow students, including those who were not part of the special study group, was at least as important as what she learned in class. When some thirty-five years later she was invited to speak to the first-year students at Queen's about the process of obtaining a legal education, she told them:

> You will find that the study of law is quite different from any other subject you've taken on. You cannot do it by yourself. You can't just retire to a quiet corner and mug it up. You've got to talk about it with others – form a small group for discussion and debating purposes. Don't just accept what the professor says is gospel – think about it, add a few variants to the facts and inquire: would the answer still be the same if this and so. This is stuff you have to really understand. You have to reason it through and make it part of your own intellectual experience ... You can plumb the depths of your intellectual capacities and achieve the joy and satisfaction in knowing that you've really got it – that this new piece of knowledge will from here on be part of a richer and profounder you. That is what I mean when I say that law is part of a liberal education. It's more than just a subject; it's a growing experience.[18]

There was one class which she did regret missing out on. At that time, the only optional courses at Dalhousie law school were offered in third year: students could choose a seminar on labour law, international law, or land use. Lilias Toward influenced Bertha to join her in taking Professor Murray's seminar in town planning in her third year. Wilson became intrigued with new developments in nuisance law and in zoning restrictions as a taking of property. 'A Choice of Values,' a revised version of the paper she prepared for this course, was one of Wilson's earliest scholarly publications. It appeared in the *Canadian Bar Journal* in 1961.

Wilson always regretted that she had been unable to fit into her law school schedule a course in labour law. No subsequent reading and reflection or continuing legal education courses, she thought, were adequate to fill the gap. In Wilson's own mind, theoretical legal education belongs firmly in the law school which offers the best and only opportunity of acquiring a solid conceptual foundation in all the various areas of law. Procedural training is quite properly the purview of the bar admissions and articling and early associateship years. However, Dalhousie during Bertha Wilson's era made an effort to integrate the two strands. Articling commenced with some practical training during third-year law school, followed by a full year of apprenticeship during which the student was attached to a particular articling principal.[19]

Wilson's experience at Dalhousie did not change the opinion she had expressed to Horace Read at her admission interview. For years afterwards, in fact, she has sustained her belief that the study of law, because it touches on peoples' lives at every significant point, ought to be part of the liberal education offered routinely to all students in a democracy. Wilson defines liberal education as an 'education for living ... [to provide] basic ground rules for individuals living in society.'[20] As we have already seen, Wilson credits her experiences as a minister's wife at Macduff as initiating her own real education for living and as essential to her subsequent professional life as law school itself.

GRADUATION AND ARTICLES

The news report of Bertha Wilson's graduation notes that 'two of the lady lawyers were prize-winners in their final year and all ranked high in the 58–member class'; Wilson, of course, was one of these and Lilias Toward, who won the Sir James Dunn, Bart. scholarship to complete an LL.M. at Dalhousie, was the other. Moreover, Dean Horace Read is quoted as saying graciously of these lady lawyers that 'they all did extremely well.'[21]

But if law school had not changed Wilson's mind about the value of studying law as an aspect of a liberal education, Read had not entirely changed his mind about Bertha Wilson either. She had been offered a scholarship to Harvard to complete an LL.M., where she very much wanted to pursue her interests in property law and nuisance, but Read discouraged her from accepting. He told her, 'There will never be women academics teaching in law schools, not in your day.' Purdy Crawford, however, had gone off to Harvard for the LL.M.; he chose not to teach, but the nature of his practice in labour, securities, and corporate law meant that his public profile during the Osler years was always considerably higher than Wilson's.

In fact, all the women graduates, no matter how well they had done, had some difficulty getting articles; because of her age and her lack of local connections, Bertha found it even harder than the others. There was a short period of some anxiety which must have been discouragingly similar to the search for work she had already experienced in Ottawa. Realizing that her own interests in law were primarily academic, she did briefly consider post-graduate studies back home in Aberdeen.[22] But Dalhousie Professor Lorne Clarke, who had taught her corporate law, was able to persuade his friend F.W. Bissett QC to take her on as an articling student.

It was not the kind of practice best tailored to Wilson's inclinations; she confesses, laughingly, that she may have become a bit of an intellectual snob as a result of all the heady theoretical studies at Dalhousie. Bissett's grubby downtown offices on Barrington Street shared a single washroom with other offices in the same building. A chain smoker whose false teeth clicked incessantly, he loved to think through a case out loud with his feet on the desk. He practised almost exclusively low-end divorce law and criminal work, including prostitution cases, buggery charges, and drunk and disorderlies; criminal law had been one of the few areas of law not of much interest to Wilson.

Bissett cultivated his reputation as an eccentric single practitioner who was so resolutely non-intellectual in his approach to law that he tended not even to prepare legal briefs. Nevertheless, he was well regarded among the local bar where he was known for his integrity, his sheer courtroom ability, and his willingness to do more than his share of pro bono work. His representation of his underdog clients was tenacious; Bissett pursued their defence without regard for the additional expense which would inevitably be absorbed out of his own pocket.[23] At the same time, he delighted in taking Bertha down a peg or two if she attempted to engage him in any abstract or conceptual discussion.

At first he permitted Bertha to accompany him to court while she learned the ropes; Lorne Clarke can recall seeing the two of them walking along Barrington to the Spring Garden Road provincial court-house. Bissett would be in his overcoat and Homburg hat, chain smoking as always, stooped and talking non-stop to the fresh and youthful Bertha who always looked very trim and proper.

But Bissett, later leader of the Conservative Party of Nova Scotia, already had political ambitions. The Liberals were entrenched in Ottawa and (with the exception of Robert Stanfield) in Nova Scotia as well. Bissett soon discovered that he could leave this competent, mature articling student alone to manage the office and even to appear in court while he pursued his other interests. His standing with the local bench was such that Bertha was permitted to represent clients and argue cases even though she was not yet qualified as a lawyer. Bissett's first woman student may have been foisted upon him, but the story has it that he took great pride in her and voluntarily sought out women for the next three articling positions to come up in his firm.

All of this provided excellent procedural experience even if on something of a self-help basis. Bertha was grateful for the opportunity to complete bar admissions, whatever the nature of the case load and the sporadic quality of guidance offered by her articling principal; she must have realized that there could be no future in a partnership with Bissett. She wrote the final round of examinations and was called to the Nova Scotia bar in 1958. However, as it turned out, Bertha and John scarcely had time to attend the celebration party before they were on the move again back to Ontario, this time to Toronto.

4

The Osler Innovations

The Honourable John Arnup's cottage near Fenelon Falls figures large in any account of his eminent career as a lawyer and as a judge. In itself it is a modest enough dwelling, not a show piece but the kind of place where a family has enjoyed many good times around a fieldstone fireplace.

Called to the bar in 1935, John Arnup established himself as one of the leading litigators in Ontario. A partner at Weir & Foulds, he was frequently retained by other law firms who sought him out for his expertise when faced with a complex legal battle, especially a battle where credibility might be at issue. Any firm wishing to retain Arnup did so on the clear understanding that he would be largely unavailable for July and August and that he would expect work to continue on the case in his absence in accordance with the directions he had left behind. He could be contacted for advice if absolutely necessary, but the process was a cumbersome one which no junior would lightly undertake twice. A telephone call was placed to the nearest general store which would send a young lad across the lake in a boat. Arnup, summonsed, would bring his own boat back across the lake and return the call. He was noted for his patience and his courtesy, but any query directed his way during the summer months better have been an important one.

It was Arnup, called himself directly from practice to the Ontario Court of Appeal in 1970, who was quick to welcome Bertha Wilson to the bench in 1975. He had become familiar with Wilson's work in 1966, two years after he was retained by Osler, Hoskin & Harcourt in 1964 to act as principal for its client in a difficult mineral claims case; Wilson had provided the research memos. But as we sit in the sun porch of his Fenelon Falls cottage, an expanse of lawn stretching down to the smooth silvery lake, Mr. Arnup tells me that he had already heard of Bertha Wilson in 1958 within months of her arrival in Toronto. Because she had not practised for three years in Nova Scotia before moving to Toronto, she was required to article again for fifteen months, attend the preparatory lectures provided for admission to the Ontario bar, and then pass the examinations all over again. Arnup received an urgent call from a senior partner at Osler, Hoskin & Harcourt. Bertha Wilson had was in grave danger of failing one of her bar admissions examinations; she had been doing outstanding work for them and they did not want to lose her. What could be done? Arnup suggested a tactful program of remedial tutoring be put into place, to be conducted by two or three lawyers at Oslers.

ESTABLISHING A RESEARCH PRACTICE

In 1957 John Wilson's hitch in the navy was up, with little opportunity for renewal given cutbacks in military spending during the Diefenbaker era. The ecumenical atmosphere of the navy had appealed to him and he was by no means interested in returning to a conventional ministry in a Presbyterian parish church; he and Bertha had joined the interdenominational United Church (comprised, as it was, of the more liberal wing of the Presbyterian church together with Methodist and Congregationalist factions) during their years in Halifax.

On a trip to Ontario for his last naval chaplains' conference in October of 1957, he happened to spot an advertisement in a Toronto newspaper for Wells Canada, an organization seeking expertise in interdenominational church fundraising. With his longstanding interest in business ethics, the job immediately appealed to him. Impulsively he arranged for an interview, was hired on the spot, and on the strength of his new appointment persuaded Bertha to take off for a month's holidays in Europe.

They returned from the beaches of Spain and Portugal and found an apartment in Toronto in the Rosedale Ravine Apartments at 4 Sherbourne Street North in December of 1957. Unfortunately, once again her brother and his family were living elsewhere and so unable to assist the Wilsons in getting resettled; Jim Wernham had taken a position in the philosophy department at Carleton University in Ottawa in 1954 and the families continued their pattern of regular but infrequent visits. In any event, according to nephew Chris, his parents were quiet and retiring people and not likely to have had contacts in the legal community that might have led to an articling position for Bertha.

By January she was attempting to set up an appointment at Blake, Cassels with Arthur Pattillo, who was an acquaintance of Fred Bissett's and her only legal contact in Ontario. But Pattillo was in Vancouver for a year, she was told. And so Bertha began leafing through the yellow pages looking for another large-sized law firm, on the grounds that a big firm would be less likely to reject her with the excuse of lack of wash-room facilities for women. Oslers was then still in the old Dominion Bank building at the corner of King and Yonge. She had never heard of the firm before, but Osler, Hoskin & Harcourt was just about as big as Blakes and looked as though it might fit the bill. And there was a further piece of good luck in that when she called Oslers, Mr Hal Mockridge, the senior partner and probably the least amenable to hiring a woman, happened to be in New York on business for Inco, one of the firm's major clients.

She did deserve a chance to qualify, she was told by the partner who interviewed her. Gordon Wotherspoon (known as Swatty among his intimates but always 'Mr Wotherspoon' to Bertha Wilson) signed on as her articling principal but wanted her to realize unequivocally that she was accepted for the purposes of articling only. And if Wilson was a lit-tle annoyed at this cautious foreclosure of all possibility that she might be hired back, considering that she had not even been given the oppor-tunity of showing what she could do, she replied with some spirit that the arrangement would suit her fine. She might not like it at Oslers, she told Wotherspoon, amazing herself a little with her own impudence. Although she did not know it, Oslers had taken her on reluctantly, as much for John's record of service in the navy as for her performance at law school.

And so she started the very morning after she had met with Swatty Wotherspoon, working at a small desk moved into a hastily converted supplies cupboard with pebble glass in the door for a little privacy. It was not much but even so may have represented a certain gallant defer-ence to her sex. Bertha Wilson was the only articling student provided with a separate office; for many years, the males were expected to func-tion in an open bullpen.

Her first assignment came from Wotherspoon who asked her to write a memo on the topic, 'What is a bond?' The result was apparently satis-factory and more research requests were funnelled to her, not only by Wotherspoon but also by other lawyers in the firm. Mr Mockridge himself was sufficiently pleased with her research that on one occasion he called her into his office and praised her for the excellence and thoroughness of her work.

But Wilson found it a rather dry and academic exercise to prepare research memos without any understanding of the client context which had given rise to the inquiry. She soon discovered that Oslers had a policy of storing all client files centrally; this had to do with the firm's philosophy that clients were clients of the firm rather than the property of a particular lawyer, although some files containing highly confidential information were of course not so readily accessible. The central storage meant that when presented with a research question Wilson could retrieve the file, discover the factual background to the research query, and discern the legal options open to the client and the pros and cons attaching to each. Wilson provided an objective view of the law but never lost sight of the client's interest; she is remembered as a logical thinker who wrote quickly in response to the pragmatic demands of practice and seldom had to revise her first opinion.

As she launched into this research function, it became apparent to her that the same kind of legal issues were recurring for different clients. What was worrisome was the potential for various Osler lawyers to provide conflicting legal opinions to various clients on the same legal problem, or even worse, conflicting legal opinions to the same client if the same problem should recur. Wilson realized that the firm's reputation depended upon consistency. She also knew that she could save time and provide a more efficient service to the other lawyers in the firm by establishing an information retrieval system so that the basic research product needed only adaptation and perhaps updating for the particular client situation. Early during her articling year Wilson began to organize and cross-reference her memos so that she could produce a response to a research request quickly.

At the same time, part of her work for the bar admissions exams required her to get up to speed on the statutes and procedures in Ontario in so far as these were different from the Nova Scotia regime. Oslers had many corporate clients who were operating interprovincially but it occurred to Wilson that no one at the law firm had taken on the responsibility of coordinating information on provincial variations in statutes and regulations or the stage which various bills might be at in the different legislatures; she began to organize and cross-reference this material as well. Not surprisingly, the quality of her research was enhanced when it incorporated the most recent legislative amendments to the relevant statutes bearing on the client's problem, even though these added considerably to her workload.

By the end of her term of articles Wilson had made herself indispensable without realizing it. She had passed her examinations, in May 1959, and submitted the required affidavit and certificate of service in preparation for her call to the bar. A few days before the ceremony, Wotherspoon confidently and enthusiastically presented her with a complex research project; he knew her well enough by this point that he was sure it would prove interesting to her. And Wilson agreed that it did look intriguing, adding regretfully that she wouldn't be able to follow through on it:

> I said, 'You should have given this to someone else because, of course, I won't be here next week.' And he was just horrified, because of course he wasn't paying any attention. I said, 'Well, you know, I get my call to the bar this week and our deal was that I was here just to article.' 'Oh,' he said, 'don't go away.' So he beetled off, I guess to talk to the other senior partners, 'We all just assumed that you are here permanently.'

They did keep her on, of course, and she stayed at Oslers for another sixteen years. Wilson never abandoned her own scholarly interests and managed somehow to find time to write and publish a number of learned articles during the early Osler years. 'Equity and the Tenant for Life' was a useful guide for practitioners faced with the problem of drafting a will which provided for a tenant for life and successive residuary beneficiaries. A year later, her property law paper based on her Dalhousie interest in nuisance and zoning regulation appeared.[1] Then, in 1962 in 'The Accountant as Executor,' Wilson provided a straightforward description of the duties of a trustee required to take inventory of an estate which may be comprised of intangible as well as more conventional types of property.[2]

All this time, Wilson continued to develop her research and legislation files. Eventually they formed the nucleus of a separate legal research department, at that time a new concept in Canadian legal culture. The legislation cataloguing function was hived off under the separate supervision of Verna King, a secretary with additional paralegal training. Eventually Wilson was able to hire a legal librarian and several competent research lawyers for Oslers. In 1972 Maurice Coombs, who had been at the Ontario Law Reform Commission for some five years assisting with research on reforms in family law legislation and new initiatives in the development of condominium and consumer protection law, heard from friends that Bertha Wilson was interested in expanding her department. He called her and told her that he felt ready to move out of government into private practice. She was immediately interested in his experience, told him she would like to meet him, and after an initial interview called him back to tour him around the firm and see how he might fit in. An affable Fred Huycke offered Coombs an expensive cigar which he accepted gratefully. And then he panicked a little – clearly it would not do for a junior applicant to wander around puffing on a stogie as he met with the senior partners. 'I'll just tuck it in my pocket for later,' he announced and Bertha beamed approvingly: he had passed the test. Coombs was taken on.[3]

Coombs recalls that he did more real research during that first year at Oslers than in his entire government stint. All of a sudden there was the pressure of meeting client deadlines. He worked long hours and many weekends gradually helping to amass the index system on multiple cards in a huge Rolodex-like contraption which constituted the heart of the internal information-retrieval system. Once Wilson's own research memos were cross-filed, she and Coombs began to solicit similar materials hidden away in the desk drawers and filing cabinets of the firm's other lawyers; two articling students proved so useful in this task that Wilson initiated a more general rotation of articling students through both of the departments which she continued to manage.

In the early 1970s, while on a trip to Cincinnati, Wilson heard about a fledgling program under way in Columbus, Ohio, for recording legal research on the earliest typewriters with rudimentary memory capacity. She flew up to Columbus, learned all that she could in a day or so, and persuaded Oslers to approve funding to begin the process of converting her manual cross-referenced catalogue into the first computerized research library in any Canadian law firm.

Wilson also had the idea of developing for Oslers a bank of precedents, focusing particularly on trust law, wills, and estate planning but also on corporate precedents and new property concepts in condominium law relating to the ownership of air space. This innovation made it possible for a lawyer working with a particular problem to call down and obtain half a dozen different precedents, markedly reducing the time required for the drafting from scratch of complex documentation. The cataloguing of legal research and opinions, the tracking of legislation, and the establishment of precedents are ideas which have now been adopted by all major law firms, but they were extraordinarily innovative at the time. Wilson was generous in welcoming to Oslers representatives from other firms who were considering setting up their own similar departments. But the key to the success of the Oslers research department was the support it received from the most senior partners and their acknowledgment of research as a central function.

FROM FAMILY FIRM TO CORPORATE CULTURE

In 1958, however, before Wilson had initiated these innovations, Oslers was still a tightly controlled family firm with Mr Mockridge the head of the firm in all but name. Five of the eleven partners were family members; others had close relationships to the firm's major clients which included Eaton's, Molsons, Kodak, Coca-Cola, the Toronto Dominion Bank, and Inco. Osler lawyers were Conservative, white, and almost all Protestant; they and their clients had often attended the same private boys' schools. The postwar years were a period of enormous corporate growth in Canada and it was slowly becoming obvious that the old family firms would have to open up and become more democratic. They would have to change the way in which they did business or acknowledge that they were unable to keep up with the increased volume their clients demanded from them.[4] What was required was a fairly rapid transition from clan to club and then from club to corporate mentality.[5]

Bertha Wilson had fitted into the almost exclusively male world of law school very well. Similarly, she admired her new colleagues and certainly did not nurture any feminist resentments about the situation at Oslers:

> When I became the first woman to be hired as a lawyer in Osler, Hoskin, I did more than enter an all-male preserve. I became associated with a very remarkable and highly respected law firm headed by families whose names were synonymous with service to their country and their profession. They were, to use an old fashioned phrase, 'Gentlemen of the old school.'[6]

Her teacher's college training in respect for her elders together with her traditional Scottish reticence meant that she saw nothing at all inappropriate in the deference she was expected to accord the more experienced lawyers; it was a matter of seniority, not sexism. There were other ethical issues which did arise from time to time for Wilson at Oslers. Often she kept quiet, but on occasion she had to speak up.

The Oslers lawyers generally met for lunch at Child's Restaurant, gathering at a round table for twelve in various combinations and permutations; Wilson frequently joined the group, expressing her opinions firmly when the topic was law but not particularly comfortable when the conversation veered to the previous weekend's sports scores. According to Stuart Thom, Oslers' tax law expert, she was considered by other lawyers at the firm as a feminine woman but never a flirt and never the kind of woman to resort to feminine wiles to get her own way.

In subsequent years Bertha Wilson delivered a number of convocation addresses in which she pointed out to graduating classes that success in their initial jobs would depend primarily on their individual capacities for personal responsibility. They would need to take responsibility for getting along with other people at the work place, tolerating the minor injustices to which they would inevitably be subjected; all but the most serious of these should be accepted with good humour as part of 'the messy contingencies of life'[7] and so trivial as to be properly beneath notice. And they would need to impose upon themselves the discipline of being patient, waiting for the promotions which would eventually come their way without slackening off in their duty to the client or to the firm.

When she started at Oslers Wilson was thirty-five, ten years older than the average articling student. She clearly put this advice into practice in her own first job. Nevertheless, she was disappointed not to make partner for nine years; she justified the delay in her own mind on the grounds that the kind of work she was doing was different from the traditional career path followed by other lawyers in the firm, some of whom made partner in five years or less. In fact, it was as she began building the information retrieval and legislation departments that her delay in attaining partnership really became a problem; in order to recruit the first-rate lawyers she needed to work with her, Wilson had to be able to assure them that their own paths to partnership would not be delayed by taking the research route.

It is generally accepted that Purdy Crawford, Allan Beattie, and Bertha Wilson – none of them related to the founding Osler family – did the most to bring about reform in Oslers' management structure.[8] Crawford was the rainmaker, Beattie the conciliator and consensus builder. As Wilson became the in-house lawyer's lawyer, she sat in on sessions with clients more frequently and advised the lawyer who was acting directly on the file. This developed her reputation outside the firm as the 'brains behind the big names,' but she had to be sensitive not to outshine the lawyer whose client she was advising. Wilson's research innovations and her willingness to be of service were so obviously useful in streamlining Oslers' procedures that it was not long before the executive committee realized that central cataloguing and quick retrieval of research had the potential to increase the profitability of its corporate files.

The Oslers Wilson had joined was a firm noted for its integrity; Mr Mockridge, for example, would not permit Osler lawyers to construct tax avoidance schemes for its corporate clients even though they might be strictly speaking within the letter of the Income Tax Act and even though he himself was strongly of the opinion that the policies underlying the tax were economically indefensible.[9] Given the firm's pride in this reputation, it must have been somewhat galling to have their junior lawyer and only woman challenging the firm periodically on ethical grounds. Ironically enough, the multiple reuse of legal research made possible through her information retrieval systems created for Wilson an enormous dilemma which finally blew up in her dealings with the senior partner, G.M. ('Mossy') Huycke.

Mr Huycke specialized in wills and estates and often had legal problems for which he sought out Wilson's research skills. This was an area of particular interest to Wilson in which she did take on clients of her own; generally clad in dark V-necked jumpers with white blouses or unremarkable tweed suits, her colleagues knew that Wilson was coming out of the back room when she arrived at the office in her formal navy 'meeting-with-clients' suit. Her gender could be advantageous in assisting the wives of corporate executives, who were generally more comfortable confiding their wishes to another woman. It was she who recognized that because husbands and wives do not necessarily have the same testamentary intentions, their will instructions should therefore be taken separately.

However, Huycke also had some responsibility for the financial management of the firm during Wilson's early years of practice, especially in requiring compliance from juniors with the docketing system customarily used to track lawyers' billable hours. Very little work in law firms is done on a flat fee basis; lawyers customarily charge on an hourly basis against a retainer which is deposited in the firm's trust account. If the lawyer does not keep track of every unit of time he or she expends on working for a particular client, then the firm cannot recover its expenditure for the associate's salary and of course there is correspondingly less profit to be distributed among the partners net of the expenses of doing business. With large corporate clients who have retained a law firm on an ongoing basis, there may be a number of lawyers working on various aspects of the client's work over any given period of time. Billing involves a collection and compilation of all these individual dockets and might occur only at fairly long intervals of six months to a year.

At first Wilson's speed and thoroughness in generating the research memos and opinions made her a profit centre for the firm and accordingly her work was lauded. But as she built up her information retrieval system her profitability fell off. She could bring herself to charge only for new research required by a particular client but not for the value of research which she had already done, beyond the time it took her to retrieve the original memo and rework the information into a problem-specific opinion. To her, charging full price a second or third time around smacked of the Macduff draper's assistant required by her boss to sell off special sale merchandise as if it were quality goods.

Wilson recalled Huycke's rebuke for her billings on one particular file:

> I realized that I couldn't charge this client for [time] that I hadn't spent and the firm presumably had already been paid for that by somebody else, so what I started doing was not putting in my charges and one day I got called up before a senior partner and he wondered what had gone wrong, because from being a profitable servant I had become an unprofitable servant ...
>
> It had been a phone call that [Mr. Huycke] had received on a matter that needed an opinion very fast and he had come down the hall to my office and said, 'Well, I want you to drop everything you are doing and look into this because I promised them that I would phone them back today.' Which I did. As it turned out apparently it was a very important issue for them, financially and I hadn't spent very long on it because I think he had come to me almost at lunch time and I had probably spent an hour or an hour and a half or something, checking this out in the library. And I charged accordingly.
>
> Months later ... he had been putting out the great long account that these permanent clients receive ... he saw this charge of mine and was absolutely furious and I was hauled up to explain how ... I know I started off at $5.00 an hour and then I crept up to $10.00 an hour and so on, so I had probably put in a charge of $15.00 or $20.00, something like that ... So I explained how I reached the figure ... and of course he was just livid. And he said, 'Don't you recall that I told you how important this was to the client, how he had to have the answer right away, how you were to drop everything else you were doing?' And I said, 'Yes, I recall all that.' And he said, 'Didn't

you realize that this was a matter of great value then, to this client? ... This is what you have been doing?' And I said, 'Yes.' So of course they realized then how I had become a non-productive person and they decided that I was to record my hours only, I was to put no monetary value and they would decide the value to the client ... They said that I was incapable of valuing my own work.

Wilson may have capitulated but she did not change her mind. Because she had little choice, she consented to the firm valuing her time for billing purposes, but from Allan Beattie's account she never did so willingly. Beattie recalls another occasion when Huycke chastised Wilson for carelessness in her handling of her dockets, exploding at her as the paper slips fluttered about her, 'These are like five dollar bills!'; When Beattie was appointed chairman of the executive committee in 1972 and managing partner after 1973, he himself had to deal with her directly on the same billing issues. He found it very frustrating until he came to realize that she was simply modest, not only about the quality of her work but also about the amount of time she had spent on it.

Beattie recalls her working ferocious hours and understating the time, while other lawyers had a tendency to exaggerate both their time and the value of that time to the client. On at least one occasion, when Wilson had stayed late to prepare an opinion for a client and sent it off in the mail, she found herself unable to sleep once she arrived home. Perhaps there was another angle she should have considered; maybe she should have consulted an additional source or two. By two in the morning she had woken John and asked him to drive her back to the office. Delving into the library, she put in an additional three hours or so, satisfied herself that she had got it right the first time and had John drive her home again, presumably without changing the original docket of her time that she had first prepared.

This issue of value billing for women's work and also the presumption that billable hours were the only measure of worthiness for promotion from associateship to partnership was one Wilson was to revisit with particular insight during the preparation of the gender equality study for the Canadian Bar Association she would chair later in her career. Her own experience at Oslers underlies some of the most controversial recommendations made in that report.

One method of assuaging her conscience over the billing issue was the opportunity Wilson found in her wills and estates work to present to

Oslers' wealthy corporate clients opportunities for charitable donations which might not have occurred to them independently. She was particularly interested in the use of trust law in estate planning in order to minimize taxation and experienced no ethical conflict in taking advantage of variations in international tax laws which could benefit Oslers' clients; the relevant legislatures could always choose to amend their statutes if there were loopholes to be closed, but in the meantime, she reasoned, clients had no obligation to make donations to government entities.

Quite often this estate planning involved the purchase of real estate overseas to be vested in the trust. Wilson began to realize that it was necessary to travel with one or other of the partners (all of whom were, of course, male) to explain the rationale and appropriate mechanisms for these purchases; she had done the research and often established the contacts and the male partner needed her for backup. However, to her surprise it turned out this raised a very controversial issue. Hal Mockridge worried about the potential for gossip within the firm and perhaps more publicly if a female lawyer were to travel with a male lawyer. Initially, he refused his permission.

Wilson seldom engaged in head-on confrontation to protect her own interests at Oslers or anywhere else, but this restriction was not in the category of minor injustice to be tolerated. The question was how to go about persuading Mockridge to reverse his decision. She was quite sure that his stance was not indicative of any serious questioning of her personal morality or the state of her marriage; she understood his preoccupation with propriety and decided not to take his edict personally. Instead, she went to him and appealed to his sense of professionalism and his fair-mindedness; if she were not allowed to do the travel necessary to follow up on these files, not only would the scope of her practice be unreasonably constricted but the clients' interests might be fatally compromised. Faced with these arguments, Mockridge agreed to let her go. However, he did require both John Wilson and the male lawyer's wife to grant permission, indicating that neither of them was troubled by the joint business trips of their spouses.

DEVELOPING PHILANTHROPY: A CONSERVATIVE SOCIALIST AT WORK

Wilson's trust work also involved visiting clients in their homes. Although Wilson always found it difficult to be at ease with the wealthier members of the congregation at Macduff or Renfrew, she had no hesitation in making it clear to Oslers' wealthy estate-planning clients that she was not a typical member of the firm but a socialist; in fact, she and John Wilson by this time were card-carrying members of the New Democratic party. Beattie can recall occasions when Wilson was quite frank in expressing her political views.[10] But Oslers' clients were invariably charmed by her humorous self-deprecation moderated by her perpetual sense of duty, and tended not to take offence. Wilson might say, if the issue arose: 'It's not that I don't approve of you personally, but perhaps I don't approve of everything you stand for, but that doesn't mean that I am not going to be completely dedicated to achieving the results for you that you want.'

Wilson was always interested in encouraging private philanthropy. As a result of the estates aspect of her practice, Wilson worked with John Hodgson of Blake, Cassels to establish the charities subsection of the Wills and Trusts section of the Canadian Bar Association (Ontario) and its magazine, the *Philanthropist*, of which she became the first editor. It took a lot of time and effort to persuade people to write articles for the magazine, but her efforts in promoting the work of the *Philanthropist* had the side effect of further raising Wilson's profile outside her research role at Oslers.

When it became apparent that there was no central clearing house for charitable foundations, Wilson, John Hodgson, and new contacts they made through the *Philanthropist* turned their energies towards the founding of the Canadian Centre for Philanthropy, a Toronto-based organization which has developed courses in private sector fundraising and grant application techniques. The law of charities is an old and academically interesting area of law, not much revised over the centuries.[11] Wilson had a pragmatic and non-judgmental understanding that people are motivated to give to charities because of the tax advantages which accrue to them from doing so. Like the great economist Adam Smith, she realized without particular shock or disapproval that pure altruism is a rare phenomenon. However, altruism may not be necessary to the functioning of a civil society; the desire for recognition is often sufficient to motivate individuals to engage in good works.

Wilson preferred not to draft the legal documents which arose out of the legal research and opinions she provided and she did not question the firm's decision to make use of her talents primarily as a lawyer's lawyer.[12] She seldom spoke up in partnership meetings although if someone presented a position which troubled her, she might seek him out the following day and let him know her opinion privately. During all the years she worked at Oslers, Wilson had very few clients who were completely her own. She was made a partner on 1 January 1968 and named a Queen's Counsel in 1973, but was never a senior partner or appointed to the firm's management committee.

In fact, despite her success, Wilson says she preferred a minimum of client contact in her legal work, especially relishing her freedom from any of the social responsibility of rainmaking such as taking clients out to lunch. Bissett may have poked fun at her intellectual pretensions; at Oslers she was free to consider herself an academic lawyer, immersed in the intellectual challenges she would have enjoyed had she pursued postgraduate studies at Harvard. In Coombs's opinion, it was the knotty intractability of the legal issues which interested Wilson most intensely rather than the clients themselves; this was an enthusiasm he fully understood and shared. On one occasion, he recalls, Bill Bryden, a particularly compassionate lawyer, had come to them for help. He outlined the situation and Coombs responded eagerly, practically wringing his hands with excitement. 'That's a great problem!' he blurted out. Bryden was taken aback and Wilson took Coombs aside, explaining that propriety required a little more sympathy and restraint.

Even though she had been assigned a fair amount of court work while articling for Fred Bissett in Nova Scotia, Wilson did not seek to continue that experience in Ontario. Occasionally she would go into court with the firm's litigation lawyers as research backup, but even then she would not likely sit at the counsel table. Stuart Thom, Oslers' tax expert, worked very closely with Bertha on a number of complicated trust matters and had a huge respect for her abilities; he would have liked to see her take an active litigation role, especially in the wills and estates area.[13] Allan Beattie believes that only when she went to the Court of Appeal did she realize for the first time that she could have been a first-rate courtroom lawyer.

Beattie probably knew Wilson better at Oslers than anyone else – there was a friendship between the two couples focused in part around their shared religious beliefs and the Wilsons and the Beatties travelled together on a number of occasions – and Beattie stresses that it would be a serious misreading of her history at the firm to perceive that Wilson was held back in any way. Her Osler role can be viewed fairly only in the context of the times; the 1960s and 1970s were a transitional period in terms of women's liberation and their entry into the professions. The legal world in particular was still a male preserve.

Oslers, like most law firms, was conservative; it is also the case that Wilson was herself quite conservative – if not politically, then personally. She had no desire to assert herself as equal in the sense of being

identical with the more prominent male lawyers.[14] Wilson was permitted to carve out the role she wanted, a different role. She was respected
for her expertise in that role and built her own bailiwick within the firm.
And as far as Beattie is concerned, she became very influential at Oslers.
But it was typical of Wilson that at work she invariably addressed Allan
Beattie as Mr Beattie; on social occasions, he says wryly, she tended to
avoid calling him anything at all. And in fact, she accorded the same
courtesy to her junior, addressing Maurice Coombs punctiliously as Mr
Coombs on every occasion, professional or social, for the entire first year
of his employment, until finally one of the senior partners suggested
that she might use his first name.

COURTROOM STRATEGY: *TEXAS GULF SULPHUR*

There was, during her time at Oslers, one famous litigation file which
Wilson did work on over several years, *Leitch Gold Mines* v. *Texas Gulf
Sulphur*.[15] It was on this case that she got to know John Arnup. Arnup
had been retained by Oslers in 1964 on behalf of its client, the defendant.
Bill Bryden went to see him at his house as soon as he discovered that
J.J. Robinette would be representing the plaintiff. Bryden had been a
partner at Oslers for almost ten years at the time and was himself a competent and experienced lawyer, but with Robinette on the other side he
knew that he would need help.

The case concerned a massive mineral claim near Timmins, Ontario,
with an estimated value of some $450 million which was then the largest
claim ever to be adjudicated in a Canadian court. Texas Gulf had con-
tracted with Leitch to provide it with aerial surveys over a large area of
the surrounding country extending into Quebec, but the contract specified that Texas Gulf was permitted to exclude the transfer of geophysi-
cal information pertaining to certain subsections of the area surveyed. It
was probably inevitable that Texas Gulf discovered valuable copper,
zinc, and silver deposits in one of these excluded subsections which it
promptly developed on its own behalf into an extremely lucrative mine.
Leitch claimed that there was confusion concerning the excluded area
and in its action sought an interest in the Texas Gulf mine based on constructive trust principles.

The case, which turned largely on the issue of whether or not the area
in question had in fact been contractually excluded, was extremely complex. The plaintiff argued that the contract and the location maps incorporated within it were both ambiguous in key respects. For Arnup to

make his case required very painstaking coordination of data derived from the electromagnetic survey instruments (the 'fids,' or correlated fiducial numbers) as they related to those physical anomalies on the ground signalling the likelihood of mineral deposits which could be observed and photographed from the air (the 'pics'). This was, of course, an era without any computer-assisted document management or imaging capabilities. A second major issue revolved around the credibility of the various witnesses for each party in so far as their testimony provided evidence of verbal modification of the contract. Assessing their expertise required Arnup to gain considerable familiarity with aspects of cartography and geophysics; real property law also came into play. It took the better part of two years after Arnup came on board before he considered that the case was adequately prepared for the trial, which began in 1966.

At the time of the trial the University Avenue court-house was still quite new and there was some unfinished open space on the sixth floor, roughly the area of two courtrooms, which was turned over to Oslers. This war room was known within the firm as 'the gymnasium.' Film flight strips from the aerial surveys were pieced together on acetate overlays in giant mosaics and pegged up with clothespins for ready reference throughout the trial; additional documentation was stored in ten legal filing cabinets and there was a large conference table where the Osler team could meet to discuss what had happened that day in court. Putting in the evidence alone required 130 days of meticulous attention to detail, the kind of work for which Arnup was renowned. He himself reviewed the transcript as soon as it had been prepared from the previous day's hearing by the court reporter and compared it with his own notes. His first submissions to the court as a preliminary matter each day of the hearings concerned corrections to the transcript which he considered necessary.

As Arnup recalls it, all the evidence for both sides was in and he was developing his final argument when he first met Bertha Wilson. She and her team of researchers had prepared a number of excellent legal memos concerning the few purely legal points which were of concern. During the course of her research, Wilson had uncovered another legal argument which she thought that Robinette might make and which she was afraid could be fatal to the Texas Gulf position. Oslers had a duty to do its very best for its client; she must have known that her discovery would not be welcome news but she believed it was necessary even at that late date to amend the statement of defence and that accordingly it was her duty to raise the issue with the senior lawyers.

The argument Wilson had discovered had never occurred to Arnup or to any of the other members of the Osler team.[16] Judging from his observations of Chief Justice Gale and his note-taking activities as the evidence was presented, Arnup believed that the case was going well for his client. Amending the statement of defence would make obsolete a good deal of the work the judge had already done in preparing his draft judgment and Arnup did not think that could be helpful to his client.

Arnup was taken aback at Wilson's suggestion. From a legal perspective, he had to agree that her novel argument had merit. As a litigation strategy, on the other hand, this proposal for a late amendment to the statement of defence seemed to him to be a very poor idea. It would require the bringing of a motion, would interrupt the flow of the proceedings, and could suggest to Gale and to Robinette that he had lost confidence in his case. Gale would be puzzled; Robinette, overjoyed.

Bill Bryden, Dennis Lane, John Arnup, and Bertha Wilson spent half a day sitting around the conference table in the gymnasium considering the pros and cons of accepting her suggestion. It was Arnup's belief that if the argument had not occurred to him, it probably had not occurred to Robinette either. That was the gamble he had to take; it was Bill Bryden, however, who made the decision that because Oslers had retained Arnup to represent its client, Arnup's position should prevail.

Robinette's closing argument took ten days. He did not once refer to the argument suggested by Wilson. Arnup wrapped up in thirteen more days for the defendant without, of course, mentioning the Wilson argument either. Gale found entirely for Texas Gulf on the main issue, ownership of the lucrative mine in question, although there was a small award to the plaintiff for damages for potential land speculation profits. The judgment did reveal, however, an understanding of the commercial reality that if Texas Gulf had pushed too hard in its negotiations to acquire those lands where it had determined economically viable mineral deposits were located, it would have tipped off its competitors and inflated the prices of the lands it wanted to acquire. Gale held on the facts that there was no patent ambiguity and no relevant latent ambiguity in the contract. According to Arnup, this section of the judgment is derived almost in its entirety from the superb legal research provided by Bertha Wilson and her team.

The remainder of the case turned on credibility. With his carefully acquired grasp of the relevant scientific principles and his painstaking organization of the detail generated by the data, Arnup was able to demonstrate that the testimony of the Leitch witnesses had been tainted by opportunism. It is difficult to overturn a decision based on findings of fact, particularly if the judgment states that where facts were in dispute the trial judge has determined the facts by weighing the relative credibility of the witnesses. Despite the value of the claim at issue, Gale's judgment was on its face impregnable and the case was never appealed.

Some sixteen years after *Texas Gulf*, Wilson made an after-dinner speech to a group of newly appointed trial judges in Quebec which she called 'The Unappealable Judgment.' In this wonderfully mischievous speech, she advised the new judges to avoid successful appeals by controlling the shape of the case and confining their findings, as much as possible, to the facts rather than to findings of law or findings of mixed fact and law:

> The tool for shaping the case is, of course, findings. Let that word be indelibly imprinted in your mind. Say it over and over again as you bump your head on the pillow before you go to sleep. It is your secret weapon. Every case is, as you know, made up of two elements – the facts and the law. Appellate courts may be able to overrule you on the law but on the facts you, the trial judge, are supreme. Now you are all thoroughly familiar with the law before you got to the bench. Obviously, you have been outstanding practitioners or you would not have been appointed to this high office. The law therefore is not a problem, and for the odd one or two judges to whom it might conceivably present some difficulty, there are always the law clerks. No, the real challenge is finding the right facts, the facts that are going to paralyse the judges on appeal and leave them gnashing their teeth in frustration![17]

She does not name *Texas Gulf* in this speech, but it seems very likely that she had begun learning these lessons from Chief Justice Gale long before both of them were to meet at the Court of Appeal.

Although Arnup did not agree with her, he did not dismiss her suggestion out of hand as the presumption of a junior. Later, she recalled the trepidation she had had about working with him on the *Texas Gulf* case:

> At that time a woman in the legal profession was still something of a *rara*

avis and I wondered before I met him how he would react. I need not have been concerned. I found in this man a true servant of the law and what mattered to him regarding any of his associates was their measure of devotion to that service. It was not a relevant factor whether they were senior or junior, male of female. He was always kind and courteous, ready to accept any contribution that seemed to him to have merit. And it was a sheer joy to see how the various strands of input were carefully wrought and crafted and given direction and shape in his later presentation, all the while displaying those natural gifts of orderly analysis that he seemed to summon without apparent effort.[18]

John Arnup and Bertha Wilson recognized in each other a congruence of values and attitudes which cut across hierarchy: Arnup was also a staunch adherent of the United Church, his father having served as moderator. Moreover, John Arnup remembered from his own early years as a junior lawyer how much the rare and exquisite courtesy of Mr Justice Middleton had meant to him.[19] Throughout his career he quite deliberately modelled his own behaviour as a lawyer and later as a judge on Middleton, Wilson, as we will see, would learn a great deal more from Arnup on the bench.

THE CONSCIENCE OF THE FIRM

Wilson continued to function, in the words of Allan Beattie, as the conscience of the firm. In Coombs's opinion, although there is no question that his principal loved the law, she seemed on occasion to be even more interested in the dynamics among the partners and staff, and the necessity of encouraging the firm to live up to its larger responsibilities. She perceived Oslers and other large law firms as 'skimming the cream'[20] from legal practice, dealing almost exclusively with huge clients who had no difficulty in paying the hefty fees which they were charged but offering little to ordinary people with serious legal problems which quite often had a traumatic impact on their personal lives. It troubled her a great deal that law was becoming more of a business than a profession. Together with a few like-minded lawyers she tried to encourage Oslers to set up store-front community legal services on a pro bono basis to compensate for the rarefied practice the firm was able to enjoy, but she had to acknowledge in the end that the typical Osler lawyer would not have been either comfortable or effective in such a role.[21]

This was, in fact, the kind of issue on which Beattie and Wilson sharply disagreed. Beattie believed in consensus-building, in getting a little bit agreed to and then moving ahead slowly and surely; his job, as he saw it, required him to get the idea sold to the appropriate constituency within the firm. Beattie sees Wilson's style as more impetuous, in part because she had a natural ability to see the big picture and the courage to leap ahead, but in part because she was at times a little naive or impractical. She might enunciate the principles of incrementalism, but during the Osler years she was often impatient about the time it took to achieve change, especially when she believed that change to be urgently required. Beattie's approach was more gradual but his fundamental values not very different from Wilson's and he has devoted a very great deal of his own time to charitable causes.

Beattie was also able to achieve some consensus on the store-front proposal. He suggested an inventory be made within the firm of all the contributions made by Osler lawyers in their free time to their various charitable endeavours outside of practice. When it was completed, Wilson had to admit her critique had been harsh. She was not only impressed but comforted to realize the extent of her colleagues' contributions to the Toronto community. Wilson also had to acknowledge that it was Oslers' well-heeled clients who were able to fund the kind of legal research which she herself found so intellectually stimulating; there were parallels here with the Macduff church elders whose business ethics made her uncomfortable but who nevertheless were the financial pillars of the church.

Wilson was more successful in her internal efforts within the firm to transform what had been a benevolent dictatorship into a more democratic management structure. Oslers had moved across the street to the Prudential Building at the corner of King and Yonge in 1961 and continued to expand. By the mid-2970s there were thirty-eight partners and a great deal of the real work of managing the firm was being handled by mid-level committees. But the labour of these committees could still be overturned by policy fiat imposed from above. It was becoming increasingly clear that not all partners shared Wilson's philosophy that the interests of the firm as a legal entity ought to be placed ahead of personal interest and individual career development.[22] She saw this trend, which she deplored, as further evidence of the transition of the practice of law from a profession to a business.

Wilson was one of four lawyers who signed a memo in 1975 addressed to the executive committee through managing partner Allan Beattie which sought to combat that attitude. The group proposed expanding the executive committee and opening it up to more constituencies within the firm so that the majority of the members would be elected, rather than appointed simply on the basis of their seniority. They offered two sound reasons for doing so. First, it was not economically or professionally good practice to continue to appoint all the senior partners to the executive committee for an indefinite term of office; it meant that they were preoccupied with management to the detriment of their practices and their important rainmaking functions in client development at the very point in their careers when they were at the peak of their professional expertise. Secondly, some junior members within the firm had a genuine interest in and flair for law office management. They wanted to serve as conduits for more diversified and imaginative solutions to various challenges facing the firm. It took many months of debate and Wilson had herself left before Oslers' management reforms were completed, but the changes suggested by the junior group were implemented pretty much as recommended and they opened the firm up to an increasingly democratic form of governance.

There were a number of women who joined Oslers as associates and eventually became partners during the early 1970s. Wilson was successful in having the firm introduce appropriate maternity leave policies; from Allan Beattie's perspective, the primary problem was in persuading the women to take all the leave from practice which Oslers was prepared to fund. The firm still subscribed to a somewhat paternalistic belief that, at least towards the end of their pregnancies, women ought to be taking it easy; on the other hand, many of the younger women in law still subscribed to the sameness feminist philosophies which were endemic during that era.[23]

Above all, Wilson's chief source of power and success within the firm was her skill in letting everyone know what she was working on. Out of her work cataloguing changes to statutes and regulations she developed a synopsis service targeted towards Oslers' clients whose business interests might be affected. This was an excellent external marketing tool providing clients an added value for no additional fee. With the increase in desktop publishing capacity, it is now routine in law firms of all sizes, but at that time it was very new.

And Wilson had so much intellectual enthusiasm for the law that she also spent many hours talking informally to everyone within the office about her current research projects. Her immense capacity for personal warmth meant that when people came to see her about legal problems, the consultation often moved into a consideration of personal problems.

Wilson spent many hours with lawyers and staff at all levels within the firm listening to them, advising them, and consoling them. As Coombs, not a sentimental man, describes it very simply, 'Everybody loved her.'

Although not craving direct client contact in her work as a lawyer, Wilson always liked people and cared about them; even senior members of the firm became accustomed to confiding in her. Allan Beattie considers that Wilson was not ambitious in the normal sense while she worked at Oslers, but that she was not above taking the opportunity of using this network of people who poured into her office to advance her own agenda of ideas which she considered to be for the betterment of the firm.

She wanted to be good at what she did, she worked very hard, and as her staff expanded she was unusually skilled at delegating tasks to others. In ordinary business transactions outside her informal counselling role, Wilson sustained a crisp professionalism on the job which left no ambiguity about the standard which she expected on the assignments which she distributed.

PUBLIC COMMITMENTS, PRIVATE LIFE

Although the volume and the quality of work Wilson produced remained high, due in part to her remarkable ability to concentrate on the task at hand, her health was not good for much of the time she spent at Oslers. She suffered from high blood pressure from the early 1960s on; she was hospitalized for several serious operations which required lengthy periods for recuperation; and her arthritis was severe enough that she was often unable to sleep, getting up several times during the night for hot baths and tea to ease the pain.[24] By 1974 she realized that her workload was too strenuous. Then aged fifty, she was already considering retirement or a reduction in her hours. She had approached Hal Mockridge about stepping down at the next partnership renewal. In part, this decision may have been related to her sense that she had gone as far as she could within the firm. It was important to her also that she had received assurance that what she had done was more than adequate to justify her parents' financial sacrifices and satisfy their ambitions for her.

During the years at Oslers several of Wilson's trips on estate files involving international tax planning were to the United Kingdom. She was able to visit with her parents in Aberdeen from time to time. Her mother's dismay at the time of her marriage had given way to pride in

Bertha's new accomplishments at law school. Christina Wernham took real pleasure in learning that her daughter had been made a partner. And her attitude towards John had also softened a little. Moreover, Bertha's father had more sympathy for John's socialist politics after he had himself retired to enjoy the benefits of an improved old age pension scheme and free medical care introduced in the United Kingdom by a Labour government.

By this time Bertha's oldest brother, Archie, was long since married. He and his wife Hilda had two boys. Their family was living in Aberdeen, where Archie taught philosophy and served as dean at the university after his stint at St Andrew's. Archie's rather lofty disdain for those who professed religious faith had been somewhat moderated even before Mr Wernham's death in the late 1960s. Rather belatedly, Archie seemed to become aware that his focus on intellectual activity to the exclusion of all else had cramped his ability to make satisfying connections with other people.

Christina Wernham died in the mid-1970s, shortly before Wilson was appointed to the Court of Appeal. Bertha remembers travelling to Aberdeen when Archie and his wife needed a hand with the nursing at the end of her mother's life. Probably because of the wartime deprivations she had endured with baby Archie, Mrs Wernham had always had a special fondness and a fierce protectiveness for her first-born. She believed him to be a genius, moved the family to Aberdeen to enrol him in private school, organized the household so that he could study, raised the money for his school fees by taking in paying guests, and then looked after him all his life. There was never any question that Archie would care for her when she was dying, but he needed a respite. Bertha arrived to help.

Brother and sister sat talking around the fire, recalling some of the philosophical arguments that they had shared with their brother Jim (and occasionally with John Wilson) which their mother had once found so infuriatingly impractical; they concluded, oddly enough, that it was from their mother that all three of them had inherited their philosophical 'bump.' This was the occasion of the most intimate conversation she was ever to have with Archie and it was deeply satisfying to tell him a little about her success in law. And Archie had a confession to make. He had realized during their early philosophical debates that she was not herself very interested in the intellectual concepts they were batting around and had not done the reading or the thinking about them in which the three young men delighted. Nevertheless, for the first time he admitted that she had on several occasions contributed points to the discussion which had not occurred to him. Without realizing it (and despite the fact that they had been loathe to acknowledge it even to each other at the time) she had regularly dumbfounded them all. And then all of a sudden he added, as if it was a recognition which still surprised him, 'You know, you have the best mind of the three of us.'

What a tribute to savour. Moreover, it is easy to understand why Bertha was ready to consider slowing down when we think of the pace of her life with John and in the larger community outside Oslers during these years. She spent three years on the Ontario and National Councils of the Canadian Bar Associations, three years as a member of the board of trustees of the Clarke Institute of Psychiatry, and six years on the board of the Toronto School of Theology. But her major contribution outside law was still to church work. During the entire period she was in practice there was never a time when she was not serving on some United Church committee or other. More often than not she was engaged in contributing her legal expertise to the resolution of immediate problems and formulation of church policy on complex issues such as the preferential taxation of church property, which Wilson considered discriminatory in an increasingly secular society.

The Royal Commission on the Status of Women had been created in 1967 with a mandate 'to ensure for women equal opportunities with men in all aspects of Canadian society.'[25] Bertha Wilson thoroughly enjoyed her role as chair of the committee researching and preparing a United Church position paper. This was the only instance after her call to the bar in which she acted as a traditional counsel, representing the United Church of Canada in its submissions to the commission at the February 1968 hearing held at the St Lawrence Hall in Toronto. The United Church brief stated that marriage should be considered an economic partnership with all property acquired during the marriage – including savings, businesses, and employment income – deemed to be joint property of the husband and wife. Only such a policy could give women equal status with men and the economic freedom to leave unhappy marriages so that they no longer would need to endure intolerable home conditions, stated 'Mrs John Wilson,' according to a contemporary news report.

The commission released its report on the Status of Women in 1970 and Wilson served as chairman of the Committee for the Implementation of the Recommendations arising out of the report in 1971–2. She successfully urged the establishment of a minister responsible for the

A plump Bertha, aged about two, scowling in her scratchy handknitted leggings, with brothers Jim and Archie, in front of the Hendry Road flat in Kirkcaldy.

Christina Noble Wernham with Bertha, aged about three. The stern young matron insisted that her daughter get just as good an education as her brothers, and she was fiercely proud of all her children's accomplishments.

Bertha has a deep affection for her father, Archibald Garden Wernham, whom she remembers as a gentle and kindly soul who would do anything for anybody.

At the Wernhams' small granite bungalow named 'Raith' on Cheyne Road in Aberdeen, Christina grew roses, cultivated her strawberry patch, and even took in summer visitors to help pay for Archie's private school fees.

John Wilson met beautiful Bertha Wernham through her scholarly brothers, classmates at Aberdeen, when she was just sixteen. He kept this photograph of her on his desk for many years.

After a six-year courtship steadfastly opposed by her mother, Bertha married John Wilson in December 1945, at King's College Chapel, University of Aberdeen.

Built in 1805 and dominating the highest point of the hill of Doune, the Wilsons' first parish soon became a beacon for the spiritual, educational, and social life of Macduff.

There were ten gloomy rooms heated only by peat-burning fireplaces at the Manse of Doune, outside Macduff in northeast Scotland, where Reverend Wilson and his bride took up their first parish in 1945.

The Wilsons worked extremely hard every day of the week at Macduff. Bertha (second from the left) took two weeks at summer Guide camp and that was her only holiday.

The Wilsons missed their beloved pets, which had to be left with relatives when they immigrated to Canada in 1949. Bertha was especially fond of stripy Satan, so named because (as the Wilsons discovered at Macduff) sin is always shades of grey. The incorrigible Lorna Doune acquired her glossy coat through raids on the family hen coops.

Welcomed to Canada by the Presbyterian minister from Arnprior in late August 1949 and by the friendly deer in Algonquin Park, nevertheless at first the Wilsons found the immigrant experience a bewildering one.

In 1949 Renfrew Presbyterian Church had already been built in Ottawa Valley stone. Unfamiliar with the Scottish tradition of the actively engaged minister's wife, the congregation did not expect much contribution to its activities from Bertha Wilson.

The Canadian winters were cold and snowy but Bertha and John Wilson took great pride and pleasure in their first car, a Prefect.

With no particular demands on her time for Presbyterian parish activities, Bertha Wilson entered tournaments with ladies of all denominations in Renfrew and became something of an expert curler.

Laying the Corner Stone - Presbyterian Manse, Oct 21-50.

In October 1950 successful fundraising activities by the Renfrew parishioners finally made it possible for John to lay the cornerstone for the manse. Completed in late 1951, it was occupied by the Wilsons only briefly before John set off for Korea to serve as a chaplain in the Royal Canadian Navy.

John spent a year serving as a Presbyterian chaplain during the Korean War. While he was away, Bertha had supported herself working as a dentist's receptionist in Ottawa. In December 1952, she drove the Prefect to Halifax and greeted John in the wardroom of HMCS *Nootka*.

When Bertha graduated from Dalhousie Law School in 1956, the photographer himself grabbed his scissors and sheared her hair in a Portia-style crop.

Bertha Wilson was highly respected for the sheer labour she put into establishing the research department at Osler, Hoskin & Harcourt. On the wall of her office she hung reproductions of Van Gogh's hardworking peasant labourers. (Howard Anderson Photography Ltd., Toronto)

Bertha Wilson's parents, Christina and Archibald Wernham, taken the year before their golden wedding anniversary (circa 1964). (Jim Wernham)

status of women to review all federal programs and policies for their effect on women.[26]

During this period, Wilson was appointed the United Church's representative on the board of governors of the Westminster Institute for Ethics and Human Values which met at the University of Western Ontario. The board included prominent members of the medical, legal, and business world. Given the long-term fascination she shared with John for issues of business ethics, this seemed to her to be a golden opportunity. But although during her tenure the board scheduled seminars for the public in both legal and medical ethics, she was unable to persuade it to schedule a seminar on the topic of ethics in advertising or on any other area of business which had the potential to interfere with the pursuit of profit.[27]

The most controversial United Church work in which she was involved was the report on the church's position on abortion, an issue with which it had begun to wrestle in the late 1960s. A commission, initially chaired by Wilson, was appointed in 1974; it was a position she relinquished when she was appointed to the Court of Appeal in 1975. The final report (with a minority dissenting position set out by one of the five commissioners) was not submitted to the Moderator of the United Church General Council until February of 1980. The majority examined with great sensitivity and thoroughness a full range of theological studies of the abortion issue, accepting that moral dilemmas are not neatly resolvable with hard and fast rules. It concluded that the taking of life is almost always wrong but that in some instances, considering the quality of life as a whole and when it is the most responsible alternative available in a particular situation, abortion may be the lesser of two evils. The report recommended that the Criminal Code be amended to remove all sanctions against women and medical personnel performing abortions in licensed facilities within the first twenty weeks of pregnancy.[28]

There were considerable overlaps and intersections between Bertha Wilson's professional and volunteer work and John Wilson's career path during the Osler years. While she worked long hours he was quite regularly on the road for Wells, thoroughly successful with his church fundraising and thoroughly enjoying the ecumenicity of the projects. He raised funds for the building programs of churches of every religious denomination all over the country. His job was to develop the marketing plan and then pin down the pledges up front before the building itself got under way, a process which generally took about a month or perhaps six weeks for a larger church.

This mix of business and religion exactly suited John's interests and was incidentally much more lucrative than the ministry had ever been. He was making $7,000 a year, a large salary in those days, which made it possible for him to buy a rather flashy Porsche – not new or even second-hand, he hastens to say, but a vivid red one. He loved driving it; Bertha was never allowed behind the wheel. It was this Porsche, driven by the avowedly socialist Reverend John Wilson on a fundraising mission to Kitchener, Ontario, that steered him into his next, entirely secular, career. A potential donor spotted him in the parking lot, asked if he was interested in sports cars, and offered him a position heading up the fundraising for the Mosport racetrack.

He accepted with alacrity. John educated himself about all the small constituencies within the industry; there were the race car clubs, the rallying clubs, and the motorcycle clubs around the province, all potential fundraising groups within a larger structure not very different from individual parish churches within a denomination and imbued with an almost equal fervour for their cult of speed. When he saw that, the rest was a snap; the Mosport land was bought, a prospectus prepared, and John began selling bonds on commission. He doubled his salary from Wells, bought a new suit, and obtained corporate sponsors from all the major oil companies. And in eighteen months, once the racetrack was up and running, he was offered the job of managing it.

But this would have been too drastic a departure from the principles of his Presbyterian forebears. John Wilson did not attend a single race at Mosport. He had never been particularly interested in cars, only enamoured of his own red Porsche, and was just beginning to contemplate where to turn next when once again fortuity stepped in.

The United Church had by this time decided to save money by establishing its own internal fundraising arm. John was the only United Church clergyman with the training and experience to do the job and just as the Mosport fundraising project ended, the phone call came offering the position to him. It meant a return to his former modest salary but John was content; feeling comfortable and at home once more was more important than the cash. He spent the rest of his career during Bertha's Osler years working out of United Church headquarters near Avenue Road and St Clair, managing a staff which grew to twenty at the height of the postwar baby boom bulge of church building and then shrank again with the drop in church attendance in the mid to late 1970s. His final assignment in the Golden Horseshoe area between St Catharines and Oshawa was a series of projects involving land or sometimes buildings on a shared-use basis between the United Church and various other denominations.

During the Osler years the Wilsons had moved from their first apartment on North Sherbourne Street to a new flat on Lowther Avenue in the Annex area which was on two floors of an old mansion. They very much enjoyed their spiral staircase, high ceilings, sun room, and Italianate garden. Unfortunately when the owner died, his widow wanted to sell the property for development. John set about the task of finding them another place.

As it turned out, there was money enough to purchase their first home. It was white stucco, on Moore Avenue, and described by John as a large-small house; there were spacious rooms but not too many of them since it had been architecturally designed with just two people in mind.[29] And the Wilsons took enormous pleasure in ownership of this very special space. Part of the living room was converted into a library of wall-to-wall books with a ladder for reaching the top shelves. Two bedrooms were full of books as well. Their formal dinner parties were held in another room located up a half-flight of stairs over the garage. When they were home alone (and they did not entertain often) the Wilsons generally ate in the kitchen which had its own collection of five hundred or so cookbooks covering every conceivable type of ethnic cuisine, health cuisine, and drinks with a special focus on single malt Scotch.

They began to put down roots. The garden was professionally landscaped[30] and backed on to Mount Pleasant Cemetery. The Wilsons had every expectation of staying on Moore permanently, joking that they did not have far to go for their last resting place. Bertha did all her own housecleaning, which she said she enjoyed as a break from law. John continued to handle the grocery shopping and cooking in accordance with the pattern established at law school. They might give a small dinner party on a Friday night after work. But almost without fail and no matter how late, every weekend they would head north to the boat house which they rented for twenty-seven summers in Bobcaygeon, beginning in 1962, from Herb and Norma Orgill. From the minute they walked up the ramp into the airy screened verandah with its expansive views up the Trent Canal and then stepped inside the single room with its lofty beamed ceiling, the two of them were absolutely enamoured with it. Its tiny and rather primitive kitchen and bath, tucked into a little annex under low ceilings, represented no drawback. What mattered was the soothing sound of the water underneath and a luminescent quality of reflected light which coalesced into an almost mesmerizing tranquillity.

Over the years the Wilsons furnished the boat house to their own taste. There was an especially comfortable upholstered arm chair for reading; two round backed Muskoka chairs for the verandah; a sideboard for their dishes and wine collection; a small desk with a good lamp; and a huge collection of books, including everything from philosophy and theology to atlases and bird books and murder mysteries. Bobcaygeon was a real refuge and tonic to both of them after a week in the city; they picnicked on the islands, took short drives, and mostly listened to music and read and read. From early spring to late fall they wanted to wake up Saturday mornings in their retreat with the drawbridge ramp figuratively, at least, pulled up.

But the Wilsons were generous in sharing this cottage with their Wernham nephews from Ottawa who frequently came down to spend the weekend. When Chris and Richard were small Aunt Bertha and Uncle John had been inspired gift-givers and an important family presence, but always at a distance. Now they were equally skilled in making young people feel at home. The cottage was quiet but not too isolated for growing teenagers or (later) young men from the social life of the summer resort town. Chris Wernham remembers this as the period during which he really came to know and love his aunt and uncle. And although there was certainly nothing pretentious about the cottage, it was unusual and notably suited to this unusual couple. The Wilsons created an atmosphere with a certain glamour that the nephews had not experienced before. It was obvious that this was a couple who read widely, enjoyed challenging conversation and good meals and wine, and lived life zestfully in a somewhat epicurean style. In sum, they 'did everything differently' from everyone else; for Chris, it was his first recognition that adult relatives could be people.

Did these contacts during their teenage years help shape the young Wernhams in their career aspirations? Richard studied law at University of Toronto, met and married a fellow law student, and then pursued a notably successful career in finance. Chris recalls a trip to visit his aunt in her office at Oslers, by this time a large and impressive space kept in immaculate order, where she was obviously held in considerable esteem by her colleagues.

Among the Wilsons's Toronto friends there was a group of people who met regularly to read and discuss feminist theology. However, aside from their evolving relationships with their nephews, the Wilsons were essentially a very private couple and their weekends were most typically spent enjoying each other's company. No longer active church-goers (although still personally deeply religious) they read widely and listened to their vast collection of recorded music. Chris Wernham remembers his uncle's particular passion for Wallace Stevens, whom he himself found impenetrable. Bertha says she and John would spend days mulling over a single passage from Heidegger.

It was into this situation that an unexpected appointment would drop like a rock thrown into a mill pond.

PART TWO

On the Bench:
The Ontario Court of Appeal and
the Supreme Court of Canada

5

The Ontario Court of Appeal

One day in 1975, Bertha Wilson's nephew, Richard, who was at that time a fellow at Massey College at University of Toronto, encountered a lawyer from another firm at a social event. This man knew Bertha Wilson's work and asked Richard if he thought she would be interested in a judicial appointment. Richard said he did not know, but he reported this rather peculiar conversation to his aunt. She was not interested in a trial division appointment.

Then one of the firm's lawyers received a call from a government official late in the fall of 1975; a political decision had been made, there was to be an appointment of a woman to the Court of Appeal, not many women were eligible, and the official was terribly worried that the wrong woman might be selected. Would Bertha Wilson be interested? Inquiries were made; the response was more favourable and a discreet report followed. But Wilson did not consider this to be a serious overture. And nothing further came of the preliminary inquiry for some considerable time.

The next contact was a flurry of pink telephone messages from an 'Ed Ratushny in Ottawa' to Bertha's office at Oslers. The name was not that of an existing client and she was deeply engaged in a complex tax law project with Stuart Thom. It was getting late in the afternoon and she hated to break off their discussion but began to feel guilty about failing to return the call. She mentioned the name to Thom.

Thom was well connected in the legal profession and certainly knew that

Ratushny was then advisor to the minister of justice, Ron Basford. When Wilson called Ratushny back, he sounded her out. Three people were under consideration for the Court of Appeal appointment, Ratushny said, but Wilson quite definitely got the impression that the job was hers if she wanted it.

The provisional offer put her into a state of shock and she did not know how to reply. What came out of her mouth may have been 'the most idiotic unfeminist answer' of her entire life: 'I'll have to ask my husband,' she said. When she spoke to John he was very enthusiastic and only wanted to know why she hadn't accepted straight away. After the appointment was confirmed she told Stuart Thom and then went to Allan Beattie. Beattie broke the news to Hal Mockridge, who was stunned; although still titular head of the firm he had heard nothing at all about it.

And the response around Oslers was not all positive once the news was out. Some of the lawyers who had come to rely upon her research work were disappointed; Coombs himself was delighted for her and considered that her appointment certainly contributed to the prestige of a research practice but on a personal level would have preferred that she might have continued in the firm for a few more years. Others who had viewed her as a powerful ally in promoting the cause of the middle or junior lawyers of the firm perceived her departure as a personal loss.

But there was no denying that it was a great honour for the firm to have Bertha Wilson appointed directly from the practice, the first woman on any appellate level court in Canada. They did her proud with a gracious send-off at the York Club including a memorable meal and speeches by all the senior partners. The renowned photographer, Cavouk, was commissioned to take a portrait of Wilson in her legal robes and in it Wilson looks every inch the polished professional she had become.

The swearing-in ceremony had been several weeks earlier. In her speech on that occasion, Wilson had paid full tribute to Oslers for the unique opportunity which it had afforded to her. She refused to be apologetic about her lack of courtroom experience, stressing instead the value in her new role of her immersion in pure legal research and her prior career working with people in the parish as a minister's wife:

> I hope that you will forgive me if I confess an element of unreality. Other than the occasion of my call to the bar, this is the only time I have worn a gown. I have never argued a case in court. Indeed, I have not even practised law in the way most solicitors practice ... [However] when one becomes immersed in the pressures of daily practice, there may be a tendency to emphasize the form over the substance, and the letter of the law over the spirit, and to lose sight of that larger dimension ... Perhaps

the unusual nature of my practice has helped me to retain this perspective, and to remember that people and the law are inextricably intertwined, and that the role of the profession is essentially to serve the needs of the people.

Of all the judges on the Ontario Court of Appeal, Wilson knew only John Arnup personally and he was the only judge to call and welcome her. She suspected, quite rightly, that not all her new colleagues would be as receptive to her presence as he had been.

APPOINTMENT TO THE COURT OF APPEAL

Oslers was still in the Prudential Building at Yonge and King when Bertha Wilson moved north to the Court of Appeal at Osgoode Hall in early January of 1976. Osgoode Hall is named for William Osgoode who served as Upper Canada's first Chief Justice between 1792 and 1794. It houses Ontario's Superior Courts, the domed Great Library, and the Law Society of Upper Canada which has statutory authority to govern the profession through its elected Benchers. And there are many who would be prepared to argue that Osgoode Hall is still the most beautiful building in Toronto.

The six-acre site on Queen Street West was acquired by the Law Society of Upper Canada 1828. By fall of 1832, the Benchers could meet in convocation in the newly constructed east wing and the Law Society could offer classes to aspiring lawyers. During the 1840s and 1850s the Law Society received grants of public monies to expand and provide a number of court rooms. A central pavilion and west wing was added, and the Law Society funded the building of the Great Library with a moderate dome. Eventually, the Society ceded to the crown ownership of all but the Great Library and the Benchers' quarters in the east wing. With substantial design modifications by architects Frederick Cumberland and W.S. Storm, Osgoode Hall was extended northwards behind an impressive stone-columned and triple-porticoed facade set atop massive rusticated arches. The central pavilion was rebuilt with a soaring two-storey rotunda surmounted by a rose, yellow, and blue stained-glass dome and a colourful tiled floor. A final embellishment – the elaborate iron fencing with its famous 'cow catcher' gates – was not completed until 1867. Contrary to popular legend, this fencing was no longer necessary to keep out livestock which might choose to graze on Osgoode Hall's luscious green lawns and flower beds. The surrounding neighbourhood had become thoroughly urban. Instead, the fence was an assertion of the professional dignity thought appropriate to the Law Society and the Superior Law Courts, separating off law from life in the streets. And this professional dignity was very explicitly male; it took another thirty years before Clara Brett Martin was called to the bar, in 1897, the first woman barrister in Ontario.

By the time Bertha Wilson was sworn in to the Court of Appeal there had been a few further incursions of female presence into the cloistered realm of Osgoode Hall. The previous year Laura Legge had been elected the first woman bencher of the Law Society. There were two women judges at the trial division of the Superior Court at Osgoode Hall, Mabel Van Camp (who had been appointed four years earlier) and Janet Boland, and outside Toronto there was the pioneering Madam Justice Helen Kinnear who had been appointed to the bench in Haldimand County as early as 1943.

ON-THE-JOB TRAINING: MAKING A PLACE

Dalhousie Law School had been pretty much an all-male preserve before Bertha Wilson's arrival with five other women students in 1954; even so, though they had no access to the common room, a women's washroom was provided. When Bertha Wilson articled with Fred Bissett on Barrington Street in Halifax, there was only one washroom for all of the offices in the building. During her search for articles in Toronto, she took into account that a big firm like Blake, Cassells or Osler, Hoskin & Harcourt would not be able to use lack of washroom facilities as an excuse to refuse to hire her. Her first office at Oslers had been a hastily converted storage cupboard; her office on the second floor at Osgoode Hall was small and looked out across a window well to a rather uninspiring yellow brick wall.[1] But washrooms were not a concern for Bertha Wilson on her move to the Court of Appeal. She knew there were certainly women on the clerical staff at Osgoode Hall in 1976 and assumed they were appropriately accommodated.

Chief Justice Gale was one new colleague who had not been at all concerned about the appointment of a woman judge. At the time of her investiture, he handsomely described Bertha Wilson in the press as 'a very bright person and a magnificent lawyer.'[2] But, to Wilson's own merriment, Gale was extremely agitated about the delicate issue of providing her with a private toilet. At that time, there were only two en suite washrooms on the second floor, one attached to Gale's own quarters and one adjoining the office occupied by G. Arthur Martin, plus two general washrooms for the use of the remaining judges.[3] A decision was made that one of these general washrooms, suitably renovated, would be set aside for Bertha Wilson's exclusive use:

> So in due course what they did was they took over one of the male staff's washrooms and they just pulled out the urinal things, left these great holes in the wall of course, and he very proudly took me along to show me that they had done this, and he thought that I might have some ideas of what more they could do ... And I said that you don't need to make major alterations, you know, for my coming, but I would appreciate a mirror, that would be a useful thing, why don't you put a mirror, and then maybe a few shelves would be useful and so on.
>
> And that was done and the funny thing was that the two women judges who were on the trial division, Madam Justice Van Camp and Madam Justice Boland, they had come to see, to make sure that they had done an appropriate job to provide facilities and of course were absolutely shocked when they saw this, so much so that when the Court of Appeal invited guests as we often did to lunch in the judges' dining room, if they were women, they said to me, 'Now, you must not show these women this place, send them down to our washroom facilities downstairs.'

Madam Justice Van Camp's private washroom was adequate although nothing special. But Madam Justice Boland's 'was absolutely beautiful, all done in pink and carpeted and she had all kinds of perfume and stuff,' Wilson reports. During her entire time at the Court of Appeal her own washroom was never much improved.

Chief Justice Gale was worried about washrooms but he was also anxious to encourage collegial relationships. He had invited Wilson over to the court for a lunch to meet all the judges. Unfortunately, John Arnup was unable to attend that particular day, and for a number of the other judges the adjustment to a woman colleague continued to be wrenching for some time.

Wilson was told that even before her appointment was made public, Gale called a special meeting of all the Court of Appeal judges to warn them (without specifying any name) that the new judge would be a woman. When her name was released, there arose from the bench a chorus of 'Bertha Who?'. It was reported to her, no doubt in the interests of simple candour, that one of the most senior judges had added balefully, 'No woman can do my job'; he was, however, among the quickest to change his mind and to support Wilson once he saw what she could do.[4]

At first the new judge was particularly conscious that fully 40 per cent of Court of Appeal cases are criminal appeals and that she herself had a serious dearth of experience in criminal law. She had not been in a criminal court since the Bissett days in Halifax or been called on at Oslers for much in the way of research on criminal topics outside white-collar corporate crimes relating to monopolies and competition law under the Combines Act; during her era, Oslers did not have a criminal law department.

The expert in criminal law on the Court of Appeal was G. Arthur Martin. Rather unfortunately, after one criminal hearing which took place early in her tenure at the court Martin overheard Wilson saying outside the courtroom, 'I don't really find the criminal cases all that interesting.' Martin was very upset and he reported the comment to Arnup whom he knew was a Wilson ally. Arnup soothingly suggested that Martin give her some time to adjust and that he also consider offering her some assistance to get up to speed. And then Wilson, perhaps at Arnup's tactful suggestion, approached Martin with her own request for special tutoring. She confessed that she was terrified of the complexities of the Criminal Code and even fretted that her lack of familiarity with the law might impose an unfair burden on the other two judges on a panel when she was assigned a criminal appeal.

Martin never ate lunch. Criminal defence counsel and Crowns alike knew that he was likely to be available for consultation over the noon hour and quite frequently would call on him for emergency assistance midway through a trial which they sensed was not going well. He was legendary for his helpfulness at Osgoode Hall and he was very kind and reassuring when Wilson approached him. 'You mastered the Income Tax Act, didn't you?' he reminded her. 'The Criminal Code is child's play in comparison.'[5]

Martin recommended a basic text to her, gave her a list of the leading criminal cases, and then discussed them with her after she had read them so that she could be confident she had grasped the fundamental principles. Eventually Wilson came to enjoy criminal cases and admire some of the outstanding criminal counsel who appeared before her. But Wilson knows of no comparable instance of any newly appointed male judge on either the Court of Appeal or the Supreme Court who was prepared to acknowledge the shortcomings of his prior experience as she was and to seek out timely remedial assistance, even though in her opinion a number of them were not at all familiar with the intricacies of a solicitor's (as opposed to a barrister's) practice.[6]

Arnup, who admires Wilson but is frank about her shortcomings, recalls that it took her some time to understand the collegial approach which had evolved under Chief Justice Gale and the necessity of accepting that the ultimate decision was ideally to be reached by three judges. For many years she had been running her departments at Oslers with full authority; she was exceptionally good at delegating tasks to the staff and the associates working with her and had become quite accustomed to the weight accorded her voice behind the scenes in the management of the firm as a whole. When she first came to the Court of Appeal, Arnup considers, Wilson had a tendency to make up her own mind and be somewhat intransigent about modifying her initial decision based on discussion with the other members of her panel, but eventually she got used to the system. From Gordon Blair's perspective (and he was sworn in to the Court of Appeal the same day as Wilson) it was not intransigence but Wilson's extreme conscientiousness which compelled her to write dissents or diverging reasons so frequently once she had come to a firm decision in her own mind about what ought to be done.

It was Arnup's view that what judges write is the only way their worth can be measured, and this was a key aspect of his philosophy of 'serving the work.'[7] Although the enormous volume of Wilson's extrajudicial writing indicates that she did not fully subscribe to this view, she certainly agreed that lawyers and judges ought to serve the law and she took as much trouble with her judgments as Arnup himself. Arnup's help in integrating Wilson into the collegial system was discreet and she herself may not have fully realized all that he did; in contrast, his assistance with writing judgments was quite explicit.

Arnup had taken the American Bar Association course in judgment writing for appellate judges in Boulder, Colorado, and he provided regular lectures on judgment writing at the judges' continuing education seminars. Both Blair, who had joined the Ontario Court of Appeal directly from his Ottawa practice in administrative law, and Wilson herself enrolled in the Boulder course in 1976. They were the only Canadians, and Wilson was also the only woman in attendance. She was astonished that the basic drills provided in remedial grammar and logic could be necessary at that level – and it was very obvious to her that they were. Blair reports that Wilson wowed the other student-judges at this course, making an outstanding impression through her contributions to the seminars and more informal discussions; she was selected to deliver the closing speech at the final dinner, a task which she carried out with her customary good humour and graciousness.

When it came to writing judgments, Wilson had somehow survived the nit-picking thoroughness inflicted upon her by Jock Robertson at Aberdeen Central. Arnup recognized early that she loved language as much as he did. While she was at the Court of Appeal, and even if he did not agree with her reasoning, at her request he might look over her first draft of a dissent (when he himself, of course, was not serving on the same panel) and suggest revisions to improve its clarity. Later he would write to her from time to time to comment on her choice of a word or phrase which he thought deserved praise or should have been sharpened.

At Osgoode Hall the trial division and appeal court judges share a burl-panelled third-floor dining room. The room, pleasant enough but certainly not luxurious and somewhat long and narrow for its height, has a wall of windows overlooking a protected court yard. During Wilson's tenure, most judges ate their lunches in this dining room every day. And Wilson considered that one of the great benefits of this common space was the opportunity of participating in informal discussions around the lunch table. Trial judges required different skills from appellate judges. Wilson recalls in particular how on occasion Mr Justice Edson Haines called in question her idealistic concept of the role of a trial. 'A trial is a search for proof,' he said, 'not a search for truth.'[8] But by meeting regularly all the judges gained a broader perspective on the work of the superior court as an integrated whole.

Distinguished guests were regularly invited to lunch simply to raise the awareness of the bench on current social issues. Wilson took an active role in ensuring that more and more women were invited. When this overwhelmingly male group of judges had had the opportunity of meeting with individuals as impressive as astronomer Helen Hogg, they began to realize that Bertha Wilson was not the only women to have broken into the first ranks of professional life.

Osgoode Hall also provided a more formal continuing education program, organized by the trial judges but with a standing invitation to everyone at the Court of Appeal as well. There was generally an early evening dinner followed with a lecture offered by one of their own number or another legal expert who surveyed current developments in some area of the law. It was through these working lunches and dinners at the Court of Appeal that Wilson came to be accepted by her new peers, particularly when they realized how much she had to contribute.

CRIMINAL LAW: A PROVOCATIVE DISSENT

Martin's rapid acceptance of Wilson's participation in criminal appeals resulted not just from the clarity of her judgments: they shared many views about the necessity of protecting the rights of the convicted to the fullest extent and the desirability of encouraging rehabilitation whenever possible. For security reasons a panel of three Court of Appeal judges would frequently travel to the penitentiaries to hear criminal appeals in person. Because of his expertise, Martin would almost inevitably be among the panel and Wilson often joined him on these trips. She took great satisfaction in her ability to influence the humanity of the procedures put in place for these appeals.

Each prisoner was accompanied by two security guards. Wilson found it unnecessary and degrading to have the prisoners brought in in leg irons and when she raised the issue with Martin he immediately agreed. Martin was so highly respected by the Crown attorneys that when he would on occasion point out some aspect of the case which should have been raised at trial they would quite often agree with him. Even in the absence of a defence counsel appointed to represent the appellant, it was sometimes possible to obtain Crown consent to reduce sentences and Wilson appreciated Martin's role in this respect. Wilson herself had excellent contacts through the United Church and the Toronto School of Theology with the prison chaplain system. When she believed that a prisoner was the victim of circumstances and could benefit from a break in his incarceration she tried to arrange for the reduced sentence to be served out of a jail cell, working in the fields or at some other community site.

Wilson continued to find criminal appeals difficult. She never forgot that 'the liberty of the subject is at stake.' In a speech delivered to a group of church women just two years after she had gone to the Court of Appeal she sounded rather like the mother of one of John Wilson's sailors explaining her son's misdemeanours, although a mother with some familiarity with the blurring of sociology and law advocated by the Scottish Enlightenment Lords Monboddo and Kames:

The criminal lives by different rules and subscribes to different loyalties. Somewhere he or she has gone off the track and, although we now know

many of the root causes of this, such as economic and emotional deprivation – broken homes, drugs, alcoholism, poverty – we have no cure for
those who have already gone that route and now are totally caught up in a
life of crime ...

What we *can* do, of course, and what we *must* do, is work to eradicate the
conditions that spawn the criminal mentality. And we should be able to
achieve this, you know, in a wealthy country like Canada if our priorities
are sound and our motivations sincere.[9]

But in the criminal context, Wilson also retained a certain pragmatic
agnosticism about the value of sociology to the development of the corrections profession; she had noted in another speech just a year earlier
that although she admired the determination and optimism of experts
in that field, nevertheless she had observed that 'the confidence we developed in the behavioral sciences over the last decade seems to be
waning.'[10]

Wilson sat on many criminal panels at the Court of Appeal but she
did not write many criminal judgments. Nevertheless (and perhaps
because of her improved relationship with him), Wilson did somehow
find the temerity to dissent from the Martin majority decision in *Olbey*,[11]
one of her early criminal cases at the Court. Two excellent counsel were
in court, Clayton Ruby for the appellant and David H. Doherty (later
himself of the Court of Appeal) for the Crown. Both would develop a
deep respect for Wilson. In fact, Doherty named one of his beloved bas-
set hounds 'Bertha.'

The case was an unsavoury one. At trial, Olbey had been convicted of
the murder of one Patterson, a rival drug dealer. They had both
attended a party where the guests were under the influence of alcohol
together with barbiturates, amphetamines, heroin, and marijuana. There
had been an ongoing altercation between the two men, but the evidence
indicated that Olbey shot Patterson only after Patterson had called him
a 'two-bit nigger punk.'

Olbey pleaded self-defence on the grounds that he believed Patterson
had accepted a contract to kill him. The appeal resulted from the trial
judge's failure to instruct the jury to consider intoxication in relation to a
possible defence of provocation. In a brief judgment Martin (writing for
himself and Dubin) upheld the guilty verdict, which they found would
have been the same even if the trial judge had related the principle of
reasonable doubt to provocation, especially since the accused's own evidence did not establish that his behaviour was a reaction to the insult.

Wilson's dissent looked at the relationship between intoxication and the subjective element of provocation; she argued that the accused did not deny hearing the epithet or being affected by it but was merely silent about whether he heard it or not. From the trial transcript of the evidence presented by the chief witness, Wilson focused on the specific circumstances of the quarrel and certain ambiguities apparent from the chief witness's description of the sequence of events. Because ingestion of drugs in large quantities is known to slow reaction times, she reasoned, the trial judge ought to have instructed the jury to consider whether Olbey's response to the insult was delayed. Through sympathetic inference, the jury ought to have taken into account the subjective experience of the accused. Since a properly directed jury could have concluded either that Olbey acted in response to provocation (and brought in a verdict of manslaughter) or that they were not satisfied beyond a reasonable doubt that he had not responded to provocation, Wilson would have allowed the appeal.

She acknowledged that it would have been highly improbable for a properly instructed jury to have found him not guilty of murder. Her recognition that self-defence and provocation could co-exist and be co-determinative of the appellant's behaviour suggest a much more Humean notion of causation than is customary in our law courts.

This dissent is thoroughly congruent with Wilson's Scottish Enlightenment roots. At the Supreme Court she would be consistently vigilant in protecting the rights of accused criminals as a marginalized group. And although it is in the Charter context that Wilson is considered to have first explicitly articulated a contextual balancing of competing rights,[12] this consciousness of contextuality is characteristic of Wilson's analysis right from the beginning of her career as a judge.

It was because of Wilson's dissent in the Court of Appeal that Olbey could appeal, again unsuccessfully, to the Supreme Court of Canada. However, Wilson's courage in dissenting was vindicated when Chief Justice Laskin also dissented on the same issue, stating that he adopted in its entirety all that was she had said on the law of provocation. He agreed with Wilson that the weighing of the evidence of provocation ought to have been left to the jury so that the accused could have benefited from any reasonable doubt and had the charge of murder reduced to manslaughter.

Almost twenty years later, six years after she herself had left the bench, and following significant changes in British case law, a Wilsonian and nuanced version of the defence of provocation was finally endorsed in the Supreme Court by Justice Cory in the *Thibert* case.[13] Norman Thibert had been convicted of second-degree murder in the death of one Alan Sherren, his wife's lover, who had taunted Thibert while swinging the woman back and forth in front of him as a human shield, saying 'Go ahead, shoot me.' Thibert did shoot him and pleaded provocation as his defence; the majority concluded that these insults were sufficient that an ordinary man in the same circumstances might lose his power of self-control. It was a highly controversial judgment with a sharply split court and the press response was somewhat critical. However, it is hard not to consider that Wilson's temerity in her *Olbey* dissent at the Court of Appeal had finally been rewarded.

COMMERCIAL LAW: CONSISTENCY AND CONTEXTUALITY

If Wilson was conscious of her lack of expertise in criminal law when she went to the Court of Appeal, she certainly did not accept Justice Arthur Jessup's assessment of her abilities in that vast area of corporate and commercial law which integrates various elements of law and economics. From the beginning to the end of their association, it was Jessup who had the most trouble of all the judges in accepting a woman colleague. He made it clear that he never relished the necessity of sitting on panels with her and was heard to refer to her from time to time with considerable exasperation as 'that woman.' On at least one occasion Jessup himself told Wilson he had suggested to the chief justice that she be replaced on a particular case because he considered that the subject matter was too complex for her to grasp.

Wilson was thoroughly familiar with Jessup judgments from her research before she came to the Court and was prepared to respect him. She found his 'stony-faced stare' when she refused to withdraw and his 'great skill in ignoring her completely' when he was compelled to serve on the same panel with her very distressing.[14] However, she and John had evolved a well-tested formula for dealing with such personalities. Some people are simply born with a nature which they themselves find very difficult to manage. They deserve more sympathy than condemnation; and suitable allowances have to be made in dealing with them. Wilson observed that Jessup's attitude seemed to extend to other women and was not personal to her. She was prepared to accommodate Jessup and to learn from him, regardless of his opinion of her.

But of course she had spent seventeen years at Oslers steeped in corporate and commercial case law, memo and opinion writing. The more complex the issue, the more likely it would have been sent to her by the lawyer on the case. In this area she rightly considered that Jessup did not have much to teach her. Moreover, because of her perceived short-comings in criminal law, she had all the greater duty to bring her solicitor's expertise to the bench.

So when the troublesome issue of contribution among concurrent wrongdoers in a contractual relationship came to the Court of Appeal early in her time there and Jessup told her that he thought she was not fit to participate in the decision, Wilson merely replied mildly, 'Oh, I think I know a bit about the subject.' The panel for both *Dominion Chain*[15] and the *Dabous* v. *Zuliani*[16] cases, which were heard consecutively, consisted of justices Jessup, Zuber, and Wilson; Wilson dissented in part in both.

To understand why, it is useful to have a little understanding of the relationship between tort law and contracts. Conceptually, these two regimes are very different. A successful plaintiff in a torts action is entitled to full recovery 'jointly and severally.' Each wrongdoer who has caused the plaintiff loss and who reasonably ought to have realized that his behaviour could damage that plaintiff is on the hook; generally speaking, both will 'contribute' but if one is unable to do so (perhaps because of bankruptcy) then the other is liable for the whole loss. Tort liability is based upon the claims of those 'neighbours'[17] who are foreseeably within the ambit of the duty of care and who have suffered damages because the tortfeasor[18] has negligently failed to meet the objective standard of the reasonable person; both statutory and common law may apply. Liability in contract, on the other hand, results from the breach of the terms of a specific and private and negotiated relationship in which two equal parties themselves have freely decided upon the rules governing their relationship.

However, in the 1960s and 1970s this bright line between contract and tort law was dimming with the recognition that there is a potential for the same instance of misconduct to give rise to a cause of action both in contract and in tort. And yet the common law was not clear on the equitable right of contribution (how much each party should have to pay) in cases of concurrent breach of contract and tort.

Dominion Chain involved the defective construction of the roof of a building. The contractor (Eastern Construction) had protected itself with an exculpatory clause in its contract but the consulting engineer (Giffels Associates) had not. Dominion sued in negligence against both the contractor and the engineer and was successful against the engineer alone; the engineer, in turn, sued for contribution and the trial judge had applied negligence analysis to award a hefty 75 per cent from the contractor. At the Ontario Court of Appeal, Jessup and Zuber found that both the contractor and the engineer were liable in tort as well as in contract, but that the contractor's exculpatory clause protected it from contribution.

Wilson agreed that contribution was not available but she did not rely on the exculpatory clause to reach that conclusion. In her opinion, the contractor was not liable in tort because the alleged wrongdoing was not an independent tort unrelated to the performance of the contract. She argued that the liability of the contractor had to be confined to the contractual relationship because 'the acts or omissions complained of by the plaintiff are in relation to the very matters covered by the contract.'

Her reason for doing so was based on a very careful analysis of the current case law dealing with breach of the contractual duty of care, which she reasoned is independent from tort law's duty of care in the professional context, and from a careful examination of this specific term in the contract at issue:

> The borderline of contract and tort in my opinion exists where a contract either expressly or impliedly imposes on A a duty of care vis-a-vis B, the other party to the contract, to do the things undertaken by the contract without negligence and there is also coincidental with, but independent of, the contract a duty of care upon A in tort. This latter duty may exist by virtue of A's professional status or the fact that he is pursuing a so-called 'common calling.' We are not in my view concerned here with the duty of a defendant not to injure his 'neighbour.' ... It is true that if A has contracted with B to perform certain acts in relation to B's person or property, then B may be characterized as a member of a class of 'persons who are so closely and directly affected by my act that I ought reasonably to have them in contemplation as being so affected when I am directing my mind to the acts of omissions which are called in question.' However, where the person to whom the duty is owed, the scope of the duty and the standard of care have all been expressly or impliedly agreed upon by the parties, it appears to me somewhat artificial to rely upon Lord Atkin's 'neighbour' test to determine whether or not the duty is owed to the particular plaintiff and as to the requisite standard of care the defendant must attain.

The writing is lucid but the concept complex; this is not at all easy reading. It is perhaps not surprising that when *Dominion Chain* went up to the Supreme Court of Canada two years later, Justice Laskin simply affirmed that the contractor had excluded its liability through the exculpatory clause without deciding the question of under what circumstances there might be concurrent liability in contract and tort.

The issue was thrown into much sharper relief in the companion *Dabous* case. Jessup and Zuber again found for the majority that a clause in the builder's contract, providing that the issuance of the architect's certificate constituted a waiver of all claims by the owner, did not exclude the builder's liability for damages caused by his negligence. The builder and the architect were held to be concurrently liable to compensate the homeowner for fire damage resulting from an incorrectly installed prefabricated fireplace chimney.

Wilson again dissented in part. She concurred with the majority in dismissing the architect's appeal against liability but would have found that the breach of duty sounded only in contract and not in tort. In her opinion, the fact that the builder had protected himself with the waiver clause ought to have deprived the architect of the status to appeal against the dismissal of the plaintiff's action against the builder.

The issue of whether or not one ought to be able to contract out of professional negligence is not so much a problem of social justice as an issue of business justice of considerable moral complexity which Wilson takes very seriously. These were not unsophisticated parties suffering from inequality of bargaining power or information asymmetry or coercion; in Wilson's view, the parties ought to be held to the contractual terms to which they had agreed.

The topic of concurrent liability in contract and tort and resulting liability for contribution interested Wilson enough that she later delivered a speech on it. In her view, the courts had not supplied enough guidance to signal for contracting parties when common law tort duty might be superimposed upon the negotiated terms, and the tacit solution – that tort duty might be applied when it was a third party outside the contract which had suffered the loss – does not seem to her an adequate solution to this situation of uncertainty.

Her solution would have been to exclude tort liability and contribution as between the contracting parties whenever the alleged tortious behaviour was the very subject of the contract and its negotiated terms. Wilson believes that, in the commercial context, deference is required to the expectations of the parties as clearly articulated in their contractual arrangement which has determined its own optimal distance and propriety. She could not agree with those commentators who argued that the difference between contract duty of care and tort duty of care was illusory, nor with the proposition that general tort law duties which the parties could have overridden by contractual agreement continued to co-exist with contractual liability unless they had done so. But she also considered that the business community could adjust to either a concurrent liability or no concurrent liability regime so long as the approach was clearly decided one way or the other.[20]

As might be expected, given her background from Oslers, Wilson went on to make solid contributions to corporate and commercial jurisprudence while she was on the Ontario Court of Appeal. What is interesting about many of these cases is Wilson's increasing recognition that to do justice in complex circumstances requires an integration or even a blurring of the sharply defined categories of law (contracts, torts, property, family law, and so on) as she had studied them at law school.

Wilson helped to clarify for Canadian courts the doctrine of misrepresentation or negligent misstatement, another point of intersection between contract and tort law; a plaintiff may recover damages if he has been induced to enter into a contract upon some assurance made by the defendant which the defendant knew or ought to have known would be to the detriment of the plaintiff.[21] When there is inequality of bargaining power between the parties to a contract, Wilson reasoned persuasively in several early cases, it may be necessary to import concepts from equity relating to unconscionability and fiduciary duty to set aside contracts which would do injustice to the weaker party if they were to be upheld.[22] She struggled hard in the *Chomedy Aluminum*[23] case to come to terms with the emerging issue of fundamental breach in contract law: under what circumstances does an exclusion clause survive the disintegration of the entire contractual setting? Wilson wrote the unanimous judgment for the court, allowing the appeal and holding that the waiver could not bind the appellant once the respondent had clearly refused to perform its basic obligations under the contract.

Wilson's major focus of interest at Dalhousie had been property law and she wrote a number of important decisions at the Court of Appeal in this area which again demonstrate her understanding of the integration of ethics and economics arising out of her Scottish Enlightenment roots. Indeed, her work in property law is so important that a study could be made of her property cases alone. Unfortunately, space does not allow any detailed analysis here.

Labour law was the area Wilson had not covered at all at law school. Although one might assume that a card-carrying member of the New

Democratic party would be consistently pro-labour, she signalled in the early Court of Appeal judgments that this would not always be the case. Unions had come into existence for the collective protection of the rights of workers faced with the powerful economic clout of their bosses, but if on occasion unions failed to act on that mandate, Wilson could be relied upon to champion the individual.

In *Downing*, for example, an employment equity case decided in 1978,[24] – Wilson and Blair joined in a majority judgment which upheld the appeal of the dismissal of an application for judicial review made by a young woman employed in a framing shop. Her pay was 15 cents less an hour than that of male workers performing exactly the same job. The decision considered clearly for the first time the issue of equal pay for equal work six years before the report of the Royal Commission on Equality in Employment.

The relevant provisions of the Employment Standards Act at that time did not provide for a full hearing into the prohibited issue of wage discrimination. Therefore the complaint was dismissed by the Ontario Labour Ministry's Employment Standards Branch after a confidential investigation did not permit the complainant to make any oral presentation and did not inform her as to why her complaint had gone nowhere. Wilson leaves full analysis of the applicable law to Blair, but her brief concurrence is characteristic of her nuanced and contextual approach to such issues and also, from Blair's perspective, characteristic of that sense of duty which drove her to write diverging reasons even when she concurred with the majority. She stressed that implementation of the requirement of natural justice that both sides be heard can only be determined in the context of the individual case. She added that in view of the many different tasks the employee was required to perform, the complainant should also to have been permitted to make representations as to the nature of the actual work performed by the males and females in the shop in order to demonstrate that they were in fact doing equal work. The case attracted considerable attention in the popular press; one anonymous lawyer was quoted as stating that it gave people a whole new set of rights.[26]

ALL IN THE FAMILY

Wilson has always considered family law to be one of the most difficult and also one of the most important areas of law. It is difficult because the sheer complexity of intimate family relationships makes them opaque to outsiders and malleable in the hands of skilled counsel advocating a particular point of view. Judges 'half the time ... don't know what we are doing,' she says, despite the psychological assessments which the parties may submit in evidence to the court. In an adversarial system, the assessments themselves may be of questionable value. While Wilson's record on Charter cases demonstrates her openness to the introduction of many new forms of evidence (especially through expansion of the intervenor process), in the family law context Wilson was equally sceptical about the contribution the behavioural sciences could offer as she was in the criminal law context.

Wilson had a difficult time persuading some judges that the family law cases were important and that in fact nothing could matter more than to settle the law in these areas. Swift and certain resolution offers the possibility of reducing the potential for psychological harm generated by a liberalized divorce regime, especially for children, although Wilson was well aware that there are no winners in a divorce case and that after family litigation neither party was ever the same. Wilson always considered family law cases the quintessential situation in which 'judges are most conscious of sitting in judgment and playing God.'[27]

Division of Property

One major area of concern for Wilson was integrating the issue of division of family property with the issue of spousal support upon marriage breakdown. Among her unpublished papers is a set of detailed notes prepared for a speech to the Women's Canadian Club on 'Recent Developments in Family Law' delivered in Ottawa in February 1979. In those notes Wilson makes it absolutely clear that women need to know what property will be theirs and what support they may be entitled to so that they can have the security and sense of independence necessary to leave violent or unhappy marriages. The certainty which her analysis of concurrent contract and tort regimes indicated was essential in the commercial context was every bit as essential here and she could unhesitatingly adopt the language of economics in the marriage context which the new legislation required.

The 1970 incorporation of liberalized no fault grounds within federal divorce legislation was followed in Ontario by the Family Law Reform Act[28] in 1978 and then by comparable provincial statutes across the country. Together, this legislation redefined marriage as an economic partnership, demanding equal division of property acquired during the course of the marriage upon its dissolution, and entailed the expectation that women achieve some measure of economic self-sufficiency after marriage breakdown. Wilson believed that the new laws reflected a profound shift in social consensus and accordingly that the courts had a duty to enforce this duly authorized legislation.

The Legislature had made inquiries throughout the province and determined that people generally did not think title to property should necessarily determine the allocation of its value on dissolution of a marriage. Surveys recommended some distinction should be sustained between so-called family assets, used and enjoyed by all members of a family, and those other assets which did properly belong solely to the spouse who had acquired them – through inheritance, perhaps, or through labour in a business which was completely separate from the family. However, fairness required adjustment of the division of the value of property when acquisition by the titled spouse had been made possible by the contributions of the non-titled spouse.

In 1978 the *Becker* v. *Pettkus*[29] case made new law on the issue of division of property after dissolution of a relationship between an unmarried couple when title to the property had been held by only one of the common law spouses. The decision was unanimous, but Wilson wrote the judgment and she generally gets the credit for her novel application of constructive trust principles.

The opening of Wilson's judgment is memorable for its simple, unadorned recitation of the facts found by the trial judge. She takes us back to the early days of the romance between Rosa Becker and Lothan Pettkus:

> The parties to this appeal emigrated to Canada from central Europe in the early fifties. The appellant was 26 years of age when she arrived. The respondent was 22. The appellant got her first real job in 1955 working in a lace factory in Montreal. She earned $25 to $28 a week and lived in a rented room costing $10 a week. She met the respondent at a dance in March of 1955. He had found a job as a garage mechanic at $75 a week and was sharing a room with two other young men. After a few dates, he moved in with the appellant. Her rent was raised to $12 a week.[30]

Wilson sketches the history of the parties' twenty-year common-law relationship, paying particular attention to the ordinary details of their domestic arrangements. Rosa Becker's salary increased to $67 a week and she continued to pay all the couple's living expenses for food and rent and clothing while Lothan Pettkus deposited all his earnings in a savings account in his own name. Becker wanted to marry Pettkus and he held out some hope but said he needed to get to know her better; as Wilson phrases it, 'the defendant said that he might consider it after a more thorough acquaintance.'

By 1960 Pettkus had $13,000 in his bank account and he suggested that the two of them take a vacation out west. The holiday turned out to be a three-month apprenticeship at a bee-keeping operation where they both learned the business. They were paid, Pettkus for helping with the bees and Becker for assistance with the meal preparation and house-keeping for the hired hands as well as for her assistance in the apiary, but Pettkus accepted the pay cheques for both of them and deposited the money into his account.

They returned to Montreal and successfully developed their own bee-keeping business on a small acreage southwest of Montreal purchased by Pettkus with title in his name alone. Becker made frames for the hives and negotiated with neighbouring fruit farmers to arrange placement of hives in their orchards; she assisted with the extraction of the honey, marketed the processed honey, and helped renovate the farm house on the property. But even though Becker was a full partner in the labour of the business, Pettkus controlled the accounts and retained title to the property and the new equipment in his own name alone.

With the profits of a bumper honey crop Pettkus bought a new acre-age in Ontario, again taking title in his own name. The couple made plans to build a more comfortable home and began moving the bees. However, the relationship had become troubled. There was one brief separation. Soon, faced with all the work of managing the operation on his own, Pettkus asked Becker to come back. She returned, assisted again with the bees and the domestic chores, and helped to build the new house.

Within eight months of its completion, the relationship had deterio-rated to the point that Becker moved out permanently, taking the car and just $2,600. Regardless of the fact that legal title to the property was in Pettkus's name, Becker was determined to obtain justice; she believed passionately that it would be only fair for her to receive half the value of the property she had helped to acquire and to develop.

The trial judge had rejected the claim, indulging in an implicit sneer at the immorality of the common-law relationship. He characterized Becker's support of her partner during the first five years of their cohabitation as 'risk capital invested in the hope of seducing the younger defendant into marriage.'[31] He awarded her forty beehives without the bees and $1,500 with no ongoing support.

In Wilson's opinion, the trial judge had grossly underestimated the value of Rosa Becker's contributions. She therefore allowed the appeal, finding that Becker was entitled to a one-half interest in the capital and revenue of the bee-keeping operation. She based her decision on constructive trust principles, then a relatively new kind of unjust enrichment analysis. If Pettkus were allowed to keep all the value of the property, he would be unjustly enriched by the contributions Becker had made. Wilson referred to passages from the transcript of the cross-examination at trial in which Pettkus admitted he would not have been able to save the capital to purchase either of the farms but for Becker's assumption of all the expenses of everyday life and that the business would not have become so prosperous if she had not contributed her labour for nothing.

Wilson's judgment represents a calculated risk. In the *Murdoch* case a few years earlier, the majority at the Supreme Court had rejected a farm wife's claim for an undivided half interest in the family farm which belonged to her husband, even though she had worked it with him, because he had expressed no intention of sharing it with her. The court had held that an express common intention was necessary for an untitled spouse to make out any claim in what was called 'resulting trust.' And Pettkus had never expressed any intention of sharing his property with Becker.

But Wilson knew that Laskin had dissented in *Murdoch*, finding that an express intention was unnecessary and that the husband should have been deemed to hold the property as a constructive trustee for the benefit of his wife.[32] Wilson's initiative, following Laskin's dissent, was to find that even in the absence of an expressed common intention and even though the Family Law Reform Act did not explicitly provide for common law couples to share assets equally, the support and labour which Becker had contributed constituted a constructive trust sufficient to make out the claim. If the case were to be appealed further from the Court of Appeal to the Supreme Court, Wilson believed there was a good chance of establishing this incremental development in the common law.

When Wilson released her judgment in 1978 there was not much publicity. The flood of public reaction came two years later with the Dickson judgment,[33] unanimously affirming her decision and awarding Rosa Becker a half-interest of $150,000 together with all her legal costs. One reporter called Wilson 'quite possibly Canada's most competent female judge,' New Democratic member of Parliament Pauline Jewett said in the House of Commons that more women judges needed to be appointed if the courts were to ensure impartiality in the treatment of women; Lynne Gordon, head of the Ontario Status of Women Council, and Doris Anderson, president of the Canadian Advisory Council on the Status of Women, both praised the decision but still warned common-law wives to insist upon cohabitation agreements to protect their interests. Even the editorial in the notoriously conservative *Globe and Mail* concluded approvingly: 'Miss Becker has won her case. She has received her fair due.'[34]

But Rosa Becker, still working as a hired hand on a dairy farm, realized that her battle was not over until she had her money in hand. For six more years Jerry Langlois, her lawyer, fought tooth and nail to recover on the judgment.[35] He found Pettkus, to be a thoroughly unpleasant individual who was simply determined not to pay. There were innumerable judgment-debtor examinations during which Pettkus stolidly or screamingly asserted his inability to pay. The house was sold and Becker realized $60,000, most of which went to pay off her legal bills. The bees in their hives were seized to be sold by court order but Pettkus refused to feed them and they all died so recovery was minimal. Eventually there was an auction and a tractor and a lawnmower and various other smaller items were sold with some money flowing to Becker.

By 1986 the frail Miss Becker was exhausted and discouraged. She was sixty and the hard physical labour required by her job was too much for her. Langlois had spoken to her on the phone almost every day for thirteen years but on 16 November he was travelling in Europe; if she called, he was not at home that day to console her. When he was reached by a reporter for the Montreal *Gazette* and told that his Rosie had committed suicide, Langlois was distraught.

Rosa Becker had no living relatives. Langlois had prepared her will. She had wanted to leave her estate to Langlois's young daughter, Veronica, but Langlois quite properly refused. Instead, she bequeathed all her possessions to a couple of friends who had emigrated to Canada on the same boat with Lothan Pettkus and whom she knew from the old dance hall days when she had met him in Montreal. And Langlois continued to pursue justice for Rosie even after her death, hounding Pettkus mercilessly and finally settling for an additional $36,000 which was paid to the estate.

Langlois had spent six years pursuing the judgment. He ran up over $26,000 in disbursements out of his own pocket, comforted her when she was discouraged, and mourned when she died. And he fought for six more years to see justice done even after her death. Not surprisingly he considers this to be the greatest case of his life, combining a sympathetic client with a compellingly interesting legal doctrine of constructive trust. *Becker* v. *Pettkus* changed the direction of Canadian family law and had a huge impact on constructive trust applications in other areas of the law as well.

This constructive trust matter was certainly one of the highest profile cases Wilson would ever decide and it established her expertise in property division. On 16 December 1980 she delivered a paper in the Continuing Education Program on Family Law to the judges of the trial division of the Superior Court dealing with a tricky aspect of property division under the Family Law Reform Act which applied only to married spouses.

Wilson distinguished two lines of jurisprudence which were beginning to evolve. One section of the act permitted the court to make an unequal division of family assets under certain enumerated circumstances in which an equal division would be inequitable, concluding with a rather ambiguous phrase referring to 'property' which seemed to give the court wide discretion; another section of the act required that the court resort to non-family assets (such as a business owned by the husband) to remedy any inequity which could not be satisfied by unequal division of family assets alone. There was also a section of the Act setting out the presumption that child care, household management, and financial contribution were the joint responsibilities of the spouses giving rise to the *prima facie* division of family assets on dissolution of marriage. The question was whether a wife's extra effort in contributing to the acquisition of family assets could be satisfied only through an unequal division of the family assets, or: whether it could be compensated with access to non-family assets even when she had made no direct financial contribution to the acquisition of those assets. The issue was not fully resolved until the Supreme Court in affirmed

Ontario Court of Appeal's strict interpretation of the act in *Leatherdale* v. *Leatherdale*,[36] finding that non-family assets could not be tapped to top up an unequal division of family assets unless the spouse had made a direct contribution to their acquisition.

Spousal Support

Clarification of the division of property issue was certainly not Wilson's only significant contribution to family law in her Court of Appeal days. She gave a great deal of thought and contributed extensively to the debate on the bench about the purposes, the methods, and the effects of the implementation of many other aspects of this new family legislation. Among Wilson's personal papers is a series of memos she wrote to other members of the Supreme Court of Ontario between 1979 and 1981 on the subject of the interaction of maintenance awards and welfare assistance. She pointed out that appeals naming former wives as the parties seeking increased maintenance were in many instances initiated by the welfare authorities to replenish their own coffers; the wives were often unwilling of their own accord to place further financial pressure on their former spouses. Wilson also circulated a paper on 'The Variation of Support Orders'[37] which she had delivered at a Judicial Conference on Family Law in Vancouver in August 1981, setting out the principles which form the basis of her analysis of such cases.

There were two non-contractual spousal support matters decided by Wilson when she was on the Court of Appeal which may seem to point in opposite directions. The endorsement in *Welsh*[38] looks at first blush like a case which favours women. Wilson (sitting as a single judge as is customary for appeals of motion decisions) confirmed that the appropriate standard for interim maintenance under the new legislation set aside the former 'modesty and retirement doctrine'; support was to be determined in accordance with the means of the husband and the standard of living to which he had accustomed his wife during the course of the marriage.

This particular wife had enjoyed a home with a swimming pool, golf and bridge club memberships, and travel. A back injury prevented her from returning to her former occupation as a hairdresser and at age fifty-seven it seemed unlikely she could retrain to return to the work force. Her husband's after-tax income was over $55,000 a year and he had assets of some $275,000. Wilson interpreted the relevant provision of the Divorce Act[39] as requiring the judge to exercise his or her discretion. But although a support payment of $1,400 resulted in this instance – much more generous than average – Wilson's analysis makes it clear that the level of support was determined by the particulars of the situation: that is, by Mr Welsh's substantial income and the fact that he had kept his wife in relative luxury. In other words, a careful reading of the judgment reveals that the approach she applied was mandated by statute and factual context, not feminist principle.

Cure,[40] on the other hand, was a relatively brief Court of Appeal decision in which Wilson gave the unanimous oral judgment for the court. At trial, on the breakdown of his second marriage, the husband had been ordered to transfer to his wife a $20,000 lump sum support payment to compensate her for loss of the capitalized value of a pension which had been awarded after the death of her first husband. That pension had terminated on her remarriage, but the second marriage lasted less than a year. At the appeal, Wilson decided that a payment of just $10,000 was fairer. The wife, who would have shared in the prosperity of the second marriage if it had continued, had made the decision to remarry in full knowledge that she would lose her pension. Wilson therefore held that she ought to have shared equally in the economic losses resulting from that second marriage's failure; the loss of the pension did not result from the breakdown of the marriage but from the fact of the marriage, which meant that the compensatory provision in the Family Law Reform Act was not applicable.

It is not clear from this judgment whether the court took into consideration the differential impact that the loss of $10,000 would have for a fifty-nine year-old husband earning (in 1979) $15,000 a year and for a fifty-nine year-old wife who was unemployed and had been able to earn only $2,400 a year before her second marriage. What *Welsh* and *Cure* have in common is their strict application of the relevant statutory provisions which in Wilson's view indicated a shift in legislative policy resulting from a new social consensus about the ability and the duty of women to achieve economic independence as autonomous agents. She looked to section 21 of the Ontario Family Law Reform Act, which required that there be either a material change in circumstances as justification for any variation in a spousal support order or fresh evidence of economic circumstances not available at the original application for support.

As a matter of broad public policy, she wrote, the courts ought to allow variation of support orders only in situations when there had been a substantial change in the circumstances of the recipient spouse which was both unforeseen at the time of the original order and likely to be ongoing. Variations are not appeals, so propriety demands that an original order made by a court must be assumed to have been appropriate at the time it was made.

The legislation also provided that the courts could set aside domestic agreements where one of the spouses would otherwise become a public charge. However, Wilson was obviously sympathetic to the then-emerging policy in English case law which assigned responsibility to the welfare state to support needy spouses after a divorce, particularly when a substantial award may force the husband himself below a subsistence level and onto welfare rolls, or when a second family's claims mitigate obligations arising out of the first. Wilson wrote a series of memos to the Court of Appeal judges on assessment of maintenance when the recipient spouse was receiving social assistance. These memos reveal that in her opinion the existing assessment form provided an adequate standard of living – because the amount of support paid to recipients was above sustenance level.

Given Wilson's view that private philanthropy ought not to relieve government of its duty to provide appropriate levels of relief and her belief that it was doing so, it is predictable that she would consider that the husband's required contribution ought not to plunge him into penury. In the memo which she distributed to the Court of Appeal judges, she incorporated a contextual logic to the issue of mode and duration of spousal support which she believed should be determined in part by the age of the recipient spouse:

> I was interested to discover at the conference substantial support for the lump sum maintenance or support payment for the spouse as opposed to an award of periodic maintenance or support. The thinking behind this is that the maintenance and support should be viewed as *rehabilitative* only and not as a permanent meal ticket. However, I think a great deal depends on the age bracket of the wife. A rehabilitative approach to support is not realistic where the wife is older and has been a housewife all her life. In the case of younger women I think it makes excellent sense. There is, however, the difficult question as to the power of the court to vary a lump sum award. For this reason some judges expressed reservations about it at the conference.[41]

With respect to privately negotiated support contracts (not the situation in either *Welsh* or *Cure*) Wilson explicitly warned that in her view 'the courts in the past had been far too ready to interfere with the arrangements the parties have themselves made to settle their financial affairs.' It was not until she was at the Supreme Court of Canada that Wilson had the opportunity of putting this aspect of her theory fully into practice, much to the dismay of some feminist supporters who had applauded the *Becker* v. *Pettkus* decision. But that case, because it dealt with a common-law couple outside the statute, had been decided in the absence of specifically applicable legislation by developing the common law in accordance with the legislative policy direction.

Custody of Children

If Wilson's attribution to younger women of a greater capacity for reha-bilitation and economic self-sufficiency was in part coloured by per-sonal experience, she may have not taken sufficiently into consideration that most of these women would have had young children. Arrange-ments for care of the children when their mothers have been home with them and are forced back into the workplace after divorce is both costly and emotionally wrenching. It was not until the implementation of the Federal Child Support Guidelines in 1997 that these cost issues were at least partially addressed but the shortage of certified childcare space continues to be an issue.

Wilson was in other respects extremely sensitive to children's needs arising out of divorce and there were a number of Court of Appeal deci-sions concerning custody in which this sensitivity pushed her into dis-sent. As she said as early as 1976, whether or not Canadians considered liberalized divorce laws a good thing for husbands and wives, everyone seemed to agree that 'the casualties of marriage break-down are chil-dren.'[42] Almost a decade later she was to use this phrase as the title for a scholarly paper[43] on the topic, but her Court of Appeal jurisprudence demonstrates that her views on the issue had substantially been formed at that time.

Part of the problem of adopting an economic model which views mar-riage as a partnership requiring division of family assets on its disso-lution is the difficulty of fighting custody issues within this scheme. Children are not property to be divided, but neither are they partners with a direct claim to the assets. Children are not even shareholders in a corporation with access to an equitable oppression remedy if they believe that the behaviour of their parents has unfairly disregarded their interests. On the other hand, because concepts of custody are usually associated with criminal law, such language seems particularly dissonant in the family law context, where parents anxiously attempt to reduce psychological harm by assuring their children that they are not to blame for the dissolution of the marriage.

The doctrine of the best interests of the children purportedly governs all court proceedings relating to custody and child support. But as Wilson pointed out in her dissent in the *Kruger*[44] case, the winner-takes-all mentality of adversarial litigation fails to take into consideration that 'in some circumstances it may be in the child's best interests not to choose between the parents but to do everything possible to maintain the child's relationship with both parents.' She also pointed out that the adversarial process, requiring each spouse to attack the other in order to protect his or her economic interests, results in too much emphasis on the husband-and-wife relationship and not enough on the parent-and-child relationship;[45] as she commented in an interview much later:

> I always felt that the adversary nature of the husband and wife disputes had considerable effects on the children and that when you had an adversary proceeding on divorce or separation, it was in the interests of each spouse to make the other look the worst that they possibly could, that was the whole aim and object of winning your case ... even down to, you know, saying they were unfit parents and so on. And I realized from a number of the cases I sat on that this had a terrific effect on the custody issue of the children and it practically made joint custody impossible, and I always viewed joint custody as being the highest and best answer because the whole purpose of the thing was that the best interests of the child be the dominant feature.

Kruger was a case in which a psychological assessment had determined that the parents had the capacity to cooperate in a joint custody arrangement with shared responsibility for all major decisions concerning the children's health, education and religious upbringing. Indeed, they had done so with very little difficulty for the two years between the date of separation and the date of trial; interim custody was awarded to the father who had remained in the matrimonial home but the children spent half of their time with their mother and there had been no quarrels about schooling or attendance at church or physical care. Each spouse candidly acknowledged that the other was an excellent parent.

Kruger had by his own admission been a drinker and adulterer during the first nine years of his marriage and had caused his wife a great deal of pain. Eventually and under her influence he joined her church and became a Jehovah's Witness. At that point he belatedly transformed himself into a model father to their two children, a nine-year-old daughter and a six-year-old son. The assessment showed that the children undoubtedly loved their father.

He tried to become a good husband as well, but it was too late for Mrs Kruger; without doubting the sincerity of his conversion, she decided to leave him. He would not permit her to take the children, although during earlier discussions he had originally agreed that she should have custody. But at the point of separation Kruger changed his mind on the advice of a church elder who informed him that ensuring the appropriate religious upbringing of the children was his duty as spiritual head of the household. His wife did not quarrel that this was an issue of conscience for her husband. And then, some time after she left him, there was one incident of adultery which resulted in her being shunned by the church.

The possibility of joint custody was raised in only a cursory manner before the trial judge. Believing that he had to make an either-or decision, he awarded sole custody to the mother on the rather weak grounds that the father had originally agreed to that arrangement.

Wilson looked to the development of the case law both in Canada and in England to support her belief that the time was ripe for a new approach to this issue. Three years earlier, Wilson had expressed the view that the courts had a duty not only to reflect public opinion but also to guide and lead it. This is an approach fully congruent with her philosophical training and in particular with Adam Smith's concept of the rolling evolution of the law which sometimes leads and sometimes follows public consensus.

But in this instance Wilson might have known that she would be sitting out in dissent. Some six months earlier, in *Baker*,[46] the Court of Appeal had reversed a decision by Madam Justice Janet Boland who had made an award of joint custody not sought by either the husband or the wife. Justice Lacourciere had written that unanimous judgment allowing the appeal. He criticized Boland sharply for failing to cite any legal literature in support of her assertion that there should be a presumption in favour of joint custody, which she had justified on the grounds that children fare best after divorce when they sustain loving relationships with both parents.

Wilson had the greatest respect for Boland role as trial judge in custody cases; but even though she was in sympathy with Boland's decision in *Baker*, she had to find a way of distinguishing it on the facts from *Kruger* because the reversal by the Court of Appeal created persuasive precedent. She admitted that there was some evidence that the Baker parents were incompatible and unable to cooperate and therefore that the imposition of a joint custody order might not have been appropriate. In *Kruger*, however, there was every reason to believe that the parents could cooperate.

Wilson also supplemented any deficiency in the authority underpinning Boland's judgment in *Baker* by providing a review of current English case law in which joint custody orders had been imposed, pointing out they were no longer confined to exceptional circumstances but were made more routinely whenever the best interests of the children seemed to require it. She referred, as well, to the 1976 report of the Law Reform Commission of Canada which advocated a more flexible approach to determinations of custody. In her view, just as parents have a duty to subserve any mutual hostility in the interests of their children, so too does the court have a duty to make a contextual assessment that recognizes the broad variety of options always available, and then to select the option which best meets the needs of the children. If the court effectively permits one of the parents to refuse to cooperate, it is abdicating its own responsibility and failing in its institutional role of modelling (as well as demanding) an appropriately moral standard of behaviour in a matter of crucial importance.

Justice Thorson wrote the majority decision in *Kruger*, affirming the trial judge's award of custody solely to the mother on the grounds that willingness must be sincere and genuine to make joint custody work, that the cost to the child of its not working is potentially very high, and that accordingly it cannot be imposed by the court. Thorson fully understood that Mrs Kruger was unwilling to give up custody on appeal; 'it is only human nature for the "winner" at trial not to be willing to accept "something less" later on.' But Thorson also threw in a gratuitous critique of Wilson's understanding of human nature:

[M]y colleague Wilson J.A. has stated her view that our Courts should 'reflect in their orders a greater appreciation of the hurt inflicted upon a child by the severance of its relationship with one of its parents.' With respect, I think that our Courts do appreciate, and very keenly so, the hurt that can be inflicted in this way … The difficulty is that all too often in the cases that come before the Courts in this Province and elsewhere, the facts are such as to leave the courts with little or no realistic expectation of being able to devise workable custody arrangements that will avoid the need for hard choices. It is this reality, in my opinion, which had bred the 'healthy cynicism' referred to by my colleague as to the practicality of joint custody orders ... With great respect to my colleague Wilson J.A., it is not cynicism but observed human behaviour that causes me to question her expressed view that 'most mature adults, after the initial trauma has worn off, overcome their hostility attendant on the dissolution of their marriage or at the very least are capable of subserving it to the interests of the children.[47]

The majority decision is anything but respectful of Wilson's optimistic assessment of the general ability of parents to act in the best interests of their children. This is an optimism we can trace back to the kind of simple propriety which, for Scottish Enlightenment philosopher Adam Smith, was a pragmatic if not completely altruistic adjunct to moral behaviour. But Thorson clearly believed that Wilson was merely naive, inexperienced as a judge, and perhaps also inexperienced because she was not a parent. His judgment incorporates an injudiciously personal rebuke, suggesting that he was somehow stung by her dissenting opinion. She herself could not help but consider that the majority judgment hit rather close to home although in the interest of judicial decorum and collegiality she kept her response to herself at the time.

Contemporary press coverage of *Kruger* was fairly even-handed, simply setting out the facts of the case and the reasons for the judgment and dissent. However, because joint custody since *Kruger* has increasingly become the solution reached through negotiation in amicable divorces, current legislation may be lagging behind social consensus on this issue. To date, the issue of whether joint custody must be voluntary or could work if imposed mandatorily has been revisited periodically both in the courts and discussed in the press without resolution. At the political level, proposed revisions to the federal Divorce Act move away from the language of joint custody to consider a shared parenting model which may be more congruent with developments in the common law.

Beginning in 1987 there has been an interesting line of cases in British Columbia, very compatible with Wilson's dissent in *Kruger*, in which the courts have held that an order of joint custody may be imposed when both parents are excellent parents with a history of cooperation with respect to their care of the children and there is no valid reason to exclude one of the parents from continued involvement at that level in the lives of the children.[48] This signals a clear conflict at the provincial level. However, because the Supreme Court has articulated its commitment to the 'maximum contact' principle, reaffirming the presumption that it is in the best interests of a child to spend as much time as possible with both parents after a divorce, there is some reason for optimism that the philosophy of the Wilson dissent in *Kruger* will ultimately prevail. Wilson's dissent in *Kruger* still seems to capture best the true intent of the best interests doctrine: there is an unseemly manipulation of the courts and an abandonment by the courts of their statutory duty to decide in the best interests of the children when one parent is permitted to deprive the other parent of meaningful involvement in the lives of the children because he or she prefers not to undertake the difficult task of cooperating on decisions affecting the children's welfare.

A number of other significant Wilson pronouncements on child custody emerge from her Ontario Court of Appeal jurisprudence and further demonstrate that she was ahead of her time on this issue. Wilson was aware of the weight accorded by trial judges to continuity of care and their general reluctance to disturb interim custody arrangements which seem to be working well for the children in question. Nevertheless, she recognized that a fixed policy of never disturbing custody arrangements would only escalate manoeuvrings to establish *de facto* possession and undermine the court's proper authority to make decisions in the best interests of the children.

In the *Ishaky*[49] case a Jewish father had inveigled his wife and two younger children (then aged fourteen and eighteen) into travelling to Israel with him, purportedly in order that his son could make his bar mitzvah there. He had bought round trip tickets and the understanding was that the children were to be enrolled in school back in Toronto once they returned. However once they were in Israel, Ishaky refused to allow his wife or his children to return to Canada, invoking the jurisdiction of the rabbinical tribunal and seeking to have Mrs Ishaky declared a 'rebellious wife' ineligible for maintenance and even seeking to have criminal conspiracy charges levied against her after the eighteen-year-old was somehow able to escape and return to Toronto.

When he himself returned to Toronto to sell the matrimonial home, his wife had him served in Ontario with an application for spousal and child support, custody, and interim disbursements pending divorce. A master granted the child support; the trial judge granted interim custody to the mother and made an order that she and children were to be returned to the jurisdiction of the Ontario courts, their place of ordinary residence, and a further *ex parte* injunction preventing Ishaky from leaving Ontario pending resolution of the matter. The father appealed on the grounds that the custody issue had been decided without sufficient evidence as to the best interests of the children.

Wilson referred to the ample evidence contained in eight affidavits which had been filed by the wife and upheld the interim custody order of the Ontario trial judge. As in *Kruger*, decided two years later, Wilson invoked the full normative force of the law in articulating a standard of parental care which in her view the father simply had not met: 'The husband is engaged in conduct which not only exacerbated the gulf between himself and his wife but has shed a somewhat unkindly light upon his disposition and called in question his ability to form a considered judgment as to what is best for this family.'[50] If the father was not able to manage his apparently difficult disposition and to behave appropriately towards his family, then the courts could compel him to do so by substituting its judgment as to the best interests of the children; she therefore dismissed the appeal.

A few months later, in *Bezaire*,[51] Wilson dissented from the majority judgment of justices Arnup and Weatherston in a case involving a lesbian mother who was originally awarded custody of her children conditional on her establishing a more stable home environment. When she failed to do so, the trial judge had directed that the father take custody; the mother appealed and the appeal was dismissed. Wilson considered that the Court of Appeal had failed to take into account the psychiatric evidence filed in an affidavit and arising out of investigations undertaken by the Official Guardian which had been appointed to represent the children on the appeal, in so far as it conflicted with a responding psychiatric assessment provided by the father. She would have referred the matter back to the trial judge for a full hearing of the fresh evidence. And Wilson concluded pointedly: 'I would like to add as an addendum to these reasons that in my view homosexuality is a neutral and not a negative factor as far as parenting skills are concerned. To the extent the learned trial judge proceeded on a different view I would respectfully disagree with him.'

This comment gave heart to the gay community, but not for another fifteen years did the courts deal in a systematic way with the evidence on the relevance of sexual orientation to the relationship between parent and child, upholding Wilson's insight.[52] However, it ought to be noted that Arnup had specifically dissociated himself from any connotations in the trial judgment which might be interpreted as denigrating homosexual parents, holding that in each instance the judge should take this factor into consideration only in relation to evidence showing the effect that the particular lifestyle of the gay or lesbian parent had had or might have on the children. Arnup also specifically held that the mother in this instance was granted leave to apply for a variation of the custody order whenever she could show that her living circumstances had changed in such a way that she was able to provide a more appropriate situation for her children.[53]

Finally, in the *Cooney*[54] custody case heard close to the end of her period on the Court of Appeal, Wilson felt compelled once again to write a dissenting judgment. This was an appeal from a final order of custody of a ten-year-old son to his father; the majority dismissed the appeal out of the same deference to the trial judge's responsibility for the finding of facts. Arthur Jessup, Wilson's sharpest critic, served on the *Cooney* panel but it was the generally mild-mannered Peter Cory who wrote the judgment. It amounts to a rebuke of Wilson for her failure to accord due respect to the reality that only the trial judge can weigh credibility because he alone has had the opportunity of observing the witnesses during *viva voce* testimony:

> The factual findings of a trial judge should always be given great weight and should not be lightly disturbed by an appellate court. This is particularly true in a case involving custody for he is in a uniquely advantageous position to assess the parties.
>
> An award of custody must be based in large part upon an appraisal of the parents. Such an assessment can only really be made by someone who has seen them and heard them. It is easy to be critical after the fact and to meticulously note the errors of omission and commission made during a trial and in the reasons for judgment. Yet, how little is really conveyed by the transcript. An appellate court will look in vain for the brief pauses, the changes in the inflections or tone of voice of a witness that may be so revealing in an appraisal of this sort. The most scrupulous search of the arid typewritten page will not yield any indication of the gestures, the deportment and demeanour of a witness which may be critical to the eventual findings of the trial judge.[55]

Wilson, of course, had never served as a trial judge; although Cory does not personalize the criticism by naming her, the implication is that this lack of experience makes her unduly harsh in her assessment of the trial judge's decision.

But the crucial omission pointed out by Wilson in her dissent is the failure of the judge in his reasons for judgment, which are based on consideration of some three hundred pages of transcript from the trial, to signal that he has taken into consideration the best interests of the child in making his decision. In addition, she points out the commission of a clear error of law. The trial judge had peremptorily silenced the mother's counsel when he had attempted to introduce evidence that she was seeking to protect her boy by removing him from a frightening instance in which her husband had been violent towards her in the child's presence; he told counsel that the welfare of the child was not the point. As far as determination of custody is concerned, of course, the welfare and best interests of the child is the only point.

The Cooneys had been high-school sweethearts. Cooney had successfully taken over the management of a family stationery business originally owned by his wife's parents and she had continued to work there. Both spouses had privately discussed their marital difficulties with another employee and sought his advice. Their marriage had broken up because Mrs Cooney subsequently had an affair with the confidant; understandably, Mr Cooney felt doubly betrayed.

The Cory judgment recounts in some detail the history of the affair, Despite the no-fault divorce regime, it covertly imputes blame to the wife by deeming this relationship the real reason for the break-up of the marriage. The only evidence that Mrs Cooney may have been an imperfect mother was an incident in which she had been a little late in picking her son up at the local arena because she had been with her lover; however, the boy had been unaware of the reason for the delay and apparently filled in the time happily enough watching a hockey game.

As Wilson states with some indignation, 'We don't know whether Mrs Cooney was a wonderful mother or not'; what is far more significant is the trial judge's failure to acknowledge that marital misconduct is not relevant to a custody issue unless it has a direct bearing on the spouse's ability to be a parent. In fact, Mr Cooney had written to his wife assuring her that he knew she was a good mother but that evidence was not persuasive to the trial judge. The judge had also been swayed by the future financial prospects of the child who stood to inherit the family business if he sustained a close relationship with his maternal grandmother, who lived next door to his custodial father's house and had taken the side of her son-in-law. But these were not the kind of best interests that the statute had in mind. The courts in this instance permitted the father to exercise his vindictiveness against his wife and former employee through his child; they sought to exert the normative force of the law in an anachronistic condemnation of the wife's adultery rather than to uphold their statutory mandate of considering the psychological well being of the child in relationship to both parents.

In the notes which she had prepared for the 1979 speech to the Women's Canadian Club, Wilson had written:

> It is said by many that we have come through the era of women's rights and that we are now entering the era of children's rights – that the child will be the focus of the next decade. This may well be so and certainly the Ontario legislature is actively engaged now in reviewing the position of this most defenceless member of the family unit. There is no more difficult task a judge has to face than to decide which parent should have custody of children when a marriage collapses. Here is one instance where a judge is expected to have the wisdom of Solomon. All of us agonize over custody applications. There are no winners in a divorce case but there certainly are losers and these are the children.[56]

Wilson was too optimistic in anticipating that the decade of the 1980s would be an era of children's rights and that significant developments would occur in the law of custody in that time frame. In the event, real change has taken longer and the most significant changes are still rising over the British Columbia horizon.

As Osler managing partner Allan Beattie noted, Wilson has a remarkable ability to see the big picture, which she combines with a cheerful confidence about the capacity and the willingness of others to do what ought to be done once it has been made evident to them. It is only too clear that many parents still consider custody of their children a right rather than both an obligation and a privilege. Nevertheless, during her years at the Supreme Court she continued to try to move the law along in many areas relating to children and to family law more generally.

THE HUMAN RIGHTS CASES

Wilson's most significant human rights decisions at the Court of Appeal were heard in 1979, all of them involved discrimination against females, and all of them attracted considerable public attention. In two test cases, boards of inquiry at the Ontario Human Rights Commission had decided that two organized sports associations were in breach of the Human Rights Code because they had prevented young girls from participating in boys' sports teams. The Divisional Court had allowed an appeal. The cases were then heard by a panel comprised of justices Houlden, Wilson, and Weatherston.

In 1976 Gail Cummings,[57] then aged ten, had been prevented from playing for the Huntsville Atom All-Stars because the Ontario Minor Hockey Association rules denied teams with female players affiliation with its association. Although the OMHA would have waived its right of appeal on the technicality, the court held (with Wilson writing the unanimous judgment) that the relevant provision of the Ontario Human Rights Code which prohibited discrimination on the grounds of sex was not applicable, given that only legal or natural persons were prohibited from exercising such discrimination and the unincorporated hockey association was not at law a person. Wilson provides a thorough overview of the applicable case law relating to unincorporated associations; the appeal was dismissed accordingly with the *obiter* advice that the complaint ought to have been laid against named officers or directors of the association. The decision, when it came three years after the original complaint, made Gail rather sad but by the age of thirteen she had come to realize that many other girls were also prevented from playing competitive minor hockey. She had signed up for a girls' hockey team and redirected her athletic talents to the Huntsville All-Star Lacrosse Team, where the policies were more enlightened and she had the opportunity of travelling across Canada. But the principle still galled her: 'Girls should have just as much rights as boys,' a reporter quoted her as responding to the decision.

In the companion case[58] also initiated in 1976, then nine-year-old Debbie Bazso, who was the star player on the Waterford Squirt All-Star Softball team, had disqualified her team by participating in the baseball play-offs organized by the Ontario Rural Softball Association; as a female she could not be registered in accordance with ORSA's rules, and ORSA as an incorporated association was a legal person which could be sued for alleged discrimination. Her coach, Brett Bannerman, was anxious to have her play and he had initiated the complaint.

This time judges Weatherston and Houlden both dismissed the appeal although for separate reasons. For Weatherston the issue turned on the intention of the regulations which was to create fairness of competition taking into account the differing rates of growth of girls and boys and providing separate leagues for each (although the nearest girls' team was twenty miles away from Debbie's home); that some discrimination had resulted was inevitable. Houlden reasoned that the service provided by the ORSA was merely the provision of play-off schedules; such a service was not comparable with the services provided in a hotel or restaurant which were properly caught by the prohibition.

Wilson dissented. It was clear to her that Debbie's application was denied not on merit but solely because of her sex. She would not buy the argument that ORSA could determine the scope of the services which it wished to provide. As she inquired indignantly, reasoning by analogy to the racial situation in which discrimination would certainly not have been permitted,

> Is it open to ORSA to say: 'We provide softball for whites and softball for blacks and that is the scope of the service we have decided to provide'? I do not think so. I do not believe that the services provided in a public place can be circumscribed on the basis of the prohibited criteria. Certainly, any organization can determine what services it is going to provide and to whom, but I think what the Legislature is saying in s. 2 is: if you are going to provide them in a place to which the public is customarily admitted, then you cannot exclude anyone from them solely on the basis of race, creed, colour, etc.[59]

The newspaper coverage was generally sympathetic to Wilson's point of view. An editorial in a Brantford paper stated that the Human Rights Code should be amended so that it could prevent discrimination against young girls seeking to play on boys' teams. The *Toronto Sun* deplored the discrimination encountered by these young athletes as emblematic of the larger difficulties encountered by women in employment and politics. The *Globe and Mail* editorial pointed out that the sports leagues in practice monopolized public facilities in most small towns and their failure to provide equal services effectively shut girls out of organized sports.[60]

The Ontario Human Rights Code was amended with the addition of a provision specifying that the right to equal treatment was not infringed by restricting participation in an athletic organization or activity to persons of the same sex.[61] But in the meantime, Charter guarantees of sexual equality had been enacted and were in force. Once again, a thirteen-year-old female hockey player challenged the Ontario Hockey Association ruling that she could not play on the boys-only teams. This time, she won,[62] and the reasoning of Justice Dubin echoed the approach comparing racial discrimination to discrimination on the grounds of sex which had been taken by Wilson in the Bazso case seven years earlier.

If one were to identify a single case which stands out as the best-known contribution Wilson made at the Court of Appeal, it might be *Bhadauria* v. *Seneca College*[63] in which she wrote the unanimous judgment for the plaintiff and recognized a new tort of civil discrimination. Pushpa Bhadauria had emigrated to Canada from India. She had a Ph.D. in mathematics from an Indian university, an Ontario teacher's certificate, and seven years of teaching experience. Between 1974 and 1978 she had on ten different occasions applied for teaching positions at the Seneca College but had not once been granted even an interview although her education and experience more than met the requested qualifications.

On this occasion Bhaduaria opted not to file a complaint under the Ontario Human Rights Code alleging racial discrimination. Instead, in her statement of claim she sued for $1 million in damages, alleging that Seneca had breached both its common law duty and its statutory duty not to discriminate against her. Seneca had moved successfully to have the statement of claim struck for disclosing no reasonable cause of action because the judge found that the Ontario Human Rights Code had established a comprehensive code for dealing with issues of discrimination which precluded Bhadauria's resort to the civil courts.

Wilson's analysis of the case law and the history of civil rights legislation demonstrates that the code only evidenced Ontario's public policy of recognizing the fundamental human right to be free of racial discrimination. She pointed in particular to the judgment in *Re Drummond Wren*, decided after Ontario's first civil rights legislation had come into effect, in which Justice Mackay had struck down a restrictive covenant prohibiting transfer of a particular property to Jews on the grounds that it was offensive to public policy even though the legislation did not specifically provide such protection from discrimination at the time. Because that right had independent pre-existence in the common law right to service provided other members of the public, Wilson held that the code could not exclude the common law tort remedy which Bhadauria wished to invoke. Of course, Wilson's judgment allowing the appeal did not amount to a finding that Seneca College had in fact discriminated against Pushpa Bhadauria, but it would have permitted Bhadauria to pursue her civil suit.

The public response was overwhelmingly positive. Civil rights lawyer Joseph Pomerant considered the judgment 'the most important decision for the little guy on the street in the history of this country.' Allan Borovoy, general counsel to the Canadian Civil Liberties Association, said it was 'a creative and progressive application of the best public policy principles in the development of the common law.'[64] On a private level, Wilson received letters of congratulations from Ed Ratushny, who had recruited her for the Court of Appeal, and from Clayton Ruby, one of the lawyers whom she most respected.

It had been assumed that, if the Court of Appeal judgment were to be appealed, the Supreme Court would affirm Wilson's analysis. Instead, Chief Justice Laskin held that the code mandated the complaint route through the Human Rights Commission because the code itself laid out the procedures to be followed in vindicating the public policy it embodied; only if the complainant were able to demonstrate that the findings of the board of inquiry were in error could she access the civil courts through the process known as judicial review.[65]

There was more press coverage which brought out additional information apparently not before the courts, or at any rate not referred to in the judgments. The weak explanation for the lack of any invitation to interview over the four years of Bhadauria's applications which was offered by Seneca's personnel department was that a degree in pure mathematics would not likely be useful in teaching the applied courses that the college offered. In fact, Mrs Bhadauria had received letters stating she would be contacted for an interview with no subsequent follow-up and with no reason ever offered for her rejection. According to the executive director of the commission, Bhadauria had on twenty-two previous occasions filed complaints relating to her failure to obtain employment teaching mathematics at several Toronto high schools and another community college. In each instance, the complaint had been investigated and turned down for 'lack of substance' without a board of inquiry ever being held. The director expressed his opinion that Bhadauria's failure to obtain employment related to her poor grades in obtaining the teaching certificate .[66]

Given this candid and rather indiscreet disclosure that the issue had been prejudged, it is little wonder that Pushpa Bhadauria had not gone to the commission on this occasion: 'Those people are hopeless, [she said] ... You come here young, ambitious and full of hope and then you discover that all doors are closed to you.' Bhadauria had had other offers of teaching positions from various educational institutions in both India and the United States, but as a Canadian citizen she wanted to stay in Canada; she considered the ruling at the Supreme Court to be 'a loss for all Canadians, not just for ethnic minorities.'

The Ontario Human Rights Commission was notorious for its backlog of complaints. There is considerable consensus among human rights lawyers that organizational problems, together with endemic delays, mean that commission procedures continue to hold out empty remedies; there is even evidence to indicate that the headway which has been achieved in reducing the backlog may result from a more aggressive invocation of the code provisions permitting the commission to decline jurisdiction altogether.

Nevertheless, there is some reason for optimism that the Wilson approach at the Court of Appeal may yet be vindicated through incremental developments in the common law which have resulted from careful drafting of pleadings. In a number of recent cases the courts in Ontario have upheld the right of a plaintiff to initiate a claim in the civil courts simultaneously with a complaint at the Ontario Human Rights Commission so long as the civil claim is separately actionable. The *Bhadauria* doctrine does not necessarily foreclose simultaneous civil action when the defendant's behaviour is discriminatory but also constitutes a breach of an employment contract or a separate actionable tort such as constructive dismissal, damage to reputation, breach of privacy, breach of fiduciary duty, or the intentional or negligent infliction of harm. This development is very much in accordance with the long-established common law tradition permitting great flexibility in the development of novel torts; to avoid the *Bhadauria* doctrine, which still has precedential weight to foreclose the civil action, a lawyer need only take care that the novel tort not constitute one of the varieties of discrimination as defined within the code. Would Pushpa Bhadauria's civil action be allowed today in the context of this evolving dual regime? In her pleadings, she had alleged that Seneca's refusal of her application for employment deprived her of the opportunity of earning a livelihood and caused her mental distress, frustration, and loss of dignity and self-esteem; these claims today might be reframed as intentional or negligent infliction of harm.

The harms inflicted upon her have indeed been long-lasting. The legal costs were devastating. Although she has done some occasional supply teaching in the intervening years, Mrs Bhadauria has never obtained a permanent job and remains convinced that the notoriety of her name prevents her from doing so. She remains, not surprisingly, bitter about the Supreme Court reversal and even sees in it evidence of conspiracy.[67] But despite her disappointments with Canadian law and Canadian government, throughout the years Pushpa Bhadauria has sustained a deep sense of gratitude towards Bertha Wilson, the judge who over two decades ago found in her favour at the Court of Appeal.

THE SUPREME SACRIFICE

Mr Justice Allen Linden,[68] a hearty and outgoing man, had been at Osgoode Hall in the trial division from 1978 on. He came to know Bertha Wilson well through conversations in the judges' dining room and meetings at the judges' continuing education seminars and he shared with her a desire to make the law more friendly to ordinary Canadians. Before he went to the bench Linden had been a distinguished academic and tort law professor at the York University Faculty of Law; he was particularly delighted with Wilson's *Bhadauria* decision which, as he recalls, had people dancing in the streets.

Linden was disappointed but not surprised by the Supreme Court decision to dismiss the appeal. From Linden's perspective, Bora Laskin was no great friend of the common law of torts. Laskin genuinely believed that the administrative tribunals were the best defenders of civil liberties and human rights, and that the court had 'a duty to see that statutes if at all possible are given an operative effect.'[69] Laskin could see a worrisome erosion of tribunal authority in the labour relations area. Accordingly in *Bhadauria* he had wanted to assert the important principle of judicial deference to what he considered the statutory mandate of the commission.

Linden had known Trudeau as a fellow law professor. Both of them were active in the Liberal party in the early 1960s, and Linden shared Trudeau's federalist philosophies, his dreams of law reform and the hopes for a just society Trudeau articulated during his term as minister of justice. After Trudeau's election in 1967, Linden served as chair on a policy committee working towards participatory democracy. He was involved in a lot of the backroom discussions initiated by Trudeau concerning constitutional reform and a Charter of Rights and Freedoms.

If Wilson's appointment to the Ontario Court of Appeal came almost completely out of the blue, that was certainly not the case with the Supreme Court appointment. In 1981 Mr Justice Ronald Martland was approaching the mandatory retirement age of seventy-five. There had been unprecedented speculation and lobbying about the appointment of his replacement, heightened by the growing public awareness of the new role the courts would play after the patriation of the Constitution and the coming into force of the Charter scheduled for April of 1982.

Sandra Day O'Connor was newly installed at the United States Supreme Court; in early March of 1982, Conservative member of Parliament Flora MacDonald rose in the House of Commons to demand of the then justice minister, Jean Chrétien, when the Canadian Supreme Court would follow suit. Chrétien replied that his government had wanted to consider a woman when the previous appointment had been made in 1981, but simply could not find anyone sufficiently qualified. Canadian feminists were furious at this slur.

But Trudeau had, in fact, been looking for a suitably distinguished and experienced woman and he called upon his old friend Allen Linden to help him in the search. When they met that year at the Toronto Film Festival, it quickly became apparent that this issue was very much on Trudeau's mind. He asked:

> By the way, do you know Bertha Wilson? I am thinking of putting her on the court, what do you think of her? I have read some of her judgments and they seem to be very good in commercial law, she seems to be a very sound scholar of commercial law, but what about human rights and civil liberties, what would she be like there?

Linden was amazed that Trudeau had been reading Wilson's judgments. He knew, of course, that Trudeau wanted to appoint someone whose intellectual and philosophical background was congruent with an expansive and innovative development of the Charter. In Linden's opinion, Wilson was supremely competent in commercial law but her heart was in human rights; there could be no one finer. Trudeau was not familiar with the Wilson judgment in *Bhadauria*; when Linden described it to him, he requested that Linden forward a copy of it to him. Within a few days, the Wilson appointment had been announced.

Bertha and John Wilson received word by telephone in Arizona where they had retreated for a holiday and in order to get out of the eye of the increasingly intrusive publicity which had been swirling around them in Toronto. But by the time they reached the airport to return home, there were newspaper reporters and photographers already waiting for them. Although thrilled about the appointment and much less equivocal than Bertha herself, John was 'mad as a hatter' at this intrusion; Bertha had to tell him, 'For God's sake, John, smile.'

Wilson had come to love her work at the Ontario Court of Appeal which she considered to be the leading court in the country.[70] Her participation in the informal dining room conversations and the judges' continuing education seminars provided the intellectual stimulation she always craved. In 1980 she had been honoured with the first of her twenty-nine honourary doctorates in law, fittingly from her own law school, Dalhousie. All in all, Bertha Wilson had reason to be richly contented with her work and the recognition she had won.

Scared stiff when she was appointed to the Court of Appeal, admittedly frustrated by the compromise necessary to get signatures on judgments, Wilson had slowly made a place for herself inside the cowcatcher gates on Queen Street West, just as she had done earlier at Oslers and Dalhousie and Macduff. She enjoyed the way the 'fellows' would drop into her office or invite her to theirs for lively discussion of particular cases or more general social conversation. Bert MacKinnon, whose office was kitty-corner from Wilson's, reports that when he regularly heard bursts of laughter and giggling (male giggling, he specified) coming from her room, he would be unable to resist setting aside whatever task he was doing in order to rush across and find out what was going on.[71]

Chief Justice Howland, who replaced Gale on his retirement, had also been a solicitor and he fully valued the particular contributions Wilson brought to the bench; Wilson reciprocated his esteem.[72] She had become completely at home in the collegial atmosphere she had helped to create and would have been very pleased to have worked out the rest of her career on the Court of Appeal.

But her colleagues at the Ontario Court of Appeal and other judges were openly pressing her to accept appointment to the Supreme Court if it were to be offered. Gordon Blair recalls attending one of the French language courses which were held twice a year to encourage bilingual capacity in all the federal courts. Both the Wilsons were there. When the impending Supreme Court vacancy became a topic of conversation over lunch, all those present joined in urging Bertha to accept the promotion if it came her way, although she quite naturally remained noncommittal as to her intentions. A number of issues made her hesitate.

The workload at the Court of Appeal during her tenure was certainly not light but it was manageable. Wilson was still not in robust health. Seven years earlier she had already been talking to Hal Mockridge about early retirement or at least cutting back on her practice. And when she had accepted the appointment to the Court of Appeal in a rather dazed state of mind, as much from shock as from her sense of duty, she had not realized she would need to work fifteen more years before she would become eligible for a pension. With the advent of the Charter, Wilson could anticipate that serving on the Supreme Court would require unprecedented hard work. She was never a slacker, but she had serious doubts as to whether she would be able to handle it. Moreover, in Ottawa she would be a pioneer once more. Experience had taught her she would have to prove herself to a new group of men unlikely to assume that she had won the position on her merits:

> I don't believe that when I went on the court that the male judges took it for granted that I was going to be able to do the job. I think, maybe, that the view was contrary. So, to go on there and start throwing your weight around when you were, in their eyes, a novice ... Well, you have to gain acceptance through your ability first and they will listen to you ... A lot of women, I think, are of the view that as soon as you get into a group, you can start trying to change things. I don't think it works. I think you have to go through this process of proving yourself first.[73]

For all of these reasons she had profound misgivings. The appointment was not one that Bertha coveted in the slightest; what made it worse was that she was acutely aware that there were others who very much did. And acceptance would create considerable dislocation on a personal level, both for her and her husband. She and John were happy with their house on Moore Avenue and in fact had just begun to think about expanding their kitchen. They loved their weekends at the beloved Bobcaygeon boathouse retreat, which they had continued to share or make available to nephews Chris and Richard Wernham through their teenage years and early adulthood. They had a close circle of Toronto friends and above all enjoyed a pace of life which made possible their quiet times together for reading and thinking and listening to music.

When his fundraising work for the United Church of Canada had come to an end, John Wilson had taken on a job as director of the Consumers' Association of Canada, a lobby association that worked hard to achieve legislative reform for consumer protection and handled various kinds of consumer inquiries out of a downtown Toronto office. It was, once again, work that he thoroughly enjoyed, entailing the coordination of submissions from smaller constituency offices located all over the province. He could see pragmatic results from his efforts to integrate the ethical and economic issues which had fascinated him from his earliest days at Macduff.

But at the end of the day Bertha and John both knew that if she was appointed she had to serve. It was her duty.

The swearing-in ceremony took place on 30 March 1982. All the Wernhams attended: brother Jim and his wife Rosemary were still living in Ottawa; nephew Chris and his wife, Monique were also in Ottawa; nephew Richard and his wife, Julia came up from Toronto. Oslers assisted with the travel arrangements for the Toronto Wernhams and hospitality for everyone. It was a proud moment for both her law firm and her family.

Nevertheless, the remarks made that day signalled mingled respect and wariness on the part of the chief justice. Laskin's somewhat pointed suggestion that the new judge take on her role as a team player must have been unintentionally ironic after Wilson's dissent in the girls' softball case. Laskin earnestly recommended that she conform to the existing traditions of judgment which had been established by the hitherto exclusively 'old boys'' club:

> We are sustained by a long tradition in which we embrace our new colleague. It is a tradition that has manifested itself in an easy informality, in a reciprocal cordiality and in a mutual deference, all of which make for cooperative and effective adjudication, but with due allowance for individual independence of judgments ... Nous espérons tous que la Cour et le pays ont tiré profit de nos contributions personnelles, et notre nouvelle collègue ajoutera, je le sais, sa propre contribution à l'ensemble qui a donné et qui continue à donner a la Cour suprême le caractère qui lui est propre.[74]

Similarly, Minister of Justice Jean Chrétien's address contained a remarkably overt direction to the new judge that, should her personal life experience ever conflict with her legal training, the rule of law had to triumph:

> You, Madame Justice Wilson, as with your colleagues before me, have been appointed as a result of your distinguished career in law. The wisdom and knowledge that you bring to this Court results in part from your life experiences. The influences of such things as place of birth, residence, age, sex, religion are balanced by your training in the law and the commitment to the rule of law over and above the concerns of special interest groups or governments of the day.

And Chrétien mischievously tweaked Laskin with an implicit reference to the still-fresh *Bhadauria* reversal:

> Although I know that Madame Justice Wilson will work closely with her new associates, her service on the Court of Appeal demonstrates that she will not hesitate to write clearly and compellingly in dissent. My Lord the Chief Justice has been recently aware of the persuasive innovation which his new associate can bring to her judgments, and in the future, he may find it more difficult to resist the kind of reasoning which he recently characterized as a bold and commendable attempt to advance the common law.[75]

What mitigated Wilson's innovative creativity, in Chrétien's view (and what this praise implicitly recommends that she sustain) was the fact that 'her innovations result from carefully-reasoned legal analysis – meticulously researched and scrupulously fair' together with her 'deep respect for the rule of law, and an appreciation for the stability which characterizes the common law at its best.'[76]

Wilson was aware of the general discomfort and nervousness surrounding her appointment to the Supreme Court. In her response she was notably circumspect. Her carefully selected words acknowledged the advice she was being given without in any way foreclosing her intention to explore new legal directions in accordance with the fervent aspirations and expectations of all those who had lobbied for her to be offered this ultimate judicial appointment. She stressed that her own experience both as a woman and an immigrant symbolized the diversity inherent in the Canadian concept of cultural mosaic and added: 'I trust that within the collegial structure of this national Court I can be a faithful steward of the best of our legal heritage interpreting it responsibly according to the rule of law and in the context of a contemporary pluralist society ... as a true servant of the law.'[77]

Her commitment, then, was not to *all* of the legal heritage urged upon her, but only to the best of it and as a servant who would be purposively true to its underlying principles as an expression of fundamental social value. She deliberately excluded anything abrasive or confrontational in her manner which might have offended against the decorum of the occasion. And John, who was watching in the crowd, told her later that Laskin obviously had been dreading what she might say and that he heaved a sigh of relief when panic failed to erupt. She had intended a certain equivocation, Wilson admits now, but it was carefully calibrated so that it was not really enough to worry Laskin.

John had taken early retirement. The Wilsons packed their bags, put their Toronto house on the market and moved first into a hotel and then into a winterized summer cottage while they began house hunting in Ottawa; fortunately, the weather was uncharacteristically mild with little snow for much of that year. Their new place, when they found it, was pretty but more conventionally so than Moore Avenue. It was of white stucco with leaded, diamond-paned windows, a stone-trimmed arched door, and high cedar hedges all around the garden. Considerable renovations needed to be done; Chris Wernham jokes that the foundations required shoring up to take the weight of John's library. There was a conference in Newfoundland that summer which both Wilsons attended and the work was completed while they were away.

Unfortunately, Jim Wernham was shortly to retire from his teaching position at Carleton University, and he and Rosemary moved back to Toronto. But one good thing about the move was that Chris and Monique Wernham, still in Ottawa, were happy to welcome this favourite aunt and uncle. They loved the Wilsons' new house and were regular dinner guests there; the relationship deepened. The Wilsons were aware that Chris was not happy in his job teaching French language and literature, but at first they did not know that, like his brother, he had begun to explore the possibilities of law by taking a few arts program courses in legal studies at Carleton.

Chris felt deeply ambivalent about the shift. While pursuing postgraduate studies in France he had met his wife, who was then working as an archivist at the University of Ottawa. Chris had also planned on an academic career but in the late 1970s the kind of job he wanted wasn't available. All that was on offer was part-time and sessional work at Carleton or a full-time position teaching engineering students at Royal Military College in Kingston. That meant he could be home only weekends. But now in his early thirties, Chris worried that it was too late to change gears. The preparatory courses quickly dispelled that worry. Immediately he loved the law as much as Bertha had when she enrolled at Dalhousie. Not surprisingly he did well.

Nevertheless, it was not until he had finally made up his mind to pursue professional legal training and get called to the bar that he confided in his aunt. Only then did he understand, with a certain awe, how remarkable her career had been. She, too, had taken up a new career late in life, and now she was very encouraging to Chris. By the fall of 1983 he had enrolled in the faculty of law at the University of Ottawa. Throughout his law school career, however, Chris kept his connection at the Supreme Court quiet from his classmates and the university professors; he never even visited the Court or Wilson's chambers although he certainly followed her judgments with keen interest.

John settled more fully into the role of house husband, adding to his shopping and cooking chores. Bertha had helped him at Macduff and Renfrew; now it was his turn to take on the supportive role. He stepped up the clipping service by which he had always kept Bertha apprised of social trends and data which should appropriately be brought to 'judicial notice.' What is particularly endearing about the boxes and boxes of clippings from this era is their homeliness and the integration of life with the law. Mixed in completely at random with obituaries of former judges and editorials pronouncing on recent judgments and letters calling for sentencing reform are new recipes for soups and scones, advertisements for executive patent leather pumps or ingenious wheeled shopping bags, restaurant reviews, art gallery reviews, and articles about country inns around and about Ottawa. But although John Wilson liked to present himself to the other judicial spouses and to the Supreme Court law clerks as immersed in routine domesticity, this was in large part a ruse; he continued to read both widely and deeply and to think profoundly about all the issues of the day. Allan Beattie believes that John Wilson contributed immeasurably to the work Bertha Wilson was able to perform at the Supreme Court.

By the end of the summer of 1982 John's new study on the third floor had been made ready for him with exposed wood beams and lots of shelving for his enormous collection of books. Bertha realized that she would no longer be able to do her own cleaning and for the first time hired help. Once again, she had to begin the hard work of making a place for herself, this time burdened by the expectations of so many Canadian women that she would also be able to make a place for them in the development of Canadian law.

6

A Canadian Philosophy of
Judicial Analysis

Mr Justice James MacPherson of the Ontario Court of Appeal knows
Bertha Wilson well. He served as executive legal officer at the Supreme
Court of Canada between 1985 and 1987; he was dean of Osgoode Hall
Law School and teaching constitutional law there in 1990 when Wilson
delivered her controversial 'Will Women Women Judges Really Make
a Difference?' speech; and on a personal level, the Wilsons and the
MacPhersons are friends who generally get together each year at the
end of December for a proper celebration of Hogmanay, the Scottish
new year.

In late 1991, at the symposium Dalhousie hosted to honour Wilson
when she retired from the Supreme Court, MacPherson spoke about her
contributions in the context of the Charter of Rights. Enacted two weeks
after her appointment, the Charter in his view irrevocably transformed
Canadian public affairs. Its impact has been four fold: political (in urging legislators to consider not whether they *could*, but whether they
should, enact a particular law); legal (in improving, through litigation,
the lot of marginal and hitherto neglected groups in Canadian society);
judicial (in raising the profile of the Supreme Court of Canada as an
institution) and educational (in reminding Canadians of their better
selves both as rights-bearing and as rights-protecting citizens).[1]

Wilson, says MacPherson, illuminated all four of these functions.

Accordingly, he concluded, she was a perfect judge for her time. What made it possible for her to do so much were three personal qualities which he considers her to possess to an unusual degree: a formidable intellect, a profound compassion, and a passionate boldness.

MacPherson's analysis more or less mirrors the evolution of Wilson's personality we have been tracing before her appointment to the Supreme Court. Her compassion was first deeply engaged by the social problems she encountered as a minister's wife at Macduff. Her intellectual capacities were awakened by her law studies at Dalhousie. At Oslers, Wilson's principled boldness over issues such as billing and business travel and organizational structure kept pace with her growing professional confidence. But writing judgments at the Court of Appeal demanded the integration of all these qualities. The complexity of law and fact required thinking cases through from many different perspectives. And because Wilson's life experience brought new perspectives to that court, it is not surprising that she sometimes found herself in dissent.

Wilson's Osler colleague Allan Beattie also knows her well. In his opinion, it was not so much Wilson's multiplicity of perspectives but her longer perspective which could give rise to conflicts with colleagues in 1982, when she was heading to the Supreme Court. Wilson could be restless and impatient. If something was unfair, unjust, or outmoded and needed to be changed, she tended to look beyond the limitations of the particular situation. However, he admitted, very often what had appeared to be a conflict between the idealistic and the pragmatic vanished when viewed from her longer perspective.

In Beattie's view, that longer perspective had continued to be Wilson's contribution to Oslers long after she had left the firm; he humorously anticipated that the Court of Appeal would experience a similar lingering influence after Wilson had departed for the Supreme Court.[2] And in fact Wilson's enduring contributions to Canadian jurisprudence since she left both courts can only be understood by tracing the incremental development of the common law in the directions she initiated.

Wilson herself fully recognized the difficulties of integrating the inconveniently contradictory elements of human personality, her own included. But she also considered it essential to try for that longer perspective. At a number of convocation addresses, she recounted an anecdote about an Edinburgh brain surgeon performing a long and difficult operation with 'cool flair and calm confidence.' His intern, observing, was repelled by the doctor's apparently dispassionate skill and commented, 'My goodness, but you are an unfeeling creature.' The surgeon replied, 'Young man, years ago I learned to lose my sympathy as an emotion and to gain it as a principle.'[3]

After she had left the bench, Wilson herself gave considerable consideration to formulation of a contextual definition of what might constitute merit in a particular judicial appointment. Borrowing from the contextual approach to jurisprudence she had learned from W.R. Lederman at Dalhousie, she reasoned it was a given that all judicial candidates seriously in the running would possess the basic criteria required. She acknowledged also that no single candidate could possibly possess all the desirable characteristics. The best appointment at any particular time, she concluded, will be the one which fills an existing gap or meets a particular need on the court.[4]

When Wilson was appointed, the Supreme Court needed a judge capable of interpreting the new Charter contextually. Paradoxically enough, only a contextual reading of the Charter could be true to its fundamental principles. And with great fortuity, that is what it got. Contingency and contextuality run as deep as principle in Wilson; for her, in fact, contextuality *is* principled and in many instances only contextuality *can be* principled. These were attitudes engrained in her long before law school through immersion in a culture shaped by Scottish Enlightenment philosophy, and then further reinforced by her deep religious values and by her interdisciplinary program of studies at the University of Aberdeen. It was there that she learned about the great Scottish economist Adam Smith and absorbed his notion that law shifts and changes in accordance with changes in social consensus. Wilson also adopted Smith's theory of moral sentiment. Both she and John have throughout their lives been fascinated with issues of business ethics, founded on Smith's doctrine of the invisible hand integrating economics and ethics through reliance on self-interested propriety so long as people lived in close proximity to one another.

On a more personal level, circumstances have created in Wilson a particularly vivid awareness of life on the margins. She was the first woman to become a partner at Oslers, yet never a member of the management committee. She was the first woman to be appointed to a provincial or national Council of the Canadian Bar Association, the first woman to be appointed to any appellate court in Canada, and, as we are about to consider, the first woman on the Supreme Court of Canada. There is no question that she broke traditional gender boundaries.

It has generally been overlooked, however, that Wilson was also the first working-class immigrant judge at the Supreme Court. For Bertha

Wilson, avowedly not a feminist, immigration to Canada was the big event in her life – an event which had far greater weight than the fact of her gender. Wilson has sustained a perpetual sense of herself as a multiple immigrant, first grafting herself onto the Scottish root stock of her new country, then repeatedly transplanting herself into what had been traditionally male preserves and finding new ways to flourish.

Elements of her characteristic contextuality, her attentiveness to marginality and her willingness to transgress boundaries were already apparent in Wilson's Court of Appeal judgments when she was appointed to the Supreme Court. These were approaches we have already seen her applying, no matter what area of law she was called upon to adjudicate.

What was Wilson's dissent in *Olbey*, for example, if not an assertion of the court's moral duty to attend to the particular social and racial characteristics of the accused? What were her commercial law judgments if not an assertion that the context of business requires certainty? And yet Wilson's commercial judgments also signal that the court should attend to the evolving social consensus that fairness sometimes required breaking down boundaries between rigid categories of law. In family law, she did not flinch from applying equitable constructive trust principles to division of property division to create justice for Rosa Becker. *Bhadauria* tackled racial discrimination by demonstrating that tort principles had never been excluded from the human rights arena by operation of the common law; although the Supreme Court reversed that decision, Wilson signalled an alternative pathway for the development of simultaneous civil actions which has been followed in recent years with some success. All of these elements are derivative from her immersion in Scottish culture and philosophies. We might call Wilson's characteristic stance one of principled contextuality.

Wilson's approach to judicial analysis is also congruent with a widespread contemporary cultural development called postmodernism; in Scots-saturated Canada, postmodernism has evolved in peculiarly ethical and principled directions. There has been some general scholarly writing, but for the most part fairly fragmentary and tenuous to date, on the connections between Scottish Enlightenment philosophy and postmodern thought,[5] but we need not concern ourselves with being particularly scholarly here. Nevertheless, these are ideas which it is useful to explore a little if we want to understand Bertha Wilson's place not only in Canadian legal history but more generally in the evolution of Canadian cultural history.

PRINCIPLED CONTEXTUALITY

Contingency and contextuality run deep, not just in Wilson's own life but in the history of Western civilization, emerging most predictably in eras of expansive social change when political and economic boundaries become permeable to outside influences. Although the connections between Scottish Enlightenment thought and contemporary postmodernism are not yet well articulated, the historic links backward from the Scottish Enlightenment into the Aristotelian origins of its philosophies of moral sentiment and provisionality are much more explicit.[6]

Wilson most emphatically does not consider herself to be a feminist. However she may have been mislabelled one because of the mistaken assumption that an ethics of care – which Wilson certainly does display – is inevitably a product of feminist sensibilities. Instead, and as philosopher Joan Tronto explains it,[7] it is more useful to think of the Scottish Enlightenment as representing the emergence of a persistent but frequently subterranean tradition of moral thought initiated by Aristotle in Western philosophy, which is not the exclusive preserve of women.

Aristotle believed that morality is highly dependent upon context, virtue is achievable only in action, and that complete wisdom (what all good judges despair of but aspire to achieve) requires a case-by-case contextual integration of practical with philosophical wisdom. It may be that these Aristotelian forms of moral thought are constant elements in the human psyche which we cannot choose to eliminate by an act of will; the Canadian philosopher Charles Taylor certainly thinks so.[8]

Part of what makes Wilson's life and work so interesting is that her stance of principled provisionality is not merely personal to her. Such a stance has become required of all of us by the provisional and complex times we live in and by the multiplicities of the uniquely Canadian culture developing around us. Postmoderisms can only be understood in relation to the particular culture which gives rise to them; different societies produce different postmodernisms.[9] It has, in fact, become commonplace to say that Canada is a postmodern nation[10] and to note with pride Canadian accomplishments in postmodern architecture[11] and in postmodern literature.[12]

But not in law. Certainly legal academics have produced reams of scholarly papers on the relationship between postmodernism and law. Unfortunately, much of this work is incomprehensible. And in Canadian legal circles the short answer to the question, 'What is postmodern-ism?' might still very well be, 'Something which it is best to avoid.'

And yet Canadian legal postmodernism might be more palatable if it were recognized not as a dramatic break with the past but a resurgence, like the Scottish Enlightenment, of that Aristotelian integration of emo-tion and rationality in moral thought which comparably complex societ-ies have evolved before us. Indeed, Canadian writer John Ralston Saul has said that 'the essential characteristic of the Canadian public mythol-ogy is its complexity' and that 'to the extent that it denies the illusion of simplicity, it is a reasonable facsimile of reality': this quintessential 'reversal of the standard nation-state myth' is what he considers to con-stitute the Canadian 'act of nonconformity.'[13]

But the big stumbling block to acceptance of postmodernism in law is law's reverence for dispassionate neutrality. In fact, objectivity *is* law in the eighteenth century modernist tradition initiated by Kant; neutrality and rationality have traditionally been considered the essential attributes of the modernist judge charged with the power of adjudicat-ing disputes between rational, autonomous, freely choosing legal sub-jects who are responsible for their actions precisely because they have the rational ability to choose.

Postmodern approaches to law are both more radical and more dif-fuse. They draw attention to the infinite variability of *legal subjects*, tak-ing into consideration relevant aspects of the personal identities of the parties to the litigation and also the effects of judicial decisions on par-ties not directly tied to the dispute. They encourage a contextual consid-eration of *legal texts*, including statutory language determining both substantive and procedural matters relating to a dispute. They expand our awareness of *legal facts* beyond the immediate events giving rise to the dispute by interpreting those facts in the larger social climate in which the events occurred; this may be necessary to do justice in the specific circumstances of a specific case and help a court to predict the social effects on other subjects of any specific decision. And if legal sub-jects, legal texts, and legal facts can all be characterized contextually, how can there be the certainty and the objectivity fundamental to the principle of justice which requires treating like cases alike? That is what causes the legal profession to reject postmodernism so vehemently.

Elements of Wilson's judgments and even of her post-judicial work have been derided for their characteristic contextuality; invoking the modernist principles of objectivity and neutrality, University of Western Ontario law professor Rob Martin has probably been her most persistent critic.[14] Nevertheless, we may be able to sharpen our understanding of the postmodern by considering a little more thoroughly the assumptions underlying modernism.

Modern law is based not only on the assumption that autonomous legal subjects can make rational choices, but on the logically associated common law doctrine of precedent.[15] The doctrine of precedent functions as a tacit acknowledgment that there are simply too many stories – too much variety in human contingency – for legislatures ever to be able to draft statutory law that can cover all the possible disputes which may arise between citizens or between a citizen and the state. But, as Wilson sees it,

> The legal system has been unable to respond to the increased pace of change in the twentieth century and the increased complexity of its social and legal problems. The doctrine of precedent has discouraged the progressive development of old principles and the creation of new ones. We still cling stubbornly to the 'purity' of the law and refuse to baptize it with the insights of more modern disciplines. We are, accordingly, becoming increasingly irrelevant and further removed from the 'Weltanschauung' of the people.[16]

Modern law's strength – its predictability – is also, paradoxically, the source of its inertia. It may work fairly well in homogeneous societies where all those accorded the status of legal subject share similar characteristics: maleness, for example, and whiteness and the financial means to purchase property. But this is no longer the kind of society in which we live. Instead, we are experiencing a general decline of deference towards authority, together with a demand for involvement by the multiplicity of people whose needs are to be served by law. Non-regulated paralegals or accountants encroach on professional turf marked out as their exclusive domain by previous generations of lawyers; do-it-yourself litigants, well-educated and confident of their own abilities to search the Internet, represent themselves in court; and mediators, many of whom are not lawyers, offer to resolve disputes swiftly and economically outside the courts.

Even if Kantian rationality is the defining element of what it means to be human in modernist law, historically the pursuit of modern law's purity based on the application of precedent to resolve disputes was made possible only by a relatively recent technological development – the publication and the widespread availability of case reports. The modern scientific casebook method of teaching law, which Wilson encountered at Dalhousie was ostensibly entrenched in Toronto only in 1949, when Caesar Wright finally abandoned Osgoode Hall to become University of Toronto's dean.[17]

But Wilson, of course, had also been exposed to a different tradition of legal scholarship at Dalhousie in the mid-1950s; Lederman had advocated a contextual approach to constitutional law and to statutory interpretation. His course in jurisprudence was designed to be fully integrative, to give students an overview of the legal system as a whole, to look at analytic logic and social utility and the value systems of various systems of justice and to raise students above the particulars of a specific subject or a specific case.

Modernism insists on dichotomy and logical forks in reasoning; legal method is the act of discerning dichotomy and the kind of thinking law students enmeshed in modern legal education are still taught how to do. That is why, for Rob Martin, Wilson's candid acknowledgment in 'Will Women Judges Really Make a Difference?' that pure judicial objectivity is never achievable necessarily constituted a collapse into its opposite, pure subjectivity. But although training in legal method is a useful and even an indispensable skill, we need to consider why, in a post-Charter postmodern society, it is no longer enough. We can begin with acknowledging that there is no necessary contradiction between modernist legal method and postmodern contextuality; after all, if the context of business is business, it is equally self-evident that the context of law is law.

A contextual (or postmodern) approach to law incorporates modernist methodologies of statutory interpretation or deference to precedent without abandoning principle or collapsing into modernist dichotomy: Wilson, like all great judges, did just that over and over again. And such an approach is principled. But in a postmodern legal system, what is just as principled is a sensitive attention to the constantly changing nature of our social problems. Justice cannot be done in a multiple and complex society without admitting new evidence and granting standing to new parties. It was Brian Dickson at the 1991 Dalhousie Symposium who noted of Wilson that she advocated neither judicial activism nor judicial restraint for its own sake, but elegantly sidestepped that false dichotomy.[18]

If understanding postmodernism is facilitated by looking to its modernist roots, it may also help to consider how postmodernism first emerged as a cultural movement most visibly in architecture during the 1970s. The phenomenon is usefully described in *What is Post-Modern-*

ism?,[19] a readable handbook by Charles Jencks published in 1986, just four years after Wilson went to the Supreme Court of Canada. Postmodern buildings, Jencks makes clear, don't abandon historical precedent; they just make use of old architectural elements in surprisingly new ways. They offer a pastiche of mixed and integrated historic references which generates a variety of shapes and spaces for different purposes, making them available to an inexhaustible multiplicity of interpretations and uses. But postmodern architecture does not abandon the strengths made possible by scientific engineering, structural steel, and glass curtain walls. Instead, it seeks to create more human and satisfying spaces which acknowledge human differences rather than imposing a sterile equality of sameness.

Postmodern law in Canada builds on the rational structure of common law precedent and statutory interpretation in just the same way. It relies on precedent and statute for the moral strength forged through the modernist, rational principle of justice as fairness – treating like cases alike. But our citizens and our courts are developing a greater awareness of the multiplicity of identities of the legal subjects relying on and restricted by the law, and a greater acknowledgment of the multiplicity of interpretations which need to be brought to bear on the words of a statute or the facts of a case to do justice in accordance with the principles of equity.

Just as academics and cultural commentators have already begun to identify the local and provisional but nevertheless unique characteristics of a Canadian postmodern architecture, so we are also evolving a unique postmodern law which does not abandon its modernist traditions. As good modernists (and we remain modernists within our increasingly postmodern society), we are accustomed to think about rationality as a process of making choices between categories; if that were so, then postmodernism would by definition have to be something radically different from modernism. But part of what makes postmodernism both deeply traditional and yet profoundly subversive is that it continues to be nourished by and dependent upon the roots of modernism.

Some postmodernisms have given up on attempts to find any meaning at all; that is the unCanadian kind of postmodernism most derided and also most feared by those who seek to reject it. Other postmodernisms optimistically assert the possibility of determining some meanings even while acknowledging that meaning can no longer be unitary or universal. And this is the approach (earnest, polite, understated, but stubbornly respectful of difference) which is already typical of Canadian postmodern architecture and literature.

Our emerging Canadian legal postmodernism is an enlightened (if diffident) postmodernism. And it is the sometimes uneasy integration of modernist rationality and modernist consistency with postmodern contextuality and postmodern multiplicity which is uniquely characteristic of our Charter. Earlier, we used a horticultural metaphor of grafting and uprooting to describe Bertha Wilson's immigrant experience and her repeated transplantings into previously all-male zones. There is, of course, ample justification in Canadian law for evoking such imagery, dating back to the famous 1930 description of our constitution as a 'living tree, capable of growth and expansion within its natural limits' which Wilson herself so heartily endorsed.[20] But in the post-Charter era the limits began to expand. We need a new plant metaphor, something which grows a little closer to the ground.

One might think of postmodernist law spreading itself by travelling runners like a strawberry patch growing out of its neat rows; the parent plants (like modernist principle) remain as a source of vigour while the new plantlets extend themselves tentatively across well-trodden pathways, putting down roots in more friable soil or locations with more favourable microclimates where they ultimately produce greater yields. The role of the 'judicial gardener' has changed; there is no longer just one noble tree sheltering the few, but a network of interconnected growth capable of nourishing us all, although still transplantable back into neat rows for greater efficiency in cultivation or harvesting. Bertha learned how from Christina at Cheyne Road.

Given Adam Smith's observation that law shifts in accordance with social consensus at the same time social consensus shifts in accordance with law, it ought not to surprise us to find elements of postmodernism in Canada's new constituting statute, its Charter. If Bertha Wilson was the perfect judicial appointment in 1982, it is because the contingencies of her own life and the multiplicity of perspectives she brought to the task of judicial analysis had uniquely prepared her to be a postmodern judge in a postmodern time.

THE CHARTER: PRINCIPLED CONTEXTUALITY,
NATIONAL FEELING

In her speech on the Scottish Enlightenment, Bertha Wilson noted proudly that during the eighteenth-century 'law in Scotland became identified with Scottish national feeling, as well as with creative and intellectual progress in the most general sense.'[21] Part of the reason why law was particularly identified with Scottish national feeling is that the 1707 Act of Union between England and Scotland did not impose English law on Scotland but left pretty much intact the much more scholarly and erudite traditions of Scottish law. Two main characteristics differentiated Scottish law from English law and reveal its fundamentally Aristotelian roots. In the Scottish system, there was much less slavish adherence to precedent. Secondly, equitable issues were always addressed within the general law courts; there were never separate courts of equity. Both of these elements signal a culture which was less amenable to the more rigidly modernist rule of law established in England and in the United States.

Given that Scots immigrants have been influential out of all proportion to their numbers in shaping key Canadian institutions, it would not be surprising to discover that our Charter as a constitutional document has evolved and continues to evolve in a manner which gives evidence of those lingering Scottish traditions. And if there are particular affinities between contemporary postmodernism and the contextuality and contingency of the common sense Scottish Enlightenment philosophies which those immigrants brought with them, based in turn as they were on Aristotelian sources, then Bertha Wilson's judgments can be seen as reinforcing what was already a very old tradition of moral sentiment and common sense in Canadian culture.

Are there parallels between the historic events which moulded Scots society in the eighteenth century and Canadian society over the last century? It has to be admitted that it is hard to identify any specific triggering political event in Canada comparable to the 1707 Act of Union. However, if there has been a period of cultural flourishing in Canadian history comparable to the Scottish Enlightenment, we might look for its initiation to the founding of the Canada Council in 1957. Buoyed by a robust tax base, the Canada Council organized competitions, provided grants for study and travel, purchased or commissioned various cultural artifacts, and funded the expansion of universities to accommodate the offspring of the baby boom generation.

There did follow an era of development in painting, sculpture, and architecture as well as in literature, literary criticism, philosophy, and technology. Expo 67, sited in Montreal to acknowledge Canada's centennial, coincided with a mood of unprecedented Canadian optimism and pride in these cultural achievements. And there was a parallel evolution in law based on the quiet work of various committees and law reform commissions which to an unprecedented degree based their recommendations for statutory change on public input.

In 1967 Pierre Trudeau became prime minister. Lawyer and law professor, he was probably the most academic and intellectual political leader ever elected in Canadian history although these qualities were little understood at the time. It was his sophistication and *savoir faire* which established Canada for the first time as a fashionable political presence internationally. Michael Adams of Environics Research, a national pulse-taker, went so far as to call Trudeau the first Canadian postmodern, so multifaceted in his abilities and accomplishments that he has redefined what Canadians consider most admirably human.

Liberal party policies of bilingualism and multiculturalism during the Trudeau era, fuelled in part by generous immigration policies, established an ideology of Canadian culture as a mosaic. Canadians have loved to congratulate themselves on the contrast between our mosaic and the American ideal of a melting pot, our tolerance and the American history of racism, our socialized medicare and the profit-driven American health care system, our peaceable society and soaring American crime statistics fuelled by the constitutionalized American right to bear arms. However, many Canadians have conveniently ignored that many of these differences are founded in fiction.

A new ethnic multiplicity permanently fragmented the old dominance of English Canada at the same time as various provincial premiers began to flex their regional political strengths and set about dismantling the Pearson legacy of negotiated, executive federalism. Trudeau's concept of federalism was a more abrasive and confrontational one; the sheer intellectual power of his leadership may have been necessary to the repatriation of the constitution and the entrenchment of the Charter in 1982, but these goals were achieved only through tenuous political compromises. We are still in the process of evolving a notion of federalism which permits regional variations in autonomy, creating a unique multinational entity which is less a sovereign state than an agglomeration of collectivities cherishing cultural identities of their own.

Canadian unity as we know it depends upon shifting accommodations and perpetually renegotiated consensus among those collectivities.[22] And in Canada, particularly in this post-NAFTA era, Canadian national feeling has become more and more identified with the Charter. Wilson anticipated this stance in 1983 as the courts had just begun to interpret the new constitution when she said Canadians viewed the

Charter as a statement of faith that they expected would 'usher in a new era in the quest for equality.'[23]

But if the Charter epitomizes a characteristically Canadian approach to human rights, we can also see it as the culminating work-in-progress of an historic evolution in human rights legislation over almost four decades.[24] Again, there has been no sharp rupture with the past. Saskatchewan was the first province to enact a Bill of Rights as early as 1947, two years before the Universal Declaration of Human Rights adopted by the United Nations. Parliament enacted a Canadian Bill of Rights in 1960 but its impact was disappointing because of confusion about whether the bill could be overruled by later statutory pronouncements. Ontario had enacted a Racial Discrimination Act in 1944, a Fair Employment Practices Act in 1951, and a Fair Accommodation Practices Act in 1954. It was the first province to consolidate its human rights legislation into a comprehensive code in 1962, with a commission to enforce it and carry out investigative and educative functions. By 1970 British Columbia, New Brunswick, and Nova Scotia had followed suit, in part inspired by the recommendations of the Royal Commission on the Status of Women which reported that laws prohibiting discrimination against women were toothless without agencies to administer them. That 1970 report was also instrumental in the establishment of a federal human rights commission.

The entrenchment of our 1982 constitution is best understood as the legislative culmination of a long evolution in Canadian social consensus about human rights. The early Charter cases, setting down the fundamental principles for interpretation of the constitution, simply continued that process. And the Charter itself certainly does not break with the legal traditions of the past. Instead, it integrates elements of modernist rule of law within a postmodern acknowledgment of our commitment to cultural mosaic and social context.

Before we look to the interpretive jurisprudence which Wilson helped develop at the Supreme Court, then, it will be useful to take a look at the specific provisions of the Charter itself. Our three basic principles of principled contextuality will serve as useful guideposts: we are looking for provisions which permit and even require an expansive definition of who constitutes legal subjects; which permit and even require an expansive interpretation of meanings contained within legal texts; and which permit and even require an expansive inclusion of legal facts. And because postmodernism incorporates modernism and builds upon its underlying structures, we are also looking for those reassuring provisions which sustain the modernist commitment to the objective, neutral, and universal rule of law. The preamble itself, of course, does that. And there is also the 'supremacy clause' (section 52), which asserts that the constitution is the supreme law of Canada and provides that any law inconsistent with the provisions of the constitution is, to the extent of that inconsistency, of no force or effect.

The Charter protects fundamental freedoms of conscience, religion, thought, belief, opinion, expression, peaceful assembly and association.[25] It ensures the rights essential to the operation of a representative democracy: the right to vote, the necessity of holding elections at least every five years, and of annual sittings of legislative bodies (sections 3–5). It recognizes the right to mobility of movement from one region to another within the country (section 6). It guarantees the right to life, liberty, and security of the person (section 7). At the core of the Charter is the assertion of equality rights without discrimination based on race, national or ethnic origin, colour, religion, sex, age, or mental or physical disability (section 15). For greater specificity, the Charter guarantees the rights of English and French groups to the use of their language and to education in that language within geographic areas where they are minorities (sections 16–23), the rights of aboriginal peoples, including but not limited to treaty rights (sections 25), and the protection of Canada's multicultural heritage (section 27).

The substantive content of these provisions fits comfortably enough within the old liberal humanist tradition of rights, but they also acknowledge the multiplicity of characteristics Canadian citizens have, not merely as implicitly white, heterosexual, English-speaking Protestant 'rational men' but as people of all religions and races and colours and sexual orientations and abilities who nevertheless desire the same opportunities of participating in society through expression of their varied opinions and thoughts and beliefs. In the language of postmodernism, the old concept of the single legal subject at the centre of the rule of law has been fragmented.

Other elements of the Charter articulate a postmodern indeterminacy of meaning. The notwithstanding clause permits a province, after a court has determined that an act of its legislature is in contravention of a Charter guarantee, to sustain the impugned law's operation for five years and then to renew its operation. What does this mean if rights guaranteed by a supreme law can be selectively overridden, province by province, for an indeterminate period of time? One preliminary answer is that postmodernisms are regional and local; another more modernist interpretation would point out that any provincial government which attempts such a move is checked at the polling booth by the democratic discipline of the renewal requirement.

The 'remedies' provision (section 24) determines what can be done once it has been found that a guaranteed right or freedom of an individual has been infringed. There has been an expansive interpretation of this text. The Charter accords a court extremely wide latitude to order whatever it 'considers appropriate and just in the circumstances'; the equitable intention is clear enough. Accordingly, the jurisprudence has established an enormous flexibility of sanctions: stays of proceedings, awards of damages, grants of injunctions, declarations of invalidity of statutes in whole or in part, to take place immediately or prospectively, and even constitutional exemptions. But this remedies provision also sustains modernist rule of law in its assertion that evidence can be excluded altogether if it has been obtained in a manner which would bring the administration of justice into disrepute; more important than the conviction of any individual is the protection of the legal system's reputation for fairness, and this is a provision which Wilson was to consider often in her judgments.

The tightest integration of modern and postmodern elements in the Charter is found in the ambiguous section 1. It is not surprising that Wilson delivered several speeches and prepared a number of academic papers concerning this provision, and that she frequently wrote separate concurring or dissenting judgments when section 1 was at issue. This section specifies that all of the guarantees of rights and freedoms are subject to 'such reasonable limits prescribed by law as can be demonstrably justified in a free and democratic society.' One might assume that to accord a right logically entails the notion of absolute entitlement but it is not so; in our constitution we make it explicit that rights cannot be absolute. However, section 1 specifies that any limits on rights must be 'reasonable' and 'prescribed by law,' which sounds modernist enough.

But there must be evidence brought forward to prove that the potential effects of a particular decision are justified. It throws wide the courtroom door to admission of a multiplicity of legal facts outside and beyond the nexus of the dispute before the court. And because these additional legal facts can only be brought forward by interested parties, this clause required expansion of the notion of legal subjects to permit much broader engagement through intervenor groups. Again, as we will see, Wilson was in the vanguard in supporting this procedural development.

A biography is a narrative account of an individual's life, with events unfolding in time; Wilson's story, like the account of any life, can be told only in fragments. What I am attempting here is to suggest how those personal and professional fragments fit into our evolving understanding of the story of Canada as a political and legal and historic entity.[26]

Interjected into the narrative of Bertha Wilson's life these observations and speculations constitute a kind of theoretical interlude. It was in 1982, with the advent of the Charter, that the covert postmodernism of Canadian law (reflective of the developing postmodernism of Canadian society) first became explicit; and 1982 was also, of course, the very moment when Wilson was about to shoulder her duties at the Supreme Court. That is why this seemed the right time to offer a summary of the postmodern elements in Wilson's life and work up to and including her work at the Ontario Court of Appeal, to sketch out some of the historical antecedents and defining characteristics of postmodernism, and to consider in a preliminary way why and how the Charter is a uniquely postmodern constitution requiring and rewarding postmodern interpretation.

In law, the persistent demands of modernist rationality and consistency-as-fairness which continue to coexist with postmodern demands for contextual equities ensure that legislated shifts in social consensus will be conservative and incremental; changes in the common law will be slow. Nevertheless, Dalhousie professor Shalin Sugunasiri has recently and persuasively argued that 'the move to contextualism represents the [Supreme] Court's single greatest analytical shift in its one hundred and twenty-four year history'[27] and further, that this contextualist approach has become pervasive.

Wilson's influence on the Canadian legal landscape has been pervasive. Of course not all of the cases in which Bertha Wilson participated at the Supreme Court of Canada were concerned with Charter issues. But as we will see, Charter considerations have become inextricably interwoven with every area of Canadian experience as Canadians have come increasingly to identify Canadian law with Canadian national feeling. Charter values, explicitly or implicitly, form the backdrop of expectations shaping our society.

The liberal humanist concept of the autonomous legal subject deemed responsible for his legal actions because he chose them has not been extinguished. It continues to inform our understanding of law and justice, but it no longer occupies the field. A principled and postmodern contextualism, Bertha Wilson's chief contribution to the development of a distinctively Canadian jurisprudence, has now unequivocally been prescribed by the Supreme Court.

7

The Supreme Court of Canada

The Supreme Court of Canada is housed in a magnificent dressed-stone build-ing just west of the Parliament Buildings, on a high bluff overlooking the Ottawa River. First occupied by the Court in 1946, its twin bronze entrance doors are set into a façade of six pilasters and flanked by two projecting wings. The whole is crowned by a steep extravaganza of copper roofs, chimneys, and towers. Litigants seeking justice at the final court of appeal in the country approach up two shallow flights of stairs flanked by tall sculptures of Truth and Justice. At that point they must choose to turn either left or right and continue up a further flight past fluted metal light standards towards one or other of the doors. The overall effect is certainly symmetrical and ceremonial. It signals reassuringly to the embattled legal adversaries bringing their case to be heard from two opposing perspectives that the judicial processes followed inside will adhere to due process and that judgments will be reached through logical and incremental steps.

Once inside the east or west door one enters a grand and lofty entrance hall with floors and walls of marble, fluted marble columns and richly coffered ceil-ing. The precedent of the facade is followed; moving towards the centre, liti-gants must choose again to turn east or west and approach up two further shallow flights of stairs. But these stairs reverse to converge on the central por-tal that opens through double doors into the walnut-panelled main court room that occupies the heart of the first floor of the building. Raised on a dais is the gently concave curve of the bench with its nine high-backed chairs to accommo-

date the nine justices of the Supreme Court of Canada.¹ The chief justice sits in the centre and the remaining judges are seated in order of their seniority of appointment to right and left. When Bertha Wilson was sworn in, she took her place as junior judge at the east end of the bench on the far right. Antonio Lamer, who had been appointed just the year before, moved over as second most junior judge to the far left.²

All the Supreme Court Justices were wearing their ceremonial bright scarlet robes trimmed with Canadian white mink and their black tricorn hats. It is customary, in accordance with the conservative continuity of the law – and it is also, of course, thrifty in accordance with the best Scottish Canadian tradition – for the new judge to inherit the robe of his predecessor. In Bertha Wilson's case, that was Ronald Martland. However because he was considerably taller than she, a new robe was made for her incorporating only the Martland mink.

Shortly after the swearing in, a glass of champagne at a brief reception, and a quick lunch, Wilson returned to the court room with the other judges. Now clad in their 'working' black silks, they began that afternoon hearing an intellectual property case, Shell Oil Company v. Commissioner of Patents.³

Once a hearing has been completed, the judges retire to their conference room directly behind the court room where they seat themselves in nine red leather chairs around a round table. At Wilson's first judicial conference, she was the last to enter the room. As she came through the door, all of the judges rose except Lamer.

He remained seated. In his opinion, it was inappropriate to show traditional gallantry by standing to honour Madame Justice Wilson as a woman. By remaining seated, he explained,⁴ he meant to show her the greater courtesy of according her full professional respect as an equal colleague on the Court. His failure to rise certainly was not intended to communicate any resentment over the fact that the male Supreme Court justices had just lost two of their toilets, the space severed off to create a private facility for the new judge.

INSIDE THE COURT

Few people other than Wilson herself have written about the inner functioning of the Supreme Court or the process by which Supreme Court judges prepare their judgments.⁵ It is a process which she believes strongly should to be described more openly because she is persuaded that the methodology followed 'in some cases conditioned the judgment that we ended up with.'

The *Shell* hearing concluded the day after Wilson's swearing in. Wilson herself says that when she joined the Court she knew nothing of patents. However, with the departure of Martland there was no one else on the court with expertise in the area or willing to take it on. As Wilson describes the situation with her characteristic self-deprecating mirth:

> I remember the silence when Bora Laskin said, 'Well, who would like to take this,' and nobody wanted to take it because it was a highly specialized field. And that was when Bora said, 'Well, Bertha, you have come out of a great big corporate commercial law firm, you must know all about ... the law of patents.' And he said, 'Why don't you write it?' And of course, I was so new that I couldn't possibly say, 'I know nothing about patents either.' So I said, 'Fine,' and I remember how hard I had to work on that, because it was my first case and it was a subject with which I was quite unfamiliar.

The call to begin proving herself all over again had come immediately. But *Shell* is written in a tone of scholarly zest which reveals how thoroughly Wilson always enjoyed the opportunity of researching and teaching herself a new area of law.

Shell had been denied a patent for its plant growth regulators, on the ground that the compounds involved were not themselves new and that the company was only proposing a new use for the compounds in a new composition. Wilson determined that the traditional Canadian dichotomy between patentable 'process' and 'product' could not assist her and turned instead to the definition of 'invention' in section two of the Patent Act as 'any new or useful art.' With characteristic Scottish Enlightenment enthusiasm for the contributions of learning to the betterment of society, Wilson interpreted art to include knowledge or learning. By categorizing Shell's discovery of the application to which the compounds could be put as an advance of knowledge, she was able to conclude that both the process of combining the compounds and the use of the new product demonstrated inventive ingenuity; therefore the patent ought to have been granted. With due respect for the constraints of modernist statutory interpretation, this decision provides a typically Wilsonian solution which embodies Aristotelian practical wisdom through the convergence of reasoning from a postmodern multiplicity of directions.

During her first two years on the Court, before the Charter decisions had begun to work their way up through the lower courts to Ottawa, Wilson says that she was allowed to write one judgment after another in the commercial areas of law, particularly in contract and tort matters. In 1982 Wilson was joining Chief Justice Laskin and justices Ritchie, Dickson, Beetz, Estey, McIntyre, Chouinard, and Lamer, all of whom seemed happy enough to defer to her experience at Oslers and the heavy commercial weighting of the judgments she had written at the Ontario Court of Appeal. Unfortunately, Bertha Wilson's bench book from March 1982 to October 1982 (which would have included her initial notes made during the hearing of the case) has not survived; however, these early judicial conferences followed a fairly predictable pattern.[6]

When the Supreme Court justices retired into their conference room after the close of argument to exchange their preliminary and tentative opinions, they were invited by the chief justice to speak up around the table in reverse order of seniority[7] in order that the more junior judges would not be inhibited by hearing first the opinions of their seniors. The chief justice is 'first among equals,' providing leadership and direction which sets the tone of the Court but possessing no more power or authority to affect a judgment than any of the other judges.

Even at this early stage there might be some sense that one or more judges would be dissenting from the majority judgment or that there might be a concurring judgment – that is, a judgment agreeing with the majority but reaching the same result through a divergent path of legal reasoning. If everyone was in agreement, obviously a single set of reasons would suffice. And Wilson soon discovered that her new colleagues were fully capable of looking down at the table (or even bending under it to attend to a propitiously untied shoelace) in order to avoid catching the chief justice's eye when he was seeking a volunteer to prepare the first draft. Such evasive techniques were understandable in dry or technical cases where the decision seemed relatively uncontroversial. Much more ego came into play in the post-Charter era of constitutional cases when, Wilson noted, a strong element of competition emerged, with judges jostling to write majority judgments and make legal history.

Wilson was prepared to pay her dues from the beginning. But although she had anticipated it would be difficult establishing herself in the previously all-male enclave of the Supreme Court, in some ways it turned out to be even harder than she had expected. Oddly enough, it was William McIntyre (renowned as the Court's deeply conservative advocate of judicial restraint[8]) who most genuinely and openly rejoiced at her arrival; she recalls him telling her that he had laid bets on her appointment and was so confident of her winning that he had brought in copious quantities of Scotch in anticipation of the celebration.[9] Despite the fact that, as Wilson says with only a little exaggeration, 'we didn't agree on anything having to do with the law,' she came to consider McIntyre her closest friend on the court. Wilson also had a high regard for Brian Dickson. He was quite reserved in comparison with McIntyre – 'you didn't know what Brian was thinking a great deal of the time' – but he was also more likely to share her particular approaches to the law. And later Gerard LaForest became a close academic colleague with whom she enjoyed many far-ranging legal discussions often widely removed from the cases with which the Court happened to be concerned at the time.[10]

It was not, then, that the Supreme Court was an unfriendly place, but congeniality and collegiality are not entirely the same thing. Indeed, Wilson herself says that the court was more 'collegial' during the first five years or so than it became later, at least according to her own definition of collegiality by which she means an acceptance that each judge has both the duty and the responsibility of making up his or her own mind.[11] Nevertheless, in the interests of representing regional diversity it is customary for Supreme Court appointments to be made from across the country; there are three appointments from the Quebec civil system, three from Ontario, and generally one each from the Maritimes, the Prairies, and British Columbia. Almost by definition this means that the judges have been uprooted from their familiar communities and are unlikely to have the shared experiences with their fellow judges dating back to law school and the practice of law typical of judges appointed to the trial division or provincial appellate courts. They are more likely to form congenial relationships with their new colleagues based on shared activities, and in a male-dominated group these activities will most frequently be sports-related. Such a situation predictably places a friendly and congenial woman with arthritis who does not play golf or squash or tennis and does not ski or attend hockey games at something of a disadvantage.[12] After a few lame efforts to introduce as luncheon topics the current theatre or music programs at the National Arts Centre or the exhibits showing at the Art Gallery or museums, Wilson began to regret the judges' earlier decision that there was to be no discussion of the cases at the lunch table.

Wilson had always admired Bora Laskin; the opportunity of working with him had been some consolation for her mixed reaction to leaving the Court of Appeal. But Laskin, whose nervousness about a female appointment was disappointingly obvious at the swearing-in ceremony, was seventy and had begun to fail. It was embarrassing to see him becoming increasingly testy with counsel in court. And although he was unfailingly courteous to Wilson personally (after all, he had written his fair share of dissents earlier in his career), when he chaired the post-hearing judicial conferences he could not help but show his frustration with emerging split decisions.[13]

Laskin himself had come to believe that unanimous decisions carried more weight and enhanced public confidence in the Court as an institution. On the spectrum of stances ranging between the ideal of judicial unanimity and the ideal of judicial diversity, Laskin could not help but be aware that Wilson tended more towards diversity. Dissents, obviously, are necessary when a judge is unable to agree with the majority but, in Wilson's opinion, diverging concurrences were also valuable because they created alternative pathways for the future development of the common law. The most extreme advocate of judicial diversity in decision-making was Lord Reid of the British House of Lords, who would have endorsed each judge writing a separate judgment in order to provide for the greatest possible flexibility in the application of common law precedent.

The tension between the clarity of unanimity and the flexiblity of multiple reasons certainly creates an unresolved issue about which there is still considerable debate among Supreme Court judges past and current. For McIntyre, 'the ideal is a unanimous judgment'; next best is 'a strong judgment going one way and, say, one dissent going the other way'; but 'concurring judgments are not particularly useful' because 'if you can concur in the result, you only confuse the issue by explaining why you reach it by a different route.' Because he considers it the Supreme Court's duty as the court of last resort to provide unequivocal direction for the lower courts, Cory also values unanimity if at all possible and, like McIntyre, considers a clear dissent better than a diverging concurrence.[14] For McLachlin a clearly stated difference has value but only in instances where the difference is a substantive one; otherwise, unanimity for the sake of clarity is very much preferable.[15]

In Gonthier's opinion, the appropriateness of dissents or concurrences depends very much upon the circumstances of the case, but he tends to be more sympathetic to Wilson's position; particularly for societal issues when no clear consensus has been reached about which way society wants to go, a dissent can make a decision more acceptable because it is more reflective of multiple points of view and at the same time can open doors for future decisions. And interestingly enough Iacobucci, who had been a good friend of Wilson's dating back to the Osler days and who succeeded her when she retired from the Supreme Court, reports that her advice to him at the time of his appointment was to 'do what you can to get more collegiality on the Court'; the judges during her era had not done enough, she told him.[16]

During Wilson's early years on the Court it was Laskin who decided to have a motions room on the third floor converted into a judges' dining room – to encourage the congeniality which could help build the consensus he had come to identify with collegiality, and because the press of work precluded taking time for lunch at the Rideau Club. But the dining room seems never to have become the locus of an informal exchange of views on matters of current social interest. Guests were seldom invited to attend and indeed, attendance by the judges themselves tended to drop off.

Laskin was not the only member of the Court with health problems. Part of the difficulty of managing the Court during the Laskin era and even after 1984 when Dickson replaced him as chief justice was related to illness and absences of judges. For a long period of time the Court was not functioning with its full complement.[17] As a result, it was subject to sharp criticism by those not fully aware of the situation who were impatient with lengthy delays in the release of judgments. Of course Wilson was often not well, but she kept that to herself; somehow she was always able to sustain her concentration in order to plough through the work at hand. For quite a while when Wilson was on the Court there were effectively only four stalwarts sitting and writing judgments almost continuously, carrying the load for the other judges not able to shoulder their full share of the Court's work. And yet in retrospect she considers that 'there never was a period when we were more collegial than that period when there were few people to write a great many judgments.'

The job of a Supreme Court judge obviously requires both clerical and research assistance. Judges are provided with some help, although remarkably little compared with other government or private business executives at a comparable level, given both the quantity and the importance of the workload they are expected to process. When Wilson first went to the Court she inherited not only the mink trim from Martland's robe but also his support staff.[18]

During that era each justice was supplied with a private secretary.

Although Wilson seems to have been uniformly loved by the staff at Oslers and at the Ontario Court of Appeal, and although she did her best to champion the cause of the support staff at the Supreme Court, her relationship with the secretary assigned to her for most of her Supreme Court stint can most charitably be described as a difficult one.[19]

There was also a court messenger, generally ex-military and of post-retirement age, who was expected to perform personal errands and to retrieve documents required by members of the Court when it was in session. The Court holds three sessions a year – from January to Easter, from April to June, and from October to Christmas – generally hearing two appeals a day, on a two weeks on and two weeks off schedule. Not all messengers were expected to attend every session. Ample hours remained in the day for the off-duty messengers to chat or snooze in their crowded basement common room.

Some of the court messengers had close relationships with their judges; Roland Ritchie found it increasingly difficult to keep up with the pace of work and the social obligations entailed by his position at the Court. On one occasion an invitation to a state dinner interfered with the press of writing judgments at a point when he also needed a haircut badly; Ritchie told John Wilson that he had dreamed about taking his head off and handing it to his messenger to deliver to the barber. Martland's messenger, very much of an age with Martland, had enjoyed a relaxed and jovial relationship with his former judge, smoking cigars with him in chambers; he made it abundantly clear that he was not at all pleased about being assigned to work with a woman.

In 1982 each judge was assigned only a single law clerk, generally recent and top-ranking law school graduate completing the year-long articling requirements for the call to the bar.[20] There had been law clerks available to assist with research at the Ontario Court of Appeal but during Wilson's era there was only one clerk for every four judges, rotated quarterly, a system which tended to preclude the development of any significant support function. As more law clerks were recruited to assist each judge with the expanded workload at the Supreme Court (two in 1984, three in 1989), Wison did everything possible to make the best use of the additional resources provided to her.

The Martland court messenger retired within the year. Jean-Marie Plourde, approaching the mandatory military retirement age of fifty-five, needed to keep working to support his family. Through his connections at the Court he had been anticipating the opening and he applied for the job. During the initial interview, Plourde instantly felt comfortable with Wilson. Raised as a devout French Catholic, he came from a working-class family of seventeen. Wilson looked over his resumé and noted that for his final four years in the military he had served as security officer to the minister of national defence with his own staff of eight, and before that he had been personally responsible for an annual budget of over $7 million relating to military engineering construction. Plourde had also spent four years in United Nations quarters in Paris with various military staff representing fourteen different nationalities. Beginning in the military with only a grade eight education, he had taken innumerable courses to better himself, including English courses by correspondence to become fluently bilingual.

A small and trim man with erect bearing and keenly intelligent brown eyes, Plourde combines great personal warmth with a certain formality of manner. There is little doubt that the first impression was a very favourable one, but Wilson was worried about whether the job she had to offer was sufficiently challenging for him:

'This job is not important enough for a person of your qualifications,' she told him.

Plourde thought for a few seconds. 'Is the work that *you* do important?,' he asked.

'Well, yes it is,' Wilson admitted, a little nonplussed, reluctant to sound boastful but assuming that an applicant ought to have realized the nature of her job. 'Supreme Court judges must make very important decisions, it is a big responsibility ...'

'Then if I can help you do your work, which *is* important, my work will be important, too,' Plourde replied.[21]

She hired him instantly.

Plourde soon discovered that the job description for the position had been changed about a year earlier and that nobody at the Court had taken notice that the new job title was the more dignified court attendant rather than merely court messenger. As Wilson's confidence in him grew, he set about the task of redefining his role in accordance with her needs, handling both the most trivial and the most complex tasks she sent his way with complete dedication and unquestioning loyalty. Wilson had mentioned during the interview that she started work at 8:00 a.m.; he made it a point to arrive at 7:30 to prepare her chambers, sharpening pencils, opening her mail, and making sure that her legal robes, court shirts, and tabs were in perfect order. When she put on her robes to leave her chambers for court, Plourde would assist and check that the folds were hanging perfectly behind her. John Wilson drove Bertha to work every day. But Plourde, who had a key to their home, handled her personal banking, picked up her prescriptions, and was also happy to serve as her driver for longer trips to speaking engagements, using one of the official cars if it was available or even his own. And all of these tasks were more or less within the traditional duties of the court attendant position.

Where Plourde really shone was in taking the initiative to implement new support systems for his judge. Only rarely did Wilson have to ask him to change something he had done; for example on one occasion during her absence he reorganized her bookshelves, inadvertently placing certain frequently-used sources out of her reach. But when Plourde managed to lay his hands on nine four-drawer legal filing cabinets (most judges had only one or two) and organized all of the materials she had brought with her from the Court of Appeal into a neatly labelled, colour-coded, easily retrievable information bank, she was very pleased indeed. Then he repeated the process and, having reorganized all of the internal office files with a summary index in a binder, was able to guarantee that he could find any document she needed and have it on her desk within a minute.

Plourde had retired from the military without any first-hand exposure to computers. When the Court decided to implement a new computer system, he took the manuals home and first taught himself, then patiently and tactfully instructed Wilson's secretary. The secretary continued to find the technology so confusing (particularly when the Court switched from its initial program to a slightly more complex one) that she might call on him for help as many as twenty times a day. On one occasion, Wilson even called Plourde in from vacation to assist when an important document had been printed and distributed to all the other judges with the odd-numbered pages missing. However, Plourde did not make himself particularly popular with the other attendants who preferred the slower pace of life they had enjoyed under the old regime and who resented his failure to make himself available for the rotating stints of attendance in court. There were several occasions when Plourde was rebuked or rebuffed by the administration and it was important to him that his judge would immediately speak up on his behalf, as Wilson inevitably did; his immense loyalty to her was fully reciprocated. They established a warm and mutually trusting relationship which has continued to the present.[22]

Plourde got along well with the law clerks, making it a point to be tactful and tolerant of the messiness of some or the long hair of others so long as they got their work done on time. His judge worked a gruelling schedule, arriving early and leaving late; part of Plourde's job was to ensure that bench memoranda she had assigned to the clerks were completed in accordance with her timetable so that the briefcases could be packed up with the necessary motion records, factums, transcripts of evidence and books of authorities before she left on Fridays.[23]

If the Court was scheduled to hear ten cases the following week and Wilson was sitting on every case, she would need the materials for each of those cases to prepare over the weekend. The clerks' bench memos summarized the facts and the law for the upcoming cases; ideally, the clerks also selected those cases (or passages from the cases) which it was essential for Wilson to read in advance of the hearing so that the complete factum and book of authorities need not be trundled home.

John Wilson would come to pick her up in their modest silver Toyota; the 'Friday Procession' out of her office would lead off with Plourde carrying two enormous legal briefcases, one on each side for balance, followed by John Wilson with more cases if necessary, and Bertha Wilson bringing up the rear. Once she had left, the law clerks, who often worked late, could heave a sigh of relief and take off for a more leisurely weekend. They all knew that Wilson routinely spent all day Saturday and Sunday reading and preparing for the next week's hearings; her so-called off weeks had to be spent writing and rewriting draft judgments.

The full participation of her clerks was for Wilson an absolutely indispensable contribution to the management of her workload. Without them, she candidly acknowledged, she would have been unable to function. In turn, her clerks had the impression[24] that not only did she herself work harder than any of the other judges but that she also required them to work harder than any of the other clerks. Wilson's clerks did memos on everything, including the applications for leave to appeal (for which there might be forty or more ten-minute oral hearings over two days), the civil cases coming up out of the Quebec system (even though it could be confidently expected that the Quebec-appointed judges would be writing the judgments for these cases and her clerks rarely had any familiarity with the Quebec Civil Code), and of course the bench memos summarizing the facts and law in advance of hearings to prepare her for the appeals themselves. Wilson preferred to go into the hearing knowing ahead of time the key questions which she would want to have counsel answer. It was well known among the law clerks that most of the other judges did not require any memos for the applications for leave to appeal and that many of them would tell their students not to bother with detailed bench memos on those cases for which they had already made up their minds.

Once it had been determined at the judicial conference following the hearing that she would be writing reasons for any particular case, Wilson consulted the notes in her bench book and followed the procedure she had initiated at the Court of Appeal. Preliminary thinking complete, her first step was to dictate an initial draft into her dictaphone to be typed up by her secretary. Equipped with this provisional map of the steps in the legal argument which would be required to reach the conclusion she believed to be just, Wilson would often divide the issues raised into their various components. Next, she set individual clerks the task of delving into statute, case law, and academic writings in the vast Supreme Court library to flesh out and support the argument. She had an extensive collection of legal references in her own office if she wanted to look to the sources herself.[25]

As late as 1988, before the clerks were supplied with their own computers, their bench memos or research memos would be handwritten with plenty of cut-and-paste, sandwiching photocopies of relevant passages from cases or academic authorities between paragraphs of their own legal analysis. If a clerk's writing was large, it was not unusual for these inky memos to run to a hundred pages or more. Because they were so much neater in the post-computer era, the clerks' memos seemed to become correspondingly shorter; they generally submitted these memos both in hard copy (for Wilson's annotation) and on disk (to facilitate their use by the secretary in preparation of the draft judgments).

After this first round of research memos, Wilson would often invite the clerk into her office to discuss the lines of argument he or she had developed. Setting out the facts and issues was a relatively mechanical process where the clerks' memos could be very helpful; the development of the reasoning process was where she needed to do the most work. When she was not sitting, Wilson tended to reserve the mornings when she felt freshest for judgment drafting, something which she always preferred to do entirely by herself; on average over the course of a year a clerk might meet with the judge once or twice a week, generally during the early afternoons.

These discussions were just as vital an aspect of the clerks' job as their research and memo writing, at least as far as Wilson was concerned. On one occasion when she was filling in for the chief justice at the September orientation session for all incoming law clerks, she explained to them how they could best provide their judges with psychological as well as intellectual support. They needed to be willing to 'spend a year, metaphorically speaking, inside our judicial skins.'[26] This did not mean that Wilson wanted a clerk to abandon his own convictions or her own powers of reasoning; on the contrary:

> We want your views. You have reviewed the facts, read the judgments below, studied the factums and researched the law. What would you do with the case if you were in our shoes? This is what we want to know. Don't be shy. Don't be modest. If you disagree with us, say so. If you think we've missed the point, say so. This is one of your most important functions – to be a critic and a sounding board for your judge. Through argument and discussion and debate our thinking is refined and our insights sharpened. *We try to do this with our colleagues but it's not always possible.* So we rely on you.[27]

With the initial round of research memos and discussions under her belt, Wilson would return to work revising her draft judgment, amending and annotating, then sending it back to her secretary for repeated retyping. Mulling over the drafts was something which, she says, gave her a lot of satisfaction ; she aimed, as Arnup had taught her, for clarity, succinctness, and persuasive force.[28]

Nevertheless, accustomed as she had been to client deadlines at Oslers, she was not a perfectionist who was unable to let go or get the work out the door. At some point (perhaps after a second or third round of research assignments to her clerks and more discussion), the revisions had to come to an end in order that the draft could be circulated to the other judges for their comments and suggestions. And as we review selected cases with reference to some of the clerks' memos and their memories of their years in Wilson's chambers, it will become clear that in at least a couple of instances her clerks were able to rise to Wilson's challenge – that is, to disagree on points of law and to sharpen her insights in a manner which is reflected in the final judgment she wrote.

'We try to do this with our colleagues but it's not always possible,' Wilson had said to the law clerks, perhaps a little wistfully. The question of why debating the cases with the other judges (as had been customary at the Ontario Court of Appeal) became increasingly impossible over the period of her tenure at the Supreme Court is a vital one. It goes directly to the polarity between collegiality-as-unanimity, Laskin style, and Wilson's own concept of the duty and responsibility of individual judges to make up their own minds on every case in which they participated, together with her belief that multiple judgments made an important contribution to the rolling evolution of the common law.

Perhaps the internal layout of the Supreme Court building itself, with the nine offices on the second floor, lined up sequentially off a silent marble corridor running around three sides of the building, was partly at fault. On one occasion, Estey had spoken dismissively of the judges disappearing into their gopher holes; LaForest thought it would have been better had the building been designed in such a way that it would have been impossible not to come into contact with his colleagues.[29] But in Wilson's opinion, the main problem was a certain divisiveness arising out of an escalating tendency during her later years on the Court for judges to lobby for support of their own reasons, something which she herself found repugnant.

In her early days, it had been considered bad form to begin writing a dissent or diverging concurrence before the first draft of the majority judgment had been circulated; as Wilson explained:

> Then when the judgement came around if you just had minor differences you could go along and talk to the person and say, 'Look, if you were to drop that out, I would be happy to go along with you.' Or, 'If you would add this,' and so on and so forth. And usually relatively minor things. But if it was a clear difference of view then the thing you did was indicate that you were going to be writing different reasons, and then those would be circulated and you would get a little note saying that 'I propose to concur with your reasons,' or 'I would concur with your reasons if you add this, or changed that' and what have you. And it was mostly done in that way by exchanges with pieces of paper from your colleagues indicating their intentions and sometimes someone would say, 'I am going to be really in substance agreeing but I want to write on a particular aspect so there will be concurring reasons coming around.'
>
> So everybody sort of waited, nobody signed anything until we all knew exactly what the situation was going to be. And that was the way that it worked for about the first five or six years that I was on the Court.
>
> And then it seemed to change and the concept of lobbying your colleagues to support you became an important part of the process. So people would spend quite long periods in each other's rooms, arguing about changes and amendments and so on and so forth. You might not know

anything about this, of course, and that person wouldn't come and speak to you, because they were going to speak to the person that they thought, well, this is the judgment I am going to be supporting. So there never was any kind of opportunity to explain why you didn't think that was a sound addition, or a sound subtraction. The first thing you knew was that group had now formed.

More than a decade after Wilson left the Supreme Court there still seems to be no clear consensus on this aspect of the decision-making process[30] either as it existed during her era or as the process may subsequently have evolved. Claire L'Heureux-Dubé supports Wilson's view that the protocol is for judges to wait to sign on until they have the opportunity of reading all sets of reasons which are going to be written for any given case; dissents or diverging opinions are usually not circulated until after the majority reasons and then a delay of several weeks is customary to permit all the judges to reconsider their positions. Peter Cory agrees and this is the version of the decision-making process set out in a 1992 account.[31] But William McIntyre, for one, does not believe there was any unspoken agreement to wait and see what dissenting reasons might be circulating: 'I think the idea was you dealt with them as they arrived and as you had time. Certainly I didn't wait to find out who was agreeing and who was disagreeing before I signed ... There was no rule.'

Some of the Supreme Court judges were less inclined to memo writing, sometimes because their outgoing personalities meant they found a button-holing process more congenial. Gerard LaForest, like Wilson, tended to write memos for distribution to all his colleagues because in his experience it took less time and the process of writing tended to clarify his thinking; however, he would also write a note directly to a specific judge whose draft reasons he had reviewed if there was only a small point of disagreement or if he considered it potentially less embarrassing for the drafting judge if he approached the issue on paper. Beverley McLachlin is of the view that a memo-writing process is valuable but cannot be imposed; because some judges are reluctant to increase the deluge of paper, there ideally would be time for reconferencing after initial drafts have been circulated in order that everyone could have the opportunity to speak up and hash out differences of opinion. Frank Iacobucci, who went to the Court after Wilson's retirement, believes that now there is more reconferencing than during her era; however, he sees a continued role for the small-group discussion because it is a fact of human nature that retreating from an opinion once articulated on paper (even if only in an internal memo format) can be difficult. And Cory, who is persuaded that a certain sacrifice of ego is necessary to achieve consensus, also thinks that because memo writing tends to crystallize opinion informal discussion works better.

Informal discussion can only work better when all judges are included; in Wilson's own experience, too often she was not. L'Heureux-Dubé also recalls that there were numerous consultations among colleagues in which Wilson, she herself, and later McLachlin were rarely, if ever, participants. For judges who for whatever reason were not privy to the private discussions, one indirect source of information about the coalescence of particular groups came from the law clerks. Wilson found herself depending upon her clerks in this way:[32]

It was after the lobbying started to creep in that 'the collegiality became less collegial,' Wilson recalls. Groups started to develop with some members of the Court signing on to majority judgments before they had had the opportunity to review alternate lines of reasoning. It bothered Wilson that once a particular group knew it had 'won,' there was little incentive for it to consider any diverging or opposing opinions.[33]

Wilson was steadfastly opposed to lobbying; in her view, it resulted in the Court becoming increasingly politicized. However, for those who engaged in it, the justification was that it produced clear majorities instead of split decisions even if the price was the introduction of some ambiguity into the reasons. But Wilson's own inclination was to scrutinize draft judgments rigorously, rewriting ambiguous phrases in favour of precise articulation which eliminated any possibility of misunderstanding or misinterpretation. Calculated ambiguity, as one colleague described it, was anathema to her; far better to have a range of judgments offering options, including a dissent and a diverging concurrence if necessary, as long as each judgment was written with crystal clarity.

What distressed Wilson above all about the development of lobbying was her sense that in such a climate insufficient attention was given either to the facts of a specific case or to the contextual determination of the issues. This is something which she considered vitally important in instances of novel Charter jurisprudence where rights and freedoms absolutely require such contextual evaluation because of the various balancing provisions. In her view, members of the Court, by engaging in lobbying their colleagues or being lobbied by them, were serving an agenda to which they had made an ideological commitment rather than meeting their individual responsibility to decide. She saw this as an ominous trend for the future, particularly after the retirement of Chief Justice Dickson from the Court.

Wilson concluded that the Supreme Court, especially after the advent of the Charter, urgently required the establishment of set procedures or a clear protocol determining how judgment ought to be reached by a panel of several judges. Such a protocol was necessary to preserve the duty and responsibility of each individual judge to decide, having weighed all the legal analysis brought to bear on the issues by each of the judges who chose to write reasons, before any judge signed on to any judgment. The need for such a protocol was a matter which judicial decorum precluded her addressing publicly while she was still on the Court, although she would have like to see it tackled by one or other of the chief justices under whom she served. Laskin was out of sympathy with her stance because of his commitment to unanimity. Dickson, who was not, was preoccupied with illness on the Court and the deluge of Charter decisions; his primary concern was to see that judgments were delivered in a timely fashion. And Lamer was most interested in implementing the management efficiencies which were urgently required.[34]

In her view, the Supreme Court lobbying process which had evolved ad hoc out of a collation of congeniality with collegiality was far too dependent on personalities. The institution of lobbying became a methodology accepted uncritically and perhaps unconsciously. In Wilson's opinion, more thought needed to be given to the process for decision-making by a multiple judge court, particularly a court of final resort.

It is a little ironic that Bertha Wilson, the most postmodern of all Canadian judges, emphatically advocated establishment of a rule of law that would have required judges to discipline themselves by adhering to an independent and individuated process of decision-making. But her strong desire to do so – indeed, her profound conviction that duty and the Charter both required the Court to do so – illustrates beautifully the characteristic integration of modernist structure within postmodern diversity which a principled postmodernism demands.

Whatever criticism there may be of the accommodations provided along that second floor corridor for the judges' chambers themselves, it cannot be coincidence that Cormier's arrangement of dormers across the soaring copper gable surmounting his austere and rational facade evokes the voices of those justices. His graduated dormers with their own gabled 'thinking caps' seem to articulate the individual duty and obligation of the Supreme Court Justice to decide independently and even, when necessary, to speak out individually.

In harmonizing their individual voices into majority judgments when possible or in preparing dissents and diverging concurrences when their analysis dictates it has to be so, judges ought never to lose sight of their individual duty to decide. Sustaining the potential for independent reasons by as many judges as care to speak up guarantees a diversity and flexibility of judgment essential to the development of the common law as it shifts in accordance with changes in social consensus. On occasion, such diversity may be the only way in which the Court truly can reconcile reason and passion, persuading as many of us as possible that justice has been served in the immediate case before the bar while holding out as consolation to those unpersuaded that the common law may yet develop in the future in accordance with the alternatives offered by the minority judgments. That is Wilson's conviction which seems to have been anticipated by Cormier's architectural design, so prophetically suited to our post-Charter postmodern society.

8

Diversity at the Margins

The public profile Wilson had developed during her years at the Ontario Court of Appeal was very much that of Bertha Wilson, champion of the underdog. Here was a staunch defender of individual human rights. What could be more appropriate than to appoint such a person to the Supreme Court of Canada at the same time as the entrenchment of the Charter of Rights and Freedoms – in other words, to choose someone who understood the Charter's anti-majoritarian purpose? As Wilson saw it, a legislature is elected by popular vote and accountable to the electorate which will demand that it pass legislation to the advantage of the nation as a whole. But in the post-Charter era the courts have been assigned a new responsibility; they must 'carefully scrutinize this legislation to ensure that it does not sacrifice the rights of the few simply to enhance the welfare of the many.'[1]

Under the 1867 constitution and in accordance with the division of powers between federal and provincial governments, the courts were permitted only to decide whether or not a particular level of government had the jurisdiction to pass a specific law. The Charter stood for the novel proposition that there were some laws which neither level of government could pass because they infringed the rights of its citizens. And that is why the Charter (itself entrenched by the political decision of an elected legislature) effectively constitutionalized the courts' human rights powers so that they could defend individuals and minority groups against the greater political power of the majority. But the

Court's role in the context of each case before it is to apply a close scrutiny to the meaning of the specific right guaranteed by the Charter and the purpose of that right in relation to the overall goal of creating a democratic society. The meaning of the right at issue cannot be determined simply by examining the text of the guarantee. Only a flexible approach will ensure that rights are interpreted in a way which reflects current notions of justice and fairness in response to changing social consensus. It is a approach which necessarily entails the perpetual motion of social change. Change, in Wilson's optimistic view, is not to be feared but to be welcomed because it represents an opportunity for positive progress and continuous improvement.

As we noted earlier, Wilson objected vehemently to the grouping of cases according to an ideological agenda determined by a judicial lobbying process. But at the same time, she was aware that the Court did not have the luxury of saving up cases on like issues so that they could be decided concurrently. On a few occasions multiple cases dealing with similar issues did arrive at the Supreme Court simultaneously and could be decided concurrently. However when this did not happen, Wilson was worried that 'we weren't saying something in one of these cases that was going to come back to haunt us when the same right was being put forward in another context.' It was a similar concern that had motivated her to establish the Oslers' information retrieval system.

Looking back over Wilson's Supreme Court career can offer the retrospective luxury of considering like cases together. We can organize our review of key cases from her Supreme Court jurisprudence by beginning with her concept of the individual at the centre of her human rights decisions; then move on to some of the family law cases which look to the relationships between individuals in those most intimate associations that Wilson herself always considered to be a fundamentally important area of the courts' work; consider a few of the corporate and commercial decisions, in particular as these entities create artificial persons by operation of law which sought to claim some of the Charter protections afforded natural persons; examine a number of the criminal law cases where the accused is confronted by the full power of the state or the administrative law cases where the applicant is bound up in the bureaucracy; and even explore some relatively rare situations in which our domestic Supreme Court had to consider the protection of the rights of the individual in an international context. And we will be able to see how persistently Wilson's judgments express her concern not only for proper application of substantive statutory provisions or relevant common law doctrines but also for proper interpretation of relevant procedural provisions, particularly in relation to issues such as the leave to appeal procedure or the expansion of intervenor status before the Court.

Such a sequencing will be an expansive arrangement, the reverse of the narrowing focus we used in surveying the Court of Appeal case law from criminal to human rights law. An expansive organization is particularly suitable in this post-Charter era when constitutional law (now overwhelmingly and almost exclusively human rights law) began to expand into and inform non-constitutional and non-human rights cases, presumably in response to the relatively swift shift of social consensus as Canadians began to associate the Charter as supreme Canadian law with national identity and national feeling. In fact, Wilson herself came to the view that it is impossible to hive off constitutional adjudication as a separate category of legal analysis and that to attempt to do so denies the 'crosscut' reality of people's lives.[2]

Given this integration, it is not surprising to discover ongoing evidence of Wilson's willingness to integrate other categories of modernist law by importing, for example, trust principles into both family law and corporate law. But in this survey we will also see how Wilson's equitable flexibility in adapting doctrine to changing circumstances and changing social climates remains rooted in her deference to justice-as-modernist-consistency; the variation represented by each new postmodern direction is inevitably connected to an existing and well-established modernist principle.[3]

My own impulse to create tidy categories in a sequenced pattern for discussion of the Supreme Court judgments is admittedly derived from the modernist experience of law school; students take courses in discrete areas of law and that is how lawyers are trained to think. For better or worse, however, it will be obvious that this impulse is inexorably frustrated and its arbitrariness revealed by the complex intersection of contingencies which have generated the litigation. Human rights cases often have an employment law dimension, for example; family law dilemmas frequently touch on economic issues of support and division of property and may also be interwoven with racial or religious issues; real human beings lurk behind the corporate veil; a criminal law case may be as much concerned with freedom of expression as with liberty of the person; and so on.

MULTICULTURALISM: THEORIES OF HUMAN RIGHTS

Before discussing the human rights cases, our point of departure, it may be helpful to examine briefly some of our indigenous human rights theory, which is reflective of the Canadian aspiration to create a multicultural society. Canadian philosopher Charles Taylor has argued that human identity itself is fundamentally *dialogic* in character. Identity is liminal, always negotiated with others in a manner which is simultaneously internal and external at the juction of the public and the private; we experience our identities both individually and communally. Taylor rejects the idea that a liberal equality of rights model permits only social homogenization that necessarily denies distinct cultural identities. Nevertheless, he warns, a modernist liberalism of the rational, choosing individual can be incorporated within a multicultural society only so long as liberal equality of rights does not either insist upon uniform application of rules or deny the collective goal of every distinct society which has to be its very survival.[4]

Canadian legal scholar Nitya Iyer[5] has pointed out the inherent danger of human rights protection focusing exclusively on categorization of enumerated characteristics such as the race, national or ethnic origin, colour, religion, sex, age or mental or physical disability criteria listed in sections of the Charter. The very act of categorization of these characteristics implies insidiously that there is some neutral norm from which they constitute a deviation. The so-called neutral norm is always comprised of the particular characteristics possessed by those with the power to be the categorizers. They will be insensitive to numerous differences within the categories of race or gender or class or disability which are urgently significant to the experience of those categorized; dialogue, in Taylor's sense of the word, is obscured.

Furthermore, important aspects of the identities of persons or groups whose differences are multiple remain invisible. It may be, for example, that intersections among categories of race, religion, and sex have given rise to the problem; a categorizing grid tends to focus on one characteristic only. Persons whose differences are multiple are unable, individually or communally, to obtain recognition which is sensitively nuanced in accordance with their own perceptions of the discrimination they have experienced.

But, as our earlier discussion of its provisions illustrates, the structure of the Charter articulates that very Canadian notion that almost all of us live on the margins. And if postmodernisms are specific to the cultures which create them, it is interesting that a number of American race theorists have been deeply suspicious of postmodernism's characteristically apolitical stance and its chic 'discourse of difference.'[6]

Such suspicions may also arise out of the different attitudes which have evolved in our two countries. Multiculturalism in Canada may be official public policy, but it has also been embraced by the majority of Canadians in the street and the workplace and as part of their private social experience. In Wilson's opinion, Canadians, unlike Americans do not perceive a sharp disjunction between the public and the private; they do not assume that the best government necessarily governs least or view government as an intrusion upon their private realm of freedom.[7] This stance is at odds with the public American ideal of homogeneity juxtaposed with its persistent experience of private segregation as an assertion of negative liberty even in the face of government policy instruments intended to require integration.

ADVERSE EFFECTS AND UNDUE HARDSHIP

It took Wilson some considerable time to formulate her views in a manner which satisfied her own understanding of the basic principle of human rights legislation – that is, the contextual consideration of each person as an individual to ensure an equality of treatment that takes into account each person's particular attributes. Cases dealing with visible minorities are obvious instances where diversity law approaches will be appropriate; at the Court of Appeal, Wilson had shown particular sensitivity to Olbey's race and colour in her audacious dissent based on the defence of provocation, and noted in *Bhadauria* that 'there can be no doubt that the interests of persons of different ethnic origins are entitled to the protection of the law.'

But Wilson was not at all happy with the decision in *Bhinder*.[8] Although she wrote separate reasons (for herself and Justice Beetz) she joined with the majority at the Supreme Court (Justices Estey, McIntyre, and Chouinard) in deciding that CN's work rule requiring all employees to wear hard hats on the job did not constitute racial discrimination. Bhinder, a Sikh, had to wear a hard hat instead of a turban if he wished to retain his job as a maintenance electrician in the Toronto coach yard.

Wilson began by examining the statutory definition of a bona fide occupational requirement (BFOR) set out in the Canadian Human Rights Act. If the hard hat was genuinely necessary because of the demands of the job, then it was not a discriminatory practice for the employer to insist that Bhinder wear it; only if the employer had been found to discriminate did the statutory duty to accommodate – that is, to meet the reasonable costs incurred by any alternative method of meeting the job requirements without discriminating against the employee – kick in. As Wilson concluded with an almost palpable reluctance, 'The legislature, in my view, by narrowing the scope of what constitutes discrimination has permitted genuine job-related requirements to stand even if they have the effect of disqualifying some persons for those jobs. This was a policy choice ... I do not believe it is open to the courts to query its wisdom in this regard.' Significantly, Dickson and Lamer dissented; in their view, any interpretation of a specific provision of the act which had the effect of obliterating the duty to accommodate or diminishing the protection of the individual from 'adverse effects' discrimination had to be contrary to the overall purpose of the act. The majority decision was sharply criticized by Gordon Fairweather, chief commissioner of the Canadian Human Rights Commission. He stated that 'equal opportunity will not be established in this country unless employers are required by law to accommodate differences.'

Justice McIntyre had written the majority judgment in *O'Malley*[9] which was decided concurrently with *Bhinder* but in favour of the appellant by adopting the then-new concept of adverse effects discrimination from American jurisprudence. Mrs O'Malley was a Seventh Day Adventist who celebrated her Sabbath on Saturday and objected to her employer's requirement that she be available to work two out of every three Saturdays. McIntyre found that the employer could organize its business as it saw fit and seek out employees available to work such hours but that Mrs O'Malley was entitled to be free from the compulsion to work on her Sabbath day contrary to the requirements of her religious faith. Working on Saturdays was not an occupational requirement relating to the safety or the reasonable efficiency of the workplace in the same way that wearing a hard hat was thought to be a legitimate safety issue.

Adverse effects doctrine distinguished instances of direct discrimination, where a workplace rule was found to be discriminatory on a prohibited ground and was simply struck down, from instances in which an apparently neutral employment rule was not discriminatory on its face but unintentionally discriminatory in its effect, given the circumstances of a particular employee. In such cases, when the rule was bona fide and met a genuinely work-related purpose for the employer it did not have to be struck down for the majority of employees whose rights it does not offend. But the employer did have the duty to accommodate the adversely affected employee up to the point of undue hardship; Simpsons-Sears could not show that its business profitability was put into serious jeopardy if it was compelled to permit Mrs O'Malley to work the other days of the week.

It was not until the *Dairy Pool*[10] case in 1990 that Wilson had the opportunity of applying this adverse effects analysis in an employment law context which also involved the issue of freedom of religion. The appellant, a Mr Christie, was a prospective member of the World Wide Church of God which expected its adherents to attend services on certain religious holidays, including Easter Monday. This requirement conflicted with his job at a milk-processing plant which closed down over the weekend and therefore was particularly busy dealing with the pent-up supply on Mondays. The employer accommodated Mr Christie's absence for one of the pre-Easter holidays but when he failed to show up on Easter Monday he was fired.

Wilson wrote the majority judgment. She reviewed the facts, the relevant legislation, the decisions at the board of inquiry, the trial level, and the court of appeal. She isolated the issues and surveyed all the recent Canadian case law as well as the Canadian Human Rights Commission report, together with the leading academic interpretations of the employer's duty to accommodate in instances of adverse effects discrimination. In *obiter*, she set the record straight on *Bhinder*; 'it seems to me in retrospect that the majority of this Court may indeed have erred in concluding that the hard hat rule was a BFOR,' she wrote, pointing out that in fact the hard hat wasn't necessary to his job as an electrical technician and that there would have been no additional risk to his fellow employees or the general public had he not been compelled to wear it. And in *Dairy Pool*, given that the employer had in place alternative arrangements to cope with the Monday absences of employees due to illness or scheduled vacation time, there could be no bona fide occupational requirement of attendance.

But, as *O'Malley* had established, if the employer could have demonstrated a genuine occupational requirement of Monday attendance at the workplace, then the onus would have fallen upon him to accommodate any employee (like Christie) who suffered adverse impact discrimination from this otherwise neutral rule. This duty to accommodate extended up to the point of undue hardship. Although in subsequent case law the Supreme Court of Canada eliminated the dichotomy

between direct and adverse effect discrimination, the concept of undue
hardship developed by Wilson in *Dairy Pool* still takes into account a
multiplicity of contextual factors:

> I do not find it necessary to provide a comprehensive definition of what
> constitutes undue hardship but I believe it may be helpful to list some
> of the factors that may be relevant to such an appraisal. I begin by adopt-
> ing those identified by the Board of Inquiry in the case at bar – financial
> cost, disruption of a collective agreement, problems of morale of other
> employees, interchangeability of work force and facilities. The size of the
> employer's operation may influence the assessment of whether a given
> financial cost is undue or the ease with which the work force and facili-
> ties can be adapted to the circumstances ... Where safety is at issue both
> the magnitude of the risk and the identity of those who bear it are rele-
> vant considerations. This list is not intended to be exhaustive and the
> results which will obtain from a balancing of these factors against the
> right of the employee to be free from discrimination will necessarily vary
> from case to case.

It is clear that she contemplates accommodation that goes far beyond
that which can be provided by the employer alone.

The employer's duty to accommodate was not mitigated by the fact
that Christie had only a recent and somewhat prospective interest in the
World Wide Church of God, nor by the fact that the church was not as
punctilious as Christie felt necessary, since it did not impose sanctions
for disobedience relating to its preference that no work be done on religious festivals. Issues of conscience and religion go to the core of the
individual's definitions of self and the courts ought to take them seriously, acknowledging that such definitions are often in a state of fluctu-
ation and change.

In *O'Malley*, McIntyre had spelled out a reciprocal duty on the part of
the employee to compromise with the employer who had gone some
distance to accommodate in instances of adverse effects discrimination:

> The employer must take reasonable steps towards that end which may or
> may not result in full accommodation. Where such reasonable steps, how-
> ever, do not fully reach the desired end, the complainant, in the absence of
> some accommodating steps on his own part such as an acceptance in this
> case of part-time work, must either sacrifice his religious principles or his
> employment.[11]

Wilson cites this passage in *Dairy Pool* but she does not comment on McIntyre's implication that at some point the plaintiff must weigh his own convictions and provide some accommodation of his own. Nevertheless, based upon other judgments which Wilson wrote relating to freedom of religion one can infer that the degree of accommodation required by the complainant would be proportionate to the significance of the civil right which had been infringed. Some moderate compromise of freedom of religion might be justified under certain circumstances, but the section 7 guarantees of liberty of the person ought to be protected with the utmost vigilance.

IMMIGRATION: LIBERTY AND SECURITY OF THE PERSON

Wilson's ascription of paramount importance to liberty of the person is not surprising, given that one of her most significant (and controversial) decisions had been *Singh*,[12] another visible minority case decided a few years earlier, in 1985. A group of Sikhs who were denied refugee status appealed the decision of the Ministry of Employment and Immigration on the grounds that the redetermination process was contrary to the section 7 principles of fundamental justice because applicants were not offered a full oral hearing under circumstances which resulted in deprivation of security of the person. Although the merits of the claim were not the major issue, the fear of persecution was undeniably well-founded: some twenty-five hundred Sikhs seeking refugee status had been expelled from Canada back to India using the ministry's streamlined redetermination process between 1981 and 1984, a period in which four hundred people had died because of clashes between the minority Sikhs and the majority Hindus. Herself an immigrant though not a refugee, the experience of war in Aberdeen was something neither she nor John could ever forget.

Ed Ratushny, now a law professor at the University of Ottawa and director of its Human Rights and Education Research Centre, had released a report to the minister of immigration in June 1984 in which he criticized the entire system for evaluating refugee claims made within Canada as 'wasteful of time, resources and goodwill.' He pointed specifically to the absence of oral hearings at which claimants could respond as a fundamental omission going to the issue of procedural fairness.[13]

Justice Beetz (writing for Estey and McIntyre) found for the appellants through application of the Canadian Bill of Rights which still continued in effect, avoiding the issue of whether the Charter applies to persons who are in the country but are not Canadian citizens. Wilson (with Dickson and Lamer concurring) wrote an exhaustive judgment setting out the facts and issues, the scheme of the Immigration Act, all the associated international treaties and conventions, and all the case law which had a bearing upon the circumstances.

However, it is Wilson's examination of the shifting and contextualized meanings of the key concepts from section 7,[14] especially liberty and security of the person, which is of particular interest. She insisted that these concepts are capable of a broad range of meaning and rejected the single-right theory of the ministry. Although not prepared to argue that a full oral hearing is an indispensable attribute of fundamental justice in every situation in which these issues come into play, the oral hearing was essential in this adversarial refugee determination context, whenever facts are in dispute. Fundamental justice demands that an applicant have the right to state his case and to know the case which he has to meet.

Wilson sternly rejected the ministry's characterization of the procedure as a purely administrative one. Nor was she impressed by the ministry's assertion that providing a full oral hearing would dramatically increase the costs of the refugee determination process. Her application of Scottish Enlightenment pragmatism is not reducible to the kind of calculation characteristic of mere utilitarianism.

Wilson was well aware that she had opened the door to a broad interpretation of section 7 rights and in particular a profound and prophetic expansion of security of the person': in speaking about this judgment not long afterwards, she said:

> The judges who relied on the Charter stated that security of the person encompasses freedom from the threat of physical punishment or suffering as well as freedom from such punishment itself. If Canada deports an individual to a country where there is a threat of physical punishment or suffering, we concluded that there is a direct causal link between Canada's action in deporting them and the threat to that individual's security of the person ... Accordingly, in view of the potential consequences to an individual of a denial of that status if he or she is in fact a person with a well-founded fear of persecution, an individual is entitled to fundamental justice in the adjudication of his or her status. In reaching this conclusion we rejected the notion that procedural protections did not apply to immigration because immigration is a privilege and not a right. This distinction between 'right' and 'privilege' has plagued both administrative law and

Bill of Rights jurisprudence for years and, in our view, was inappropriate in the context of a constitutional document protecting fundamental rights.[15]

Wilson went on to point out that *Singh* was then the only case to consider the meaning of the phrase 'security of the person' and speculated about whether it might be interpreted as including the economic right to a minimum standard of living.[16]

The immediate reaction to *Singh* was positive. The *Ottawa Citizen* praised Wilson for affirming that the Charter rights held by citizens and landed immigrants are to be extended to anyone who is in Canada. Ottawa immigration lawyer Hugh Fraser described how the emotional impact of his clients' testimony was lost when they were required to speak into a tape recorder about the torture they had experienced and their words were reduced to cold pages of transcript; Montreal lawyer Steve Foster and Toronto lawyers Barbara Jackman and Lorne Waldman also expressed their relief and pleasure in the decision. But the government had adopted the transcript procedure because it was faced with a backlog of some thirteen thousand appeals. It was estimated (accurately, as it turned out) that the requirement of oral hearings would cost additional millions of dollars.[17]

In response to the *Singh* decision, the federal government has developed stringent guidelines defining the degree of persecution necessary to meet refugee status and reduced the number of board members required for each hearing from two to one 'protection officer' for inland claimants while eliminating appeals for overseas claimants who (not yet on Canadian soil) do not qualify for Charter protection. These measures predictably increased the number of refugee claimants making their claims from within the country, setting off fresh controversy as boatloads of Chinese in particular slipped through the misty islands off the coast of British Columbia at regular intervals throughout 1999. The *Singh* decision was resurrected in the popular press only to be condemned, with a good deal of the criticism aimed pointedly and personally at Wilson. It was considered that she had been wrong to afford Charter protections to refugee claimants who should be jailed and shipped home on arrival: many refugees assert sham claims and are fleeing not political persecution by rather seeking economic betterment. The three provinces which absorb 95 per cent of the twenty-five thousand refugees who arrive in Canada each year – British Columbia, Ontario, and Quebec – have joined forces to demand that the federal

government pay all costs arising out of federal refugee policies including social assistance, housing, and legal aid.[18] What no one seems to
have noted is that although the six judges participated in the *Singh* decision split evenly, the Beetz alternative under the Bill of Rights was
equally committed to the full hearing process.

FREEDOM OF RELIGION

If visible minority cases such as *Singh* are obvious candidates for application of diversity law analysis, *Bhinder* could also have been framed in
relation to freedom of religion in the employment law context. But during the 1980s many retailers, particularly members of ethnic minority
groups, wanted to assert their right to operate their businesses on a
schedule in accordance with their own religious holidays or with no
restrictions on opening hours at all. *Big M Drug Mart* was one such case
decided in 1985.

It is not surprising that the effects-based analysis which drove the
result in *O'Malley* appealed to Wilson, who had only a few months earlier agreed with the majority in *Big M* that federal legislation prohibiting
Sunday sales infringed religious freedom. In fact, Wilson's brief but
important concurrence was concerned only with analytic method; she
expressed the view that for Charter litigation 'the appropriate analytic
starting point is the effect rather than the purpose.'[19]

In 1986 the Supreme Court, in *Edwards Books*[20] upheld Ontario's Retail
Business Holidays Act. The act, wrote Dickson for the majority, had the
secular purpose of creating a common pause day. The fact that this day
happened to be Sunday did not offend religious freedom because there
was an exemption provided within the act for small retailers (defined in
relation to square footage of the store and number of employees),
so long as they had taken a pause for twenty-four hours previous to
Sunday, thus accommodating Jews or Christian Saturday Sabbath
observers.

In Wilson's view, the size restrictions had the effect of providing religious freedom for some and not for others based on totally extraneous
considerations. She was compelled into outright and indignant dissent:

[I]t seems to me that when the Charter protects group rights such as freedom of religion, it protects the rights of all members of the group. It does
not make fish of some and fowl of the others. For, quite apart from considerations of equality, to do so is to introduce an invidious distinction into

the group and sever the religious and cultural tie that binds them together. It is, in my opinion, an interpretation of the Charter expressly precluded by s. 27 which requires the Charter to be interpreted 'in a manner consistent with the preservation and enhancement of the multicultural heritage of Canadians.'[21]

Wilson makes reference here to legal philosopher Ronald Dworkin's distinction between external compromises in law – policy decisions about what system of justice to adopt, such as she thought she faced in *Bhinder* – and internal compromises, like this one or the lobbying issue in the decision-making process, which can break law's 'seamless web,' threatening the coherence and the very integrity of law itself. A law which may once have worked well enough no longer functioned because the social context which had once been overwhelmingly Christian had changed to a secular and multicultural society. She would have allowed any merchant who closed on Saturday to be open on Sunday, regardless of size.[22]

The reaction in the popular press to this majority judgment indicated overwhelming approval for Wilson's sole dissent. The *Ottawa Citizen* endorsed Wilson's compromise as a principled solution which would not have resulted in wide-open Sundays; the *Globe and Mail* editorial considered that Wilson's move was in the right direction, but argued that the law should be abolished altogether; the *Toronto Star* pointed out that the decision of the majority focused on freedom of religion without adequate consideration of other aspects of discrimination and called it a bad law.[23]

WRONGFUL DISMISSAL

If there is no constitutional right to a common pause day, the framers of our Charter also and quite deliberately excluded specific economic protections; there are no guarantees of food and shelter, no right to work. There is a long established common law principle in the employment context that, unless a contract makes specific provision to the contrary or the situation is one of dismissal for cause, the expectation of employment continues indefinitely. Nevertheless, an employer has the unilateral right to end that employment and can satisfy any ongoing obligation to the employee through payment in lieu of notice. If wrongful dismissal is litigated, the appropriate notice period will be calculated by the court taking into account such factors as age, length of service, inveiglement from previously secure employment, attempts to mitigate loss by seeking new employment, and the likely difficulty of obtaining new employment at a comparable level.[24] And although a number of Supreme Court cases during Wilson's era were concerned with the right of retail businesses to open their doors in accordance with their owners religious beliefs, there were other cases in which individuals sought the right to continue their employment or sought novel remedies when they had been summarily let go.

Vorvis[25] must have been a particularly sympathetic case to Wilson. Like her Dalhousie classmate, John Charters, Eonis Vorvis had entered law school in his mid-thirties as a mature student after a successful career; he had been an engineer with Dupont and was reluctant to accept a transfer out-of-province. And like Charters, he appears to have found the stresses of practice too much for him.

After graduation and call to the bar, Vorvis took a job as in-house counsel with Insurance Corporation of British Columbia. His work involved routine preparation of leases and real estate purchases which he performed satisfactorily, receiving regular merit pay increases until a new broom came sweeping through his workplace. Greater management efficiencies superseded meticulous attention to detail as the measure of excellence. Vorvis was required to report to a new general counsel who expressed his dissatisfaction with the pace of his work.

Vorvis did his fair share of the work and met his deadlines but only by putting in very long hours. In Wilson's words, 'he was simply conscientious to a fault.' The new supervisor set up Monday meetings reviewing his productivity in relation to time spent on each file, riding herd on him in a manner somewhat similar to the billable hours controversy Wilson herself had struggled with at Oslers, but far less pleasant. The trial judge found that these meetings were conducted as inquisitions. It did not take long before the unceasing pressure of his supervisor's complaints distressed Vorvis enough that he required medical attention and tranquillizers. Then, after almost eight years of employment and at the age of forty-nine, he was abruptly dismissed with just two weeks' notice; moreover, he was unable to find new employment as a lawyer.

Vorvis had won his suit for damages arising out of the wrongful dismissal; the trial judge found that he had been a hardworking and sincere employee. The Court of Appeal had made a further award for lost overtime benefits. At the Supreme Court, Vorvis pursued his claim for lost pension rights, aggravated damages for mental distress, and punitive damages. The majority found against him. McIntyre reasoned that the pension benefits were excluded by the terms of the pension agreement itself; that an award of aggravated damages is a contractual remedy intended to compensate for intangible injuries (limited to the period of notice) when the acts complained of are independently actionable and directly related to the method of dismissal; and that punitive damages are by definition rare in instances of contract because they are a torts remedy intended to express public condemnation of extremely offensive conduct – conduct sufficiently offensive to constitute a separate actionable wrong, a test which he did not consider had been met in this instance.

Wilson, with L'Heureux-Dubé concurring, dissented in part. The contract clearly did exclude an award of pension benefits, they agreed. Aggravated damages were also excluded but Wilson would have made an award in punitive damages in order to fulfil one of the purposes of the Court which, she argued, is to 'punish high-handed, vindictive or otherwise shocking and reprehensible conduct.' Wilson provides a thorough and scholarly analysis of current and contradictory developments in British and Canadian case law, pointing out that the Court had a duty to clarify whether or not there was still a firm prohibition against such awards in a contractual setting and if so under what circumstances.[26]

Wilson stressed that the wrongness of the conduct did not inhere in the legal characterization of the particular acts which were performed:

[I]n my view, the correct approach is to assess the conduct in the context of all the circumstances and determine whether it is deserving of punishment because of its shockingly harsh, vindictive, reprehensible or malicious nature. Undoubtedly some conduct found to be deserving of punishment will constitute an actionable wrong but other conduct might not ... The very closeness engendered by some contractual relationships, particularly employer/employee relationships in which there is frequently a marked disparity of power between the parties, seems to me to give added point to the duty of civilized behaviour.[27]

There ought to be a kind of benevolence automatically arising out of the closeness of collegial work relationships. If it has not evolved, then the state (through its courts) has a duty to educate its citizens to behave in accordance with our consensus about minimal standards of civility: Adam Smith would applaud this ruling.

Eight years later, in the landmark Supreme Court ruling on *Wallace* v. *United Grain Growers*[28] (a case which set employment law on its ear) Wilson's interpretation in *Vorvis* was indirectly vindicated. Wallace, in his mid-forties, had been encouraged by United Grain Growers to leave secure employment to head up its publishing division with the promise that he could continue until retirement. Top salesman for fourteen years, he was fired suddenly and without explanation. When Wallace sued for wrongful dismissal the company alleged dismissal for cause: Wallace, it maintained for two years up until the date of trial, was let go because he was unable to perform the job satisfactorily. Wallace was so humiliated by this allegation that he required psychiatric treatment for mental distress. Moreover, he was unable to obtain similar employment.

Justice Iacobucci, writing for the majority, articulated a doctrine of 'bad faith conduct,' finding that employers ought reasonably to be aware that employees at the point of dismissal are extraordinarily vulnerable and in need of protection and that accordingly employers should be held to an obligation of fair dealing in such circumstances. He held that in instances where the manner of dismissal has been markedly reprehensible, the censure of the court ought to be expressed through an expansion of the period of reasonable notice.

EQUALITY, CITIZENSHIP AND ANALOGOUS GROUNDS

Andrews,[29] concerning a lawyer who wanted to work, was an extremely important case in the development of Charter jurisprudence. A white male British subject resident in Canada challenged the Law Society of British Columbia because it had refused him admission to practise law in the province in accordance with the provincial Barristers and Solicitors Act on the grounds that he was not a citizen; the judgment provides the first elaboration of the meaning of equality under section 15 of the Charter.

The Court held that section 15 does not provide a general guarantee of equality but focuses only on the application of law. The appellant must show that the impugned law itself is discriminatory. The analytical procedure involves a two-step process: first, it is necessary to determine whether an infringement of an equality right has occurred, and second, to consider whether that infringement can be justified under the section 1 test.[30] Discrimination results from distinctions which impose disadvantages on individuals or groups based on personal characteristics outside the control of the individual (such as, in this case, citizenship) and not based on merit or capacity, since these distinctions are usually not discriminatory. The Court rejected unequivocally the 'similarly situated' equality test which had been put forward at various trial and appellate levels.

Citizenship, of course, is not an enumerated section 15 characteristic; the judgment also established the doctrine of 'analogous grounds' discrimination to expand upon the categories which are actually listed in section 15 – a significant move which subsequently enabled the court to read in sexual orientation, for example, as an expansion of the enumerated ground 'sex.' In this instance, the requirement of citizenship was found to be discriminatory and the law was not saved by section 1; Andrews was called to the bar.

For our purposes, what may be most interesting about this case is the expansive approach to the definition of analogous grounds Wilson set out here: 'It can be anticipated that the discrete and insular minorities of tomorrow will include groups not recognized as such today. It is consistent with the constitutional status of section 15 that it be interpreted with sufficient flexibility to ensure the 'unremitting protection' of equality rights in the years to come.'[31]

MANDATORY RETIREMENT

Age is one of the enumerated section 15 characteristics and in the McKinney[2] group of cases which went up to the Supreme Court together, the justices had the luxury of considering mandatory retirement policies in public educational and health care institutions from many different angles. What is particularly difficult in finding discrimination based on age is, of course, that because all of us move through the various age categories during our employment careers we can all be said to benefit at one stage from age provisions which work to our disadvantage at another. If senior employees are not retired out of the workplace there may be no entry-level positions available when we want to start our careers. But when we are compelled in turn to retire there is no requirement that our employers evaluate our individual circumstances or capacities before imposing the exit.

McKinney is the dissent which Wilson herself humorously identified in a 1993 speech as 'the high-water mark to date in the Court's elaboration of context to support a Charter challenge.'[33] The threshold issue here concerned whether institutions such as hospitals and universities should be treated as government pursuant to section 32 of the Constitution Act, 1982 which stipulates that the Charter applies only to government action. The Court had already wrestled with Charter applicability four years earlier in *Dolphin Delivery*, and Wilson cites a passage from McIntyre's judgment in that case to support her contention that the Charter can apply in private litigation when one of the parties relies on governmental action:

> It would seem that legislation is not the only way in which a legislature may infringe a guaranteed right or freedom. Action by the executive or administrative branches of government will generally depend upon legislation, that is, statutory authority. Such action may also depend, however, on the common law, as in the case of the prerogative. To the extent that it relies on statutory authority which constitutes or results in an infringement of a guaranteed right or freedom, the Charter will apply and it will be unconstitutional. The action will also be unconstitutional to the extent that it relies for authority or justification on a rule of the common law which constitutes or creates an infringement of a Charter right or freedom. *In this way the Charter will apply to the common law, whether in public or private litigation. It will apply to the common law, however, only in so far as the common law is the basis of some governmental action which, it is alleged, infringes a guaranteed right or freedom.*[34]

It was Wilson's view that McIntyre left the door open for counsel to invoke Charter protections on behalf of their clients whenever they can argue that some degree of government action has been involved in the private litigation, although she concedes that it is not at all certain what the minimum degree of government action might be. 'Because private discrimination is hardly trivial and is just as pernicious as discrimination caused by government' – and because support of an interventionist role for government is a general characteristic of Canadian national feeling, a broader rather than a narrower definition of what constitutes government action triggering Charter protection is appropriate.

The majority in *McKinney* held that universities and hospitals are not government; if they were, the universities' mandatory retirement policies would indeed have been found to be discriminatory because they do make a distinction which disadvantages individuals over sixty-five; but that mandatory retirement could be justified under section 1.

In her dissent Wilson argues that the Charter should apply to public institutions whenever one or more of three tests are met: general control of the institution by one of the branches of government; performance by the institution of a responsibility generally ascribed to government; or functioning of the institution pursuant to some statutory authority linked to achievement of an identifiable government objective.[35] In her view, universities, colleges, and hospitals easily meet these tests.

Secondly, Wilson believed that the mandatory retirement policies in place at these institutions had the effect of law and infringed the guaranteed right of freedom from discrimination on the basis of age not saved by section 1; mandatory retirement is an affront to the dignity of the individual. Moreover, those sections of the relevant human rights codes which fail to protect workers younger than eighteen or older than sixty-five also contravene the Charter guarantees.

But in the context of age discrimination, Wilson's judgment zeroes in on the interrelationships between race and gender that compound the discrimination of mandatory retirement policies for women and for immigrants. She wrote:

> Immigrant and female labour and the unskilled comprise a disproportion-ately high percentage of unorganized workers. This group represents the most vulnerable workers. They are the ones who, if forced to retire at age 65, will be hardest hit by the lack of legislative protection.
>
> In addition, even in relation to the organized sector of the work force, serious problems remain. The statistics show that women workers gener-ally are unable to amass adequate pension earnings during their working years because of the high incidence of interrupted work histories due to child bearing and child rearing. Thus, the imposition of mandatory retire-ment raises not only issues of age discrimination but also may implicate other section 15 rights as well.[36]

Wilson must have been vividly aware of the irony of a group of Supreme Court judges, themselves not required to retire until age sev-enty-five, determining this issue – an irony compounded by the health difficulties which had prevented a number of those judges from carry-ing out their responsibilities. Moreover had she herself been compelled to retire at age sixty-five Wilson would not have been able to compile the fifteen years required to obtain her judicial pension.

MINORITY LANGUAGE RIGHTS

Wilson had been mulling over the issue of minority language rights for some time. This is clear from her diverging concurrence in the *Acadiens*[37] case decided in 1986, which could be characterized as an employment law case asserting the right of unilingual judges to keep their jobs. The dispute centred around the issue of whether section 19(2) of the Charter entitles a party in a court proceeding to be heard by a judge who is bilingual enough to understand all the evidence and the argument in whichever official language the party elects to use. At that time the vast majority of judges outside Quebec had little facility in French. An affirmative decision would have called their competence into question in many situations.

The French-speaking Justice Beetz, writing for the majority, distinguished between section 7 guarantees of the legal right to procedural fairness, which he considered to be rooted in the principle of fundamental justice, and language rights which resulted from mere political compromise and accordingly did not merit the same degree of protection. Wilson's spoken French (somewhat Scots-accented in accordance with her self-proclaimed status as a member of an 'oral minority') was clearly competent. She could read French slowly but confidently; occasionally she would call on her court attendant, Jean-Marie Plourde, for help when she got stuck with an idiom. But in no way did she consider herself to be bilingual, comfortably capable of following the oral submissions of French-speaking counsel or the questions put to counsel by the French-speaking members of the Court. 'There wasn't a day passed that I didn't feel that I was missing something through that gap,' she said, adding, 'I can remember counsel, one French-speaking counsel whose whole argument had been conducted in French saying one day, "I know that Justice Wilson is desperate to ask a question and she is not doing it because she doesn't think she can articulate it in French, please do it in English, I am perfectly fluent in English."' He was right; she swallowed her embarrassment and spoke up.

It was in her own mind 'perfectly unarguable that members of the Supreme Court of Canada should all be fluently bilingual.' Yet in the *Acadiens* case Wilson was vividly aware of the irony that she (who was not bilingual) was compelled to help decide that very issue.

Her own sense of Scottish propriety prompted her to attribute to the appellate judge whose language competence was impugned in *Acadiens* a sufficient understanding of the French language to enable him to follow the argument. Wilson asserted in her concurrence that 'no judge will sit if counsel alleges that he or she has a conflict of interest and there is some basis for the allegation';[38] this courteous assumption saved her from outright dissent.

Wilson's painstaking analysis of the legal issues is immense and complex, running to well over sixty pages in the English-French format of the Supreme Court reports. Only after finding that the appellant's appeal had failed on the jurisdictional issue does Wilson turn to an analysis of the language rights issue in the constitutional context. Both parties, she noted, were in agreement that the judge had to be able to understand the proceedings, evidence, and argument in whatever language was being used in the courtroom. The dispute centred on the level of understanding and who should have the power to decide whether that level had been attained. Through careful examination of the specific wording of sections 16 and 20 of the Charter, Wilson came to the conclusion that the Charter constitutionalizes a commitment to growth in the equality of use of both official languages over time. She sums up her reasoning in this way: 'If I am correct in my characterization of section 16 (1) as constitutionalizing a societal commitment to growth, then presumably our understanding of what is significant and what is reasonable under present conditions will evolve at a pace commensurate with social change.'[39]

In his 'living tree' doctrine, Lord Sankey had constitutionalized a commitment to growth in the interpretive jurisprudence; here Wilson suggests that constitutional law is tended not just by judicial gardeners but by Canadian society as a whole, a society which is committed to growth of the rights themselves in response to changes in society as they occur.

Wilson's subsequent analysis of the social consensus which already exists concerning the level of bilingual competence demanded of judges makes it clear that in her opinion a high level of written and spoken facility had already been deemed to be necessary:

[T]he judge's level of comprehension must go beyond a mere literal understanding of the language used by counsel. It must be such that the full flavour of the argument can be appreciated. To the extent that this requires what Monnin C.J.M. describes as a comprehension of the nuances of the spoken word, I would agree with him that a judge must attain that level of sophistication in order to make the litigant's linguistic right meaningful in the context of the court's process.[40]

More specifically, Wilson departed from the Beetz line of reasoning in her insistence that language rights are not merely a political compromise and that they go beyond due process considerations to embody a sociocultural content. She was also attempting to assert the principle that a legal right under the Charter gives rise to a corresponding obligation on the part of the state. This means that minority plaintiffs may not be foreclosed from bringing actions against the crown for breach of Charter rights arising out of a failure to act or for statutory omissions – for example, for failure to lay criminal charges arising out of an assault or for failure to extend the reach of legislation evenly to provide fair coverage for all minority groups.

Several editorials singled out Wilson's contribution for special praise,[41] but we are only now beginning to reap the benefits of this vigorous concurrence. *Acadiens* is one of Wilson's most far-reaching and prophetic judgments, dovetailing neatly not only with Lord Sankey's living tree approach to constitutional law but also with Wilson's fondness for the McIntyre ruling in *Dolphin Delivery* that the common law must evolve congruently with Charter principles and her characteristic Scottish Enlightenment optimism about the possibility of continuous improvement through change.[42]

ABORIGINAL LAW DEVELOPMENTS

All of these characteristics are also apparent in the aboriginal law cases where the Supreme Court was laying down important new jurisprudence during Wilson's tenure. Wilson's contributions to aboriginal law frequently deal with situations where multiple enumerated grounds of equality, including race, sex, and religious beliefs, intersect with family law, and property and employment issues. She insisted upon an expansive, contextual, and evolving interpretation of aboriginal rights which helped define and affirm their distinctiveness and yet linked these doctrinal developments to existing principles of treaty interpretation. And that is why the aboriginal jurisprudence developed during her years on the Supreme Court anticipates the themes which re-emerge in the crowning achievement of her career – her participation in the Royal Commission on Aboriginal Peoples after her retirement.

Martin v. *Chapman*,[43] a 1983 case, was Wilson's first aboriginal rights judgment at the Supreme Court. The dispute centred upon the appellant's denial of Indian status by a band registrar because he was the illegitimate son of an Indian father and a non-Indian mother. The court split four to three,[44] with Wilson holding for the majority that the appellant was entitled to Indian status. In her reasoning it was not necessary to consider whether or not legitimacy itself might be a concept specific to the dominant culture which had drafted the applicable provisions of the Indian Act because in fact it was the Indian band which sought to read in the concept from the exclusionary clause and apply it to the definition of descent clause in order to exclude the applicant. Instead, Wilson examined the intersections of the clauses very carefully in order to demonstrate that legitimacy could not be at issue in a system which defines race (in itself a cultural construct) through descent of the male line.

A much more wrenching case for Wilson decided that same year was the adoption decision in *Racine* v. *Woods*,[45] a Manitoba case concerning a young girl whose Indian mother had turned her over to the temporary custody of the Children's Aid Society when she was six weeks old, making periodic attempts to reclaim her. Wilson's first difficulty was persuading the Supreme Court to grant leave to appeal. Despite the complexity of the intersecting issues generated by the facts and the law, her colleagues indicated that this was not the kind of case they wanted in their court. Somehow Wilson prevailed and the case was heard.[46]

Linda Woods had been periodically abused by her husband, who was the father of her two older children. She admitted to a history of serious alcohol problems and agreed that she had been unable to care for her youngest child, Leticia, at birth. The Children's Aid Society had placed the infant with a foster family, the Racines; Leticia's foster mother was white, her foster father a Métis, and the evidence showed that they were well respected in their community.

When Leticia was two years old, Mrs Woods arrived on the Racines' doorstep and demanded that they give her back. They refused and heard nothing more for three years, at which time Mrs Woods initiated an application for *habeas corpus*. The Racines countered as the statute permitted with an application for an order of de facto adoption on the grounds that Leticia had been cared for by them for a period of three consecutive years as a member of their family; by the time the matter came to court, two younger children had been born to the Racines. Pending the hearing of the application, home study reports were to be prepared; in the interim, Mrs Woods attempted to abduct the child and when this attempt failed, obtained an order for supervised access. She arranged at her first meeting with Leticia for a newspaper reporter and a photographer to be present; the story was published in the *Winnipeg Free Press*. Leticia, at six, was old enough to be upset by the publicity.

Over the intervening years, Mrs Woods had sometimes lived with her husband and sometimes with her children apart from him. The trial judge was sympathetic to her attempts to overcome her alcoholism. But Mrs Woods also showed considerable anger towards whites; she had come to the view that the adoption of her child by a 'white family' was indicative of systemic political oppression of native peoples. Nevertheless, the evidence at trial showed that the Racines had been most sensitive about maintaining Leticia's cultural heritage. They were the only parents she had ever known and the assessments left no doubt that she had bonded with them psychologically.

The trial judge found that Mrs Woods had abandoned her daughter, that it was unclear whether or not she would be able to sustain her rehabilitation, and that at least in part Mrs Woods was using the adoption battle as a political issue. She made the adoption order in favour of the Racines. Mrs Woods appealed; each of the three appellate judges wrote separate reasons but the adoption order was overturned, the child was made a ward of the Court of Appeal, and custody remained with the Racines. Mrs Woods was denied access pending further appeal to the Supreme Court.

Wilson found this case a hard one. For her, there was absolutely no question of the aboriginal mother asserting any custody claim analogous to property rights; custody is determined only with reference to the best interests of the child. Nor was there any question that the Racines should be prevented from asserting their adoption claim because they had refused to return the child when Mrs Woods first demanded that they do so. Such a refusal was perfectly proper and not an assertion of proprietary 'title,' given that they had been entrusted with the child by the Children's Aid Society, believed the arrangement to be permanent, and had no way of knowing whether she would be safe if they let her go.

The best interests doctrine required Wilson to weigh the evidence of psychological bonding – at that time a relatively new concept in social science – against the issue of racial heritage. An important factor in Wilson's decision was that little Leticia would not lose her registered Indian status as a result of the adoption. The Court was obliged to make a decision; otherwise, Leticia's life would continue to be a battleground. And Wilson concluded that in an increasingly pluralist society with an increased incidence of interracial marriage, the importance of interracial adoption was fading; as one of the witnesses had testified at the trial, the case at bottom was about two women and a little girl and one of them (Linda Woods) didn't know her. But this was undoubtedly one of the cases which Bertha Wilson agonized over most in the course of her entire judicial career.

Wilson was strongly criticized for her incorporation of this new scientific evidence of psychological bonding, which some family law experts believed to have elevated the older notion of natural ties of affection to almost a controlling factor in custody disputes. While acknowledging the danger that consideration of bonding meant the courts might effectively enshrine possessory rights for the parent who had obtained interim custody, in Wilson's own view the courts were protecting the emotional rights of children according to the best interests doctrine.

The Supreme Court was very busy over the course of the Wilson years establishing guidelines for the interpretation of Indian treaties and statutes. *Guérin*[47] concerned a situation in which members of the Musqueam Indian Band of Vancouver had agreed to surrender surplus land to the crown which in turn leased the land to a golf club. But the revised terms on which the lease was finally arranged were much less favourable to the interests of the Indians than the terms which they had approved, and these revised terms were not presented for approval to the appellants before the Indian Affairs branch official concluded the deal. The Dickson judgment in *Guérin* was a landmark, affirming that aboriginal interest in land was a pre-existing and inherent right, independent of and prior to the royal proclamation of 1763 and not contingent upon its recognition by the crown; Dickson did, however, assert Canadian sovereignty over the aboriginal peoples in his finding that before 1982, when aboriginal rights were entrenched in section 35 of the Charter, these rights existed only at common law and could be regulated or extinguished by legislative authority.

The Wilson contribution to *Guérin* is another landmark for its definition of the special type of fiduciary relationship arising out of the Indian Act, which in her view imposed special obligations on the crown. Although section 18(1) of the Indian Act confers a broad discretion upon the crown in dealing with land once it has been surrendered, Wilson held that upon surrender this discretion crystallizes into a fiduciary duty (something beyond a mere political obligation) that the crown exercise its discretion for the benefit of the band. Writing for Ritchie and McIntyre, she decisively rejected the crown's position that the surrender document gave express and complete discretion to the government as to the selection of lessee and the terms of the lease:

> I cannot accept the Crown's submission. The Crown was well aware that the terms of the lease were important to the Band. Indeed, we have the trial judge's finding that the Band would not have surrendered the land for the purpose of a lease on the terms obtained by the Crown. It ill becomes the

Crown, therefore, to obtain a surrender of the Band's interest for lease on terms voted on and approved by the Band members at a meeting specially called for the purpose and then assert an overriding discretion to ignore those terms at will ... It makes a mockery of the Band's participation. The Crown well knew that the lease it made with the golf club was not the lease the Band surrendered its interest to get. Equity will not permit the Crown in such circumstances to hide behind the language of its own document.[48]

The fact that the crown agents may have been motivated by some mis-guided but benevolent notions of paternalistic protection was for Wilson absolutely no excuse. And because the Indian interest in land could not be sold or leased but was inalienable except through surrender to the crown, this restriction created a particular kind of fiduciary obliga-tion which was unique, *sui generis*, trust-like rather than adversarial, and accordingly to be exercised with even greater punctiliousness than a merely commercial fiduciary duty.

A number of important aboriginal cases were moving through the Court between September 1989 and March 1990 and the role Wilson played cannot be fully understood simply by reading her judgments. Dickson, who had pioneered much of the pre-Charter and early Charter approach to aboriginal issues, was, like Wilson, always more interested in the consistent and principled development of the common law than in placing himself front and centre. If it was possible to work strategi-cally behind the scenes to encourage his colleagues to modify their draft reasons in accordance with these evolving principles when historic cases of first instance came before the Court, he was perfectly content to allow them to take the credit for the reasons as released. And Wilson, who carried the baton for Dickson when his other duties prevented him from pursuing these important directions, was similarly prepared to behave strategically so long as she was not required to engage in per-sonal lobbying; to maintain an open process, she adopted the technique of circulating to all the other judges a memorandum expressing her views on the case before any judges had signed on to any set of reasons. It was the same method of working primarily through memos which she had evolved in practice at Oslers.

Sparrow[49] was the first case to consider the effect of section 35 of the Constitution Act, 1982. Aboriginal peoples were hopeful that with the constitutionalization of aboriginal rights, Canadian sovereignty would be repudiated and the aboriginal right to self-government recognized accordingly. The key issue in this case was whether or not the

Musqueam had an inherent right to fish with drift nets unextinguished by the comprehensive regulatory scheme governing non-native anglers; Sparrow, who was fishing in a part of the Fraser River where his ancestors had fished for generations, had been charged under the Fisheries Act of British Columbia with using a drift net longer that the band's food fishing licence permitted.

LaForest volunteered to write. Law clerk Rob Yalden met with Wilson after LaForest had written and circulated his first draft, following the meeting up with a memo to Wilson documenting the specific issues she had indicated were worrying her. Wilson decided it would be helpful if Chief Justice Dickson participated in order to ensure that the key *sui generis* notion of fiduciary duty and inherent aboriginal rights did not become diluted to a mere proprietary interest, a concern she would raise again in *Sioui*,[50] another aboriginal case, in 1990. Wilson was very strongly persuaded that the approach already developed by the Court was the right one, but she doubted that her voice would be persuasive if she spoke up. In the event, the court held that the government was not precluded from regulating aboriginal rights which were integral to the identity and the self-preservation of the aboriginal group in question, but that any action which interfered with such rights had to have a demonstrably valid legislative objective and give priority to aboriginal interests. Wilson could very happily sign on to these joint reasons.

Wilson did write in *Mitchell* v. *Peguis*,[51] a case in which an invalid sales tax had been imposed upon an Indian band for the purchase of hydroelectricity. When the government of Manitoba agreed to rebate the tax, the lawyers who had represented the bank sought a prejudgment garnishment to recover their fees which had not been paid. At trial and at the Manitoba Court of Appeal it was held that because the money was personal property situate on the reserve and given in accordance with the terms of a treaty, it could not be garnished. The Supreme Court dismissed the appeal with three sets of concurring reasons, none of which is entirely satisfactory.

LaForest, writing for Sopinka and Gonthier, looked to the underlying policies of the relevant provision of the Indian Act (to protect private property on the reserve from taxation) and concluded that garnishment of the invalid rebated tax would effectively permit indirectly what the government could not do directly. Wilson, writing for Lamer and L'Heureux-Dubé, agreed with LaForest on the issue of garnishment but was troubled by the intervening third-party claim; she concluded that the doctrine of crown immunity from garnishment was an anachronism requiring revision but that the courts should defer to the legislature in so delicate an area.

Chief Justice Dickson dealt with this issue head on; in *Nowegijick*,[52] for example, he set out the principle that ambiguities in the interpretation of treaties and statutes ought to be resolved in favour of the Indians, even if some party other than the state bears the cost. The legislative scheme set out in the Indian Act specifically mandates preferential treatment for Indians over non-Indians in such instances: Canadian society as a whole has benefited at the expense of the native people and individuals comprising that society must accordingly bear the burdens. In the *Peguis* case, Dickson is prepared to require protections going beyond what the state alone can provide.[53]

Given this tough and principled stance, it is not surprising that Dickson signed on to the Wilson dissent in *Horseman*;[54] unfortunately, it was not enough. The majority (Cory writing for Lamer, LaForest, and Gonthier) dismissed the appeal from the Alberta Court of Appeal and upheld the appellant's conviction for contravention of provincial hunting regulations, finding that these regulations did not contravene provisions within the applicable Indian treaty which guarantee Indian rights to hunt and fish for food. Horseman had been hunting for moose for food and killed a grizzly bear in self-defence at a time when he had not obtained the requisite licence to hunt grizzlies. A year later, in need of money to buy food for his family, he got the licence after the fact and sold the hide. The crown contended that Horseman was not hunting for food as the Indian Act and applicable treaty permitted him to do, but rather engaging in commercial activity not exempted from regulation by the provisions of the provincial Wildlife Act.

Yalden had written the bench memo for Wilson outlining the facts of the case together with the applicable law. It seemed clear to him that the appeal should be allowed. After the judicial conference, however, the word came back to the clerks that the appeal would be unanimously dismissed, with Cory writing the judgment. Yalden was frankly disappointed but he also accepted that his job was to assist, to accept her point of view and not to insist on his own.[55] In mid-January 1990 the Cory draft judgment circulated, Wilson asked Yalden for his comments and he replied in a circumspect one-page memo making brief reference to the alternate line of reasoning set out in his bench memo. Early the next morning, she telephoned him and asked him up to her office. They reviewed the issues, talked about the troubling points of law and Wilson sent Yalden away to prepare a draft dissent. He was delighted and plunged back into the research with renewed vigour. The resulting reasons incorporate an exhaustive survey of the general history of Indian treaties, the leading scholarly commentaries upon them, the particular terms of the treaty applicable in this case, and the contemporary oral and archival evidence of both parties' understanding of the agreements. Wilson came to the conclusion that only those restrictions on Indian hunting rights which were in the interests of the Indians themselves – because they served to ensure the preservation of the species upon which they depended for food and exchange – could be attributed to legislative intent. The government had in effect committed itself to regulate hunting for the purpose of protecting the traditional Indian way of life; thus Indians must be exempt from all non-conservatory provisions which the government might otherwise be justified in enacting and which might legitimately restrict hunting for other citizens of Canada.

Moreover, the statutory words 'for food' must include all of the activities required for subsistence as these activities have evolved in response to social change:

> The whole emphasis of Treaty No. 8 was on the preservation of the Indians' traditional way of life. But this surely did not mean that the Indians were to be forever consigned to a diet of meat and fish and were to have no opportunity to share in the advances of modern civilization over the next one hundred years. Of course the Indians' hunting and fishing rights were to be preserved and protected; the Indians could not have survived otherwise. But this cannot mean that in 1990 they are to be precluded from selling their meat and fish to buy other items necessary for their sustenance and the sustenance of their children. Provided the purpose of their hunting is either to consume the meat or to exchange or sell it in order to support themselves and their families, I fail to see why this is precluded by any common sense interpretation of the words 'for food.' It will, of course, be a question of fact in each case whether a sale is made for purposes of sustenance or for purely commercial profit.[56]

In her analysis of the meanings of the contested phrase 'for food' Wilson specifically invoked common sense and insisted upon a contextual evaluation which takes into account the relevant circumstances of each case. According to the terms of the treaty, the government is committed to protect Indian culture but it is certainly not entitled to freeze that culture out of its natural and reasonable change, growth, and development because of fear that flexibility will result in chaos or loss of control or legal incoherence. The implication of the crown that the full weight of the law had to be applied because letting Horseman off the hook would result in other Indians trying to circumvent such regulations by making duplicitous claims is an undeserved general slur upon a minority group particularly offensive to Wilson's Scottish sense of propriety and decorum.

Wilson circulated the draft judgment, responded on paper to questions and comments which the new line of reasoning raised, revised accordingly. She was as delighted as Yalden when two of her colleagues, including the chief justice, were persuaded to join her; nevertheless, they could not carry the day. But although she had absolutely no inkling of it in May 1990, within a few weeks Dickson had resigned; six months later, she herself had resigned; and shortly thereafter he had invited her to participate in the gruelling but exhilarating tasks laid out for the Royal Commission on Aboriginal Peoples.

9

Beyond Family Law:
Justice for Women and Children

Despite the fervent expectations imposed upon her by the feminist groups who were delighted at her appointment to the Supreme Court and despite the periodic accusations of feminist bias heaped upon her by REAL Women, Bertha Wilson does not consider herself to be a feminist. Yet undeniably the influence of feminist theories, a scarcely perceptible undercurrent during her Dalhousie and early Osler years, gathered strength throughout the 1970s and 1980s. Whether or not she chose to espouse feminism or incorporate it into her personal belief systems, feminism had also enjoyed considerable success in effecting statutory reform, especially in the family law area. That fact alone meant that Wilson could not be aloof from it professionally.

Given what we already know of Wilson's personality, it is not surprising that her attitudes towards the social movement collectively referred to as feminism are closely attuned to the context in which she expressed them. At times, her academic writings or judgments seem to suggest a certain affinity with the doctrines of 'sameness' feminism; at other times, strands of thought more compatible with 'difference' feminism come to the surface. But throughout her long career, on the bench and off, what is most apparent is Wilson's sustained commitment to the principle that men and women share an underlying and common humanity prior to and more fundamental than sex. As Allan Beattie said of her, apparent contradictions tend to disappear from the vantage point of this longer perspective.

Common humanity, however, certainly does not mean identical humanity. Wilson's mother had insisted that she receive the same opportunity for university education as her two older brothers but, although she absorbed its lessons, philosophy as an abstract intellectual study did not much appeal to young Bertha. Her 'people thing' (not necessarily a female trait) was the predominant element of her personality, she wanted to marry John, and she was content to be a minister's wife as long as there was a meaningful role for her. At Dalhousie the study of law which applied logical analysis to practical problems awakened her intellectual energies, but even so, she did not pursue the typical career path of the male lawyers at Oslers. Nevertheless, in her own mind and in the opinion of her colleagues there, her chosen alternative was determined less by the fact that she was a woman than by her particular capacity for integrating academic and pragmatic skills. She was genuinely fascinated by the opportunity to develop a unique client-oriented research facility at the firm and grateful that Oslers gave her the chance. That may be why Wilson was not prepared to sign on to the doctrines of the sameness feminists which dominated sexual politics in the early 1970s and continued well into the 1990s.

Still, there was an element of truth in their position which was quite apparent to Wilson. Sameness feminists assumed that a restructuring of the work force and a reallocation of gendered domestic labour was not only achievable but that such social changes would make it possible for women to function exactly like men. Sameness feminism is best understood as a variant of Western liberal traditions linked to the nature/nurture debate. The expectation was that men, as rational and autonomous moral agents, would recognize the disproportionate burden of childcare and domestic responsibility borne by women in addition to their participation in the waged work force and that they would voluntarily collaborate with women in the fairer restructuring of society. And in the next generation, after they had benefited from the more equal participation of both their parents in childrearing, grown women who had as little girls been encouraged to play with trucks would display values and attitudes very similar to those of grown men who had as little boys been encouraged to play with dolls.

Wilson was never pessimistic about social change. It is true that her own father had exemplified the old-fashioned idea; he was absent a good deal of the time serving his wholesale stationery customers but met his responsibilities to the family by bringing home the bacon. His absence made it necessary and his financial support made it possible for her mother to undertake most of the parenting. Wilson accepted that this was a system which had worked well in that era but it had more to do with mutual recognition of responsibilities than with individual assertion of rights.

In her own long and companionable marriage, however, a different system had been in place. After she entered law school in 1953 Bertha continued with the housework and from that point on John Wilson assumed responsibility for the grocery shopping and cooking chores throughout the remainder of his working life. After he retired and the Wilsons moved to Ottawa, John effectively ran the household. He had no doubt that this was the right thing to do and cheerfully followed this ideal of fairness.[1]

One of the legacies of Scottish Enlightenment philosophy was an optimism that persons would behave with propriety once they had been educated to understand the issues, together with a more general optimism that they would readily identify with progressive movements towards social change. Not surprisingly, given her philosophical training coupled with her personal experience, Wilson was confident of men's increasing willingness to take on domestic chores; it is a stance she has sustained to the present, eagerly noting evidence of the continuous improvements experienced by women balancing work and family commitments as a result of the increasing fairness exhibited by many men.

Wilson was inevitably billed as a pioneering feminist judge when she travelled to speak at law schools. This positive perspective was not particularly well received when she met with groups of those women students who had been afforded formal equality of opportunity (after all, they had been admitted to the lecture halls) but were eager to complain about systemic injustices which in their own minds denied them full functional equality. Wilson was brutally frank in advising women law students whose partners were not prepared to treat them with equal respect for their career aspirations and equal sharing of domestic responsibilities to break it off sooner rather than later; young men in the 1980s could not claim that they did not know better and if their awareness was not reflected in their actions, the situation was unlikely to improve.

But social institutions in general (and law firms in particular) were still dominated by older men whose positions of power were such that they did not have to understand women's claims. Even though there had been considerable progress towards equality in education and the workplace, Wilson was no Pollyanna. She was scrupulously fair in warning women law students what to expect in their future careers; 'I really did believe and used to say to the women that that is the difference – all your life as a woman you are proving yourself, you are proving yourself again, every fresh group, every advancement that you get, proving yourself again, that you can do it. And you get tired of it.'

This is the kind of comment which illustrates that from Wilson's perspective there was also an element of truth in the competing ideology of the 'difference' feminists who focused attention on the essential biological and psychological discrepancies between men and women, demanding that women be considered people too. Difference feminism was a truth to be approached with caution, of course. Undoubtedly some of the difference feminists went too far in assuming that women were possessed of an innately superior morality expressed in their gendered ethic of care and duty. Moreover, such an extreme stance was all too swiftly adopted by the conservative right as justification for the continuing marginalization of women based on the social imperative that they stay home in their role as sole nurturers and guardians of morality.

But in 1990 when the press erupted into a furore over her controversial 'Will Women Judges Really Make a Difference?' speech at Osgoode Hall Law School, the focus was on Wilson's temerity in voicing a much more modest suggestion that women have particular – and different – perspectives to bring to the adjudicative role. Wilson's suggestion took courage because of the potential redefinition of the traditional value of judicial objectivity and neutrality which this feminist stance entailed. And Wilson further insisted that she did not know if women judges *would* make a difference; she was merely willing to raise the question.

Little notice was taken of Wilson's explicit rejection of feminism as an essentialist lens through which every legal dispute ought to be viewed, presumably because such temporizing does not make for startling headlines. Nevertheless, Wilson also expressed considerable respect for the sound modernist structure of the law:

Taking from my own experience as a judge of fourteen years' standing, working closely with my male colleagues on the bench, there are probably whole areas of the law on which there is no uniquely feminine perspective. This is not to say that the development of the law in these areas has not been influenced by the fact that lawyers and judges have all been men. Rather, the principles and the underlying premises are so firmly entrenched and so fundamentally sound that no good would be achieved by attempting to re-invent the wheel, even if the revised version did have a few more spokes in it. I have in mind areas such as the law of contract, the law of real property, and the law applicable to corporations.[2]

Family law, in all of its permutations (custody, access, support, division of property) is intimately related to the sharp disjunction between the private and the public realm which informs so many other areas of law, including contracts and real property and corporate law. And protection of privacy in all of its aspects (freedom of religion, conscience, expression and association, liberty interests and the right to be free of unreasonable search and seizure) are constitutionalized in the Charter, whose values have come to permeate every area of our law.

Women, of course, were notably excluded from participation in the drafting of the Charter. We speak of the 'Fathers of Confederation' in 1867, but the situation had not changed much a hundred years later when, after his election as prime minister, Trudeau initiated discussions with Liberal legal academics about the new Charter of Rights and Freedoms. Women had no substantial opportunity to challenge the principle of formal equality which can never be entirely neutral and which perpetuates the false dichotomy between the public and the private. If they had been so permitted, it is possible that the section 7 right to 'life, liberty and security of the person,' which valorizes human identity as individuation most explicitly in the criminal law context might have been balanced with a corresponding right to the support of the state in sustaining those intimate connections which also inform our sense of human identity, especially in the family law context.

Reassuringly, however, the vitality of the common law offers opportunities for legal reform in response to shifts in social consensus. The analogous grounds doctrine which evolved in the human rights jurisprudence we have already considered offers one such example; omnibus legislation extending benefits to same-sex couples in response to the Court's decision that the Charter requires it is another. And Scottish Enlightenment optimism about the rolling evolution of the law has been further vindicated in the recent unanimous Supreme Court decision[3] that because security of the person encompasses psychological integrity, parents in danger of losing custody of their children to child welfare authorities are constitutionally guaranteed legal representation funded by the state. This ruling explicitly establishes that human identity depends as much upon connection as it does upon liberty and it has the potential for far-reaching repercussions.

202 On the Bench

CONCEPTS OF THE FAMILY

Wilson believed in an interdisciplinary approach to the study of law and to the legal analysis underlying contextual judgment; for that reason, the case survey which follows will also look beyond the ghetto of family law as it has been traditionally defined to consider, in particular, some of her key criminal law decisions relating to violence against women and children. But rather than beginning with a superimposed feminist lens, we will consider first Wilson's own expansive definitions of the family.

The feminist legal scholar Mary Jane Mossman did not much like Wilson's dissent at the Court of Appeal in *Kruger*; to impose joint custody over the wishes of the parents she considered (like the male judges who wrote the majority judgment) an illustration of the inappropriately idealized, aspirational and symbolic role that Wilson ascribed to the law. And the notion that law can have a normative effect on society, not just in bringing parents up to a suitable standard of selfless concern for their children in resolving child custody disputes but in improving society more generally, is a persistent principle which can be seen throughout Wilson's academic writings and legal judgments.[3]

As early as 'A Choice of Values,' the property paper which she developed out of her Dalhousie studies in municipal planning, Wilson had questioned Harvard Law Dean Roscoe Pound's social engineering definition of law in which he asserted that law is merely a social institution to satisfy social wants. A paradox inevitably arises from any legal philosophy so resolutely unidealistic, since 'those very people who clamour to have their conflicting claims protected by the law are equally anxious to be free of legal restraint.' Given the majoritarian (and covertly utilitarian) assumption that social needs ought to take priority over those of the individual, it will too often be the case that under a social engineering philosophy complex and vital legal disputes will be expediently resolved by a strategic framing of the conflicting interests as a clash of social and personal claims: 'It is always a temptation to justify the triumph of one competing interest over another by stating one in its social aspect and the other in its private aspect ... It is then apparent which must be sacrificed.'[5]

Furthermore, the very act of framing a dispute as a conflict between private and public interests presupposes that there can be some fixed consensus defining what social interests ought to take priority; this is no longer so easy in a post-Charter society which is committed to protecting anti-majoritarian rights but which is also required to consider what limits on those rights are reasonable in a free and democratic society.

Wilson's 1985 paper, 'State Intervention in the Family,'[6] reveals her interest in the Hart-Devlin debate of the late 1960s which for a decade and more dominated legal discourse on the subject of public moral standards and is still highly influential today. Lord Devlin held that the state was justified in enforcing conventional morality within the private realm whenever it deemed it necessary to do so in the public interest, because society otherwise would be in danger of disintegration. Wilson borrows from and expands upon H.L.A. Hart's response to support her own argument, which is that social consensus about a particular social convention or morality can shift or even disappear. When it does so, any justification for state intervention to sustain the original convention must then be modified accordingly. In relation to the social institution of the family, Wilson reasoned that because 'social attitudes to the indissolubility of marriage have changed ... in consequence the strictly *moral* dimension of state regulation [of the family] has been very much reduced in importance.'[7]

For Wilson, changes in law's response to the family – especially the inclusion in the 1970 Divorce Act of no-fault grounds and the subsequent shift to a concept of marriage as an economic partnership with equal division of property acquired during the course of the marriage upon its dissolution – were simply pragmatic legislative acknowledgments that social consensus about the permanence of marriage was gone. However, she pointed out that there are still other factors which courts called upon to resolve family law disputes should take into consideration and which continue to justify a considerable degree of state intervention in matters concerning the family.

A speech which she made at the Ontario Institute for Studies in Education, also in 1985, helps to fill in some of Wilson's rationale for this continued state role in the protection of the family. She endorsed the family as 'the primary institution of society ... where in a very real sense all education, moral and otherwise, begins,' adding: 'Home life is the foundation of all community life. The family is the basic social unit, the very cradle of liberty into which we grow and mature and develop into free and spontaneous human beings.'[8]

Citing with approval Lord Devlin's declaration that the institution of marriage is the creation of morality, she described the training and teaching of morality within the home by precept and example as a process which gradually widens out into the local community through the schools and larger social institutions and then into the nation as a whole. Contemporary families, she believed, had become less authoritarian from those of the past, with a more equal involvement of husband and wife in domestic chores and waged labour. For Wilson, this change was a good thing because such anti-hierarchical family modalities could also serve as a metaphor for new and less oppressive approaches to the transmission of knowledge or experience in business and education and politics. And in turn, less authoritarianism in these key social institutions offered a potential for nurturing of renewed respect for all social institutions, so long as each individual is taught within the family to maintain that respect as a personal responsibility.

It is an astonishingly optimistic and moving piece,[9] very far from the then current and despairing feminist redefinition of the family as 'a hell of oppression and brutality.' In Wilson's view, the revised role of the state ought increasingly to be the protection of the new family as a state agent of moral education collaborating in raising young people to become full citizens. Wilson made it clear, however, that the new anti-hierarchical models of moral education must still inculcate full respect for legitimate authority.

SPOUSAL SUPPORT REVISITED

If Mossman rejected Wilson's aspirational model for law expressed in her *Kruger* dissent, she disliked even more her analysis of spousal support obligations in the context of domestic contracts which emerged from her majority judgments in the 1987 *Pelech* trilogy at the Supreme Court. Nor was Mossman alone: undoubtedly these are among the most criticized of all the Wilson judgments.

When a new social consensus about the duty to accommodate emerged in the human rights jurisprudence, Wilson (in *Dairy Pool*) took the earliest opportunity to dissociate herself from the *Bhinder* judgment, where she had come to feel that the Court had got it wrong. However, anyone who had heard or read her 1981 paper, 'The Variation of Support Orders,' (written while she was at the Court of Appeal) might have been able to predict her principled and policy-driven approach in *Pelech*. Moreover, they might have seen from the Wilson Court of Appeal decisions in *Welch* and *Cure* that Wilson took seriously her obligation to apply the relevant statutory provisions when in her view they indicated a deliberate shift in legislative policy resulting from a change in social consensus about the ability and the duty of women to achieve economic independence after marriage breakdown. When she first considered the *Pelech* application for leave to appeal Wilson did not think it even necessary for the Supreme Court to grant a hearing;[10] once she recognized the degree of confusion in the profession about the statutory regime applying to variations in spousal support contracts, however, she agreed with her colleagues that it was a matter of national importance demanding resolution in order to provide guidance for the lower courts and reduce litigation costs by creating an environment of certainty.

In the 'Variation' paper delivered six years before the *Pelech* trilogy decisions, Wilson had already specified most of the elements of what came to be known as the *Pelech* test, developed out of close analysis of the statutory language of section 11 (2) of the 1970 Divorce Act and the Ontario Family Law Reform Act. The courts, as a matter of broad public policy, ought to allow variation of support orders only in situations where there had been a substantial change in the circumstances of the recipient spouse which was both unforeseen at the time of the original order and likely to be ongoing. The clean-break philosophy underlying this policy assumed (in accordance with the ideology of sameness feminism, current at the time the legislation was being drafted) that most women either were or could swiftly become as capable as men of supporting themselves after divorce. At any rate, with legal advice, women were equally capable of negotiating separation contracts that would protect their interests.

Variations are not appeals, so propriety demands that an original order made by a court must be assumed to have been appropriate at the time it was made. Particularly with respect to privately negotiated support contracts, Wilson had warned that 'the courts in the past have been far too ready to interfere with the arrangements the parties have themselves made to settle their financial affairs.'[11]

Accordingly, in only a few narrowly defined circumstances ought a domestic contract be set aside or an application for a variation order be approved by the courts. Agreements which did not adequately provide for the support of children are always open to subsequent revision, and Wilson had acknowledged that because a family is an indivisible economic unit children may be adversely affected when a custodial spouse had settled for less spousal support than she ought to have done. Legislation provided that the courts could also set aside agreements where one of the spouses might become a public charge, although Wilson herself was sympathetic to the English doctrine that the welfare state had first responsibility to support needy former spouses in such circumstances. Finally, Wilson believed that general principles of contract law could always be used by the courts to set aside separation agreements which were unconscionable or resulted from undue influence.

But it was evident that Wilson wished to accord substantial weight to the aspirational policy considerations underlying the new legislative directions. She spelled out those policy considerations with precision. The no-fault divorce philosophy signalled a movement away from adversarial confrontation which emerging sociological evidence had indicated was damaging to the post-divorce psychological adjustment of both the spouses and their children. The provisions were meant to encourage the parties to settle their own financial affairs privately, both because a private process is less costly and reduces pressure on the courts and because the parties are more likely to comply with agreements they have negotiated themselves. Parties are entitled to rely upon the courts to uphold agreements so that they can get on with their lives. *Ex post* variations in support orders are potentially unfair because matrimonial property settlements reached under provincial legislation at the time of divorce were almost certainly factored in to the spousal support award. If one of the parties had made a bad bargain, she concluded, that fact ought not to provide sufficient reason for the court to vary the order; *'it is only where the agreement struck by the parties is so manifestly unfair as to shock the court's conscience that variation should be made,'*[12] Wilson wrote.

Shirley Mae Pelech had made a bad bargain when she divorced her husband in 1969 after fifteen years of marriage. With the benefit of independent legal advice and in accordance with the Divorce Act she had contractually agreed to accept thirteen monthly lump sum payments in total satisfaction of all future maintenance claims. As it turned out, the mental health problems which she had suffered before her marriage (and which apparently exacerbated difficulties during it) were further compounded by physical health problems after the divorce that prevented her from working regularly. As a result, by 1982 she was reduced to living on welfare. In the meantime, her husband had prospered in his business – the business that Mrs Pelech had helped him to build – and had become a millionaire.

In the Dalhousie speech, Mossman pointed out that Wilson based her decision in Pelech on the overriding policy consideration that contracts which are not unconscionable and which have been freely negotiated with independent legal advice should be upheld because 'people should be encouraged to take responsibility for their own lives and their own decisions.'[13] Through her feminist lens Mossman saw this move as an express rejection on Wilson's part of 'the need to compensate for systemic gender-based inequality' – an alternative interpretive tool coming out of a Manitoba Court of Appeal case called Ross[14] which Wilson ought to have applied.

But Wilson did, in fact, cite Ross in Pelech and explained why she felt unable to follow it:

> While I am in sympathy with [Ross appeal court judge] Matas J.A.'s concern, I believe that the case by case approach and the continuing surveillance by the courts over the consensual arrangements of former spouses which he advocates will ultimately reinforce the very bias he seeks to counteract. In addition, I believe that every encouragement should be given to ex-spouses to settle their financial affairs in a final way so that they can put their mistakes behind them and get on with their lives. I would, with all due respect, reject the Manitoba Court of Appeal's broad and unrestricted interpretation of the court's jurisdiction in maintenance matters. It seems to me that it goes against the main stream of recent authority, both legislative and judicial, which emphasized mediation, conciliation and negotiation as the appropriate means of settling the affairs of the spouses when the marriage relationship dissolves.[15]

In other words, in this instance Wilson acknowledged the obligation of submitting to properly constituted authority. The revised legislation embodied a significant shift in social consensus about the equality of women as economic actors and rational contracting parties, representing a movement away from a former presumption of inequality which had reinforced gender bias.

The final component of the support variation test which emerged out of Wilson's statutory analysis in Pelech was the extremely tough requirement of a demonstrable connection between the changed financial circumstances of the indigent former spouse and the relationship between the spouses during the marriage itself – the so-called causal connection test. One might consider this requirement to be at odds with Wilson's endorsement of a more Humean scepticism about causality in the Olbey case; but if she was not always so single-mindedly linear, she did consistently display her respect for policy embodying properly constituted legislative authority. On the facts in *Pelech*, the appellant's hardship arose out of her mental health problems which predated the marriage and were not directly caused by it, although they may have been exacerbated by it. Wilson was invariably compassionate towards those with mental health problems, a possibility she considered here and rejected based on the trial judge's finding of fact that Mr Pelech had not been cruel to his wife. Accordingly, given that Mrs Pelech could not demonstrate causal connection, she could not succeed in her variation application.

Wilson had suggested that standard principles of contract analysis might be used to set aside support contracts without offending policy considerations. A party bringing an application to vary tacitly acknowledges in doing so that the original contract is valid. But would the contract in this case have been deemed valid if the cause of action had been framed differently? Surely the very fact that Mr Pelech knew that Mrs Pelech had suffered from substantial and incapacitating psychological illness before and during the marriage and that she was still so afflicted at the time the contract was negotiated ought to have raised the issue of whether there could have been effective equality of bargaining power at the time the contract was negotiated. The trial judge who had originally granted the variation order, which was subsequently overturned on appeal, had found that the mere existence of independent legal advice was sufficient to rebut any suggestion of unconscionability but no evidence seems to have been led as to whether or not Mrs Pelech's lawyer was even aware of her history of mental illness. If Mrs Pelech had brought an application to set aside the contract, contract analysis could have been applied to determine whether the particular contract between Mr and Mrs Pelech was unconscionable because of the failure of the negotiating process to take into account her mental disability.

Was Mrs Pelech (without denigration of the rational capacity of women generally, but in the context of her particular circumstances) capable of rational and autonomous choice? Had the correct issue been remitted to the Court for decision, there might very well have been sufficient evidence of improvidence coupled with inequality of bargaining power to challenge the validity of the contract so that it might have been set aside without disturbing the aspirational force of the normative legislation relating to applications for variation which Wilson wanted to uphold. A number of cases had already established that improvidence plus inequality was the appropriate test for unconscionability in the matrimonial contract context and Wilson's 'Variation' paper indicates that she was familiar with them.

The judgments in the two remaining cases in the trilogy – *Richardson* and *Caron* – are much shorter. Both are contractual spousal support cases, both were applications for variation and not applications to set aside, and in each instance there were also factual circumstances which could have permitted the Court to find the contract void had it been offered the opportunity of doing so.

Certainly the facts in *Richardson* were troubling. Upon separation after a marriage of twelve years but with the benefit of independent legal advice, the forty-six-year-old wife signed a contract relinquishing all her rights to the matrimonial home. In return, she was provided with only modest spousal support for a period of only one year. The husband's evidence indicated that he anticipated that his wife would be able to support herself by returning to the kind of clerical work she had engaged in prior to her marriage and for brief periods during the marriage, but there was no evidence at all of the wife's expectations.[16]

No job materialized and Mrs Richardson was on welfare at the time of her application for a variation order. In Wilson's view, the possibility that Mrs Richardson would not be employed at the end of the one-year period was not unforeseeable and therefore her unemployed status could not constitute a radical change in circumstances. She considered that Mrs Richardson's record of sporadic employment during the marriage ought to have been sufficient to sustain her clerical skills; therefore her inability to find work was not necessarily permanent and not causally connected to the fact of the marriage.

The dissenting judgment by Justice LaForest pointed to the rapid changes in clerical skill requirements which had evolved out of the computerization of the workplace during the period of Mrs Richardson's absence from it. In his view, Mrs Richardson's inability to find work was causally connected to the domestic arrangements which the parties had agreed upon during the course of their marriage. Moreover, LaForest took into account the ongoing childcare responsibilities which would impede her job search and her employment flexibility in an increasingly competitive job market.

Causal connection aside, if the case had been brought as an application to set aside there would have been the option of declaring the contract void, by using the contract principle of unilateral mistake. There was also evidence that counsel for Mr Pelech had inserted into the typewritten version of the Minutes of Settlement a finality clause which had not been included in the original handwritten draft and which Mrs Richardson might not have understood, although she signed it.

In *Caron*,[17] Wilson framed the issue of the Court's residual discretion to vary based upon a change in circumstances causally connected to the marriage. What is a little confusing, however, is that a good deal of her own analysis is most obviously relevant to the issue of validity of contract which was once again not before the Court. The husband had invoked a clause which provided that support payments would be permanently discontinued if the wife either remarried or cohabited with a new partner as man and wife for a period of greater than ninety days. Mrs Caron did enter into a sexual relationship but her new partner did not provide her with any financial support. Although it would have been open to her to do so in an application to set aside, Mrs Caron failed to argue that this new partnership did not constitute cohabitation within the meaning of the contract clause; Wilson wrote:

> I should emphasize at this point that the appellant did not argue that on a proper construction of the agreement 'cohabitation' meant more than simply living together and included the notion that the wife would be supported by her new partner. In fact, it is agreed that she received no support from him. It might have been argued, therefore, that the conditions for the cessation of maintenance from the husband were not really met. Parties to a contract are, however, free to give their own meaning to a word and have that meaning govern. Neither has disputed the fact that the contingency in paragraph 3 which disentitled the wife to maintenance took place. Each accepted that 'cohabitation as man and wife' meant simply engaging in sexual relations while living in the same dwelling. The clause as understood and intended by the parties would appear, therefore, to have been properly invoked by the respondent.[18]

Of course, Mrs Caron's failure to challenge the husband's cessation of maintenance was not necessarily evidence that the two parties to the agreement were of the same mind on the meaning of the cohabitation clause; she was bringing an application for a variation and had not contested the validity of the contract. The judgment did not take into account the possibility that, even though she had had legal advice, Mrs Caron might not have realized that she had the option of attacking her husband's interpretation of the clause. And it could not, given that the issue before the Court was whether or not to vary the maintenance which contractually had been eliminated upon commencement of the cohabitation.

In this instance Wilson reasoned:

> I think the appellant must be taken to have been aware of the significance of the latter provision [that each party was free to bring proceedings against the other to enforce any of the terms of the agreement] in the context of her agreement in paragraph 3 that cohabitation for a period in excess of 90 days would disentitle her to maintenance. She must have envisioned that if she cohabited for the prescribed period of time with another man, she was putting her right to maintenance from her husband in jeopardy.

The Supreme Court justices found these cases disturbing and there was considerably more discussion about them, particularly between Wilson and LaForest, than was customary. Each of these cases evoked sympathy for the impoverished women. Analysis of the facts in light of contract doctrine could have made it possible to attack the spousal support agreements themselves. Unfortunately, all the causes of action were framed as applications for variation resting on the parties' implicit acknowledgment that the contracts were valid when made. None of the appellants' lawyers made application to set aside the spousal support contracts; had they done so, Wilson herself believes that one or more of the appellants might have been successful.

That Wilson decided these cases as she did could not be a failure of feminist principle, given that she did not subscribe to such principles in any conventionally politicized sense. Instead, we can see in these controversial judgments a reflection of Wilson's respect for the duly constituted authority of a legislated policy reflective of a shift in social consensus about the role of the family and the relationship between public and private responsibility. And we can see also her somewhat reluctant acceptance of the fact that a judge cannot substitute as advocate when the appellant's own counsel has made a fatal error in preparing the pleadings.

In 1993, six years after *Pelech*, came the Supreme Court decision in

Moge.[19] These were six years of enormous change in social consensus about both the legal and the moral dimensions of spousal support, based in part upon new data demonstrating the gap between the earnings potential of men and women. Mrs Moge, in late middle age and relatively destitute after a long marriage during which her own employability was diminished because she had taken most of the responsibility for childcare, was found to be entitled to ongoing and permanent support from her former husband, although in a relatively small amount. *Moge* initiated a compensatory model, taking into account economic disadvantage to women arising out of the circumstances of the marriage in determining support awards when the parties had not come to any binding agreement. It is the domestic labour associated with child-rearing which generates the economic tensions throwing into sharpest relief the conflict between sameness and difference feminisms, the judgment noted. And after *Moge*, in noncontractual situations this compensatory analysis largely replaced the self-sufficiency model; in general, spousal support decisions resulted in larger awards for longer, indefinite and even permanent time periods.

There is a wryness in Wilson's acknowledgment of the criticisms which the *Pelech* trilogy had attracted: 'The Court was called upon in a trilogy of cases to determine the binding effect of domestic contracts' is her phrasing, not claiming credit or admitting blame, although most Canadian students of law would remember she had written these controversial judgments.

But Wilson still subscribes to the view that the courts cannot and should not interfere with the parties' right to negotiate a contractual resolution to their own affairs at the end of a marriage, particularly when they have obtained independent legal advice. The concept of unconscionability is sufficiently flexible, in her opinion, to permit the courts to take into account Charter principles of equality and fairness without assuming a wide-open discretion to make whatever contract for the parties it considered appropriate. And in particular, Wilson would like to see the Supreme Court provide leadership to the courts below in articulating what role the principle of equality should play in relation to the economic equality of the parties after dissolution of a marriage, taking into consideration their relative economic situations before and during their marriage.

But the Supreme Court seems to be more and more off on a frolic of its own. In *Bracklow*,[20] a unanimous 1999 Supreme Court decision, McLachlin found that in a post-divorce situation when the facts fell short of triggering a compensatory award and there was no separation agreement establishing contractual entitlement to spousal support, a healthy ex-spouse might still remain on the hook to support a sick spouse long after a marriage has ended. The wife seems to have been deemed eligible for support simply because she was disabled with psychiatric problems, unable to support herself, unquestionably in need, and had a former husband with the ability to pay.

Is this shift in public opinion, if it has occurred, the result of ethical concern about endemic poverty among elderly women? And if so, does it reflect merely a self-interested rejection of shared public responsibility for relieving that poverty in favour of shifting that responsibility back to a blameless former spouse on the part of those who have somehow managed to keep their own marriages intact and want to keep their taxes as low as possible? The problem with a standard case-by-case means and needs analysis is that it abandons the principle that the parties have both the right and the corresponding responsibility to settle their own affairs; it commits the courts to a permanent supervisory role. The Supreme Court decision in *Bracklow* seems adrift in unanchored contextualism; Wilson's contextualism had always required the application or the modification of an established legal principle to the contingencies of the specific fact situation.

THE BEST INTERESTS OF THE CHILD

As we have seen, the family is the central institution of society for Wilson, primarily because of its traditional role in the protection and nurturing and moral education of children. In her 1985 paper 'Children: The Casualties of a Failed Marriage,'[21] she reveals how troubled she was by the unprecedented increase in the dissolution of family homes which had followed the liberalization of divorce laws in 1968. Parents were asserting their legal right to end their marriages but neither parents nor the courts had accorded sufficient attention to the responsibility of ensuring that marriage breakdown did not impoverish children financially or traumatize them psychologically.

The paper surveys the subject of child custody following divorce. In her view, children's custody law must adopt a strongly normative stance 'to encourage separated or divorced parents to co-operate in the upbringing of their children.' She justifies this public intrusion into the private realm of parent-child relationships on the grounds that child custody affects the whole community since 'what is in the best interests of our children is surely in the best interests of us all.'

Wilson was to dissent in *Frame* v. *Smith*,[22] another custody case and another instance in which she expressed zealous concern to protect the interests of men – this time as fathers – at least insofar as these interests are inextricably related to the interests of their children. This was a case in which the wife had been awarded custody of the three children of the marriage with generous access privileges afforded to the husband. However, the husband alleged that upon remarriage the mother had done everything possible to frustrate his lawful access to his children. She told them he was no longer their father. She moved them to distant cities without notifying their father, changed their religion and last name, intercepted his letters and refused his telephone calls. Mr Frame sought to recover damages in tort from his former wife, the new Mrs Smith, for the expenses he had incurred in seeking to exercise access and for his severe emotional distress. The majority of the Court held that the family law legislation constituted a complete code barring further civil action and found also that to permit such an action would in itself not be in the best interests of the children because it would exacerbate emotional upheaval and divert financial resources from their support.

In her dissenting reasons Wilson agreed that the tort action was not contemplated by the legislation, was not congruent with its best interests rationale, and was unlikely to generate the desired remedy (since costs would not compensate for continued denial of access). Wilson nevertheless would have allowed fiduciary principles to be applied in order to effect the access ordered by the Court when such orders are deliberately flouted in a manner constituting intentional infliction of mental suffering. The custodial parent has a fiduciary duty to exercise his or her custodial rights in the best interests of the children; the right of the child to sustain a relationship with the non-custodial parent ought to be afforded the protection of the courts. Her succinct formulation in *Frame* v. *Smith* of the three elements of fiduciariness has become the standard test applied in almost every subsequent case which invokes fiduciary duty across all categories of Canadian law.[23]

Once again, Wilson advocated a strong normative role for law, this time in creating incentives for custodial parents to permit the exercise of rights accorded to non-custodial parents by court order. Since the order is made only after court determination that it is in the best interests of the child to maintain a relationship with the non-custodial parent, the court has in effect been shirking its obligation to ensure that the order is carried out. Because any breach of a fiduciary duty triggers an equitable remedy which can be specifically tailored by the courts to the actual circumstances of the breach and to the best interests of the child, Wilson was confident that judges could be creative in designing appropriate incentives if this new avenue of redress were opened up.

As a further safeguard for the economic security and emotional health of children, she specified that she would restrict a cause of action for breach of fiduciary duty in the context of obstruction of court-ordered access to those cases where there could be no risk of interference with the financial support of the child and no danger that it would invoke a harmful conflict of loyalties in the child between the custodial and non-custodial parents. And certainly (unless there was fresh evidence indicating that the custodial parent had fallen down on the job in many aspects of the child's care) it would be wrong to reverse a custody order to punish a non-cooperative custodial parent, since such a variation would assume that the original order had not in fact been in the child's best interests.[24]

The remedy for a breach of fiduciary duty is an equitable rather than a common law remedy; the relationship between the child and the non-custodial parent is not a creation of law but exists independently of it prior to the court order. Wilson contemplated a quantum of compensation which would be sufficient for the non-custodial parent to recover out-of-pocket expenses incurred in the frustration of his access and added on a further award for any pain and suffering resulting from the loss of his relationship with the child. In total, the sum could very well be enough to provide a substantial incentive to the custodial parent to acquiesce. And for Wilson that would be a good thing, given that the relevant legislation creates a properly constituted authority reflecting a social consensus about the role both parents should play in the lives of their children after the dissolution of the original family unit. Unfortunately, however, given that post-divorce poverty is frequent in women-led households, one cannot imagine many situations in which the criteria she establishes to protect a child from harm arising out of such an award could be met.

The analysis might be different if one considered the child rather than the non-custodial parent (generally, the father) in the role of beneficiary. The access order is made for the benefit of and in the best interests of the child. The custodial parent (generally the mother) as fiduciary is in a position to exercise unilateral power which affects the child-beneficiary; it is the child who is extraordinarily vulnerable to the fiduciary and unable to challenge the power without further threatening the security of his relationship to his mother. If the child is the beneficiary and the child's equitable right has been breached, then the equitable remedy is owed to the child.

An equitable remedy need not be a financial one; the court can make binding declarations of right (the child's right to the court-ordered access) or order specific performance, requiring the mother to deliver up the child for the access. In equity, of course, a court can also order damages, damages which might be placed in trust to provide the child with the psychological help he may well require if his ongoing relationship with his father continued to be thwarted. One can imagine that a mother required by court order to place some portion of her income into such a trust would take very seriously indeed the potential of psychological harm created by her non-cooperation with the access order.

Not all the cases involving children which Wilson was called upon to decide arose out of divorce situations. Early in her tenure at the Supreme Court a rather sad saga came up out of the Newfoundland courts[25] involving a small boy who had been removed because of allegations of abuse from the home of a couple, a Mr and Mrs Beson, who wished to adopt him as a brother for their older child, Larry. It was agreed that these allegations were unfounded. Nevertheless, during the investigation of the allegations and without informing the Besons, the Newfoundland director of child welfare had placed young Christopher in a second home. The second set of parents, a Mr and Mrs Jones, were also eager to adopt him. The trial judge had recommended that the director reverse his decision permitting the Joneses to adopt the boy but found he had no power to make an order returning the child to the Besons. The Court of Appeal had held that as a matter of administrative law the relevant statutory provisions provided a complete code and that even though it was found as a fact that the director had made the decision unfairly (acting upon completely unsubstantiated allegations from a source known to be unreliable), the action was within the scope of his statutory discretionary power and the court had no power to review his decision or to substitute its own opinion. The Court of Appeal confirmed the trial judge's disposition.

Once again, Wilson had a real battle trying to persuade her colleagues that leave to appeal should be granted and that every effort should be made to ensure that the best possible counsel were retained; fortunately, the attorney general of Newfoundland was convinced that this was an important case and offered to pay the lawyers representing both sets of parents.[26] And once the case had been heard, Wilson wrote the unanimous decision of the Court finding that Christopher should be returned to the Besons for adoption.

Her reasoning invoked a 'legislative gap' approach. The adoption legislation was deficient because it had failed to incorporate the best interests of the child doctrine as enshrined in the more general child welfare statute. In Wilson's analysis, the trial judge had a positive obligation under the circumstances to intervene through the court's inherent power to fill gaps, as specifically justified by the *parens patriae* doctrine (the state's residual duty to take on parental responsibilities) which is the most explicit common law justification for state transgression into the sanctity of private family life. What was necessary was a determination whether or not it had been in the child's best interests to remove him from his first adoptive home.

The function of the lawyer appointed to represent a child is not to determine the child's best interests, Wilson cautioned, but merely to put forward the child's wishes. In cases where the child's wishes cannot be determined, the child's lawyer must ensure that complete information (usually obtained through psychological assessment) is placed before the court. But it is always the court's duty to sift through the evidence to determine the option which in the long run will best protect the child's interests. Wilson was aware that for young children judges are in general reluctant to make a change in custody arrangements after six months, but she also recognized that a fixed policy of never disturbing existing custody arrangements would only encourage manoeuvres to establish de facto possession and undermine the court's proper decision-making responsibility. In this instance Christopher had spent only six months with the Besons prior to the intervention of the director and his most recent ten months had been spent with the Joneses. Nevertheless, Wilson found that it was in the child's best interests to return to the Beson family, in part because Mrs Beson did not work outside the home as Mrs Jones did, and because the Besons had the financial resources to ensure Christopher an opportunity of pursuing post-secondary education in the future.

In other words, despite her principled embrace of a variety of family arrangements, her analysis led her back to a preference for full-time mothering and economic security, just as it did in the aboriginal case of *Racine* v. *Woods*. And there is considerable evidence that Wilson's understanding was not at odds with a broad social consensus on the topic then or for some time to come.

These are hard cases where a judge can never be sure she has made the right decision. It must have been reassuring to read the story of young Christopher's reunion with the Besons the day following release of the judgment. By this point the little boy was five and he had not seen the Besons for twenty-two months. But he immediately recognized them as they walked towards him, calling out eagerly, 'There's mom and dad and Larry.' Among the Wilsons' papers was a clipping from the front page of the *Gander Beacon* with a picture of Christopher grinning widely as he nestled into Mr Beson's arms beside his big brother, his mother, and his new baby sister.

VIOLENCE AGAINST WOMEN AND CHILDREN

A number of the cases which Wilson helped to decide at the Supreme Court involved violence against women and children and for the most part these are the cases in which her judgments won her the praise of the feminists. *Lavallée*,[27] which introduced a significant shift in the standard of gendered subjectivity on the Canadian law of self-defence, received almost unanimous approval.

Angelique Lavallée, only twenty-two, had been living with Kevin 'Rooster' Rust for three or four years. Their relationship had been tempestuous, marked by arguments and physical violence. Lavallée had required hospital treatment for severe bruising and contusions, a broken nose, and a black eye. On at least one previous occasion a witness had seen Rust threaten Lavallée with a gun.

Rust was killed when the couple got into a fight after a party. Almost everyone had left but a few remaining guests heard shoving and thumping and yells from the couple's bedroom. Neighbours had also heard the quarrel and testified that Rust sounded argumentative and Lavallée sounded frightened. Lavallée told the investigating police officer that Rust had found her hiding in the closet, yanked her out, pushed her around, and slapped her on the head. He handed his gun to her. She was very frightened and thought about shooting herself. He told her, 'Wait till everybody leaves, you'll get it then. Either you kill me or I'll get you.' Then as he turned to leave the room, she shot him in the head.

At the trial Lavallée was acquitted, based on the defence of self-defence. Lavallée did not testify. Some of the expert evidence tendered by a psychiatrist with experience in the treatment of battered women was held inadmissible because not supported by the factual foundation, but the trial judge had refused the crown attorney's application to have the evidence withdrawn in its entirety and instructed the jury as to what evidence should be considered. The Manitoba Court of Appeal ordered a new trial on the basis that the expert evidence should have been excluded in its entirety or that the charge to the jury should have been more specific with respect to those elements of the expert's testimony which it ought to have ignored. Lavallée appealed to the Supreme Court. At issue was the question whether the expert's testimony ought to have been admitted and if so whether the trial judge's charge to the jury had provided sufficient warning that in reading a verdict it ought not to rely upon facts that had not been proved in evidence.

The appeal was heard on 31 October 1989 and Wilson's bench notes were relatively brief. At the judicial conference following the hearing she volunteered to write the judgment. Everyone headed for their offices. The other judges frequently took the stairs for exercise but Wilson's arthritis and Dickson's war wounds meant that they quite often rode up in the elevator together. As Wilson remembers it, Dickson turned to her and asked with astonishment, 'Why on earth would you volunteer to write on that one?' After the customary initial polling of reaction, it looked as if the chances of the appeal being allowed were negligible. 'He thought it was an open and shut case. That she [Lavallée] had had it.'

The decision was released on 3 May 1990 and during the intervening months, Wilson had done a great deal of reading for her 'Will Women Judges Really Make a Difference?' speech. As she prepared for this lecture she began to reconsider *Lavallée* from a fresh perspective:

It was when I was writing that [speech] and thinking about it that I realized that there were quite a number of aspects of the law that needed to be re-thought from a gender perspective and that was one, that was a chance to begin doing it by looking at the defence of self-defence and how it was essentially male oriented. And I thought to myself, now here is a chance to give some leadership to what I have said in my speech that some aspects of the law must be reviewed because of the male bias and that was a chance to do that but you know the more I thought that the more I realized how many areas that needs to happen.

Of all the Wilson judgments, this is the one in which the outcome relies most heavily on expert testimony from the social sciences. Shifts in

social consensus cannot be effectively legislated but properly constituted authority in law depends in part upon common law responsiveness to shifts in social consensus. And if the law has a duty to create
such shifts, then the courts can influence the current state of consensus
through judicial admission of relevant sociological and psychological
studies.

Criminal law is primarily concerned with subjective guilt, and intention is a required element for conviction in most criminal offences. But
central to the statutory defence of self-defence is the objective standard
of the reasonable person. The accused will be exonerated in his use of
force to repel assault if he has a reasonable apprehension of death or
grievous bodily harm from his assailant and if he believes on reasonable
grounds that counterattack is his only alternative to suffering serious
injury or death. As Wilson explained, what made expert evidence necessary in this case was the lag between general social consensus and new
scientific research:

> Expert evidence on the psychological effect of battering on wives and com-
> mon law partners must, it seems to me, be both relevant and necessary in
> the context of the present case. How can the mental state of the appellant be
> appreciated without it? The average member of the public (or of the jury)
> can be forgiven for asking: Why would a woman put up with this kind of
> treatment? How could she love a partner who beat her to the point of
> requiring hospitalization? We would expect the woman to pack her bags
> and go. Where is her self-respect? Such is the reaction of the average person
> confronted with the so called 'battered wife syndrome.' We need help to
> understand it and help is available from trained professionals.[28]

Drawing upon the testimony of the expert witness, Wilson pointed to
the assessment of the degree of threat which an abused woman must
decide she is under, and she alone is able to predict the onset of a subsequent attack. Only she can judge whether a novel form of violence signals that the degree of danger to her in a given episode was different
from the episodes which she had previously survived. So it is up to the
jury to decide whether or not it is reasonable for a battered woman in an
abusive relationship – taking into account the relative size and strength
of the woman and her assailant – to act when she has the opportunity or
to wait until the promised assault is under way.

This is an extremely contextual standard which nevertheless does
retain residual traces of objectivity. Such an act of self-defence would be

justified, in Wilson's view, not whenever any reasonable battered woman would have perceived her life to be in danger but only in those circumstances in which, according to the research, a reasonable battered woman caught up in a cycle of acts of violence would have interpreted a similar change in the intensity of a specific act of violence as signalling imminent death or serious harm requiring pre-emptive action.

And Wilson was persuasive. Lavallée's appeal was allowed and the acquittal restored. Every member of the Court signed on to her reasons for judgment with the exception of Sopinka, who wrote a separate concurrence.[29] Wilson had worked very hard and she could not help but be jubilant that justice had been done for Lavellée:

> So I have always seen that case as the biggest mystery of all my judgments because how it ended up was as a unanimous judgment when they all thought I was mad to think that there was anything that could even be said in her favour. So that was really interesting, but it did show me one thing, it showed me that if you have done your homework and you could present a case in a plausible and forceful way, then male judges would move.

Justice had also been done for women by successfully challenging the apparently neutral (but deeply gendered) standard of self-defence. Wilson herself considers her *Lavallée* decision to be one of her most important contributions to the development of Canadian law.[30] Nevertheless, the *Lavallée* battered-wife defence continues to be a controversial one where the courts are still split, sometimes along gendered lines.

Wilson was pleased when in late 1995 Justice Minister Allan Rock asked Madam Justice Lynn Ratushny of the Ontario Court to review the pre-1990 cases of more than ninety women who said that they too had killed in self-defence and requested a review of their sentences. Ratushny ultimately recommended that four women be given complete freedom, the sentence of one be reduced and that another be given a new hearing; forty-nine cases did not merit reopening and thirty women had served their full sentences, but the solicitor general opted for further review of the legal principles before acting on these recommendations. And since then, a 1998 Supreme Court judgment has affirmed a narrow application of the gendered self-defence doctrine confined to the reasonableness of the woman's expectation of violence in the context of her own experience in order to evade creation of a battered wife syndrome which might constitute a new stereotype.

There was almost no public awareness and little scientific study of wife beating when Wilson was at the Court of Appeal. Wilson's wide reading in the academic literature of the late 1980s and early 1990s on the post-divorce feminization of poverty and on family violence has persuaded her that many women are trapped in abusive relationships because of their subservient financial status, a status which often arises out of the gendered allocation of labour within the family during the course of the marriage.

A month earlier Wilson had addressed the national convention of B'Nai Brith Women on the subject of increasing violence against women and children. She condemned the treatment of women and children by law enforcement agencies and the courts after incidents of rape and incest and the shortfall in funding for shelters and foster homes which closes down avenues of escape. Both of these factors were connected in her own mind with the historic separation of the private and public realms, as this separation redounds to the benefit of men and the disadvantage of women and children:

> I believe that ultimately we must give full effect in our society to the principle of equality. Women will never have equal status with men in the home if they don't also have equal status with men in the world outside. Violence against women in the home is an expression and manifestation of power and is perpetuated by the fact that men do and women do not have power in our society. The economic, political and social inequality of women both fuels and justifies violence against women in a society which values power over all else. Saddest of all, those groups of women who are more unequal than others – women who are disabled, women who belong to ethnic minorities, and women who are senior citizens – are the most vulnerable and the most in need of support.[31]

Her analysis reveals the problem to be a systemic and public rather that a personal or private one and illustrates once again Wilson's sensitivity to the potential for multiple discriminatory effects arising out of the intersecting factors of gender and race and class.

Even so, Wilson retained her characteristic Scottish Enlightenment optimism about the possibility that men –through education, once they have come to see the injustice which the current system perpetuates – would voluntarily relinquish their power:

> Men must work along with women to achieve sexual equality because the problem is one between the sexes. Men must come to acknowledge that the

problem is really theirs; women are simply the victims of a system which has traditionally reflected male interests and favoured the male viewpoint. In the search for systemic remedies men must be willing to cast aside their own system for the simple reason that justice demands it.

This is not a feminist rant, although it might read as one to those unfamiliar with Wilson's equal fervour for defending the rights of men. It is typical of Wilson's peculiarly pragmatic and postmodern faith in the common humanity of men and women that she remains confident that men can be just as decent as women or that (failing altruism) propriety alone will be sufficient to motivate moral behaviour.

This optimism was most fully tested in the criminal cases involving violence against children which Wilson worked on very hard and where she was successful more often than not in achieving a majority. Her judgments show that she took a hard line in cases where children experienced the damaging betrayal of violence within the family and in the institutions closest to it – the neighbourhood, and the school. On the other hand, in cases involving absolute liability for consensual sexual activity with under-age girls she expressed considerable concern for the protection of the rights of the accused – a stance which might have disappointed those who expected her to be an overtly feminist judge. And Wilson's dissent in *Hill*,[32] in which she would have allowed the defence of provocation by a teenager who murdered his Big Brother after a homosexual assault, was a grave disappointment to supporters in the gay and lesbian community.

PROSTITUTION AND FREEDOM OF EXPRESSION

Although it was frequently difficult for Wilson to persuade her colleagues to hear family law cases – many of them believed that these matters were simply not important enough to take up court time – when violence triggered criminal charges, the cases obviously ought to be heard. Wilson, although labelled a feminist judge, was consistently concerned to protect the rights of the accused, who were overwhelmingly male. And for Wilson, this commitment is a kind of test of the civility of a society, linked to the anti-majoritarian nature of rights and to the common humanity which all judges ought to seek to uphold:

As judges, we should ask ourselves which groups are most likely to be ignored in the making of legislation. The poor, the oppressed, the powerless, racial minorities, accused criminals – even in the healthiest of democracies, these groups are typically shut out of the political process. When assessing the rights of individuals from these groups, we must be particularly vigilant. I believe that the true test of rights is how well they serve the less privileged and least popular segments of the society.[33]

Neither 'women' nor 'children' were groups included in Wilson's list of the oppressed and powerless. Nevertheless, prostitution and abortion are both issues which could be framed in relation to violence experienced by women and children and also in relation to attempts by the state to control women's sexuality. Children have never been provided with any direct voice in the political process, and there is little doubt that women had been shut out of the political process of drafting the applicable legislation. But in several of Wilson's most notable cases at the Supreme Court she was compelled to deal with these hot political issues.

In late 1988 a trilogy of cases[34] concerning prostitution came up to the Supreme Court. Municipalities were struggling to control an ever-increasing problem with prostitution-related street nuisance, complaining that property values were lowered, sidewalks blocked and children exposed to degrading practices because of the sex trade. They had welcomed the Tory government's 1985 introduction of amendments to the Criminal Code which made communication for the purposes of solicitation illegal. These were huge cases, with submissions from attorneys general across the country, and there was an enormous amount of public interest even before the hearings. The judgments were not released until late May of 1990. The majority at the Supreme Court held that the impugned Criminal Code provisions did not infringe Charter guarantees. And not surprisingly, Wilson dissented in all three.

Wilson had had a particular interest in prostitution from her period of studies with the United Church theology group during the early years at Oslers and she was aware that her attitude to prostitution was different from the other members on the Court. She was particularly offended by the indirectness of the analysis dealing with freedom of expression in the *Reference* case majority decision. In her opinion, no government could be justified in attempting to control a social problem (street congestion from cruising johns, the substantial street nuisance created by used condoms and hypodermic needles) by specifying which meanings of certain expressive activities are permitted and which are not:

I believe we see in this case a good example of government's attempt to deal with the harmful consequences of expressive activity, not by dealing directly with the consequences, but by placing constraints on the meaning sought to be conveyed by a particular expressive activity. Rather than deal directly with the variety of harmful consequences which ... flow from the communicative act, [the statute] prohibits the communicative act itself ... [T]his is a case where the government's purpose is to restrict the content of expression by singling out meanings that are not to be conveyed in the hope that this will deal with the physical consequences emanating from expressive activity that carries the prohibited meaning.[35]

The provision permitted a criminal sanction to be imposed without any onus on the crown to show that any particular expressive act – perhaps a nod or a wink of an innocent citizen or someone seeking to flag down a taxi – had in itself led to the undesirable consequences which the legislation purported to control. For example, in neither *Skinner* nor *Stagnitta* was there evidence to show that the activities of these two accused persons had in fact stopped traffic or contributed directly to any of the other adverse impacts associated with prostitution. Even if these impacts were a legitimately pressing and substantial concern, the proportionality test in section 1 could not possibly be satisfied by a provision which criminalized communication in any place open to public view whether or not it had in fact occurred in public view:

Such a broad prohibition as to the locale of the communication would seem to go far beyond a genuine concern over the nuisance caused by street solicitation in Canada's major centres of population. It enables the police to arrest citizens who are disturbing no one solely because they are engaged in communicative acts concerning something not prohibited by the Code. It is not reasonable, in my view, to prohibit *all* expressive activity conveying a certain meaning that takes place in public simply because in *some* circumstances and in *some* areas that activity *may* give rise to a public or social nuisance.[36]

Prostitution is not a crime, and Wilson speculated that this is so perhaps because society recognizes that the real victim of prostitution is often the prostitute herself; that it would be wrong to jail female prostitutes and permit their customers to go free; or that prostitution is a time-honoured and generally private activity which meets a social need. For

Wilson, the deliberate omission of prostitution from the Criminal Code signals a consensus that activities only tangentially associated with prostitution cannot possibly warrant severe punitive sanctions. The provision for actual deprivation of liberty based upon an unwarranted curtailment of freedom of expression must necessarily also offend the section 7 guarantees.

Wilson applied a similar kind of analysis to the freedom of association issue discussed in *Skinner*, with a characteristic insistence on the necessary intersection of Charter rights, which she justifies in part with reference to an earlier Supreme Court decision.[37] In Wilson's view, the right to freedom of association is not limited to the right to create or belong to an association; any 'coming together' is protected (although there is no guarantee that the actual activities that the individuals wish to pursue together are protected) because 'in a wide range of instances the freedoms guaranteed in section 2 of the Charter would be of little value if one could not engage in them with others.[38]

Once again, as in the *Big M* freedom of religion case which had challenged Sunday closing laws, Wilson turned to a purposive and effects-based approach as primary stage analysis that requires a pragmatic and contextual awareness of outcomes in particular circumstances. Whether or not the purpose of the impugned legislation had been to curtail freedom of association in connection with the legitimate commercial negotiations necessary for the sale of a legal service (and Wilson clearly thought that it was), the statutory definition of public place is so expansive that the effect of the provision restricts association severely. In any event, the proportionality test embedded in section 1 could not be met because the crown was not required to show in any given instance that the negotiating process has actually given rise to the street nuisance which the legislation purportedly intended to control. The *Globe and Mail* editorial denounced the anti-soliciting law as a 'sledgehammer,' expressed its disappointment with the majority decision upholding that sledgehammer and singled out Wilson for particular praise.[39]

Nevertheless, the two clerks Wilson had assigned to work on this trilogy of cases were disappointed that she had not been willing to expand the definition of section 7 rights to include an economic right to earn a living, given that there can be little meaningful security of the person without financial security. Although the clerks worked hard to make their economic analysis persuasive, ultimately she remained unconvinced. Wilson concluded that the reading-in of an economic right simply could not be reconciled with the jurisprudence already in place dealing with section 7. This was an incident which confirmed that Wilson took her responsibility as a judge very seriously and that, although she welcomed the opinions of her clerks, she was always in control of her own chambers and her own reasons for judgment.

ABORTION, PRIVACY, AND THE AMBIVALENCE OF CHOICE

The 1988 *Morgentaler*[40] decision, in which the Supreme Court struck down the provisions in the Criminal Code that made abortion illegal on the grounds that they offended basic freedoms entrenched in the Charter, was for Wilson 'the most important decision to date in Canada dealing with woman's privacy rights as against the state.'[41] Wilson knew the dilemma of abortion and realized that it is always a hard choice but thought for some women under certain circumstances it may be the most responsible alternative. She had never forgotten the anguish of her friend who had sought her out for advice when she was working as the dentists' receptionist in Ottawa in the early 1950s. She could not withhold her support, and had to acknowledge that the pregnant woman was in the best position to decide whether or not she could cope with the birth of a child.

And abortion was an issue which she had also explored from a more academic and theoretical perspective when she had begun chairing the United Church committee on abortion shortly before her appointment to the Court of Appeal. The report was released in 1980 but remained highly controversial; it was certainly not uniformly endorsed by church members. In 1985 at the height of the demonstrations held in front of the Toronto Morgentaler clinic, the Wilsons were proud when their good friend, the Reverend Stanford Lucyk of Toronto's Timothy Eaton Church, preached a courageous sermon explaining why the official United Church position on human sexuality incorporated a pro-choice stance on abortion.[42]

Morgentaler had first begun performing abortions in a Montreal clinic in 1968, been charged and then acquitted by a jury in 1973, with the acquittal overturned by the Quebec Court of Appeal in 1974. Sentenced to eighteen months, he served ten, suffered a heart attack and was acquitted at a retrial on the original charges in 1976; the Parti Québécois government declared an end to prosecutions of Morgentaler because the law was unworkable. With abortions available almost on demand in Quebec, Morgentaler set out to extend reproductive freedom to women throughout Canada.

In June of 1983 he was charged after opening a clinic in Winnipeg; the following month, he was charged at his Toronto clinic. But by 1983 Morgentaler could make use of a new legal scalpel; his defence this time was that the abortion law violated Charter rights. At trial, although the Ontario court held against him on the Charter issue, social consensus had swung in his favour: he was acquitted by a jury. The crown appealed, the Ontario Court of Appeal ordered a new trial, and Morgentaler appealed to the Supreme Court in 1986. The case was heard over four days in October, but the judgment was not released until late January of 1988.

Morgentaler, a Holocaust survivor born in 1923, had emigrated to Canada in the late 1940s; he graduated in medicine from University of Montreal in 1955 and for twelve years ran a general practice. But in 1967 he had testified before a parliamentary committee on Canada's abortion laws where his comment that abortion should be seen 'not as a privilege but as a right' was widely publicized. After that, women sought him out for abortion services and Morgentaler felt he had to help them. Over the twenty-year period leading up to the Supreme Court decision, Morgentaler had performed some twenty thousand abortions and had paid a huge personal cost for clinging to his principles. He endured two failed marriages, ill health, massive debt, and death threats.

There were floods of letters into the Supreme Court both before the hearings and prior to the release of the judgment. Wilson was still the only woman on the Supreme Court when *Morgentaler* was heard; because there was a certain awareness of her previous work for the United Church committee on abortion, or perhaps because at any rate she was considered a feminist, a lot of this mail was directed to her. Many letters were anonymous, written out of fervidly held anti-abortion conviction and illustrated with gruesome pictures of mutilated and aborted foetuses. There were threats. Wilson's secretary could not bear to open or file this mail so Wilson handled it herself. Although court attendant Jean-Marie Plourde never discussed the issue with her, his own Catholic values placed him in the pro-life camp. Remarkably enough, a great many letters (often only a little more temperate and reasoned in tone) were written and signed by officials of the Roman Catholic Church. Several of the Catholic justices on the Court were astonished that their church would approach Wilson in this way and asked if they could read her mail; she passed it along willingly enough. Unfortunately, when Wilson stepped down from the Supreme Court there was something of a scuffle among the remaining judges to have the nine filing cabinets Plourde had obtained for her redistributed; Wilson had no idea that the National Archives might have had a particular interest in this Morgentaler correspondence and she directed that it be thrown out.[43]

There certainly is no question that Wilson thought deeply about the abortion issue and her judgment shows it. Four other judges in two separate judgments agreed with Wilson that the provisions offended the procedural guarantees of life, liberty, and security of the person enshrined in section 7 and Wilson did consider this to be an important point. But only Wilson examined the section 7 guarantees substantively – a much more controversial and courageous approach.

The blunt language which opens Wilson's judgment creates a strong rhetorical frame for the analysis which follows:

> At the heart of this appeal is the question whether a pregnant woman can, as a constitutional matter, be compelled by law to carry the foetus to term ... My colleagues, the Chief Justice and Justice Beetz, have found that the requirements do not comport with the principles of fundamental justice in the procedural sense ... With all due respect, I think that the Court must tackle the primary issue first. A consideration as to whether or not the procedural requirements for obtaining or performing an abortion comport with fundamental justice is purely academic if such requirements cannot as a constitutional matter be imposed at all. If a pregnant woman cannot, as a constitutional matter, be compelled by law to carry the foetus to term against her will, a review of the procedural requirements by which she may be compelled to do so seems pointless. Moreover, it would, in my opinion, be an exercise in futility for the legislature to expend its time and energy in attempting to remedy the defects in the procedural requirements unless it has some assurance that this process will, at the end of the day, result in the creation of a valid criminal offence. I turn, therefore, to what I believe is the central issue to be addressed.[44]

Wilson was giving notice that (unlike her male colleagues) she would not be satisfied to send this law back to the legislature for further procedural tinkering. She wanted to establish, 'as a constitutional matter' that it is highly unlikely any formulation could be found which would not substantially interfere with a woman's freedom of choice.

So central is the experience of pregnancy and childbirth and childcare responsibility to the biological reality of what it means to be female that Wilson's customary faith in the power of Humean moral inference is here coloured with a somewhat Humean scepticism about the capability of males to understand it; she wrote:

> It is probably impossible for a man to respond even imaginatively to such a dilemma not just because it is outside the realm of his personal experience (although this is, of course, the case) but because he can relate to it only by objectifying it, thereby eliminating the subjective elements of the female psyche which are at the heart of the dilemma.[45]

The purposive approach which Wilson takes to her analysis of the right to liberty is, she argues, entailed by the concept of the individual which is enshrined within our Charter. In a matter so intimately connected with women's bodily integrity and freedom of conscience, state interference must of necessity infringe constitutional guarantees. The Charter integrates the proper spheres of the state and the individual by permitting state control of a wide range of individual activities, on the one hand, but then limiting the scope of that governmental control when it comes to matters with a direct bearing on the individual's definition of self. The proper role of the state, therefore is to foster the individual conscience as much as possible so that each of us generates the individual judgment 'essential to one's self-respect as a human being and essential to the possibility of that contentment.' But this refusal to pigeonhole the individual as either independent atom or collective cog is by no means some new idea growing out of feminist ideology for Wilson, who consistently rejected simple-minded dichotomies.

Although Wilson asserted that the state is required not to approve but to respect the personal decisions made by its citizens as a fundamental element of their individual privacy, it is not surprising that for Wilson this principle of respect cannot be an absolute one. It is, of course, a traditional modernist principle of law that state interference with the personal decision of one citizen will always become legitimate at the point when it is required to adjudicate a conflict with the competing interests of another individual. In this instance, the section 1 provisions of the Charter do authorize that some 'reasonable limits' be placed upon what Wilson characterized as the 'moral decision' to have an abortion. In this case she concludes that the state's interest only becomes compelling at that stage of pregnancy when the foetus could exist outside the body of its mother.

Wilson, unlike some of her colleagues, did not believe that it was ever appropriate for the Supreme Court to deliver a decision written so as to be intentionally ambiguous. When her judgment in *Morgentaler* was released both feminist groups and the anti-abortion faction across the country greeted it as a clear victory for the pro-choice position. Attempts to bring in new legislation to establish some scheme of control over abortion that would not offend Charter rights never got off the ground and Wilson, for one, was very happy that this was the case. She considered the issue a difficult one which could probably never be satisfactorily resolved; the inadvertent result was in her opinion about the best one could hope for.

Nevertheless, her judgment has a notably open-textured quality which suggests that social consensus on the issue of abortion might very well continue to shift as new scientific information becomes available about when human life begins. We can assume from all the previous indications of Wilson's deference to social consensus as the foundation of properly constituted legislative authority that with new information the law might well need to change again. Wilson argued that the decision to terminate potential life is properly allocated to the conscience of the pregnant woman early in her pregnancy because pragmatically there is no other means of protecting the rights of the pregnant woman which we at present – for lack of precise information, for lack of technology capable of non-intrusively harvesting and then nurturing embryos to maturity outside the female body – are compelled to value more highly than merely potential or pre-viable life.

However, she does not lose sight of the fact that the decision to terminate human life in any form other than the earliest beginnings of a foetus is emphatically not deemed by law (or social consensus) to be a matter of private conscience. Furthermore, she pointed out in the final paragraphs of the judgment that she had not addressed the question of whether the word 'everyone' in section 7 of the Charter included a foetus – because the crown did not argue it and 'it was not necessary to decide it in order to dispose of the issues on the appeal.' But Wilson carefully does not preclude the possibility that this issue could be revisited in the light of new scientific information that may in future help us to value more precisely (or even to protect, outside the body of the mother) the unique potential of the specific human life.[46]

What is absolutely missing from Wilson's judgment, then, is any of the self-righteous certainty that so often characterizes politicized feminisms. There is none of the crowing that the 'correct' decision about abortion had unambiguously been reached for all times in a triumph for the rights of women.[47] The *Morgentaler* judgment is moving and persuasive in part because it implicitly acknowledges that it encapsulates only a provisional and indeterminate truth. As such, its language is in turn true to the intense ambivalence experienced by most women whose circumstances have led them to seek out an abortion; as Wilson described it:

> This decision is one that will have profound psychological, economic and social consequences for the pregnant woman. The circumstances giving rise to it can be complex and varied and there may be, and usually are, powerful considerations militating in opposite directions. It is a decision that deeply reflects the way the woman thinks about herself and her relationships to others and to society at large. It is not just a medical decision; it is a profound social and ethical one as well. Her response to it will be the response of the whole person.

The release of the judgment in late January 1988 triggered another flood of letters from citizens across Canada. There are a number of comforting notes to Wilson from old friends who realized the barrage of criticism she would face and many anonymous or signed notes thanking her for 'giving women the right to choose.' However, the majority of her mail on this issue was sharply critical.

Many of her correspondents offered to pray for her. Some apparently believed her to be an elected representative with the power to enact new anti-abortion legislation; she was warned not to expect to receive their votes again unless she did. Wilson was threatened with punishment in the hereafter from A Higher Court if she failed to retract her judgment forthwith. A number of her correspondents more or less politely pointed out that she should be grateful her own mother had not chosen to abort her and a few added that perhaps it would have been better if she had. One said she had written to congratulate her when she was appointed to the Supreme Court but was now 'bitterly disappointed.' The general tone may have been one of hysteria but there were letters opposing Wilson's judgment written in a tone of unmistakably profound and compassionate conviction. There were even a few temperate essays from people who had thoroughly scrutinized her judgment and considered her arguments paragraph by paragraph, offering a reasoned response.

Henry Morgentaler had been intertwined and even enmeshed in the law for twenty years; he did not write when the judgment was released.

Touchingly, he waited until Wilson had retired when it seemed 'proper and nice' and then sent what he called a 'fan letter' to her in 1993, the year that they both turned seventy, inviting her to his birthday party:

> I wish to tell you that I found your judgment in my 1988 case inspiring and uplifting. While the other judges in the majority ruling decided the matter on narrow procedural grounds you, and only you, were upholding articulately human dignity, female self-esteem, freedom of religion and fundamental freedoms in a truly democratic society. It was a breath of fresh air and a judgment that will forever remain a milestone in Canadian history.

Wilson, not retired and still fully occupied with the Royal Commission on Aboriginal Peoples, was unable to attend. She wrote back a note of congratulations and with typically humorous self-effacement reminded Morgentaler that 'my judgment in that case received very mixed reviews!'[48]

In *Morgentaler*, through her insistence that mere procedural analysis would not suffice, Wilson provides a substantive and normative model of dignity and willed optimism going beyond gender. Wilson herself shouldered the responsibility which is indivisible from that human right and burden of choosing. Judges must adjudicate. Women faced with unwanted pregnancies want to decide for themselves and *Morgentaler* gave them the right to decide. But neither Wilson nor *Morgentaler* took away or could take away the burden of choosing. Wilson's judgment in *Morgentaler* does not so much grant women rights as assert women's responsibility to choose wisely and express Wilson's optimistic faith that they will do so.

Because Wilson's own definition of the family is expansive this survey of her key family law cases has been relatively expansive also. Although she did not think it went far enough in *Morgentaler*, Wilson did not denigrate the procedural approach and she considered it to be an essential element of the reasoning in that case. Procedural analysis in law is sometimes the best way of recognizing the common humanity which Wilson cherishes and seeks to protect. Certain provisions in the Charter mandate a contextual analysis; Wilson made deft use of these provisions in a number of judgments, including some which deal with women and women's rights, which we will consider below.

Intersecting with concerns affecting life in the family, the school, the neighbourhood, the hospital or the city, individuals in our society are inevitably affected by bigger structures – the economic entities and business organizations governed by the ancient and elaborate labyrinth of corporate and commercial law. On these areas of law there may have been no uniquely feminist perspective, but Wilson brought to them the same expansive and contextual and postmodern notion of human individuality and human relationships she applied to the human rights and family cases, dissolving as necessary the boundary between the public and the private.

10

Getting Down to Business:
Law and Economics in the Marketplace

When Wilson went to Ottawa in 1982, especially during her early years when she was effectively on probation and proving herself all over again, she prepared the reasons in more than her share of routine business law cases. These were then the bread and butter of the Supreme Court's work. There was no reprise of the struggle which she had faced at the Ontario Court of Appeal where Jessup had assumed that corporate commercial work was too complex for her to comprehend. And given how severely the Court was undermanned, even if they had been inclined to do so, her new colleagues simply could not afford the luxury of questioning her competence. Managing the Court's backlog was an increasingly serious problem because a good deal of the time only four or five judges were available to handle the workload meant to be distributed among nine. Instead, their reaction tended to be one of relief.

Without a doubt Wilson is best known for her human rights, family, and constitutional judgments; these are the cases which have most obviously helped change the public face of Canadian society, which she herself remembers best, and in which she takes the greatest pride. It is not generally understood that before the Charter the vast bulk of the case-load at the Supreme Court concerned individuals in the marketplace as economic actors. At the Supreme Court there is a huge body of Wilson civil judgments dealing with contracts, torts, property, tax, labour law, and corporate law, all of which are the stuff of mainstream commercial life. Wilson left her characteristic mark here, too. It would be a mistake to assume that she did not bring as conscientious or (when she deemed it necessary) as innovative an approach to these business law cases as to the diversity law and so-called feminist cases which made her reputation.

Fortuity has shaped the incremental development of the common law. The judicial abstraction of precedent can evolve only from the resolution of particular disputes as they happen to be brought before the courts; this is both a strength and a weakness of the common law system. On the one hand, law's flexibility and responsiveness to shifts in social consensus are enhanced by common law incrementalism. But the value ascribed through precedent to certainty and predictability can also result in rigid formalism which constrains change and can wreak injustice in particular circumstances in the short run.

Access to justice has a price tag. Bertha Wilson was very conscious that guaranteed rights under the Charter are meaningless if individuals cannot afford access to the courts; on more than one occasion she expressed her regret that 'it is too costly and too time-consuming for most people to challenge the law.'[1] But civil justice costs money too. Legal aid has generally been mandated only when the absence of legal representation impugns constitutional guarantees of freedom; until recently, section 7 rights were associated almost exclusively with criminal law. Civil cases – torts or contracts or employment law disputes between individuals – have rarely been eligible for legal aid funding. A disproportionate number of the cases which reach even a trial court involve the resolution of disputes between individuals or business entities who are able to afford legal fees and are especially vigilant about litigating those matters which touch and concern their financial affairs. That is why legislative initiatives are essential to supplement the necessarily commerce-driven locus of much judge-made law.

As we have seen, fortuity has always fascinated both of the Wilsons; Bertha Wilson was fully aware that judges must decide the cases which come before them, each of which embodies a particular legal puzzle requiring incisive legal analysis. Although Justice Jessup had been wrong about his assessment of Wilson's abilities in this area of the law, he was right in his understanding that commercial cases are often particularly puzzling and complex. Of course this commercial complexity is deliberate, especially when cases involve elaborate corporate entities relying upon precedent and the certainty of commercial law doctrine to accomplish particular economic goals for their clients.

From a postmodern perspective, one of the most pleasurable ironies of modernist law is its elevation of the individuated and autonomous liberal humanist subject, together with its simultaneous adoption of the corporate personality as a legal fiction comprised of a constellation of business entities designed primarily to ratchet up profits – generally by limiting legal liability while obtaining desired tax breaks. But in doing so, a multiplicity of individual legal subjects, diverging legal facts relating to individual circumstances and individual business purposes, and disparate legal texts (mergers and acquisitions contracts, property deeds, share prospectuses) must be accommodated and respected. And the need for such accommodation is driven by pragmatic rather than normative considerations. The commercial realities of business dictate that parties who are not satisfied that their legitimate business objectives have been integrated into the legal structure will demand some alternative form of compensation to close the deal.

Wilson, who considers herself to be a socialist, had thoroughly enjoyed serving Oslers' corporate clients by researching timely opinions relating to the drafting of just such legal documents and the construction of just such impervious commercial entities. In her own sophisticated wills and estates practice she had cheerfully scrutinized domestic and international law to set up off-shore trusts which could protect with certainty the wealth of those fine old Ontario families who relied upon Oslers to do just that. Nor did such efforts create any crisis of conscience for her.[2] Such work is principled. After all, as between the individual (whether a natural person or an artificial incorporated person) and the state, the state retains all the power to alter the statutory framework if it finds it does not like the economic results of its legislation. Wilson's stance both as a corporate commercial law practitioner and as a commercial law judge is in that sense completely congruent with the anti-majoritarianism characteristic of her human rights jurisprudence.

At the Court of Appeal Wilson had already signalled in the *Dominion Chain* case that in her opinion certainty was the pre-eminent value in the business law context, an opinion which she reiterated early in her Supreme Court career. She did not abandon effects-based analysis or contextuality in commercial law so much as exhibit a special attentiveness to the effects that a lack of certainty may create in a commercial context. Because certainty is of particular importance in business, judicial activism is all the less justified in this area of law. Nevertheless, the advent of the Charter meant that the very context of business law could of necessity and in some circumstances quite fundamentally be challenged.

We have already seen Wilson's innovative integration of constitutional issues in diversity law and family law contexts and her growing understanding that economic issues are inextricably intertwined with, for example, issues of accommodation in employment law or violence towards women in criminal law. It is not surprising, then, that the reverse is also true. The 'crosscut' realities of peoples' lives demand an integrated approach. Business law decisions are not always solely about business. Some of Wilson's most interesting and significant law and economics judgments are those in which she grappled with the intersection between corporate commercial law and constitutional law, either explicitly or, insofar as Charter values rapidly came to permeate general Canadian consensus about law, more indirectly.

The commercial law statutes to be measured against the constitutions of both the United States and Canada have by and large embodied the laissez-faire ideology most famously associated with Adam Smith. Smith's invisible hand theory, first set out more than two hundred years ago in *The Wealth of Nations,* has been used by American law and economics scholars, particularly Richard Posner and Milton Friedman, to justify the notion that the most efficient and therefore the most desirable resource allocation, economic growth, and distribution of income within any given society will result from unfettered self-interest. Because the pursuit of private interest will coincide in the long run with public interest, a laissez-faire community is absolved from any need to determine or to impose collective economic goals. Private ordering will automatically and efficiently fuse the value of individual autonomy with optimal social welfare so long as the economic actors are uncoerced and fully informed. Therefore, justice coincides with commercial certainty and the courts ought to uphold the commercial arrangements negotiated by autonomous parties: the assumption of trickle-down benefits means that wealth-maximization effectively amounts to a new categorical imperative.

Posner's version of laissez-faire doctrine omitted Smith's own profound understanding of the integration of ethics and economics which had always interested John and Bertha Wilson. It ignored the original scope of Smith's invisible hand as it had relied on the individual's exercise of self-restraint (motivated by propriety if not by altruism) in tightly knit preindustrial societies. But it was Posnerian laissez-faire which became increasingly central to the law and economics scholarship and by the early 1980s had begun to dominate commercial law and neoconservative politics, especially in the United States. This law and economics ideology infused the transnational and global capitalisms imported uncritically into some regions of Canada hot on the heels of the Charter. Quite deliberately, the Charter does not contain any explicit guarantees of economic rights, nor was Wilson able to bring herself to read them into the section 7 guarantees. And if Wilson's account of the modern Canadian state in *McKinney* is to be taken at face value, Canadians generally do not share that American belief so closely linked with laissez-faire capitalism that the best government governs least.

Nevertheless at the Dalhousie symposium held in 1991 to honour Wilson on her retirement from the Supreme Court, feminist law professor Maureen Maloney delivered a paper[3] which was highly critical of Wilson's civil judgments. Maloney assumed a close identity between Smith's economic theory and its late twentieth-century neoconservative Posnerian variant and convicted Wilson of having been captured by the contemporary law and economics agenda. She persisted in viewing Wilson's business law judgments through her own feminist lens. Like Mary Jane Mossman in her analysis of the family law cases, she praised those judgments which in her view reflected an ethic of caring appropriate to the feminist judge she assumed Wilson had aspired to be, and damned those she considered as endorsing an unredeemed spirit of self-interested individualism. Maloney on this occasion did not consider that Smith's nonlinear causality, embedded in his conception of the rolling evolution of the law shaping consensus and consensus in turn shaping law, might have offered some explanation for what she instead characterized as Wilson's vacillations. The Aristotelian subtlety and complexity of Wilson's understanding of partial goods and shifting notions of the good as ideas Maloney did not develop further.

LEAVE TO APPEAL

Before we look to some of Wilson's Supreme Court business law judgments, it is useful to consider how another legislative initiative was in the 1970s and 1980s beginning to affect the development of the common law. Up until 1982 there was a distinct bias in favour of those commercial litigants who could afford to take their cases up to the Supreme

Court and insist upon clarification and refinement of the business context of certainty as the ultimate wealth-maximizing value; after 1982, the advent of the Charter mandated the supremacy of even higher values.

Nevertheless, in Wilson's view the role of the Supreme Court had already been substantially redefined seven years earlier when an amendment to the Supreme Court Act for the first time imposed a leave to appeal requirement in civil litigation. The amendment meant that Supreme Court judges were no longer merely deciding the cases which fortuitously came before them but choosing which cases merited their attention; the process of choice inevitably pruned back the exuberant growth of the common law and imposed the new responsibility of choosing wisely. And the effect of this amendment has turned out to be so important that it requires explanation.

Adam Smith revised his invisible hand doctrine in response to the evolution of late eighteenth-century international mercantilism, acknowledging that the expansion of social distance between individuals and the corresponding erosion of interpersonal propriety would demand new kinds of control and direction on the part of the state. Similarly, if the economics-driven development of the common law can be characterized as the working of the invisible hand within our legal system, Wilson clearly believes that the new policy-making role for the Supreme Court of Canada mandated by the civil leave to appeal procedure both allowed and required the Court to become much more directive in the development of the common law, especially in the commercial context.

This was a topic which she explored in a 1983 paper, 'Leave to Appeal to the Supreme Court of Canada,'[4] written only a few months after her appointment to the Supreme Court when she was still coming to grips with her new role. From a pragmatic perspective, the leave to appeal amendment was introduced simply as a caseload control procedure; that there was a need for the Court to control its own docket could not be disputed. An overwhelming burden had been imposed upon the Supreme Court, especially in that quarter-century following the abolition of appeals to the Privy Council in 1949 which coincided with the buoyancy of post Second World War capitalist expansion and its associated proliferation of commercial litigation. The new provision required that a panel of three judges select appeals for hearing by determining which cases raised issues of national public importance. In some instances, of course – especially the interpretation of federal statutes and their intersection with provincial ones where there are conflicting decisions at the provincial appellate level, or the constitutional cases concerning guaranteed rights and freedoms – that selection is quite obvious.

What interested Wilson much more was the substantive effect of the appeal provision. No one else seemed to have given this issue any thought. Clerk Philip Bryden, whom she had asked to help her in preparing the 1983 speech, began with a thorough search of the existing British, American, and Canadian academic literature on the topic.[5] Bryden discovered that there was little assistance available to guide the Court in choosing the right cases and little awareness that formulating a strict test for national significance might 'thwart the genesis of much original doctrinal development at common law.'

What became clear in the course of the research was that the appeal provision had unwittingly transformed the Supreme Court from an appellate tribunal to a 'supervisory' tribunal[6] with an explicit duty to oversee the development of the common law in all of the everyday cases. Such cases may seem almost by definition to be of relatively small public significance because they typically involve the resolution of a dispute between two parties only; in Wilson's view, this was not so.

When the Supreme Court decided to grant leave to appeal in one of those private law disputes, Wilson explained, it should do so with full recognition that leave has become a juridical tool with an inescapable legislative component. Leave should signal both that the Court considers the law to require modification and that the Court is also prepared to implement whatever change is necessary. On the other hand, the decision not to grant leave is a decision not to open up a particular area of the law, which often amounts to an endorsement that commercial certainty trumps personal interests in the particular area of civil law which is in contention. As Wilson understood, people are much more likely to pattern their business transactions in reliance on the predictability of the law (which in this context is often more pertinent than whether or not the law is subjectively perceived to be just) rather than, for example, any decision to engage in criminal action.

Unlike some of her colleagues on the Supreme Court, Wilson had her clerks write short memos for each of the ten-minute applications for leave to appeal – as many as forty might be heard in a single week – because she took the appeals selection duty seriously. The vitality of the common law has evolved out of all the messy contingencies of human experience, sometimes from the coalescence of judgments which may not have seemed very important individually at the time they were decided, and not from externally imposed logic (as in Quebec's civil code tradition). Judicial legislation through the control of appeals, she explained, could only be justified if the Court kept in mind the 'loss of that quality of spontaneity which was supposed to bond the law to the people and give the common law its peculiar genius – general principles born and developed by sheer happenstance and buffeted and refined by a myriad of specific instances.'[7] Moreover, Wilson warned, Supreme Court judges ought to take particular care in the common law areas that their selection of appeals was not constrained by their own perceptions; only by consciously doing so could they refrain from structuring the law in their own image. It is no surprise, given her general philosophy of resisting pressure towards intracurial unanimity in order to provide alternate pathways for the development of the common law, that Wilson was just as zealous in writing dissents and diverging concurrences in these commercial law cases as in the human rights and family law judgments we have already considered.

By 1984 the Supreme Court was drowning in a backlog of impending appeals which had already been granted leave. The justices also knew they were about to be inundated by a fresh tidal wave of post-Charter applications seeking leave for future hearings. Quietly and without announcement to the public or the profession that it was doing so, the Court clamped down pre-emptively through a more stringent exercise of the leave to appeal provision provided in the 1975 amendment. And again the profession (perhaps because only a small percentage of lawyers regularly appear before the Supreme Court) seems not to have noticed.

Twice in 1984 Bertha Wilson requested suggestions from the practising bar[8] about how to deal with the problem of sorting out the frivolous or frail from the fruitful appeal in the Charter context. And she revealed in a casual and incidental sort of way that the Court had begun to exert more aggressive control of civil appeals; she asked:

> What should the Court do when leave to appeal is sought on a Charter issue but the appeal seems not to present the best factual context for the resolution of the issue? As you are probably aware, the Court in other types of civil litigation considers itself free to wait for the so-called 'good case,' the thinking being that if, due to the pressure of the caseload, we can grant leave only in one or two tax cases or bankruptcy cases or negligence cases a year, then we should select the best one, the one which will provide the greatest scope for the elucidation of the jurisprudence in that area.

Yet there seem to have been no nibbles. Then in an informal session with law students at University of Toronto Wilson expressed more directly just how troubling she considered the whole issue to be. Overwork, she said regretfully, demanded this tighter control of the appeals procedure. The Court (then and now) is able to hear only about one hundred or so new cases a year. Justices require time to research, reflect, confer with their colleagues, and write judgments. In her view, Parliament in 1975 had not fully appreciated the implications of giving the Court near-absolute control over the cases selected for hearing.

Another part of the backlog arising out of delay in the release of judgments after hearings was well within the control of the Supreme Court justices, and Wilson wrote a memo to the chief justice and to all members of the Court pinpointing the cause of the problem. Judges tended to let their colleagues' drafts sit while they focused on writing their own reasons for other cases. What was necessary, she thought, was for all members of the Court to focus on the same judgments within the same time frame and to aim for a maximum of six months (but preferably three months) from the date of hearing to the date of release, with highest priority given to the oldest matters so that judgments were released in at least a rough chronological order. She asked that an appropriate schedule be drawn up specifying target release dates and kept up to date.

No comprehensive review of either aspect of the backlog problem – selecting cases for hearing or expediting judgments once heard – seems to have occurred during Wilson's time on the bench. The post-hearing backlog issue largely resolved itself through retirements of those judges who due to illness were unable to carry a full load. But as the practising bar became somewhat better educated on the test in place for the leave to appeal procedure, the Supreme Court has of necessity focused its relatively slender resources on Charter cases, relinquishing much of its supervisory role in the development of the common law relevant to business certainty as it has devolved more and more into a criminal and constitutional court of last resort.[9]

From the vantage point of retirement, Wilson was also vividly aware of the potential problems created for the vitality of the common law by the proliferation of mandatory mediation and contractual alternative dispute resolution strategies. While recognizing that these strategies evolved to fill the gap once the Supreme Court began hearing fewer civil cases, and while acknowledging the advantages of speed and economy that they may offer, Wilson nevertheless has profound misgivings about the short-term propriety and the long-term effects of such venues which she believes merit more scrutiny and more debate in the profession.

At the Supreme Court during her tenure, 'the plain contract and tort cases, they seemed to have lost their romance compared with Charter issues,' she recalls, and this was because in many instances they 'couldn't beat the national public importance test.' But for those business law cases which could – because the law required clarification or because their factual circumstances triggered Charter considerations – Wilson continued to write many of the judgments. If they had a choice, she was well aware, her colleagues preferred the criminal cases. Although Wilson did her share there too (particularly in writing criminal dissents on procedural issues), the competition to write majority reasons was considerably less lively in the civil caseload.

Wilson's first Supreme Court case – the *Shell* patent decision heard the afternoon of her swearing-in – was a business law matter. The case reporters certainly confirm that she 'wrote a whole rash of judgments in non-Charter civil cases,' especially in her first two years on the bench but also to the end of her judicial career, many more than we can possibly consider here. Given her sturdily pragmatic understanding of the business community, one would anticipate that Wilson upheld whenever possible the value of business certainty when dealing with pure corporate commercial disputes. And a survey of a scant handful of these judgments certainly reveals that even in non-Charter civil matters Wilson was sensitive to ethical issues or quasi-rights dimensions whenever they were thrown up by the facts in the case.

TORT, CONTRACT, AND TRUST LAW

Two of her better-known Supreme Court civil decisions were in torts cases. In *Kamloops*[10] – perhaps her first big Supreme Court case – a city building inspector had noted serious structural defects in the foundation of a house under construction and issued a stop work order, which was not enforced. The house was completed and occupied without a building permit, then purchased and resold to a third party who closed the deal without noticing the defect. Wilson held for the majority that the city's breach of its duty to inspect and to enforce its stop work orders constituted negligence which was the cause of the economic loss to the purchaser, even though this negligence followed on the builder's primary negligence in building the shoddy foundation. Once the city put into operation its decision to regulate construction by by-law, it could not claim exemption from a private law duty to the purchaser because the failure to act could not be characterized as a mere policy decision made in the exercise of its statutory discretion. It was reasonably foreseeable that a purchaser of the defective house would suffer damages as a result of the breach. Accordingly the plaintiff could recover the cost of restoring the home; the limitations period did not begin to run until he could reasonably have known about the defect. Both the expansion of private law duty[11] and the expansion of limitations in accordance with discoverability have had profound and controversial repercussions in Canadian law.

In *Crocker* v. *Sundance*,[12] a judgment released eighteen months before the end of her Supreme Court career, Wilson took the opportunity of exploring the intersection between tort and standard-form contract. The facts in *Crocker* made it particularly memorable but it was also a very practical sort of issue which Wilson enjoyed tackling very much. Long after she stepped down from the bench, she has followed with keen interest the subsequent development of the legal doctrine known as host liability – the extent to which a commercial or even a social server of alcohol will be responsible for any subsequent injuries suffered or caused by the person served – which evolved out of the case.

Crocker had entered a downhill tubing contest at the Sundance ski resort by signing, several days before the race was scheduled to take place, what he thought was simply an application form. The document in fact included a standard form waiver absolving the resort of all responsibility for any damages sustained by the contestants, no matter how such damages might be incurred. But Crocker did not read the clause and it was not drawn to his attention.

At the time of the race he had already received a cut to his head and was quite clearly drunk. However, the employees of the Sundance resort kept supplying him with liquor, so that he was too inebriated to hold on to his inflated rubber tube. When it eluded his grasp and slid down the hill, the employees provided him with a second one. The resort manager, it is true, did make a weak suggestion that it might be better if Crocker dropped out of the race, but he made no serious effort to require him to do so or to draw his attention to the allocation of risk in the contract.

Crocker flipped out of his tube while riding over a mogul, injured his neck, and was rendered paraplegic. The trial judge rejected the argument that he had contractually waived his right to sue in tort or voluntarily assumed the risk of the accident. Sundance was deemed to be

75 per cent liable in tort; Crocker was 25 per cent contributorily negligent in getting drunk before showing up for the race. But this decision was overturned by the Ontario Court of Appeal, which decided that the resort had adequately met its duty to warn Crocker.

'By definition, the standard of care is dependent on context,' Wilson wrote for the Court. In this situation, 'the fact that Crocker was an irresponsible individual and was voluntarily intoxicated during the tubing competition is the very reason why Sundance was legally obligated to take all reasonable steps to prevent Crocker from competing.' The waiver clause could have constituted a voluntary assumption of the physical risks associated with tubing only if Crocker's mind had not been clouded by alcohol at the time of the race, but certainly not when no attempt had been made to draw the provision to his attention and on the facts as found at trial that he did not know of its existence. For that reason, 'Sundance had no reasonable grounds for believing that the release truly expressed Mr. Crocker's intention.'

Wilson took on the task of writing a number of debtor-creditor judgments which expanded upon the exploration of negligent misrepresentation she had initiated at the Court of Appeal. The most detailed of these was *Mason Construction*[13] in which she wrote the decision for the majority, integrating elements of contract, trust, and tort analysis and rejecting the arguments of the bank's able lawyer, John Sopinka. Mason had signed a fixed-price construction contract to build an office and retail complex for a developer but only after it had obtained written assurance from the bank (which was providing bridge financing) that the developer was adequately financed to meet its payments. Mason was not told that the bank had in fact guaranteed only a fixed sum to the developer. The bank knew at some point in the construction process that its loan would not be sufficient to cover the cost of completion but it did not tell Mason of the projected shortfall.

Wilson's initial framing of the issue forcefully established the fiduciary nature of the bank's relationship to the contractor. The evidence showed that the bank's manager was experienced, realized that the bank was inducing the appellant to enter into the contract, wanted to avoid any possibility of the bank incurring any liability to the appellant and yet wanted to protect the bank's own interest in obtaining the considerable financial benefits of this very substantial loan transaction.

At trial and appeal the courts below had characterized the relationship between Mason and the bank as a unilateral contract. Wilson agreed with Sopinka that no contractual relationship had in fact been established, applying her characteristic contextual analysis in the service of determining whether the business certainty test had been met. But in Wilson's view, the bank's behaviour amply fulfilled all four elements of liability for negligent misrepresentation – an untrue statement, negligently made, in a special relationship giving rise to a duty of care, under circumstances in which reliance was foreseeable – when all the intersecting elements of its behaviour were viewed as an integrated, coherent, and deliberate course of conduct. She concluded her judgment by determining that the damages to be awarded should be calculated according to tort principles, assuming that but for the misrepresentation, Mason would have severed its relationship with the developer, recovered for the work already completed at that date and found another project to work on, and this substitute project would have generated a comparable margin of profit that Mason would have invested, collecting the interest. This is the same effects-based approach that Wilson applied in the Charter cases.

Wilson took another crack at the perennial problem of fundamental breach in relation to exclusion clauses in the Syncrude[14] case, this time writing a strong and detailed partial dissent in which she was joined by L'Heureux-Dubé. Hunter Engineering and Allis-Chalmers were sued by Syncrude, which had entered into three contracts for the manufacture of gear boxes used in its Alaska oil sands extraction process. The Hunter contract included two warranties limiting liability to a period of twenty-four months from the date of shipment or twelve months from the date of start-up; the Allis-Chalmers contract had an additional provision explicitly excluding any other warranty, statutory or otherwise. The defects in the gear boxes did not manifest themselves until after the twenty-four month period had expired. At issue was the question of whether Syncrude could argue fundamental breach despite the disclaimer. The majority of the Supreme Court followed the English House of Lords decision and decisively rejected the fundamental breach doctrine, holding that in the absence of evidence of unconscionability, parties ought to be held to the terms of their agreements. The exclusionary clause in the Allis-Chalmers contract was enforced and Syncrude was denied damages.

Wilson was not persuaded. She pointed out that the English statutory regime was significantly different. In this instance, she agreed, Allis-Chalmers was not in fundamental breach because the gear box defects went to only one aspect of the contract and, although serious, were reparable. Nevertheless she questioned whether, in circumstances of contracts between commercially sophisticated parties in which there was no inequality of bargaining power but subsequent events gave rise to a serious breach, the courts should stand by and passively enforce a contract. Replacing the doctrine of fundamental breach with unconscionability simply failed to resolve the problem because it did not increase business certainty:

> To dispense with the doctrine of fundamental breach and rely solely on the principle of unconscionability ... would, in my view, require an extension of the principle of unconscionability beyond its traditional bounds of inequality of bargaining power. The court, in effect, would be in the position of saying that terms freely negotiated by parties of equal bargaining power were unconscionable. Yet it was the inequality of bargaining power which traditionally was the source of the unconscionability ... Remove the inequality and we must ask, wherein lies the unconscionability? It seems to me that it must have its roots in subsequent events, given that the parties themselves are the best judges of what is fair at the time they make their bargain. The policy of the common law is, I believe, that having regard to the conduct (pursuant to the contract) of the party seeking the indulgence of the court to enforce the clause, the court refuses. This conduct is described for convenience as 'fundamental breach.' It marks off the boundaries of tolerable conduct. But the boundaries are admittedly uncertain. Will replacing it with a general concept of unconscionability reduce the uncertainty?[15]

Wilson believed that there was still a vital role for the doctrine of fundamental breach in those instances when the parties were not of unequal bargaining power and yet the subsequent conduct of one of the parties would make it manifestly unfair for the court to uphold the exclusion clause as it was originally negotiated.

Also noteworthy in her *Syncrude* dissent was Wilson's explicit extension of the equitable constructive trust doctrine she had developed for Rosa Becker to this commercial law context. Two firms, the US parent of Hunter and a Canadian affiliate (whose behaviour was later deemed to be fraudulent), had both claimed the right to supply the goods under the sales contract. Pending resolution of this issue, Syncrude had unilaterally established a trust fund into which it had paid the price for the benefit of the successful party based on certain conditions which were not fulfilled. The majority held that Syncrude was entitled to the balance of the fund including the profit margin. Wilson held that to permit Syncrude to retain the trust surplus amounted to unjustly enriching Syncrude in the amount of the interest income on the money originally intended to pay Hunter.

A 'TAKING' OF PROPERTY: CONSTRUCTIVE TRUST

Breach of contract is naturaly [sic] the slightest of all injuries because we naturaly depend more on what we possess than what is in the hands of others. A man robbed of five pounds thinks himself much more injured than if he had lost five pounds by a contract.

Thus said Adam Smith in his *Lectures on Jurisprudence*, integrating nascent eighteenth-century explorations of psychology with law; he understood that the desire to retain what we already possess (or think we possess) is a much more powerful human motivation than the desire to attain what is still out of reach. And contemporary economic theorists have picked up on Smith's hypothesis that economic actors may not be single-mindedly rational in pursuing individual wealth-maximization because they tend to value losses considerably more than foregone gains and are even capable of apparently altruistic behaviours not linked to monetary gains at all.

From her earliest law school days Wilson had taken a particular interest in property law, especially government's role in the creation of new property and also its corresponding power to take away the traditional property entitlements to unfettered use and enjoyment of private property through various planning, zoning, and health regulations curbing pollution. Although her property judgments at the Court of Appeal had been numerous and varied, it was at the Supreme Court that she was given the opportunity of making new law in accordance with these new property concepts.

In 1985 Wilson wrote (for herself and Chief Justice Dickson) a diverging concurrence in *Tener*,[16] a British Columbia case in which the crown had refused to issue a permit allowing a mining company to exploit its mineral claims. According to the terms of the agreement, the title to the surface rights remained vested in the crown; it had sold only the underground mineral claims to the mining company's predecessors in title in 1937 although this bundle of rights included the right to the minerals themselves, the right to use and possess the surface for the purpose of getting the minerals out, and the right to have access to the area of the mineral claims over the surface of the adjacent land. But then the provincial government began cutting back what it had already sold.

Two years after the original grant the province, under the provisions of the Park Act, created a park which encompassed the area of mineral claims; in 1965, further legislation had been passed requiring a park use permit before any natural resources could be exploited. When in 1973 the owners of the mineral rights initiated attempts to obtain a permit to realize the value of its rights, there were delays and obfuscations. Finally in 1978 Tener received notice from the director of the Parks Branch advising that no exploration or development work whatsoever would be authorized at the site of the mineral claims.

And yet no land had been taken, the trial court reasoned, and it refused any compensation. This decision was reversed on appeal, with the majority at the Supreme Court affirming. The mining company was awarded damages based on the difference between the total value of the mineral rights less the value of the future possibility that the permit would be granted.

Wilson's reasons provided an extensive analysis of the legal concept of *profit à prendre*[17] to support her conclusion that there was a necessary integration between the mineral rights and the surface rights necessary for their enjoyment. Refusal to grant a permit constituted expropriation since the value of the mineral rights could not be realized without surface access. Her discussion moved to the thorny legal problem of distinguishing between instances of expropriation and instances of 'injurious affection' where no land is taken and traditionally no compensation has been payable. Wilson considered that the refusal to grant a permit in this instance went beyond the common regulatory effect of a rezoning because the new regulation had effectively extinguished the encumbrance of the *profit à prendre*. Even though the crown argued that it did not benefit by appropriating Tener's interest to itself, this line of reasoning was unconscionable, technical, and legalistic in Wilson's view; the crown had benefited by the extinguishment of the *profit à prendre*, a unilateral decision which effectively put an end to any further troublesome claims. Wilson would have allowed full damages in accordance with the statutory allowance for an expropriation.

In *LAC Minerals*,[18] another mining case, Wilson wrote a brief concurring judgment invoking the concept of fiduciary duty to modify the common law presumption of possession. Corona, a relatively small company, owned some mining property in northern Ontario near Hemlo and had recovered very promising ore samples from exploratory

John and Bertha Wilson together during the Osler years.

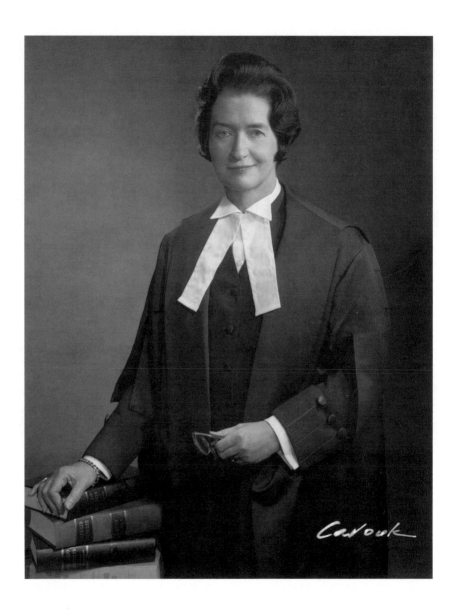

Despite their regrets at losing her, Oslers was enormously proud of Bertha Wilson's appointment to the Ontario Court of Appeal in 1975. In this photograph commissioned by Oslers, Wilson looks every inch the polished professional she had become. (Cavouk Portraits, Toronto)

The Supreme Court of Canada had just seven judges in 1946 when this building was first occupied. The facade of Ernest Cormier's evocative design seems to speak through its seven separate dormers, inviting the opposing litigants to approach up its two diverging staircases and to enter through one of its two well-separated doors. (©Supreme Court, CSS 194-2-5, Philippe Landreville Photograph Inc.)

Inside, the Grand Entrance Hall echoes the precedent of that diverging facade, but its stairs converge on a single central portal to the courtroom illuminated by natural light wells. The architecture implicitly promises a fair hearing bathed in the light of reason and a judgment in which all differences will finally be resolved through justice. (©Supreme Court, CSS 194-3-4, Philippe Landreville Photograph Inc.)

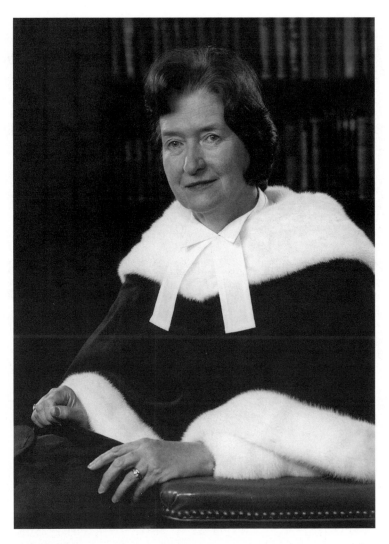

Sworn in on 30 March 1982 as the first woman to be appointed to the Supreme Court of Canada, Wilson donned her scarlet robe trimmed with Canadian white mink. Well aware of the nervousness of her new colleagues and the daunting tasks facing the Court with the entrenchment of the Charter of Rights and Freedoms, Wilson promised to be 'a true servant of the law,' but signalled that in her own mind this meant 'interpreting it responsibly ... in the context of a contemporary pluralist society.' (Michael Bedford Photography, Ottawa)

Awkwardness concerning washroom facilities was a problem Wilson had encountered with unfailing good humour at law school, during her Halifax articles, at Oslers, at the Ontario Court of Appeal, and finally at the Supreme Court of Canada. (Donato, *Toronto Sun*, 6 March 1982)

Supreme Court judges, frequently called upon to pinch hit for an absent Governor General, learn to nod assent in both official languages. Bertha Wilson had the greatest admiration for Pierre Trudeau, who had appointed her. She particularly enjoyed this occasion of GG duty required by a Trudeau-era cabinet shuffle.

SATURDAY NIGHT

$3.25 JULY 1985

MADAME JUSTICE

How Bertha Wilson's humanity is changing the
last bastion of male power–the Supreme Court of Canada
By Sandra Gwyn

DATELINE OTTAWA
Does the press gallery shape the way Canadians view their government?
By George Bain

THE $1-MILLION THRILLER
How a Canadian's first novel became a worldwide phenomenon
By Roy MacSkimming

Reserved by nature and always conscious that pronouncements by judges outside the courtroom would be scrutinized for evidence of bias, it was not until
1985 that Wilson consented to a first lengthy interview, conducted by Sandra
Gwyn for *Saturday Night*'s July 1985 issue. The lighting for the cover portrait, she
thought, was somewhat harsh; Bertha Wilson never liked having her photograph taken. (*Saturday Night*)

The Adam and Eve on Wilson's teapot was a not-so-veiled reference to the reputation as a feminist that clung to her (never endorsed by Wilson herself) throughout her legal career. In fact, far from being a typical British tea drinker, Wilson was well known for her formidable consumption of coffee. But both Bertha and John Wilson thoroughly enjoyed the series of cartoons Duncan MacPherson prepared for all the Supreme Court judges of her era. (Duncan MacPherson, *Toronto Star*)

Shortly before she announced her retirement from the Supreme Court, Bertha Wilson led a contingent of Canadian lawyers, academics, and judges to visit Lord and Lady Denning at their home in England. Wilson, often dubbed Canada's own Denning, had admired his iconoclastic judgments since law school. Still starstruck, she praised his 'pristine vigour' in speaking his mind, which made him 'larger than life.'

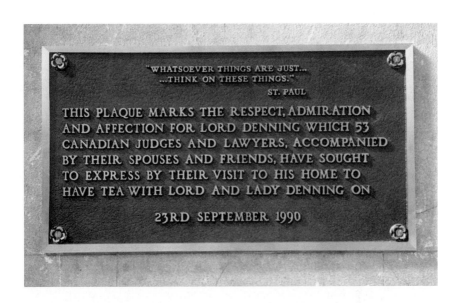

The delegation presented this plaque to Lord Denning on the occasion of the 1990 visit.

Dressed in the Gunn tartan of the Wilson clan, in 1992 Wilson was named a Companion of the Order of Canada and received the honour from then-Governor General Hnatyshyn.

The final report of the Royal Commission on Aboriginal Peoples was released on 21 November 1996, after more than five years of gruelling labour. It was met with short-lived controversy, political indifference, and slow reform. Wilson herself considers it the most important and potentially enduring work she has done. (Back) Paul Chartrand, Peter Meekison, Viola Robinson, Mary Sillett; (front) Bertha Wilson, Georges Erasmus, Rene Dussault. (Fred Cattroll, Ottawa)

Here wrapped in an Indian blanket, Bertha Wilson was eager to understand and to learn by entering into the life of the various communities the commission visited. And back in Ottawa, the commission and its largely aboriginal staff consciously adopted aboriginal spiritual values as it researched and wrote its report.

In November 1996 when the RCAP report was released, Bertha and John Wilson were far from the media on a South American cruise, somewhere off the coast of Peru. They had posponed celebrating their fiftieth wedding anniversary for a year while Bertha helped to complete writing the report.

Seen here unveiling the portrait of Bertha Wilson at Oslers in June 1999 before it travelled to the Supreme Court, artist Mary Lennox Hourd struck up a remarkable rapport with her subject. She sought to capture the many contradictory facets of Wilson's complex personality. (L. Smart)

drilling that indicated the likelihood of lucrative mineral deposits on adjacent lands. Needing capital, Murray Pezim of Corona approached the mining giant LAC with a view to entering into a joint venture; in the course of the negotiations, Corona revealed to LAC the existence of the mineral deposits. There was no contract, no documentation, not even a handshake. LAC hastened to put in a bid to purchase the adjacent property which overnight had become worth billions and developed it independently, taking the profits for itself.

Wilson found that there had been no ongoing fiduciary relationship between LAC and Corona during the course of the joint venture negotiations but she held that a breach of fiduciary duty had arisen at the point when LAC obtained the confidential information and (contrary to practice in the mining industry) used it for its own benefit. This was the kind of bad faith which eroded business certainty. She held further that such behaviour also gave rise to a common law breach of confidence but that the remedy of constructive trust was applicable for either cause of action.

TAXING BUSINESS DECISIONS

Taxes may be the quintessential example of a government taking of private property earned by a taxpayer in the interests of the public good. On a personal level, however, Wilson certainly did not consider taxation a taking; she once said, 'I could never complain about paying taxes' because 'that's the equivalent of handing out bowls of soup to the needy.'[19] She knew the Income Tax Act inside out and had a familiarity with international tax law as well. Regardless of her own view on the payment of taxes as a social responsibility, Wilson did not consider it to be any part of her role as a lawyer to preach this gospel to the clients of the firm.

Nor was the moral standard which Wilson personally encouraged by precept and example the same standard which she thought it appropriate for judges to impose upon corporate taxpayers. By and large Wilson adopted the view that the taxpayer was entitled to rely upon the letter of tax statutes for certainty in arranging its business affairs. She did not think it appropriate for judges to require corporate altruism.

In *Stubart Investments*,[20] the facts are a little complicated. Grover Cast Stone Company, sister subsidiary of Stubart, had experienced substantial financial losses. An arrangement was reached whereby Stubart sold its assets to Grover, and Grover appointed Stone as its agent to carry on the business for its own benefit. For three fiscal years, Stubart paid the net income realized over to Grover to offset Grover's previous losses under the carry-forward provisions in the Income Tax Act. On reassessment, National Revenue attributed the income back to Stubart and this reassessment was upheld at the Tax Appeal Board and at trial and on appeal to the Federal Court. The Supreme Court unanimously allowed Stubart's appeal on the grounds that the transaction was complete and had not been a sham.

Wilson (with Ritchie concurring) wrote separate reasons which provide the definitive business purposes test in Canadian law. The behaviour of Stubart and Grover was in her view neither immoral nor illegal; in justification of it she invoked what is commonly referred to as Lord Tomlin's principle: 'Every man is entitled if he can to order his affairs so that the tax attaching under the appropriate Acts is less than it otherwise would be.'[21] She added, in her own words: 'I think that Lord Tomlin's principle is far too deeply entrenched in our tax law for the courts to reject it in the absence of clear statutory authority. No such authority has been put to us in this case.'

The transaction could not be deemed to be a sham because it was intended to create legal relations and had in fact created them. A tax purpose is a legitimate business purpose because it is in the interest of the business to increase profitability where it can legally do so by reducing its tax liability. Once again Wilson rejected an artificial dichotomy, this time between tax purposes and business purposes, and asserted a pragmatic commercial reality. The context of business is business certainty. It is always and unilaterally open to Parliament to change the rules if it does not like the result.

BUSINESS ENTITIES, CORPORATE CONTROL, AND LEGAL SUBJECTS

If tax considerations often motivate the design of corporate structures, other corporate law doctrines also have a role to play. For example, *Eldorado Nuclear*[22] was a very peculiar case concerning corporate control in which Wilson partially dissented on the issue of crown immunity. Two respondent companies, both crown corporations, had been charged under the Combines Investigation Act with conspiracy to reduce competition in the production and sale of uranium. Both the Supreme Court of Ontario and the Court of Appeal had held that they were immune from criminal liability because they were agents of the crown; the majority of the Supreme Court affirmed this judgment, dismissing the appeal.

Wilson held that only Uranium Canada was entitled to assert immunity, reasoning that the statutory provision on the status of crown agents does not grant blanket immunity but requires a two-step test:

The first step is to decide whether the agent is authorized, expressly or impliedly, to perform the acts in question. In making this determination it is not enough to say that the *purpose* for which the acts are performed is an authorized purpose; the court must also determine that the *means* which the agent uses to accomplish the purpose are expressly or impliedly authorized. If as a matter of statutory interpretation the means are authorized, the agent is entitled to immunity. If, however, there is no such authorization, the Court must move to the second step. The second step is to decide whether or not the agent is, for all intents and purposes, the *alter ego* of the crown. If because of the degree of control – and by this is meant *de jure* as opposed to *de facto* control – which the crown is able to exercise over the agent it is impossible for the Court to characterize the agent's act as anything other than the act of the crown, the agent is entitled to assert crown immunity whether or not its governing statute authorized the means by which the agent carries out its statutory purposes. If, however, the crown does not have that degree of control, the agent will not be entitled to assert the immunity if the means used are outside the purview of the statute.[23]

Her survey of the relevant case law supported her position that an individual or corporation with the status of crown agent will still be personally liable for any acts carried out which are beyond the scope of its authority and that the onus is on the agent to demonstrate that it could not carry out its mandate without the commission of such acts.

Her tone was different, however, in the extraordinarily complex *Molchan*[24] case. Myron L. Molchan was a limited partner in an oil-drilling venture set up to acquire, develop, and operate oil and gas properties. After the partnership had exhausted all the capital resources it had available, the general partner offered to buy out the limited partners with shares in the parent company, Omega Hydrocarbons Limited. Then the general partner sold all the non-producing lands which had been held by the partnership to Hydrocarbons, leaving the partnership still in existence, still retaining certain lands and still receiving revenues from the oil and gas operation. Mr Molchan refused the offer to purchase and commenced an action on the issue of liability; according to Jim Phillips, the clerk who worked on this file, Molchan seems to have been 'a difficult person who was trying to hold out for a better deal than he deserved, maybe, but nonetheless he had a legal right to do that.'

What ensued was a confused trial record with the trial judge holding that the sale of the non-producing lands had breached the applicable Partnership Act, that Hydrocarbons and the general partner were in fact a single entity, and that Hydrocarbons had acquired the non-producing lands with knowledge that the transfer was in breach of the act. In other words, the trustee had effectively sold trust property to itself, a blatant conflict of interest. But on appeal the court set aside the finding of fact by the trial judge that the transfer of lands had made it impossible to carry on the ordinary business of the partnership, in effect conducting a new trial on the issue of the fiduciary duty of the general partner as trustee holding the properties on behalf of the other partners, which it held had not been breached. Molchan's claim for the return of the non-producing lands to the general partner was dismissed. The majority at the Supreme Court, per Justice Estey, followed the Court of Appeal analysis on the grounds that the sale of the non-producing lands had not made it impossible to carry on a substantial portion of the ordinary business of the partnership.

Wilson dissented. Her analysis of the procedural history of the case was a stinging critique of the competence of the Court of Appeal and, by implication, the Supreme Court too:

> In my view, the correct approach for this Court to take in such unusual circumstances is to reinstate the order of the trial judge. I say this for two reasons. First ... the trial judge's finding of a breach of the Partnership Act was not impugned at all in the Court of Appeal. While that Court has broad powers when a judgment is appealed to it, it cannot fail to address the central issues remitted to it. In this case it did exactly that. Moreover, it acted as a court of first instance on an entirely different issue from the one dealt with by the trial judge and quashed the trial judge's order on the basis of its determination of that issue.[25]

The unilateral decision of the general partner to cease acquiring and developing oil and gas properties provided evidence sufficient for the trial judge to conclude that a substantial and significant element of the business had been shut down, constituting a statutory breach of the Partnership Act and triggering liability of the general partner with the remedy of an accounting. As Wilson pointed out, the sale of lands by the general partner to itself also constituted a classic breach of fiduciary duty, even if the general partner had acted in good faith and paid a fair price. Under some limited circumstances, a court could entertain an application after the fact for approval of such an extraordinary move; but there was no evidence that it was appropriate in this instance. Had it been necessary she would have been prepared to reverse the Court of Appeal on the fiduciary duty issue as well. However, she insisted with some asperity that it would not have been necessary to do so in this instance if the majority at the Supreme Court had done its duty and reinstated the trial judge's order. Is it any wonder that judges peering into such corporate structures once their reasons have been conscientiously prepared, heave a sigh of relief and promptly forget as many of the labyrinthine details as they possibly can?

Yet one of Wilson's most interesting business entity decisions dealt with a single shareholder corporation in which the very simplicity of the corporate structure gave rise to the legal dilemma. *Kosmopoulos*[26] involved a leather manufacturer and retailer who suffered losses due to smoke and water damage from a fire in the adjacent business. Mr Kosmopoulos operated a store called Spring Leather Goods. His lawyer had advised him to incorporate Kosmopolous Leather Goods Limited and he did; but 'even though the business was thereafter technically carried on through the limited company, Mr. Kosmopoulos always thought that he owned the store and its assets.'[27] All documentation dealing with the business was in the name of Andreas Kosmopoulos or Spring Leather Goods rather than in the company name, including insurance for the contents of his business premises. After the fire his insurance company refused to pay his claim, denying liability on the ground that Kosmopoulos as sole shareholder of the corporation did not have either a legal or an equitable claim on the assets of the company and accordingly could not have any insurable interest in them. Wilson had to decide for the Supreme Court whether or not the *Macaura*[28] principle of insurable interest 'is presently the law in Ontario and should continue to be the law of Ontario.'

Insurable interest is a doctrine rooted in an economic rationale and intended to protect insurers from the moral hazard of third party claims made after a deliberate destruction of insured property in order to collect in excess of the value of that property. Unflinchingly Wilson embarked on a scholarly attack on the doctrine itself, which was weakened in her view insofar as its development had been influenced by the fraud lurking in the background circumstances surrounding the original decision.

But such fraud was not usual. She balanced the probability of moral hazard against the presumption that an insurance company's refusal to pay a claim after it had received payment of the premiums will often be a merely technical objection of potentially equal impropriety. *Kosmopolous* was a private action, not a Charter case, and yet the logic of the balancing analysis had something in common with the *Oakes* section 1 proportionality test. In this instance the means (denying insurance coverage) was manifestly not reasonable or justified in proportion to the importance of the objective of eliminating moral hazard.

At no place in the judgment did Wilson explicitly state that *Macaura* was no longer the law in Ontario; she was here merely affirming the decision at the trial and appellate levels. In his brief concurring judgment, McIntyre would have retained the *Macaura* doctrine of insurable interest but with an exception for sole shareholder corporations to be determined on a case-by-case basis; Wilson's willingness to face and resolve the issue head on is more in keeping with her pragmatic understanding of the value of certainty in commercial law situations.

LABOURING OVER LABOUR RELATIONS

Wilson felt that the Supreme Court 'failed abysmally' in dealing with labour relations during her years on the bench. Occasionally, of course, she either managed to carry the day or to concur with the majority decision. But it was a big disappointment to her to lose out in some of the major cases which dealt with labour relations in the context of Charter rights. She dissented in two of the three labour trilogy cases[29] concerned with the Charter section 2(d) guarantee of freedom of association in the context of the right to unionize and the right to strike.

Wilson did not prepare separate reasons in the *Reference Re Public Service Relations Act* case; instead, she concurred with Chief Justice Dickson's analysis, which found that the act in question did violate freedom of association and that nevertheless, because of the serious injuries to the economic interests of third parties which would result from a strike or lockout and because the impugned legislation provided for an alternate scheme of arbitration, it was justifiable under section 1 of the Charter. As Wilson put it, 'Dickson wrote a brilliant judgment with which I completely agreed, and he and I were certainly a complete identity.'

The majority on the Court denied that the act violated freedom of association; section 2 (b) simply did not include a guarantee of the right to bargain collectively or the right to strike. The judgment attempts to elucidate the issue by analogy to a golf course, discussing the circumstances under which golf might be deemed a constitutionally protected activity and whether it would be possible to design constitutional legislation to control the number of people permitted to play golf together. Wilson, long exasperated by the alliances among the male judges which formed on the golf course or the tennis court, predictably had very little patience with this logic.

In *Public Service Alliance of Canada* v. *Canada,* Dickson wrote reasons dissenting only in part and Wilson felt compelled to write separate reasons dissenting entirely. Federal legislation had extended collective agreements of public sector employees and fixed wage increases for a two-year period. The stated government objective was the control of inflation; Wilson agreed that this was of sufficiently pressing concern to justify the limitation of the freedom of employees to bargain collectively or to strike. However, there was insufficient proportionality in the legislative measures because they had not been appropriately tailored to achieve the legislative objective: 'the government conceded that the controls [applicable to only 5 per cent of the work force] were not expected to have a *direct* effect on inflation.' The kind of 'leadership by example' rationale invoked by the government simply constituted a confusion of the role of government as legislator and the role of government as employer.

What was happening here – and what was always a sure-fire trigger for Wilson's disdain – was a kind of utilitarian cooptation for unilateral gain. The workers were only a means to an end; the government wanted to make a dramatic inflation-fighting gesture to score political points and was willing to sacrifice the Charter rights of a group of its employees to do so. Briefly, at the end of her dissent, Wilson considered the 'rational connection' leg of the proportionality test. If the government's objective was to evoke voluntary compliance with anti-inflation guidelines in the private sector, then imposing mandatory compliance on public employees seemed to her a peculiar way of setting an example. The majority simply reaffirmed LeDain's analysis in the *Reference* and reiterated that section 2 (d) did not constitutionalize the right to strike; Dickson would have struck down only part of the act, given that in his view the government's anti-inflation objective and its leadership role justified suspension of collective bargaining on compensation and benefits but not on non-compensatory issues and not to the exclusion of a binding arbitration alternative.

In *RWDSU* v. *Saskatchewan* Wilson was all alone in dissent. When contract talks between the unions and the single major dairy business in Saskatchewan did not produce a new collective agreement, the unions served strike notices. The dairies responded with lockout notices and the provincial government passed legislation temporarily prohibiting both strikes and lockouts in the dairy industry. The unions applied to the court for a declaration that the act infringed their freedom of association; their application was allowed at the Court of Appeal. At the Supreme Court, however, the majority held that the act did not impugn the Charter guarantee.

Wilson's analysis in this case focused on the application of the first step of the *Oakes* test. In her opinion, the objective of the legislation was simply not pressing and substantial enough to justify overriding the Charter right. There could be no evidence demonstrating grave economic harm to dairy farmers prior to the initiation of any stoppage of work. Furthermore, Wilson questioned the progressive expansion of the concept of essential services through the characterization by the government of milk as a commodity essential to the health of the general public. She cited several pre-Charter papers written by H.W. Arthurs in which he had argued that not only the quantitative but also the qualitative element of public interest in a labour dispute must be taken into account. But Wilson disagreed with Arthur's assessment; in her opinion, 'it fails to recognize that public and private interests are not being pitted against each other. What are being pitted against each other are two different kinds of public interest, the public interest in the continuation of services and the public interest in the freedom of workers to associate and act collectively.'[30]

Those members of the public who might welcome legislative protection from any interruption of their milk supply – although the evidence demonstrated that milk would have been readily available from neighbouring provinces in the event of a strike – would undoubtedly in a labour dispute involving their own place of work wish to maintain their freedom as workers to associate and to bargain collectively. Therefore they must be prepared to tolerate a certain amount of inconvenience. And Wilson stressed that the characterization of the dairy farmers as innocent third parties to the dispute particularly vulnerable to economic harm ignored the reality that the milk-processing plants were owned by cooperative associations of dairy farmers.

However, Wilson did concur in the majority judgment in *BCGEU* v. *British Columbia*,[31] a case concerning the constitutionality of picketing in the course of a legal strike at British Columbia court houses. The labour union issued passes to permit access to the courts for urgent matters but was undeniably attempting to achieve bargaining leverage by interfering with the courts' normal operations. Believing it to be his constitutional duty to keep the courts fully functioning, British Columbia Chief Justice McEachern responded by issuing an *ex parte* injunction[32] restraining the picketing and dismissed the union's motion to set aside the injunction, a ruling upheld at the Court of Appeal. The Supreme Court also dismissed the appeal. Chief Justice Dickson wrote the majority opinion, finding that the picketing constituted criminal contempt because it interfered with other citizens' right of access to justice. Criminal contempt is a matter of federal jurisdiction outside the labour relations aspect of picketing properly within the provincial jurisdiction of a labour relations board. Sustaining the rule of law is fundamental and trumped any Charter protection of freedom of expression, given the pressing and substantial nature of this concern. In this instance, at least, Wilson did not find for the union.

Even although the constitutional labour cases were generally a profound disappointment to Wilson, she wrote the majority judgment in *Sobey's Stores* v. *Yeomans and Labour Standards Tribunal*.[33] This was a non-union labour case with a complex constitutional dimension relating not to impugned Charter rights but to the division of powers in the 1867 Constitution Act. Sobey's had dismissed Yeomans after ten years of employment as manager of its Dartmouth, Nova Scotia, grocery store. He complained to the director of the Nova Scotia Labour Standards Tribunal that he had been dismissed without cause and the director ordered his reinstatement with lost wages, a decision which was upheld at the tribunal on administrative appeal. Sobey's took the case for review to the Nova Scotia courts. It won on the grounds that the Nova Scotia labour code was unconstitutional in so far as it permitted a provincial tribunal to exercise powers reserved solely for federally appointed courts under section 96 of the act.

Wilson invoked the three-step test which had been developed by Dickson in the 1979 *Residential Tenancies*[34] case. Jim Phillips,[35] who was assigned the task of researching the historical analysis and the case law, discovered a number of interesting anomalies in the application of that test. The first step involved definition of the historic exclusive jurisdiction of the superior courts at Confederation, which might vary depending upon when a specific province had joined Canada. The case law was confused; it did not distinguish between allocation of that jurisdiction to the inferior provincial courts and to administrative tribunals. Wilson's approach was to decide that the original bargain relating to division of powers entered into by the four founding provinces applied to all, but that a frozen rights analysis was too technical given the necessity of establishing administrative bodies responsive to changing social conditions. The second step was concerned with a determination of whether the provincial tribunal was functioning judicially, since if it were not there could be no violation of section 96. Wilson determined that although the director was not exercising a judicial function at the first stage, when the tribunal as a whole heard appeals and settled them according to law, it was acting judicially. Stage three concerned an examination of that function in its broader context. Wilson looked to the substantive protections offered through the tribunal's authorizing statute relating to minimum wage, hours of work, notice periods, and the statutory right of reinstatement. She also considered the procedural protections and the rationales for them: confidentiality, speed, and the relatively low cost of resolving complaints. In her view, the judicial function of the tribunal was incidental to the policy decision of the legislature to provide minimal protections to non-unionized workers and accordingly not an unconstitutional infringement of the section 96 division of powers.

Wilson wrote one more pro-union labour decision which, even though it was not a majority judgment, did at least concur with the majority in the result. *Lavigne*[36] concerned a community college teacher who objected to the deduction from his pay cheque of that portion of his compulsory union dues which supported various causes, including a campaign against cruise missile testing and support of the New Democratic Party, which he believed to be extraneous to the purpose of the union. Lavigne argued that Charter guarantees of freedom of association ought to be construed as a guarantee of freedom not to associate; he also argued that his freedom of expression was infringed insofar as contribution to such causes constituted an expressive act. At trial he was successful on the freedom of association issue and lost on freedom of expression; the Court of Appeal reversed on the grounds that this was a private commercial matter outside the reach of the Charter altogether.

There were four sets of reasons at the Supreme Court, all converging on the same decision – that the union was entitled to enforce the mandatory dues check-off – but from different perspectives. LaForest, writing for Sopinka and Gonthier, held that the Charter did apply because the Council of Regents with overall responsibility for college administration was a creation of government; that freedom of association did encompass freedom from association because compelled association infringes human dignity and self-fulfilment; but that the infringement was justified under section 1 because it was essential to the substantial objective of workplace democracy.

Both Cory and McLachlin in separate judgments agreed with the LaForest definition of government. McLachlin, however, found that freedom of association was not impugned so long as an individual had not been compelled to adopt the ideology of the group with which the association was compelled and further, that payment was not equivalent to an expressive act in this instance. Cory adopted Wilson's reasons on the substantive issues of freedom of association and expression.

Wilson wrote for herself and L'Heureux-Dubé. She found government action triggering Charter application inhered in both the Council of Regents and the college itself as the deliverer of government-funded education. Demonstrating the same pragmatic commitment to effects-based analysis she had employed in the labour trilogy cases, she too found for the union. Freedom of expression was not impugned since no one was preventing Lavigne from continuing to object to the union's funding of activities he did not support. His freedom of association was not impugned since this guarantee could not possibly encompass freedom *from* association which by definition depends upon the perceptions of others:

> It is a fact of our civilization as human beings that we are of necessity involved in associations not of our own choosing. That being so it is naive to suggest that the Constitution can or should enable us to extricate ourselves from all the associations we deem undesirable. Such extrication would be impossible and even to attempt it would make a mockery of the right contained in section 2(d).

In any case, Lavigne could have exercised his freedom from association by declining to become a member of the bargaining unit in the first place without jeopardizing his economic interests; the legislation compelled no one to join a union and required a certified bargaining agent to represent all employees without discrimination. Furthermore, only a few cents of Lavigne's dues were actually directed towards the objectionable causes. Even if Lavigne's freedoms had been impugned, Wilson concluded, the collective bargaining objective was sufficiently pressing and substantial to withstand section 1 scrutiny. The Charter was never intended to relieve persons of trivial burdens, Wilson pointed out; the legislation provided for the appropriate balancing of public interests and left Lavigne free to balance his own personal interests.

GUARANTEED RIGHTS FOR CORPORATIONS

There were a number of significant business entity cases not concerned with labour issues which gave rise to Charter challenges. Heard consecutively on 1 and 2 November 1988, both *Thomson Newspapers*[37] and *McKinlay Transport*[38] were concerned with corporate claims to the Charter section 8 right to be secure from unreasonable search or seizure. Wilson wrote a detailed and passionate dissent in *Thomson*. In *McKinlay*, however, she was with the majority and Lamer signed on to her judgment.

Law professor Maureen Maloney provided a neat summary of *Thomson*:

> [T]he issue before the court was whether two individuals could be served with orders under section 17 of the Combines Investigation Act to appear before the Restrictive Trade Practices Commission to be examined under oath and to produce specified documents. Section 20 of the same act prohibited the use of information so obtained in future criminal proceedings that might be brought against the individual. The issue was whether section 17 offended either section 6 (the rights to life, liberty and security of the person) or section 7 (unreasonable search and [*sic*] seizure) of the Canadian Charter of Rights and Freedoms. The section has been widely used over the years by the Bureau of Competition Policy primarily as a means to obtain documentary evidence by means of a subpoena. In addition it has also been used to obtain oral testimony from individuals. These sections have been considered an important means of enforcing Canadian anti-monopoly laws. The majority of the court speaking through Mr. Justice La Forest thought section 17 did not infringe upon either section 7 or 8. In part, this was due to the fact that 'there can be only a relatively low expectation of privacy in respect of premises or documents that are used or produced in the course of activities which, though lawful, are subject to state regulation as a matter of course.' Moreover, 'in so far as section 17 is concerned ... it will be typically, if not exclusively, used to order the production of business records ... it is fair to say that they raise much weaker privacy concerns than personal papers.'[39]

Maloney quite obviously believed that the majority got it right and that there was a misplaced intensity about Wilson's dissent, which arose from Wilson's failure to recognize that the government has a right to invade corporate privacy in order to do battle against 'the undesirable monopolistic tendencies of large corporations.'

But useful as Maloney's summary is, there was one crucial point which does not accurately reflect the statutory situation which gave rise to Wilson's concern. Although section 20(2) grants protection to witnesses in subsequent criminal proceedings, Wilson pointed out, 'Nothing in the section protects the witness from the use of derivative evidence obtained as a result of his testimony. Moreover, nothing in section 20 (2) prevents the use of the documents against the witness.'[40] Almost thirty pages of her judgment were devoted to discussion of the ramifications of that omission and the potential infringement of section 7 rights which flow from that potential use of derivative evidence.

Moreover, in her review of the legislative history of the Combines Investigation Act, Wilson suggested that the initial coherence of the legislation had crumbled. Social consensus about big business had changed; the 'strong moral overtones' which prompted the first legislation in 1889 no longer existed in the same way, given the remarkable changes in size and complexity of business enterprises as they had evolved over the intervening century. Citing from her own section 7 analysis in *Singh* and in *Re B.C. Motor Vehicle Act*, Wilson insisted that some distinction must be possible between regulatory and criminal regimes:

> There is ... a vast difference between a general regulatory scheme ... designed to give some order to human behaviour and a state-imposed compulsion on an individual to appear at proceedings against his will and testify on pain of punishment if he refuses. The difference is even greater, in my view, where the compelled testimony given by the individual may be used to build a case against him in what is, in effect, a subsequent criminal prosecution. It is in my opinion that [sic] this compulsion, linked as it is to the criminal process, touches upon the physical integrity of the individual as well as that individual's reasonable expectation of privacy.[41]

She concluded that although getting at the truth is a vital element of our justice system, even that value is less important than the protection of the fundamental rights of the accused. LaForest's proposed solution to the problem of derivative justice – that it be left to the discretion of the trial judge under section 24 (2) of the Charter[42] – did not satisfy Wilson. 'The exclusion must be a matter of principle and right, not of discretion,' she reasoned, and added that the 'public repute of justice' cannot be the relevant consideration in determining whether evidence would be admitted when it is already apparent that that evidence had been obtained in direct violation of the fundamental principles of justice.

Wilson's analysis on the right to be secure against unreasonable search or seizure stressed the separability of the unreasonable search from the unreasonable seizure. When the individual seeking to avoid disclosure is compelled to produce documentary evidence, he might inadvertently release additional information giving rise to more charges than the authority ordering production had originally contemplated. In Wilson's view, then, compulsory production not only constituted seizure but might even create harsher consequences than a more conventional seizure without production ordered by authorities not sure what they are doing. In *Thomson* it was highly unlikely that an individual ordered to disclose in accordance with the provisions of the combines legislation would realize that a limited review of the order prior to disclosure was possible. Therefore Wilson would have found that the legislation did offend the section 8 guarantees and since by definition it permitted unreasonable search or seizure it could not be saved as a reasonable limit under section 1 analysis.

In her *McKinlay* reasons, Wilson reviewed a great deal of the case law with which she had bolstered her dissent in *Thomson*; she found that the demand by Revenue Canada to produce documents for an internal tax audit under the relevant provision of the Income Tax Act did not contravene the section 8 guarantee because they were necessary to the regulatory administration of the tax scheme. For Wilson, the key difference between the *Thomson* and *McKinlay* contexts was very simple; in *Thomson*, the relevant statutory provisions would have made serious criminal sanctions possible at least indirectly, whereas the *McKinlay* decision turns on the non-punitive purpose of the tax provisions intended to regulate the tax scheme set out by the act. Moreover, Wilson accepted that only random monitoring could ensure the integrity of the tax system which has to depend upon voluntary compliance given the impossibility of requiring each individual citizen and business enterprise to submit all relevant documentation for calculation of taxes owing to the ministry. A statutory requirement of disclosure was the least intrusive means of achieving the legitimate legislative objective.

In Wilson's opinion, there is a large realm of regulated social and business activity where the reasonable expectation of privacy must be very low – submission to customs procedures at the crossing of state borders, for example, or manufacturing of food stuffs for public consumption subject to health inspection. The individual or the corporation in effect tacitly acquiesces to necessary regulation as a precondition for the opportunity of engaging in that activity. Moreover these regulated activities, unlike activities relating to freedom of religion, as in *Big M* or *Edwards Books*, do not go to the core of the individual's definition of the self and therefore there is no significant loss of liberty entailed by the necessity of seeking regulatory permission or submitting to the regulatory scheme.

Both *Big M* and *Edwards Books* were decided at a point in the development of Charter jurisprudence when the Supreme Court was primarily concerned with laying down analytic procedures to be applied and also in defining the meaning of rights. There is a noticeable gap in these judgments when it comes to defining the sense in which a drugstore or a retail book outlet as commercial organizations can claim to require protection of freedom of religion. In the *Edmonton Journal*[43] case, however, the section 2 (b) guarantee of freedom of expression was so obviously relevant to the fundamental business of the appellant – dissemination of information – that it looked like an easy case for the application of Charter rights to a business entity.

The Alberta Judicature Act severely restricted newspapers from publishing details of court documents and pleadings relating to matrimonial matters and various other civil proceedings, including administrative and constitutional law cases, prior to the cases being heard. At trial and at the Court of Appeal the newspaper's claim that the act contravened its freedom of expression was dismissed on section 1 analysis; the courts found that the infringement was a reasonable one, given the competing interests of individuals in protecting their privacy and the public interest in ensuring fair trial procedures.

The Supreme Court allowed the appeal. There were three sets of reasons, two of which were already circulating by September 1989, a scant six months after the March hearing. Cory, writing for Dickson and Lamer, concluded that freedom of expression was so vital to sustain democracy that its restriction could be justified under section 1 analysis only rarely and under very clear circumstances, and not in this instance. LaForest, dissenting in part and writing for L'Heureux-Dubé and Sopinka, would have upheld that section of the act dealing with restrictions on publication of allegations relating to divorce and custody matters to protect the privacy of the parties and in particular their children, but would have allowed the appeal in relation to all other aspects of the legislation which he deemed an unjustified infringement of the freedom of expression guarantee. Wilson had read both sets of reasons and was leaning towards concurring with Cory. What made her uncomfortable was the abstract quality of his analysis of freedom of expression, which failed to confront the conflict between the competing interests at play in this dispute or to acknowledge that both values could not fully be respected at the same time. What necessitated Wilson's diverging concurrence in *Edmonton Journal* was her conviction that interpretation of Charter rights is only meaningful when competing values are weighed contextually:

> I realized how broad the rights in the Charter were, that they were set out in the very broadest terms, and that was what made me start thinking about how the same right could have different meanings in different contexts and therefore it was very important when we were addressing an argument on the Charter to appreciate the context in which it was being raised.

The contextual determination of legal facts and the contextual definition of legal subjects are approaches which we have already seen Wilson returning to again and again in non-Charter cases. She slowly came to the conclusion that it would be necessary to write separate reasons in this case and only gradually did those reasons take shape.

Wilson had great difficulty with her *Edmonton Journal* concurrence. The judgment was finally released for circulation to the other justices in late November 1989. Undoubtedly one of her most powerful and complex contributions to Canadian jurisprudence, it has been influential in its shaping of Supreme Court analysis ever since.[44] She wrote:

> One virtue of the contextual approach, it seems to me, is that it recognizes that a particular right or freedom may have a different value depending on the context. It may be, for example, that freedom of expression has greater value in a political context than it does in the context of disclosure of the details of a matrimonial dispute. The contextual approach attempts to bring into sharp relief the aspect of the right or freedom which is truly at stake in the case as well as the relevant aspects of any values in competition with it. It seems to be more sensitive to the reality of the dilemma posed by the particular facts and therefore more conducive to finding a fair and just compromise between the two competing values under section 1. It is my

view that a right or freedom may have different meanings in different contexts.[45]

Wilson's provisional process for weighing rights as it related to her highly particularized definition of rights is traceable back to Aristotelian phronesis, the subtle and shifting integration of practical and philosophic wisdoms which we saw re-emerging in David Hume's phenomenological explorations of the fragmented self, linked in turn to Hume's cheerful acceptance of the indeterminate epistemology which is all that such necessarily fragmented selves can achieve; it is akin to the writings of the best of the contemporary postmodern theorists who sustain the liberal heritage of meaning-seeking without demanding that meanings be unitary or finally fixed.

It was truly a judgment that would have been worth waiting for. Unfortunately, by the time it was released her colleagues had all signalled their support for either the Cory or the LaForest judgments. No one signed on.

In his partial dissent, LaForest had also attempted a contextual analysis. However, he evaluated freedom of expression in the context of the litigant's right to privacy, which led him to conclude that the newspaper's freedom of expression in the instance of matrimonial cases must yield to the litigant's privacy interests. His approach was in error, Wilson cautioned, because it is never possible to 'balance one value at large and the conflicting value in its context.' In this instance, she argued, 'Both interests must be seen as public interests, in this case the public interest in protecting the privacy of litigants generally in matrimonial cases against the public interest in an open court process.'[46]

Were the competing interests in this instance necessarily public interests? Does the public have an interest in protecting the privacy of litigants generally in matrimonial causes, as Wilson framed it? Or would the robust common sense of social consensus tell us that, as avid as the public might be for the prurient details of a particular divorce proceeding, it is the individuals involved who value their privacy and would wish to prevent unproven allegations about their private affairs from being spread across the pages of the local paper? Looking again at the logic of her judgment in RWDSU, where Wilson had reasoned that members of the public must be prepared to tolerate some inconvenience and interruption to their milk supply in order to sustain their own rights to collective bargaining in their respective workplaces should the need arise, might this not be a parallel instance in which members of the public should tolerate a certain restriction on the newspaper's freedom of expression in order to sustain their own privacy in the event that they themselves might become embroiled in a messy divorce proceeding?

The Court was wrestling hard with defining freedom of expression during the period when *Edmonton Journal* was being decided; Wilson herself was sympathetic to the importance of freedom of expression as a core value intersecting with other Charter values in so far as it protects and enhances them. Earlier in 1989 Wilson had participated in the majority decision in *Irwin Toy*,[47] another freedom of expression case also in a commercial context. The toy manufacturer challenged regulations in the Quebec Consumer Protection Act which controlled advertising aimed at children and the Court held that commercial expression is protected under the section 2 (b) guarantee but that the legislative restrictions constituted a reasonable limit upon that freedom because of the pressing and substantial legislative goal of protecting children against manipulation. Freedom of expression was curtailed under section 1 analysis by a narrow majority in *Keegstra*,[48] a controversial case concerning hate propaganda against identifiable groups which was preoccupying the Court at the same time as *Edmonton Journal*. Wilson did not write separate reasons but she was actively involved in the debate among the Supreme Court justices.

Although the appellant in *Edmonton Journal* was just as much a commercial entity as the manufacturer in *Irwin Toy*, the freedom of expression sought by Irwin (advertising) was incidental to its main enterprise but absolutely central to the newspaper's business. Had the competing issues in *Edmonton Journal* been framed as a contest among three competing values – the newspaper's commercial freedom of expression to sell papers based on titillating allegations; the protection through freedom of expression of the integrity of the process of fair trial; and the protection of the privacy of individuals and their children engaged in divorce proceedings – it is not so clear that freedom of expression ought to have trumped. But this was not the issue which the Court perceived had been remitted to it for decision and freedom of the press seems to have clouded recognition of the commercial dimension of the debate.

ETHICS AND ECONOMICS: WILSON'S BUSINESS CONTEXT

With the exception of a few cases, the enormous volume of work Wilson took on at the Supreme Court in the area of torts, contracts, bankruptcy, tax, property, labour, corporate, and commercial law has largely been overlooked. This was not because her Supreme Court colleagues failed to acknowledge her competence in these areas; indeed they were happy enough to have her write all the routine judgments she was willing to take on. But despite her best efforts in attempting to flag the leave to appeal issue for serious debate, she was by and large unable to persuade the Court to consider its effect as a juridical tool; it is obvious from her conscientious development of dissenting and concurring reasons in cases such as *Syncrude* or *LAC Minerals* that she herself never lost sight of the responsibility to shape the common law which had been assigned the Court through that extremely powerful 1975 Supreme Court Act amendment.

At the Dalhousie symposium to honour Wilson after her retirement it is striking how little attention was accorded the civil cases which comprised so much of Wilson's judicial career. Speaker after speaker mentioned *Singh* and *Dairy Pool* and *Lavallée* and *Morgentaler*. Yet except for Alan Watson's extended discussion of *Kosmopoulos*, only Maureen Maloney had much to say about the substantial contributions Wilson made to the development of business law doctrines. It is not so much that these cases are not interesting – very little interests us more than the protection of our own financial interests should they be put in jeopardy – as that the facts in corporate and commercial decisions tend to be enormously complex. Maloney may have adopted a deliberately provocative account of Wilson's corporate law decisions juxtaposed with the principles of feminist theory, making it difficult for her to do complete justice to Wilson's less politicized and more postmodern stance. And perhaps there was at the end of Wilson's career and even in an audience gathered to honour her an unspoken consensus that women judges are properly most interested in family law or human rights issues.

Women judges will make more of a difference when it is presumed that a Wilson tax judgment or corporate control judgment merits as much weight and respect as a Iacobucci tax judgment or a Sopinka corporate control judgment. They will make the most difference of all when all civil judgments, whether written by male or female judges, are considered in a diversity of contexts, including the context of the litigants' circumstances, the context of the common law, the context of relevant statutes and regulations, and the context of business certainty.

In *Edmonton Journal* Wilson added to the common law of Charter jurisprudence what was an essentially postmodern procedure for the contextual determination of the meaning of guaranteed rights and freedoms. But this important procedural proposal expanded upon her underlying conviction that the distinction between method of analysis and substantive result is not a bright line in any area of the law. Before we leave her Supreme Court jurisprudence altogether, we need to consider some other substantive contributions Wilson made to criminal law, constitutional law, administrative law, and even international law, which contributions were generated by her attentiveness to the substantive effects of various legal procedures.

11

Contextual Proceduralism

Drawing in part upon her experience at Oslers, where Wilson had developed a unified research department, she often wished that the Supreme Court could have had the luxury of grouping together cases on the same issue and deciding them simultaneously. Grouping is a luxury we have been granting ourselves as we surveyed Wilson's contributions to human rights, family, and business law decisions. These groupings have nevertheless been only loosely organized; legal facts stubbornly refuse to confine themselves to tidy legal categories.

Grouping of cases at the Supreme Court did sometimes occur through fortuity – in the *Pelech* spousal support contract trilogy, for example, or in the prostitution and labour cases we have already considered. But the conjunction of my tenuous organization of the case law by topic, together with such occasional and coincidental self-groupings, may have given a false impression of what it was like to sit on the Court during this turbulent period in Canadian legal history. A quick flip through any of the neat bench books in which Wilson recorded her notes from hearings would reveal how extremely varied the lineup of cases usually was; perhaps a criminal hearing in the morning, a family case in the afternoon, then the next morning a complex corporate control dispute followed by a tax law matter.

Multiple decisions concerning the definition of rights had to be made confidently, to provide guidance for the lower courts, but mostly in isolation from one another. Public expectations were high that a just society would be achieved swiftly and painlessly through the mere fact of the entrenchment of the Charter; there was little understanding that it might be difficult to determine the content and scope of the rights, or that recognizing new rights for some might entail erosion of existing privileges or impose new responsibilities on others.

In Wilson's opinion, part of the reason for the endemic delays in the release of judgments resulted from the difficulty individual justices had in setting aside work on the reasons they had volunteered to write for particular cases in order to consider thoughtfully the draft judgments coming at them from their colleagues dealing with the raft of other hearings in which they had also participated. The system of judgment writing requires each judge to take on the initial responsibility for drafting the reasons in several cases at the same time, but each judge is also dependent on the work of his colleagues; the cases are so varied and the judges' responses are also so varied that even a moderately constraining schedule may be unworkable.[1] Disciplined chambers management made it possible for Wilson to cope with her own workload; she relied upon the information retrieval systems established by Jean Plourde, the delegation of research tasks to her clerks and their cooperation with her strict Friday timetable for submission of memos, and her own long hours and formidable powers of concentration.

Still, the complexity of the caseload and the burden of responsibility were overwhelming, especially during the early Charter years which coincided so unfortunately with substantial illness and absence on the Court. Wilson remembers her colleagues at the Court of Appeal saying, 'semi-jocularly but semi-seriously, "if we have got it wrong the Supreme Court will put it right, so the public isn't going to really suffer."' The lower courts are essentially dispute resolution bodies; judges at the Supreme Court level were very aware that there was no one else to get the law right, and in Wilson's view this was an extremely onerous responsibility. It is easy to understand why she said, at a dinner party for women lawyers held during a conference in Australia when she had been on the Court for about eighteen months, that it was a hard and demanding life and 'not so much the peak of a legal career but rather the ultimate form of public service.'

The Court had become increasingly sensitive to the complexity of circumstances blurring old legal categories – the difficulty, for example, of adjudicating a contract case without taking into account aspects of tort law or constructive trust. Charter cases most obviously met the national importance test established by the leave to appeal procedure; once cases began working their way up to Ottawa after the entrenchment of the Charter and then again when the section 15 equality provisions came into effect in 1985, the Court became preoccupied with the task of defining the rights and freedoms guaranteed by the Charter.

But the very structure of the Charter demanded a methodology which integrated and harmonized the old modernist distinction between procedural and substantive elements of law. Inevitably in the Charter cases already considered, our discussion has touched upon specific provisions (in particular, the balancing exercise required by section 1 and formulated in the *Oakes* test) which required the Court to establish new procedures – procedures that were themselves in part determinative of the substantive rights or freedoms at issue.

In a 1984 speech, 'Guaranteed Freedoms in a Free and Democratic Society,' Wilson mentioned that she found very interesting political scientist Peter Russell's observation that 'the Charter guarantees not rights but a way of making decisions about rights in which the judiciary has a more systematic and authoritative role.'[2] This is a concept which Wilson would find congenial, believing as she does that methodology conditions judgments. After all, it is because there is a pressing ethical obligation to select the right methodology that she objected so strenuously to lobbying among her colleagues as a technique of decision-making. But the process of working with the Charter brought her face-to-face with the more general recognition that the dichotomy between procedure and substance is an artificial one.

Methodology conditions judgments because context also conditions rights. In *Edmonton Journal*[3] she explained that the procedure of defining rights contextually, by paying attention to the specific circumstances generated by the cases themselves, may result in the ascription of substantively different meanings to Charter-guaranteed rights in their different contexts. By 1989, the first wave of Charter jurisprudence was well under way – that is, some of the initial work of defining the substantive content of the guaranteed rights and freedoms had been done. In *Edmonton Journal* Wilson effectively requested that her colleagues reconsider the substantive effects of the procedural methods they had used to that point. And as the Court moved into phase two Charter analysis during the last years of Wilson's tenure, there were more and more cases in which she wrote dissents or diverging concurrences based on her attentiveness to the substantive impact of these procedural considerations.

Madam Justice Claire L'Heureux-Dubé recalls that when she was appointed to the Court as its second woman judge in 1987, morale among her new colleagues was so low that she would have been happy to leave after six months and return to the Quebec Court of Appeal. She might even have done so had it not been for the sympathetic welcome and the support extended to her by Bertha Wilson.[4] And L'Heureux-Dubé attributed the low morale of her colleagues almost entirely to the labour pains associated with the Charter. Coming to the Supreme Court five years after patriation, she sensed that it had all been too difficult, that the issues had been too hard, and that the Court was struggling with the divisive effects of being compelled to decide too much too soon. In hindsight, she thinks it would have been better if the early Charter decisions had been more cautious and the evolution of the jurisprudence slower in order that the Court not be compelled to reverse or retreat from earlier decisions. The heightened expectations created by the Charter's promise of a more just society resulted in a heightened scrutiny of the Court, too often accompanied by a barrage of criticism when these expectations were not met. Much of the criticism derived from confusion about the new constitutionally mandated role for the Court.

Judicial activism was the charge: judges had gone beyond their proper task of applying law and instead were usurping the democratic role of Parliament's elected representatives by creating law. Some journalists, academics, and politicians seem to have conflated the democratic process of enacting law with what they assumed ought to be a similarly democratic process of applying law. Enraged by the anti-majoritarianism inherent in Charter analysis they have not understood that such activism was not a power grab but a staggering new responsibility imposed upon judges by the Charter.

The Supreme Court can only deal with the cases remitted to it for decision by citizens or by the government which meet the national importance test embodied in the leave to appeal procedure. Nevertheless, and beginning for the first time in the post-Charter era, the Court must deal with these cases by looking not just at the dispute in isolation but also at the legality of the applicable law. As Chief Justice Antonio Lamer acknowledged toward the end of his career, 'We no longer rule on cases. Now, we rule on the laws themselves.' And although freedom of expression is one of the Charter values the Court has upheld most valiantly, Lamer and other judges on the Judicial Council have been conscious of just how damaging and even intimidating criticisms based on accusations of anti-democratic judicial activism can be both to the vigour of the Supreme Court and to social consensus about respect for law.[5]

Wilson spoke candidly about the issue of judicial activism in July 1983[6] at a conference in Australia, when the Supreme Court was still awaiting its first Charter case. Even so early she had come to the view that this controversial judicial responsibility was mandated by those little-understood procedural provisions in the Charter which require the courts to rule on the validity of laws. She warned prophetically: 'We Canadian judges are now going to have to depart the familiar harbours of contract and tort for the more treacherous waters of political, moral and social philosophy and the journey may entail more than a little discomfort and dislocation.' But Wilson was optimistic. However painful it might be, the process of struggling with these new responsibilities to balance political and moral considerations in determining norms and justifiable degrees of impairment of individual rights would help both lawyers and judges 'acquire along the way a more sophisticated appreciation of what we are about and a renewed dedication to our professional responsibilities.[7]

For her own part, Wilson got right on with the job. In her 1985 speech on decision-making she drew explicit attention to the provisions in the Charter which require the unelected courts to take on a clearly interventionist role. In her opinion, these provisions effectively ended the debate over political accountability by transforming without extinguishing the old doctrine of the absolute supremacy of Parliament;[8] the courts sustained their deference for parliamentary supremacy in the very act of carrying out the interventionist responsibilities newly entrusted to them by Parliament.

Already in this post-Charter paper, delivered when the Court had scarcely heard any Charter cases, Wilson was distinguishing between two potential methodologies while refusing to establish a sharp dichotomy between them. The Court, she said, could endorse the textual approach, seeking to define the meaning of a right by looking to the text in the modernist tradition of statutory interpretation which would show deference to legislative intent. Or it could adopt the contextual approach which acknowledges the legal framework of the Charter but 'emphasizes the context in which the dispute before the court has arisen rather than the text itself.'

Wilson considered these two methodologies as capable of being integrated and not necessarily separate and distinct, but also capable of creating significant differences depending upon which approach is emphasized. The textual approach may be necessary in some instances but is too formalistic and technical if there is nothing more; moreover, rigid deference to legislative intent can no longer be appropriate given that Parliament through the Charter has assigned to the courts responsibility for determining the constitutionality of the policy options enshrined in impugned legislation. The contextual approach she considered to be more pragmatic and functional in its power to determine the scope of rights in the multiplicity of situations which come before the courts. The question which only time could resolve was whether or not the courts have the institutional capacity to take on the demands of a contextual methodology.

In August of 1987 Wilson was invited to 'make a few remarks and not to make a speech' at a lunch held during a superior court judges' seminar in Vancouver. Her comments were theoretical but also warmly human; Wilson recognized that change is difficult and that the directions which had been emanating from the Supreme Court sometimes seemed unclear, even frustratingly so. She pulled no punches in acknowledging the difficulties the courts were having in dealing with their new Charter-mandated responsibilities and in finding the appropriate strategies to integrate its procedural and substantive provisions:

> We have now had five years' experience with the Charter and I think you will agree with me that it has been somewhat demoralizing. Pre-Charter, we tended to feel, rightly or wrongly, that we had a pretty good grasp of the law both in terms of its substance, its procedure and its techniques of adjudication. Suddenly, with the advent of the Charter, all that changed. We became split personalities almost overnight. One day we were applying the tried and true traditional analytical tools to non-Charter cases – and it's a very comfortable and secure feeling. The next day we were asking ourselves: what human or social values were the legislators trying to protect when they enacted the Charter provision? Or, where should the line be drawn between total freedom and total control in order that the public interest be best served in this particular real life context? We know that the traditional analytic tools won't answer these kinds of questions. This is no doubt why the Canadian Bill of Rights never got off the ground. So we are left groping for new techniques and new methodologies and this is going to take time.[9]

A month later Wilson was in Toronto where she had been invited to chair a session of the inaugural Canadian-American Legal Exchange organized by the Canadian Judicial Council and held at the Ontario Club. Thirty distinguished judges, academics, and lawyers gathered for a panel discussion led by University of Toronto constitutional law professor Katherine Swinton, Osgoode Hall constitutional law professor Peter Hogg and British Columbia Attorney General Brian Smith on the topic of 'The Relationship between the Judiciary and the Charter: Theories of Judicial Review.' Wilson's job was to introduce the speakers and moderate the discussion but once again she made a few telling remarks of her own on the legitimacy of judicial review:

> Canadian judges have now had five years experience with the Charter and most of us, I think are prepared to recognize that it has significantly altered the role of the courts in the overall scheme of our political institutions. But although our judges accept this as an intellectual matter, quite a few harbour serious doubts about the legitimacy of this new role. If truth were told, they don't really want to have this much power and have reservations as to whether their legal training and previous judicial experience properly equip them to handle it. They also have a very genuine concern over their lack of accountability for the exercise of their new power. I was surprised to discover on my recent attendance at a Canadian Superior Court Judges' Seminar in Vancouver how many judges considered judicial review under the Charter, despite the presence of section 1 and the legislative override in section 33, as fundamentally undemocratic and were prepared to acknowledge that their traditional posture of deference to the legislature would probably condition their approach to Charter issues.

October 1987 found Wilson addressing the American National Association of Women Judges at Seattle where she spoke at considerable length about the differences between the American and Canadian constitutions.[10] The process of balancing the constraint of precedent with the desire for improvement is necessarily more obvious in Canada because the structure of the Canadian constitution requires it. Wilson looked in particular at the section 1 provision which places the onus on the state of proving that the limitation on any infringed right is reasonable by showing that the legislative objective is pressing and substantial. American rights are framed in absolute terms and accordingly it has been necessary for American courts to read internal limits into the definitions of the rights; in Canada, she explained, the procedural filter supplied by section 1 means that the courts ought not to 'place a narrow construction on the rights themselves.'

Moreover, Wilson pointed out, our 'living tree' approach to constitutional law is sharply at odds with the conservative American doctrine of 'framers' intent.' Neither approach is completely satisfactory. The liberal anti-majoritarianism of the living tree may become simply anti-democratic if the personal values of individual judges are substituted for principled weighing of constitutional values; the deeply conservative framers' intent paradigm may freeze and blight the necessary growth of juridical analysis in response to shifts in social consensus. What is required, she said, is a purposive analysis of the allegedly infringed right linked to the particular context in which the infringement has arisen:

[C]onstitutional interpretation should be purposive. Rights should be read in accordance with the general purpose of having rights – the protection of individuals against an overbearing collectivity. Furthermore, I would submit, judges should strive to capture within their decisions the purpose of each individual right. Of course, by purpose I do not mean what some framer may have intended the right to mean in the past. Rather, I mean the best modern theory that can be devised to justify the existence of the right in question.

This task demands the continuing re-assessment of the scope of the right in light of new facts and in light of contemporary social theory. *Furthermore, a particular right may well require different meanings when assessed in different contexts.* Security of the person, for example, might mean one thing in the context of prisoner's rights and another thing entirely when addressing the validity of environmental protection legislation. But in all cases the judge must consistently ask how this particular rendering of a right will work to make society better, more tolerant and more civilized.[11]

New developments in the growth of rights must be connected to existing legal principles and rooted in new social evidence.[12]

Persuaded that this integrated textual and contextual approach constituted the only principled methodology possible, Wilson herself was not intimidated by the accusations of judicial activism hurled at the Court. Her colleagues at Oslers had noted from her earliest years in practice that she was not so much stubborn as implacable once she had thought through an issue and made up her mind. For Lamer, who completely agrees with Wilson's position on this issue, judges' tenure of office exists for one reason only – there are times when they must make unpopular decisions. With gruff admiration McIntyre, her greatest friend at the Supreme Court who (in part because he did not endorse activism) was so often unable to concur in her judgments, says of Wilson that she 'takes very, very strong positions and she can be as stubborn as a mule and that is a virtue when you have the solid base that she had got.'[13]

PROCEDURAL CONVERGENCES, SUBSTANTIVE EFFECTS

A Balancing Act: Section 1

That solid base can be demonstrated in *Perka*,[14] a 1984 non-Charter criminal case concerned with the defence of necessity in which Wilson applied a proportionality analysis analogous to *Oakes* two years before the *Oakes* test was even formulated. *Perka* was, in Wilson's opinion, one of the most interesting judgments she ever wrote because it gave her the opportunity she so much enjoyed of doing some fairly intensive research into a philosophical issue; her judgment is studded with extensive reference to relevant American and British case law, academic writings, and to the theories of Kant, Hegel, and Bentham.

The facts are simple. The four accused were attempting to import cannabis by boat into Alaska. Because of mechanical problems and bad weather they were forced into a sheltered cove off the Canadian shore, where they unloaded the cargo in an attempt to prevent their vessel from capsizing. They were charged with importing narcotics and possession for the purpose of trafficking, put forward the defence of necessity, and were acquitted at trial. The Court of Appeal set aside the acquittal and ordered a new trial at which the Crown would be permitted to call rebuttal evidence concerning the condition of the vessel. The issue on appeal to the Supreme Court was whether or not the trial verdict should stand.

Dickson wrote for the majority dismissing the appeal and finding with the Court of Appeal that there should be a new trial because the evidence concerning the boat's condition went to the heart of the defence of necessity; if it could be shown that in fact the boat had not been in imminent danger of capsizing, then an essential element of the defence of necessity could not be made out. Wilson agreed with the result. Nevertheless, she was concerned that Dickson's reasons confined the doctrine of necessity to excuse when the allegedly criminal behaviour results from moral involuntariness in risky circumstances and there is no reasonable opportunity of finding any alternative course of action which does not involve illegality.

An accused relying on excuse must prove that he was acting out of the necessity of self-preservation from imminent danger such that he had no real culpability. This involuntariness goes to the inherent 'unpunishableness' of such behaviour by invoking the court's compassionate agreement with the 'I couldn't help myself' rationale and removing it from the criminal context which necessarily requires subjective intention, Wilson explained.[15] And Wilson had her doubts that this defence of necessity based on excuse would be applicable in this instance because it should have been foreseeable to the appellants that an emergency might arise requiring them to breach Canadian law, and of course they were entirely prepared to breach the comparable American law.

Nevertheless, even though it had no application in these circumstances, Wilson was concerned that another case might arise in which the defence of necessity grounded in justification might be applicable and she wanted to preserve this doctrine in the common law for such an eventuality. Justification does not deny the unlawfulness of the accused's behaviour but captures the situation in which an individual is confronted by two conflicting duties or rights recognized in law (and this is important to Wilson: a personal crisis of conscience cannot meet the test) such that his wrongful act can be characterized as the preferable alternative available to him. The determination of justification turns on proportionality; it is wrong to steal or to trespass, but one may be justified in doing so in order to save a life (although never justified in taking one life to save another). Wilson received considerable positive response from the American legal academics congratulating her for her analysis in *Perka* and she has followed subsequent case law with interest where situations arise in which the defence of necessity grounded in justification might be applicable.[16]

If *Perka* demonstrates Wilson's anticipation of section 1-like proportionality analysis, the record certainly shows that throughout her judicial career she continued to apply the *Oakes* test in a more consistently stringent manner than the other judges on the Supreme Court. This was particularly so in the criminal context where the section 7 liberty interests most frequently intersect with one or other of the additional ss. 8–14 legal rights.

In *Bernard*[17] the facts were such that Wilson was able to agree with the majority, although she was compelled to prepare a detailed concurrence setting out variables which could have arisen that would have precluded her agreement. This was a case concerning the extremely technical issue of the distinction between specific and general intent crimes in the context of drunkenness and sexual assault causing bodily harm. The appellant admitted to having forced the complainant to have intercourse with him but argued that he had been so drunk that he did not know why he had performed the act and that it was his drunkenness which caused the assault; in other words, he claimed he did not have the *mens rea* necessary for conviction in accordance with the section 7 principles of fundamental justice or the section 11(d) guarantee of presumption of innocence. Evidence of intoxication had been excluded by the trial judge and not put to the jury. The judge drew upon the rule established in *Leary*,[18] prior to the entrenchment of the Charter, that voluntary intoxication does not apply as a defence in offences of general intent; in his opinion, this rule did not offend either the section 7 or section 11(d) principles that morally innocent people ought not to be convicted because first, a person can be presumed to intend the natural and probable consequences of his actions through inference and second, if drunkenness is at issue, then the onus shifts to the crown to prove that the accused was blameworthy because of the voluntary self-induced intoxication. The appeal was dismissed and the conviction upheld.

Wilson agreed in the result. On the facts, the kind of injuries suffered by the complainant (right eye swollen shut, three stitches required to close the wound) indicated that the force must have been voluntary; moreover, Bernard was able to walk, talk, to put albums on the record player, and to hide a bloodied towel and pillowcase from the police after the assault, which meant 'there is no evidence that we are dealing here with extreme intoxication, verging on insanity or automatism, and as such capable of negating the inference that the minimal intent to apply force was present.' Nevertheless, Wilson argued that the *Leary* rule was flexible enough to require that evidence of extreme intoxication ought to go to the trier of fact so that the onus would shift to the crown to prove the minimal intent required to make out the offence; she expressed her doubt that in such narrow circumstances the Criminal Code provision could withstand a Charter challenge. Sure enough, six years later in *Daviault*[19] and under even more egregious circumstances, the issue of extreme intoxication amounting to automatism came up to the Supreme Court, Wilson's 'flexible' approach from *Bernard* was applied, and (to cries of outrage from the public and approval from the criminal defence bar) the appeal was allowed.

There is no better illustration of Wilson's heart-felt moral compulsion to sustain the *Oakes* standard than *Chaulk*,[20] one of her last cases at the Supreme Court. *Chaulk* was a challenge to the constitutionality of section 16(4) of the Criminal Code which provides that an accused is presumed to be sane unless he can prove his insanity on a balance of probabilities. The accused, Robert Chault and Francis Morrissette, appealed their convictions for first degree murder after their defence of insanity was rejected at trial; they argued that the presumption of sanity infringed the Charter section 11(d) guarantee of the presumption of innocence because those who lack the capacity to form criminal intent ought to be acquitted. The majority agreed.[21]

Chief Justice Lamer held for the majority that the objective of the legislation was sufficient to warrant limiting the constitutionality of the protected right. Without an acceptance of this reverse onus limit, he reasoned, the crown would be faced with the overwhelming burden of disproving insanity. Accused who ought to be found guilty would be able to invoke the insanity defence too easily. The presumption of sanity might not have been the absolutely least intrusive means of meeting the objective but, within the range of means Parliament might have chosen, the presumption of sanity impaired the presumption of innocence as little as is reasonably possible, particulary since the accused seeking to make use of this provision need only prove his insanity on a balance of probabilities.

In complete agreement that section 16(4) offended section 11(d), Wilson wanted to invoke the full protections of the *Oakes* test. Where could it be more important than the presumption of innocence, which she described as 'one of the most, if not *the* most, fundamental tenets of our criminal justice system'? The government had adduced no evidence that 'perfectly sane persons who had committed crimes were in significant numbers escaping criminal liability on tenuous insanity pleas' sufficient to justify the legislation on the basis of the first *Oakes* criterion, the pressing and substantial concern test. To allow an infringement of a guaranteed right merely 'as a prophylactic measure designed to guard against a possible problem that *might arise* absent the reverse onus' would 'represent a significant departure from the approach taken to section 1 by this Court up until now,' she wrote.[22] Her judgment illustrated an ongoing procedural theme in Wilson's judgments – the need for a much expanded evidentiary base to ground the evolution of social consensus. Here we see her demonstrating how it ought to be done.

There are numerous other cases in which Wilson held out for the stringent application of *Oakes*. In a speech which she made about constitutional advocacy in 1992 she mourned the Court's retrenchment from its original and unequivocal assertion of the legitimacy of judicial review in the 1985 *B.C. Motor Vehicle* case and added:

> I think it is now fair to say that, although the Court continues to pay lip service to the strict *Oakes* test, in many of its judgments it is applied in a less rigorous fashion ... [T]here is no doubt that those who continued to cling to the strict *Oakes* test (like myself) did so out of a concern that the Charter not be emasculated, that the shift towards the much more flexible standard of reasonableness makes it increasingly likely that governments' immediate objectives will take precedence over the rights and freedoms of individuals.[23]

That same year, in the controversial pornography case *R. v. Butler*, with Wilson no longer there to dissent, the Supreme Court explicitly held that even in the criminal context of the state versus the accused, the pressing and substantial concern criterion of *Oakes* was reducible to a substantial concern test and the rational connection test to a sufficiently rational link.[24]

Remedies and Supremacies: Sections 24 and 52

Section 1 was not the only procedural provision in the Charter which gave the Court trouble and provoked charges of judicial activism. Section 52(1) specifies that the constitution of Canada is the supreme law of the land, the source of the Court's mandate to scrutinize all other statutes and common law principles in light of the constitutionally guaranteed rights and freedoms. Section 52(2), the constitutional exemption, functions somewhat like the adverse effects doctrine we have already examined in the labour law context; it provides that the Court can uphold a law which does not infringe guaranteed rights and freedoms generally, but declares that a particular law will not apply to a specific individual whose Charter rights are infringed by it.[25]

Once a court has determined that some governmental action has infringed a guaranteed right or freedom, the section 24 (1) provision gives it broad discretion to fashion 'such remedy as the court considers appropriate and just in the circumstances'; it can stay proceedings, grant injunctions, declare particular statutes invalid in whole or in part, or extend under-inclusive legislation. And this section requires the court to exclude evidence obtained in a manner that has infringed or denied a guaranteed right or freedom if to admit that evidence would bring the administration of justice into disrepute. What postmodern paradox and postmodern multiplicity: not only are the courts required by Parliament to assert their supremacy over Parliament in order to preserve the very supremacy of law asserted by Parliament, but they are given discretion to choose among an infinitely intrusive range of ways to carry out that mandate.

In the criminal context Wilson was concerned to ensure that the rights of the accused were appropriately protected from the far greater resources of the state. She was also prepared to consider the retrospective application of the Charter, disentangling the substantive guarantees from procedural provisions but acknowledging that the procedural provisions could have substantive effects if narrowly construed in a manner which denied justice. She took particular satisfaction from the majority judgment she was able to achieve in *Gamble*[26] through the broad remedial discretion available to the Court under section 24(1).

This was a case in which twenty-one-year-old Janise Marie Gamble, the getaway driver in a robbery during which her accomplice had killed a police officer, was convicted of first degree murder and sentenced under new and not-yet-enacted provisions of the Criminal Code to life imprisonment without eligibility for parole for twenty-five years rather than the ten-to-twenty-year parole eligibility period applicable at the time of the offence. In 1986, after she had served ten years of her sentence, Gamble applied for relief under the doctrine of *habeas corpus*, the section 7 liberty guarantee, and the section 24(1) remedial provisions of the Charter. The Alberta Court of Appeal agreed that because the proceedings had commenced before the new act was in force, Gamble had been wrongfully prejudiced by the application of the new provisions but held nevertheless that because of the transitional provision in the amendment act, there would have been no difference in the result. The Charter was not entrenched at the time of the offence, which meant that Gamble was effectively caught between two stools.

Wilson's analysis carried the day. She argued that it was clearly wrong that Gamble had not been tried under the rule of law in force at the time of the offence and a wrong should not be without a remedy. Accordingly, Gamble was entitled to a declaration of eligibility for parole in accordance with the flexible remedies provided under section 24(1) of the Charter because otherwise the crown would be permitted to take advantage of the uncertainty created by its own improper trial procedures. The final arbiter determining whether and when Gamble ought to be released remained the Parole Board; nevertheless, Wilson was delighted when Gamble was released after twelve years' imprisonment and sorry that she was tragically killed in a car accident some months after her release.

Even more complex than the cases requiring the Court to map out the broad and discretionary scope of Charter remedies were two cases in which Wilson wrestled with the intersection of the section 24 remedies provision and the section 52 supremacy clause, one at the beginning of her Supreme Court career and one towards the end. McIntyre considered *Operation Dismantle*[27] to be the first real Charter case and we will return to it at several points throughout this discussion because it brings together a number of elements of postmodern proceduralism. At issue was the decision of the federal cabinet to permit testing of cruise missiles by the United States in Canada. The appellants alleged that this decision violated their section 7 rights to life, liberty, and security of the person because testing in Canada increased the general probability of a nuclear war and also made it more likely that Canada would be a target for nuclear attack in the event of such a war. The majority, Wilson concurring, dismissed the appeal on the grounds that the allegations were too speculative and no direct link could be established between the decision to permit the testing and any actual increase in the threat of nuclear conflict.

In her diverging concurrence, however, Wilson pointed out that the appellants could not obtain a remedy under section 24(1) unless they could first show that a section 7 violation existed that was unconstitutional under section 52(1). The Court was not being asked to rule on the wisdom of the executive's decision to permit the testing; that would have been a political question outside its proper jurisdiction. The Court was ruling on whether or not that decision violated the section 7 rights of the appellant citizens; because section 32 (1)(a) establishes that cabinet decisions are reviewable by the courts, 'it is not only appropriate that we answer the question, it is our obligation under the Charter to do so.'[28] To come within the scope of section 52, the decision of the federal cabinet would also have to be characterized as a law that was inconsistent with the provisions of the Charter and thus to the extent of that inconsistency, of no force or effect; this is the textual part of the analysis. But then Wilson turned to the contextual element and asked whether the informal exchange of diplomatic notes, not constituting a full-fledged treaty and not implemented through any domestic legislation, did or did not constitute law. She assumed it did, and concluded with the rest of the Court that the appellants' statement of claim could not constitute a violation of section 7 because of the reciprocal and non-absolute nature of these rights:

> The concept of 'rights' as used in the Charter must also, I believe, recognize and take account of the political reality of the modern state. Action by the state, or conversely, inaction by the state will frequently have the effect of decreasing or increasing the risk to the lives or security of its citizens ... Such conduct, however, would not, in my view, fall within the scope of the right protected by section 7 of the Charter ... The state is faced with at least the possibility, if not the reality, of external threats to both its collective well-being and to the individual well-being of its citizens. In order to protect the community against such threats it may well be necessary for the state to take steps which incidentally increase the risk to the lives or personal security of some or all of the state's citizens ... The rights under the Charter not being absolute, their content or scope must be discerned quite apart from any limitation sought to be imposed upon them by the government under section 1.[29]

At some level, Wilson's analysis is always effects-based; the potential paralysis of both the courts and the legislature as a consequence of finding that citizens' groups could challenge governmental policy based on a purely hypothetical outcome would have been obvious to Wilson. Her decision implicitly endorses the existing political process; the lobby groups are free to campaign for removal of the offending government in the next election.

Not until 1990 did Wilson have another opportunity to elucidate the procedural intersection between sections 24 and 52 in *Osborne*,[30] a case involving a successful freedom of expression challenge to a provision of the Public Service Employment Act which prohibited political activity by federal civil servants. The trial judge had attempted to read down the offending provision so that only some political activities would be prohibited, but at the Supreme Court the majority (Wilson included) supported a section 52(1) declaration of invalidity. Sopinka's majority judgment left open the option of applying a section 24(1) reading down or a section 52(2) constitutional exemption in future Charter cases when a law has been declared invalid under section 52(1). However, in her diverging concurrence Wilson wrote:

I do not share [Sopinka's] views as to the recourse open to the Court once it has found that the impugned legislation on its proper interpretation is over-inclusive, infringes a Charter right, and cannot be justified as a reasonable limit under section 1. Once these findings have been made I believe that the Court has no alternative but to strike the legislation down or, if the unconstitutional aspects are severable, to strike it down to the extent of the inconsistency with the Constitution. I do not believe that it is open to the Court in these circumstances to create exemptions to the legislation (which, in my view, presupposes its constitutional validity) and grant individual remedies under section 24(1) ... The purpose of section 24(1), in my view, is to provide an appropriate and just remedy to an individual whose guaranteed rights or freedoms have been infringed or denied.[31]

What seems to be at work here, in Wilson's analysis of the intersection of the supremacy clause with the Charter remedial provisions, is her conviction that any remedial section 24(1) modification of a law or part of a law which had already been conclusively determined to be invalid could only dilute the normative force of the section 52(1) supremacy clause and by implication that vital consensus of respect for the law as an evolving and responsive social institution.

Despite her heavy workload in commercial law areas, it is not generally realized that about a third of Wilson's Supreme Court decisions were criminal law judgments with a marked escalation in this area towards the end of her career. And among these late criminal cases Wilson wrote a number of judgments in which she made a substantial contribution to the development of the section 24(2) jurisprudence, defining the proper scope of the court's power to refuse the admission of evidence obtained in a manner which could bring the administration of justice into disrepute.

One such important case was *Hébert*,[32] in which an undercover agent obtained inculpatory evidence by going into the cell after an accused had consulted a lawyer and had explicitly refused to make a statement. The entire Court invoked section 24(2) to exclude this evidence, holding that it had been obtained by infringing Hébert's section 7 right to remain silent. However, the majority judgment, held that the right to remain silent could be qualified by state interest; even if the accused had expressed his desire to remain silent, so long as he had consulted his lawyer, a voluntary inculpatory statement obtained by a cell mate or even by an undercover agent, if the agent had not actively solicited the information, could be admissible. Wilson concurred with the disposition but wrote a diverging concurrence to stress that in her view the state's coercive power could be brought to bear upon a suspect to such a degree that the right to remain silent might be infringed even prior to detention; the focus of a section 24(2) inquiry ought to be on the treatment of the accused and not on the objective of the state in preventing the administration of justice from coming into disrepute.

Her clearest expression of moral indignation over the Court's too forgiving application of section 24(2) came in *Wong*,[33] a judgment released just weeks before her retirement in November 1990. Electronic surveillance had been set up in a hotel room without authorization by police engaged in the investigation of a floating gaming house. LaForest wrote for the majority that the video surveillance violated the section 8 protection from unlawful search or seizure and that it was not justified under section 1, but that the evidence was nevertheless admissible because the police officers had acted in good faith and had reasonable and probable grounds for believing that gaming offences would be committed.

Wilson's dissent began with textual analysis of the phrase 'having regard for all the circumstances' in the section 24(2) provision, which she interpreted as requiring a highly contextual reading in order to determine in a specific situation whether evidence obtained in violation of a Charter right could be admitted without bringing the administration of justice into disrepute. Because the videotape of the gaming offence was brought into existence only as a result of violating the section 8 guarantee, it was analogous to a confession emanating from the accused and different from evidence having some independent existence apart from the Charter violation. To use such evidence goes to the fairness of the trial; the accused is in effect being compelled to testify against himself. The textual is necessarily contextual in this situation, but there is a further kind of contextual analysis relating to the sequence of events which made the Charter violation even more egregious.

The police had had two days' notice of the gambling session in which they could have obtained a proper warrant for the electronic surveillance. Wilson's review of the trial transcript demonstrated that the failure to obtain authorization did not result from a good faith misunderstanding of the proper procedure but amounted to a deliberate and blatant disregard of that procedure because the police believed that they would get away with it. There was no particular urgency and no evidence that the gambling was associated with any violent activity. Moreover, as an alternative to electronic surveillance it would have been possible to obtain the evidence through an informer or an undercover agent. The excuse provided by the police force – that no suitable undercover agent of the appropriate racial group was available – was one Wilson rejected with predictable scorn.

Wilson's belief in the normative power of the law required her to give the Metropolitan Toronto police force an incentive to improve its hiring policies; it should never be possible to exercise discrimination against racial minorities in the employment context in a manner which compounds that discrimination in the criminal context.

The Notwithstanding Compromise: Section 33

The most subversively postmodern of all the procedural provisions in the Charter may be section 33, the notwithstanding clause. On the surface, it is a democratic reassertion of the ultimate authority of the representatives elected by the people. It allows a provincial legislature to enact legislation which deprives Canadian citizens of their most significant rights by overriding the section 52(1) supremacy clause for a period of five years, and this period is even renewable so long as the electorate will put up with it.

The clause seems to respond to the charges of judicial activism as a challenge to the legislative pre-eminence in policy-making by limiting the power of the courts to strike down unconstitutional laws, but, as Wilson anticipated, the pragmatic realities of the polling booth have meant that this is not so:

Does it [the section 33 provision] not render Canadian rights completely illusory? So far, at least, the answer is no. The provision only rarely has been invoked, presumably because it might spell political suicide for any government that invoked it! Indeed, there is a strong lobby of the civil rights movement working to have it removed from the Charter. Its presence, however, has interesting implications for Canadian constitutional theory.

Decisions of the Supreme Court of Canada about the fundamental rights of the citizen are the law unless expressly overridden by the legislature. In theory, at least, Parliament remains supreme. It is hard to predict what impact this arrangement will have on Charter interpretation. Perhaps Canada's courts will be more venturesome in finding that inviolable human rights exist, secure in the knowledge that their word is less final than that of their United States counterparts. Or perhaps they will be less venturesome, feeling that their authority as a Court will be eroded by frequent governmental resort to the notwithstanding clause. It is still too early in our experience with the Charter to tell.[34]

The history of section 33 application since the enactment of the 1982 constitution suggests that the Court has been less venturesome given that the only Supreme Court ruling on this section to date has been *Ford*.[35]

Ford was a particularly sensitive case from a political perspective because it involved the enforcement of minority language rights legislation concerning commercial advertising and signs in Quebec. The courts had to decide whether the Quebec legislation requiring French only on public signs infringed the section 2(b) Charter guarantee of freedom of expression. They concluded that the language policy was a legitimate attempt to protect French language and culture but that a French-only requirement was not necessary to give effect to the policy and that accordingly these sections of the provincial legislation were inoperative. The Parti Québécois government had not participated in the constitutional conferences culminating in the adoption of the Charter and the National Assembly in Quebec had invoked the section 33 override in a blanket re-enactment of all Quebec laws with the protective notwithstanding clause inserted.

The issue was so sensitive that this was one of the rare instances when Chief Justice Dickson strongly encouraged his colleagues to strive for a unanimous judgment and, despite the interest she had already signalled in the section 33 process, there are no passages in the judgment with an identifiably Wilsonian flavour. The Court upheld the legitimacy of the National Assembly's insertion of section 33 into all the provincial legislation, interpreting it as establishing requirements of legislative form only, rather than requiring any substantive review of the legislative policy in the application of the override provision. The Court dismissed the appeal and struck down the law nevertheless; more than five years had passed since the override legislation had come into effect, commercial freedom of expression was protected under section 2(b), and the legislative objective of protecting the French language could still be met if other languages were permitted on signage, perhaps in smaller letters. Within a few days, the PQ government had re-enacted the legislation, making use again of the notwithstanding clause.

There certainly have been other instances when the courts have issued unpopular decisions and segments of the population have urged their provincial governments to invoke section 33, but so far with a conspicuous lack of success. There can be little doubt that it has sometimes suited political parties to sustain their own electoral strength by abdicating responsibility for difficult policy decisions. But this is a misuse of the Charter. Wilson had already signalled her awareness that when politicians leave issues such as abortion and gay rights to the courts the result will be a technical legal contest rather than an evolution of social consensus.

Nevertheless, when the political heat is high, legislatures can choose the luxury of not acting. The courts cannot. A court must adjudicate the cases remitted to it for decision and make difficult and unpopular policy decisions which will stand unless challenged through the section 33 override. There is considerable postmodern ambiguity about the supremacy of a supremacy clause which can be overridden selectively, on a regional basis, especially when the override can be renewed indefinitely. But there is also considerable postmodern ambiguity about the application of an override clause which can be rendered inoperative by default when governments' self-interest means they can choose to ignore it, evading their proper share of responsibility for upholding the Charter mandate.[36]

In Canada, there is an ongoing dialogue among the three branches of government (legislature, executive and judiciary) each of which has equal responsibility to carry out the Charter's mandate, according to Wilson. Legislatures have a primary obligation to draft legislation that will not infringe Charter rights; in carrying out their legislated duties, the executive (undercover police officers seeking inculpatory statements, for example) ought to exercise some judgment in ensuring their actions are constitutional; and the courts' assessment of the constitutionality of the legislation is not the last word but 'only one step in the process' because 'the matter then goes back to the legislatures for the appropriate remedial action.'[37]

Wilson compared the United Kingdom's Human Rights Act, which came into force in 2000, with the structure of our Charter and pointed to what she considered a vitally important procedural problem inherent within the British statute. The British legislators have chosen to sidestep potential charges of judicial activism by limiting the role of its courts to issuing declarations of incompatibility and assigning the compliance-monitoring function to the European Court of Human Rights. This was a serious mistake, in Wilson's view, because it extinguished the cherished principle of parliamentary sovereignty which our Charter manages to uphold. Wilson, herself an immigrant from the United Kingdom, had some satisfaction in saying:

I believe that Canada has achieved the best of all possible worlds. Parliament as the sovereign power has itself conferred the power of review on the courts, thereby recognizing and endorsing another vital aspect of our democratic system, the independence of the judiciary from the other two branches of government. It is up to the courts to use that power in a responsible and sensitive manner.[38]

Of course, in Canada the courts do not always sever the offending provision or suspend and send back impugned legislation for remedial action. Once a law is tested and found wanting under section 1, the section 52 supremacy clause triggers a wide discretion to tailor remedies. Nor is it always possible, politically or constitutionally, for a legislature to redraft impugned legislation so that it meets Charter standards.[39] Almost equally controversial is the procedure requiring the courts to exclude evidence and release an accused when it deems his or her Charter rights have been infringed.

These are the cases which give rise to charges of judicial activism and the charges show no signs of abating. If the courts had been more stringent in their application of section 1 and less forgiving of 'good faith' lapses in obtaining evidence perhaps governments would not have found it expedient to shift political risk onto the courts and instead been compelled to be more aggressive in invoking the section 33 override.

INTERVENTION AND EXTRINSIC EVIDENCE

But as difficult as the Court found it to deal with the Charter sections we have just been considering, standard textual analysis led to the inescapable conclusion that some new procedural groundwork would have to be established, and it was also fairly quickly evident that these procedural decisions would have significant substantive effects.

Postmodernism is in part about transgression of boundaries; we have seen that substantive Canadian law in the private context was becoming more postmodern because of the blurring of traditional modernist categories. But postmodernism in law is also about the multiplication and the fragmentation of legal subjects and legal facts. If the Court was to take seriously the section 1 'reasonable' limitation on individual rights, then some sort of demonstration – some expansion of the evidentiary record to justify majoritarian interests in those instances when the Court did limit guaranteed rights – would be essential. It was going to be necessary to hear from more people than the two parties engaged in a par-

,ticular legal dispute; it was going to be necessary to consider more facts and admit more evidence about the social impact of proposed decisions. Without such evidence judges could only fall back on their own subjective impressions of community standards, self-evidently not a satisfactory solution. But the question was, how it should be done and did the courts have the institutional capacity to deal with it. An expansion of the role of intervenors was the most obvious solution.

Wilson considered it a matter of duty and obligation to expand the evidentiary base. Very early on, she was pursuing vigorous initiatives behind the scenes to encourage the development of sound intervention policies and procedures. The legal framework to permit intervention had been in place long before the enactment of the Charter made it a pressing need; the Supreme Court is empowered by the provisions of the Supreme Court Act to establish a panel of five judges which can enact and amend rules governing Supreme Court procedures. Nevertheless, it is obvious that the whole process of application for leave to intervene was in a state of extreme flux and confusion during the years Wilson spent on the Supreme Court and that these issues have not yet been resolved.

Anticipating these problems even before the first influx of Charter cases, in September 1983 Wilson had taken the bull by the horns. She assigned to Diane Teeple, who was completing her articling requirements with Wilson as her principal and also serving as chief librarian of the Supreme Court library, the task of researching intervention policy and comparative intervention procedures in various jurisdictions. Teeple's work was completed and ready for distribution in early February of 1984. The following month, Dickson wrote to McIntyre stating that 'we should hold a judges' meeting and settle the policy in respect of intervention' but that his 'own view would be to grant intervention only in rare cases.' Because applications for leave to intervene were heard by individual judges in chambers, and because the judges had been unable to develop any consensus among themselves even on the threshold issue of whether the Court should be deciding on its own to admit intervenors, there was a real danger of 'judge shopping' – that is, would-be intervenors seeking out judges they believed most likely to be amenable to their applications, with those applicants who had been refused having some foundation for their belief that an injustice had been done. The leave to appeal process, in itself controversial enough, at least hinged on a fairly straightforward national importance test; it was much less clear what criteria should be applied in granting or denying leave or what the role of parties granted status as intervenors ought to be.

As Wilson explained it to a group of Saskatchewan law students late in 1984, there had long been a trend towards relaxation of the rules of evidence in constitutional law as the courts recognized that it was necessary to expand their horizons beyond textual statutory interpretation. Nevertheless, she signalled a substantial difference of opinion about what evidence could be admitted on final appeal that had not been part of the actual trial process. Distinctly different from the traditional 'adjudicative' facts (the who, what, where, why, when, and especially the how much of standard litigation), this new kind of evidence constituted 'legislative' facts illuminating the socio-political and economic environment in order to 'portray the contextual framework in which the litigation is taking place' and to 'help the court decide questions of law that have a substantial discretionary or policy element to them,'[40] she said. Wilson anticipated Canadian courts would follow the American path in expanding the evidentiary base through admission of legislative facts because, ironically enough, the problems of proof established by traditional textual statutory interpretation of the language of the Charter's procedural sections required it to do so.

Policy had not been settled in early 1985 when there was another round of memos among the judges raising some new issues with respect to intervenor policy. A lengthy and somewhat humorous memo was circulated by one of the judges who clearly wanted to shut down the intervenor process as much as possible. In his opinion, the automatic addition had meant that 'the forum now takes on the appearance of an ancient jousting contest with each side gathering up as many spear bearers as they can'; the private litigant is 'hopelessly lost in the suds frothed up by the intervention' and worse, 'presumably he has to pay his counsel to sit and listen.' The result of permitting simultaneous provincial and federal 'intervenors' had been inefficiency and obstruction of justice, particularly in the criminal context where intervention amounts to little more than a revival of the ancient tradition of 'oath pleaders.'

There were several short responding memos from justices who were similarly fed up with the intervenor process as it had evolved and similarly concerned that it was seriously straining the institutional capacity of the Court. The new chief justice proposed that the whole issue of intervenor policy and procedure be placed on the agenda of the next judicial conference for further discussion.[41]

This flurry occurred just a few months before the judgment in *Opera-*

tion Dismantle was released. The appellants there had been a group of more than twenty-five organizations and unions[42] all accorded full party standing under the procedural rule governing joinder of parties and claims and with a collective membership comprised of some million and a half individuals. Even such a remarkable multiplicity of parties was not sufficient to prevent the statement of claim from being struck out as a matter of legal interpretation and, as we have seen, weakness of the evidentiary record was a significant factor in that decision. But logistically the proliferation of documentation made this case an organizational nightmare; full party status clearly had not been the route to go.

Even a year's experience with Charter litigation had crystallized Wilson's own position. By mid-1985 she was prepared to state publicly that of all the procedural accommodations required by the Charter, by far the most important was an 'alter[ing of] the traditional two-party structure of public law litigation by giving a generous interpretation of the Court's rules governing interventions.'[43]

Exercising a proper judicial discretion, Wilson acknowledged only somewhat obliquely that 'many judges shy away from this solution on the basis that it will add considerably to the time expended on hearings.' She did not deny that multiplying parties could create problems of institutional capacity. Refusing to believe such problems were insuperable, she offered a few pragmatic solutions – such as limits on the length of oral presentation or restriction of intervention to submission in writing – which she thought could assist the Court in managing the increased burden. And Wilson believed fervently that charges of judicial activism could more effectively be countered and the Court's new countermajoritarian role more effectively be legitimized through intervention than through the section 33 override provision. The rules now provide that the Court has the discretion to determine the terms and conditions of participation by the intervenor, but wide-open discretion, of course, has simply created another opportunity for the Court's external critics to sling charges of judicial activism.

While the Supreme Court was thrashing over policy direction, intervenors themselves were not idle; the original neutral 'friend of the court' concept was rapidly evolving into a strategic litigation movement paralleling the political lobbying by interest groups pressuring for substantive legislative change. And certainly one of the cases in which intervenor groups moved most quickly to make their submissions was *Daigle* v. *Tremblay*,[44] a 1989 case which turned on an issue so sensitive that it was agreed by all the justices that judgment should be delivered unanimously by the Court as a whole.

This was another abortion case, particularly controversial in Quebec with its long-simmering resentment over what sovereigntists deemed the imposition of the Charter and against the backdrop of discussions surrounding the fragile Meech Lake Accord. Jean-Paul Tremblay,[45] a Montreal auto service representative, wanted to prevent Chantal Daigle, the unmarried mother of his unborn child, from obtaining an abortion. The couple had met in November 1998, moved in together the following month and planned to marry. But Tremblay, who had pressured Daigle to have his baby in advance of the wedding, became increasingly threatening and domineering; once she announced her pregnancy in late March of 1989 this behaviour escalated into physical abuse. On occasion the petite Daigle was thrown on the floor or grabbed by the throat and threatened on their apartment balcony. She was terrified and wanted to leave. Her family helped her move and she scheduled an abortion for a few days later in Sherbrooke.

Tremblay obtained an initial interlocutory injunction preventing Daigle from obtaining the abortion for ten days. When the case was argued before a Superior Court judge on 17 July he made the injunction permanent, citing the Quebec Charter of Human Rights and Freedoms as determinative of the foetus' right to life which trumped Daigle's liberty rights under section 7 of the Canadian Charter and drawing also on the Quebec Civil Code recognition of the foetus as a juridical person. The Quebec Court of Appeal upheld the injunction in a 26 July ruling. Chantal Daigle was already more than twenty weeks pregnant; 21 July had been the last day on which she could have been confident of obtaining a routine abortion under the regime applying in the Quebec clinics.

This time the Supreme Court received submissions from eight intervenors. Nevertheless, the list – in addition to the attorneys general for Canada and Quebec, the Court heard from the Canadian Abortion Rights Action League (CARAL), the Women's Legal Education and Action Fund (LEAF), the Canadian Civil Liberties Association, the Campaign Life Coalition, the Canadian Physicians for Life, the Association des médicins du Québec pour le respect de la vie, and the REAL Women of Canada – does reveal what seemed to be emerging as Court policy, that intervention should be granted to ensure representation from the full spectrum of opinion on a question of broad public interest. The case drew massive attention from the press. Eight of his colleagues rallied to Chief Justice Dickson's leadership, some of them travelling considerable distances to reach Ottawa on time and participate in the judgment. There was no flinching of responsibility in a situation of great urgency requiring a decision sure to be unpopular with a substantial segment of the population whichever way it went.

And there was more drama. By this point Daigle had already realized that she could not wait any longer. About an hour after the hearing commenced, her lawyer (looking rather pale and shaky) announced he had just learned that his client had a week earlier disguised herself and slipped across the border to a Boston clinic where she had obtained a late abortion. But even though their decision was rendered moot, the justices decided to hear the rest of the case, adjourned for a scant hour, and rendered their unanimous decision on the spot.[46] As a matter of general public interest, it was clearly important to resolve the issue of whether or not a pregnant woman can be restrained by an injunction from obtaining an abortion. Their answer was an unequivocal no: the appeal was allowed and the injunction lifted.

The analysis in the judgment was both textual and contextual, the language neutral and deliberately non-inflammatory. The Court held that the Quebec Charter did not include 'foetus' within 'human being,' which meant that the unborn child did not have a right to life; the Civil Code definition of the juridical person was held to be only a legal fiction to protect future interests after birth but not to accord legal personality. Because the case involved a civil action between two private parties, no state action was impugned and therefore, the Court held, the Canadian Charter had no application at all.

In writing about this case after she had retired from the bench, Wilson made it very clear that, whatever role she played in writing the judgment,[47] she herself had been vividly aware of the details of Daigle's life; as she had promised to do when she first went to the Court, she never forgot that people's lives and the law are intimately intertwined and that it is the particulars which matter to contextual justice.

In April 1990 Wilson went to New Zealand to address a Commonwealth Law Conference. Her speech was entitled 'Statutory Interpretation: The Use of Extrinsic Evidence Pre and Post Charter.'[48] This paper proves how intensively she had thought through the intersections among the procedural provisions and their substantive effects in the first place. She did not claim any credit, but by this point she must have felt some satisfaction in being able to say, 'the Court frequently confers status on intervenors who can make oral submissions and file briefs with the Court to show the larger implications of the available choice of interpretations for other individuals or groups.' She made abundantly clear the connection between so-called judicial activism and intervenor policy as a strategy essential to the implementation of the grounded contextuality she advocates, invoking the common sense of her own philosophical traditions:

> The principle of parliamentary sovereignty must clearly act as a curb upon what we might call too creative an approach to the interpretation of ordinary statutes. There is obviously a point at which interpretation becomes legislation and the legitimate function of Parliament is usurped. While this may be acceptable in Charter interpretation where the judiciary has been expressly made the custodian of the citizens' right, it clearly is not acceptable in the case of the interpretation of ordinary statutes where the will of parliament must prevail. Nevertheless one must ask oneself whether our traditional approach to statutory interpretation really does disclose Parliament's intention if indeed such a thing exists. I have been harbouring the suspicion for some time now that the sole virtue of a collection of technical rules from among which we may pick and choose at will is not that they lead us to a result but that they support a result that we have already reached ... I believe that if we are serious about giving effect to Parliament's intention, we must take a more broadly based approach and inquire into the social context in which the act was passed. We must encourage counsel to do their homework and come prepared to tell us what the legislature was trying to achieve. Legislatures seldom act in a vacuum. They are usually responding to a situation of which they are fully cognizant and of which we too, as interpreters of their handiwork, must be fully cognizant or at least try to become so through the efforts of counsel. This is not judicial creativity. This is common sense.[49]

During that conference, Wilson also participated in a panel discussion where she was invited to comment on several papers which had been prepared on the topic of judicial reasoning; she spoke of the vitality of the common law which has always been concerned both with what the law is and also what it ought to be, and the necessity for the judge to become an instrument of change by listening, keeping her antennae out and encouraging the participation of intervenors to address old problems from a variety of new perspectives. Responding to a question about the role of intervenors in Canadian law under the Charter and again without committing the Court to any firm policy decision, she indicated that the direction in which the Court was moving is to require lots of material, both from intervenors representing the legislature which had enacted the impugned legislation and also from various citizen groups representing different interests.[50]

And what is the situation on intervenors a decade after Wilson had left the Supreme Court? Is there a policy in place to permit intervenors to predict which groups will be granted leave and under what circumstances, in order that they may make strategic decisions about the expenditure of funds to amass the extrinsic evidence required for a successful leave to appeal application? While firmly denying that the Court has in any way been highjacked by special interest groups, three judges of the Supreme Court – Chief Justice McLachlin, Justice Bastarache, and Justice John Major – were in 2000 quoted as expressing the view that the Court has opened the door too widely to intervenor groups and that it may now be time to restrict access.

Does this procedural narrowing signal that we can expect a further weakening of section 1 analysis in response to the relentless criticisms of judicial activism? Bastarache and Major indicated simply that there is now less need of the extrinsic evidence intervenors can offer and that the restriction is proposed only because after years of experience with Charter litigation, the Court has developed a certain institutional competence, has absorbed within judicial notice certain socio-economic facts, and that it accordingly wants to trim the time formerly accorded to the intervention process.[51] Former Supreme Court Justice Peter Cory, who had early on after his appointment been in favour of generous intervention, with experience came to the conclusion that there was far too much political grandstanding and that intervention too often wasted the time of the Court. And former Supreme Court Justice Gerard LaForest thinks they have in a few instances been something of a nuisance which might be controlled if submissions were confined to written rather than oral formats. If these statements were a trial balloon to test public opinion and the Court is intending to curtail the intervenor process, there is still no obvious policy in place to determine when intervenors' help might still be necessary and how the Court should ensure that selection procedures create the range of perspectives appropriate in the particular circumstances before the Court.

OLD DOGS, NEW TRICKS

We have devoted considerable space to the contribution of the intervenor process to the postmodern multiplicity of parties because the

Charter brought about a novel and rapid expansion of this venerable procedure and Bertha Wilson herself considered intervention to be the most important procedural change required by the Charter. Historically, the Supreme Court's power to control procedures for both applications for leave to appeal and applications for leave to intervene was established long before the Charter was entrenched; Charter litigation merely cast light on their substantive implications. On the other hand, in the early days of Charter litigation it was not at all clear that the sections 1, 24, 52, and 33 provisions would gain their bite through the establishment of procedural methodologies. We have seen that the old modernist distinction between substance and procedure has become permeable in both directions. More generally, however, the postmodern impact of procedural manoeuvres does not depend upon the novelty of their application but rather on their purpose and above all on their effects.

There was nothing new about limitation periods, for example, which have always been intended to prevent stale claims and give repose to potential defendants; it was Wilson's application of the discoverability principle in *Kamloops* which breathed equity into the context of municipal negligence and prepared the way for the expansive interpretation of limitations periods in incest cases. Wilson was equally pragmatic in her contributions to other procedural decisions made by the Supreme Court during her tenure, many of them in the criminal context, some famous and some less well known.

Stays of proceedings became controversial in *Askov*[52] when Cory ruled for the majority that a two-year delay between committal for trial and trial date constituted an infringement of the section 11(b) guarantee of trial within a reasonable time. Across the country some 47,000 accused took advantage of this ruling to obtain stays on some very serious criminal charges. Wilson had concurred in this case but wrote a separate judgment; she would have placed an evidentiary onus on the accused to show that he had suffered actual prejudice not just by being charged and kept waiting but prejudice resulting from the delay itself. Whether or not the delay had been unreasonable, she reasoned, was contextual and dependent upon the particular circumstances.

But although common-sense analysis can achieve contextual justice by producing principled effects through fairly traditional procedures, sometimes novelty is a determinative factor. This is particularly so in cases turning on the pre-emptive procedural manoeuvre known as the 'motion to strike,' when the defendant seeks to strike out the statement of claim on the grounds that the pleadings lack 'substantive adequacy' –

that is, they disclose no cause of action known to law. This move, if successful, stops the litigation. Throughout her judicial career Wilson dealt with a number of important cases involving the motion to strike. And if intervenors and the expansion of the evidentiary record constitute postmodern multiplications of legal subjects and legal facts, these cases are primarily concerned with the multiplication of causes of action.

At the Court of Appeal in the *Bhadauria* case, Wilson had been willing to allow the new tort of discrimination as a cause of action; it was not appropriate to grant the motion to strike the pleading simply because of the novelty. As Wilson noted in *Operation Dismantle*, the plain and obvious test is determinative of substantive adequacy; that is, the court ought to assume that all the facts alleged in the pleadings are true and then dismiss the action or strike out the claim only if it is plain and obvious that there is no possibility of success even if the allegations are true. It is not the novelty of the claim or the lengthiness of the argument required to frame the preliminary issue which should determine whether the motion to strike is granted, nor the fact that some of the allegations in the pleadings are speculative or matters of opinion. What is required are evidentiary facts which can be either real facts proved by direct evidence or intangible facts which can be proved by inference from real facts or through expert opinion; once again, we see the postmodern intersection of these procedural strategies as Wilson demonstrates why intervenor evidence may be indispensable.

The majority held that these tests had not been met in *Operation Dismantle*.[53] But it was Wilson in her separate reasons who provided a blueprint for resisting the procedural manoeuvre of the motion to strike which was successfully applied by the appellant in *Hunt v. Carey Canada*,[54] a case decided late in her career and a particularly sympathetic situation. George Hunt was a retired electrician who had been exposed to asbestos fibres during his employment. Fourteen separate corporations were joined as defendants, all of which had been involved in the mining of asbestos and the manufacture of asbestos products over many decades and, Hunt alleged, all of whom had known about the health dangers associated with exposure to the fibres. He claimed that the defendants had committed the tort of conspiracy – a relatively novel tort – by withholding that health information, and that he had suffered personal injury as a result. The defendants had successfully brought an action to have the case dismissed on the basis that it disclosed no reasonable cause of action but on appeal that order was set aside.

Wilson wrote a detailed majority judgment, reviewing the legislative history and the case law on the issue of substantive adequacy in reprise of *Operation Dismantle* before turning to the emerging tort of conspiracy. In considering the application for a motion to strike she did not need to determine whether Hunt could be successful in persuading the court to extend the tort but only whether it was plain and obvious that he could not be:

> The plaintiff may have to make complex submissions about whether the evidence establishes that the defendants conspired either with a view to causing him harm or in circumstances where they should have known that their actions would cause him harm. He may well have to make novel arguments concerning whether it is enough that the defendants knew or ought to have known that a class of which the plaintiff was a member would suffer harm. The trial judge might conclude, as some of the defendants have submitted, that the plaintiff should have sued the defendants as joint tortfeasors rather than alleging the tort of conspiracy.[55]

The paragraph amounts to a checklist of the real facts and the intangible facts that the appellant needed to collate, offering implicit advice on the best strategies for building the evidentiary record and for framing the pleadings in the alternative that would be essential to the success of the claim. And on a motion to strike all of this is perfectly proper.

It is difficult to read this judgment without recalling Wilson's reputation as champion of the underdog or sensing Wilson's profound ability to put herself into the skin of this hardworking labourer who had trusted his employer and been betrayed by a self-interest endemic to the whole asbestos industry. But like the Edinburgh surgeon whose cool professionalism she liked to recommend to graduating law students, Wilson never permits her sympathy to distract her from the legal dissection at hand; in her decision to deny this motion to strike, she articulated the larger public interest at stake:

> The fact that a pleading reveals 'an arguable, difficult or important point of law' cannot justify striking out part of the statement of claim. Indeed, I would go so far as to suggest that where a statement of claim reveals a difficult and important point of law, it may well be critical that the action be allowed to proceed. Only in this way can we be sure that the common law in general, and the law of torts in particular, will continue to evolve to meet the legal challenges that arise in our modern industrial society.

And the evolutionary development of the common law in cases like this is, in turn, part of the reason why the Court must also take seriously its duty to grant leave to appeal in the first place; these procedural considerations converge from a multiplicity of directions.

THE ADMINISTRATIVE LAW PARADOX

As well as the multiplication of legal subjects, legal facts, and causes of action, Wilson was very conscious of the necessary multiplication of adjudicative tribunals in addition to the traditional law courts. This proliferation of adjudicative venues was pragmatically necessary to the administration of a complex and multi-faceted society with an absolute elasticity of citizen demand for programs and services (although correspondingly less willingness to pay the taxes which fund them). But she also knew that the administration of a welfare state can entail massive intrusions into the lives of ordinary citizens through the very agencies created to protect their interests.

The rapid expansion of the industrial economy and associated changes in social structure in Canada since 1945 required the establishment of an enormous administrative bureaucracy with authority to make most of the decisions about human rights and health care, education and immigration, agriculture and employment, municipal planning and licensing, and a host of other regulatory issues which for ordinary law-abiding citizens are likely to have the biggest effect on their day-to-day lives. This fragmentation of the adjudicative function into multiple tribunals, each assigned responsibility for the minutiae of narrower and narrower legal issues, devolves even further into procedural multiplicities. That is because for each tribunal the interpretation of its specific enabling legislation, together with the general administrative procedural statutes and the context of the preceding decisions made by that tribunal determine what procedural standards it is required to adopt. Such matters as the giving of notice, the application of the rules of evidence and disclosure, the right to counsel, or the availability of a full oral hearing may all vary from tribunal to tribunal.

This fragmentation was evolving at the very time John and Bertha Wilson emigrated to Canada and settled into their new lives here. They knew many people who were actively involved in the development of the administrative state: Lilias Toward, one of Bertha's closest law school friends, was immersed in municipal planning and tourist development administration preceding. Following their Dalhousie years, at one phase of his Toronto career, John was vitally involved in the consumer protection movement. And through her connections at the Canadian Bar Association and the Law Reform Commission, Bertha had a ring-side seat in the evolution of administrative bureaucracy during her Osler career.

The legislative intention was that an expanded administrative law regime would provide substantial advantages of economy, informality, speed, and expertise over any comparable level of service which could conceivably have been offered through the existing court structure. However, the adjudicative resolution of disputes through administrative tribunals operating without the procedural formalities of ordinary law courts not only has the potential to create injustice for individuals but may also stultify significant areas of law by cutting off incremental development in accordance with common law precedent.

And when these decisions are appealed, what are the courts to do? If deference is not accorded to the decisions of administrative law tribunals, then all the efficiencies of scale they were designed to achieve are lost as the administration of the programs and services they provide will grind to a halt. But if their decisions are accorded excessive deference in situations when the rights of individuals have been severely eroded, citizens as a whole lose respect for their governments. This is the administrative law paradox: our courts are severely criticized when they intervene and equally when they fail to do so.

When early in her career Wilson published a paper on English zoning regulation in the property law context which evolved out of her studies in municipal planning at Dalhousie, she certainly did not condemn the modern regulatory state or consider it to be merely the locus of a 'new despotism';[56] what interested her instead was the contextual definition of nuisance and the shift in emphasis away from pure private ownership to a balancing of ownership with the public good in response to a shift in public consensus about the appropriate choice of value. She also helped to decide a number of cases at the Ontario Court of Appeal which were concerned with judicial review of administrative tribunal decisions in instances where she believed the wrong value had been chosen.[57]

In her 1983 speech, 'Law in Society: The Principle of Sexual Equality,' Wilson pointed out how this administrative law paradox is particularly apparent in the human rights context because of the multifunctional nature of the roles ascribed to the various human rights commissions.

These commissions are required both to administer and to enforce human rights legislation by investigating complaints and by attempting to settle them. But the statutory pressure towards conciliation and settlement (which, because it is cost effective, is in that respect in the public interest) too often forecloses the full hearing process that may be essential to an individual's interest in public vindication, and may also erode other elements of the commissions' statutory mandate, particularly the duties of research and public education. And in speaking about the evolution and protection of democratic institutions at the Ontario Institute for Studies in Education two years later, Wilson was even more blunt in describing the extension of the administrative law paradox beyond the human rights context:

> One of the greatest changes which has occurred in the last half century is the dramatically increased expectation people have of the institution of government. They expect their governments not just to maintain order but to achieve progress ... Governments are expected to solve the problems of poverty, unemployment, housing, education, and health. They are expected to promote culture, to fund theatres, concert halls and opera houses; to provide parks, playing fields and sports complexes. In other words, they are to be concerned not only with the conditions for survival of the citizens but with their quality of life as well ... As a consequence, government is probably more involved in the lives of the citizens than at any previous time in our history, but there is a paradox – the more intimately affected we are in our daily lives by the mechanism of government, the more remote our relationship with it becomes. The vast increase in government's role has given rise to a huge, impersonal bureaucracy which threatens us with new forms of injustice and hardship.[58]

In Wilson's opinion, it was the rapid escalation of administrative law bureaucracy, with its associated devolution of the authority of the law from the court to tribunals (where decision-making was very often exercised by persons without any formal legal training at all) which made the Canadian Charter of Rights and Freedoms inevitable.

From this perspective, then, it is no coincidence that the Charter emerged as a postmodern statute, because the fragmentation of central adjudicative authority demanded by the administrative complexities of the state will both require and evoke evolution towards a postmodern legal system. But nevertheless, there are problems arising out of the administrative law paradox which are peculiarly intractable.

On the one hand, the residual responsibility of the courts to administer the law through the process of judicial review of the tribunals' decisions will, if exercised too assiduously, undermine the advantages of lower costs and increased speed and informality and specialized expertise that justified setting up the administrative law regime in the first place. Enabling statutes have been amended to award tribunals which have earned particular respect privative clauses which accord them enhanced discretionary powers. When such clauses are present, a court may not consider the merits of the tribunal's decision but only whether the choice that it made was extraneous to the purpose for which the discretion was granted. But on the other hand, because the courts have ultimate and sole responsibility for the interpretation of law, there will be circumstances when decisions – even of those tribunals with statutorily acknowledged expertise – will be found by the reviewing court to have been wrong in law.

The courts' residual duty to supervise the decisions of administrative tribunals is, of course, just another form of judicial review; here again, Wilson's stance tends to be just as contextual, purposive, and effects-based. For her, the context of administrative law is deference to administrative adjudication unless, as the *CUPE* doctrine phrases it, its decisions are 'patently unreasonable.'[59] But when there is a conflict of legal duties, then Wilson would plead the defence of necessity in justification of her decision to protect higher-level rights. Her administrative law judgments characteristically combine a section 1 style principled concern to protect the legal entitlements of individuals with a pragmatic understanding that the state will only be able to provide individuals with all the services social consensus has determined it ought to provide if the established administrative apparatus is permitted to function without excessive interference.

And that is why although Wilson sometimes endorses what we might label a postmodern devolution of authority from the courts to the tribunals, she does not consistently advocate curial deference. In fact what she understands to be the paradox at the heart of administrative law demands Aristotelian phronesis and would not admit of such simple-minded consistency. Any automatic or universal adoption of curial deference to tribunal decisions would in itself signify a perverse reinscription of modernist formalism and rigidity, with the new rule of deference to administrative multiplicity. What is consistent in Wilson's approach to administrative law (and fully coherent with her analysis in the technical cases involving limitations, stays, and motions to strike we have just surveyed) is her principled, case-by-case determination of these administrative law appeals, beginning always with the presumption that curial deference is desirable if possible but never shrinking from the obligation inherent in the Supreme Court's role as the court of last resort. If this can be characterized as a postmodern approach, legal scholars William Eskridge and Gary Peller have noted that the result tends to be a moderate position at the centre of the spectrum 'between what is perceived as an overly objectivist and conservative law and economics and an overly confrontational and politicizing CLS [critical legal studies].'[60]

In this light, we can think of Wilson's dissent in CAIMAW[61] as an illustration of her unwillingness to sacrifice specific legal entitlements for the sake of a universal doctrine of curial deference, even in the context of a privative clause. CAIMAW, the union, had entered into a collective agreement with Paccar, the employer, which included a termination clause providing that the agreement would continue during negotiations unless written notice was given by either party. Paccar laid off a large number of employees and cut back to a warehouse operation and the union was served with a notice to terminate after six months of fruitless negotiations. CAIMAW requested a determination from the Labour Relations Board as to whether the collective agreement was still in force.

The board found against the union; the decision was confirmed on review but then quashed on appeal to the Supreme Court of British Columbia, which order was upheld at the Court of Appeal. The issue for the Supreme Court of Canada was whether the decision of the Labour Relations Board, which permitted the employer to alter the terms and conditions of employment unilaterally on termination of a collective agreement, was so patently unreasonable as to exceed its jurisdiction and therefore subject to judicial review. The majority opted for curial deference and allowed the appeal, holding that the tribunal had the right to make even serious errors so long as its decision could be rationally supported by the relevant legislation. Wilson agreed that courts in general do owe deference to the policy decisions of administrative boards. But for a policy choice to be rationally defensible it must be congruent with the purpose of the relevant legislation, in this case requiring the board to make a decision that would be conducive to the collective bargaining purpose that the legislation was intended to promote. The patently unreasonable test, properly understood, requires curial deference only when the tribunal's interpretation of the relevant legislation constitutes a policy choice between equally viable alternatives. In this instance, the board's decision to permit the employer unilaterally to impose terms and conditions upon the employees after the termination of the old agreement would have had to be just as consistent with the purposes of the legislation (intended to enhance workplace democracy) as a decision that the former collective agreement was still in effect. In Wilson's opinion, there could be no question that a continuation of the old agreement would have provided a better balance of bargaining power.

But Wilson was also stung by criticisms of various academic commentators that the CUPE doctrine of patent unreasonableness and its associated principle of curial deference were being diluted by the courts through excessively intrusive judicial review. In her last year on the Supreme Court, she tried valiantly to revive what she considered to be the true spirit of *CUPE*. Her first attempt came in *National Corngrowers*.[62]

The case turned on the decision of the Canadian Import Tribunal to impose a duty upon imports of subsidized American grain that its inquiry showed were causing material injury to Canadian producers. The Supreme Court unanimously agreed that it ought not to interfere with the tribunal's decision, but was very divided in its approach. Rob Yalden recalls the discussions he had with Wilson while working on this case: 'She really did think Parliament had given tribunals a mandate and that courts should be very careful how they interfere ... Those who accuse her of judicial activism, these are very interesting judgments to look at because she is being very careful in circumscribing what she thinks is the appropriate role of the judiciary.'

Wilson stressed the vital role administrative bureaucracy plays in the running of the modern state, incorporating an explicit rejection of A.V. Dicey's classic rule of law doctrine that 'regular' law is supreme because in her opinion it amounted to a reversion to the most intrusive officiousness of the old, hierarchical-style judicial review that the Court was committed to leaving behind. Once again, we see methodology conditioning judgment:

> One must, in my view, not begin with the question whether the tribunal's *conclusions* are patently unreasonable; rather, one must begin with the question whether the tribunal's interpretation of the provisions in its constitutive legislation that define the way it is to set about answering particular questions is patently unreasonable. If the tribunal has not interpreted its constitutive statute in a patently unreasonable fashion, the courts must not

then proceed to a wide ranging review of whether the tribunal's conclusions are unreasonable. It seems to me, however, that this is what my colleague has done. And in the process he has engaged in the kind of detailed review of a tribunal's findings that this Court's jurisprudence makes clear is inappropriate.[63]

In this instance, Wilson reasoned, the Court had much less expertise in the interpretation of international trade agreements than the tribunal; therefore, if the tribunal's interpretation of the Special Imports Measures Act was not consistent with the General Agreement on Tariffs and Trade, it was up to the legislature to address the matter. The tribunal was clearly not acting outside its jurisdiction in a manner that could be deemed patently unreasonable. Wilson was very aware that permitting so intrusive a methodology of judicial review to stand unchallenged could only undermine the effectiveness and the authority that Parliament had intended to vest in the tribunal and might very well be determinative of a less acceptable judgment in future cases.

In the Lester[64] case, still trying to foster the transfer of authority from the standard court hierarchy to the more polycentric administrative law regime, Wilson found herself in dissent again. The appellant, Lester, operated two construction companies (Lester was unionized and Planet was not) functioning side by side with the same office and secretary and phone number but with separate construction employees, equipment, and finances. The reason for this structure was the practice known in the industry as 'double breasting' which enables a principal to prepare bids on projects at either union or non-union construction sites. The union which represented the Lester employees first attempted to organize the Planet employees but then withdrew its application for certification and instead applied to the Labour Relations Board for a successorship declaration. The companies appealed and at the Court of Appeal succeeded in obtaining a judgment that the board's decision that successorship had occurred was patently unreasonable. At the Supreme Court McLachlin held for the majority that the board's novel interpretation of the relevant Labour Relations Act provision dealing with successorship exceeded its jurisdiction and warranted judicial review, and that in the absence of evidence of successorship practice the board's decision was patently unreasonable.

Wilson's analysis rested upon her pragmatic understanding that the changes in the social structure within Canadian society require a comparable evolution in the structure of the law. Her interpretation of the relevant legislation was explicitly purposive. The successor provision was 'designed to prevent the loss of union protection by employees whose company's business is sold or transferred to another business concern,' she wrote, and the board was fully justified in reading into the Newfoundland statute the same 'common employer' protection which was included in many other jurisdictions to deal with the double breasting manoeuvre endemic in the industry. Curial deference is particularly necessary in instances like this one where 'the broad interpretation given to it by the Board has the merit of advancing the clear purpose of the Act.'

The *Cuddy Chicks*[65] hearing was the last case noted by Wilson in her bench book for May 1990 to November 1990 and it must have been somewhat satisfying for her. LaForest, in a significantly deferential move, found that the expertise of the administrative tribunal could offer valuable assistance to the Court in determining whether the provisions of its own enabling statute contravened the Charter, provided that the statute specifically granted the tribunal authority to deal with the Charter issue. Nevertheless, Wilson's interpretation was potentially even more deferential. She wrote a separate concurrence in which she argued that the omission of legislative authority in the enabling statute was not necessarily determinative because the tribunal might have the power and the duty to apply the Charter on other grounds. Since Wilson left the Supreme Court there have been a number of decisions of the Supreme Court in which a *CUPE*-style stringent test for judicial review has been affirmed.

INTERNATIONAL LAW: SOVEREIGNTY, RECIPROCITY, AND COMITY

The next largest structure beyond the state takes us into the international realm. And postmodernism can also be discerned both in the internal multiplicity and fragmentation of national entities evolving within the state and in the blurring of national boundaries between states. In a postmodern and increasingly global community there have been increasing pressures to dissolve old boundaries of national sovereignty while at the same time adopting some of the strategies of international law into 'domestic' law.

Nor is this idea new to Canada. Within Canada's federalist structure the 1867 constitution accorded quasi-sovereign responsibility for particular areas of law (education, health, commerce) to the provinces. More recently, principles of international law concerning comity (mutual respect for the sovereignty of nation states) have been useful for resolving certain interprovincial disputes. This was a phenomenon which was already well under way during the last months of Wilson's stint at the Supreme Court when the landmark *Morguard*[66] case was decided.

But in her academic writings and judgments we can see Wilson anticipating this development even earlier. Throughout her career Wilson always sustained a considerable interest in the evolution of international legal doctrines.

International law is quintessentially rich territory for the application of postmodern analysis for a number of reasons. First, there are the shifting and dissolving definitions of the international legal person – the various types of states and territories and intergovernmental organizations and non-governmental organizations which all acquire differing degrees of international personhood in different situations. And one of the most ambiguous and potentially most powerful legal persons is the corporation in all its manifestations: the government corporation, the intergovernmental corporation and particularly the transnational private corporation which may well be coalescing into a de facto world government in advance of the attempts of the United Nations to control it. But at the same time, in the human rights area the boundaries separating individual sovereign states have become increasingly permeable to the effects of external sanctions; as a result Canada itself may eventually modify its treatment of aboriginal peoples and acquiesce in the establishment of multiple aboriginal self-governing nations within its borders.

Secondly, a good deal of the text of international law remains substantively inchoate. The law to be applied is compiled as the situation requiring adjudication demands it in an almost ad hoc manner. In public law disputes, international law depends upon drawing together a loose amalgamation of applicable treaties, custom, general principles of domestic law, and the notoriously slippery notions of equity, supplemented as necessary with judicial decisions from the International Court of Justice (which do not have binding force) and commentaries from academic writers on international law which have more persuasive than determinative effect. In private law disputes, jurisdiction which governs procedural law will be hotly contested and the framing of the issue in contract or tort or other private law doctrine is often determinative of the substantive law to be applied. Indeed, within a few years of Wilson's retirement another landmark Supreme Court judgment in the follow-up to her *Hunt* v. *Carey Canada*[67] decision suggested that even the traditional separation between private and public international law is an artificial one, a boundary requiring postmodern transgression in the interests of doing justice.

Wilson, of course, spent her entire judicial career in what international legal scholars persist in calling 'municipal' (and what we would call federal) courts, but she did occasionally make reference in her academic writings to international law doctrines, particularly those conventions which place limits on human rights, as being most helpful to the development of a Canadian Charter jurisprudence.[68] Wilson also looked to international law to help illuminate the complex and conflicting relationship between the protection of privacy and the protection of the family which may militate against privacy when it requires exposure of family patterns of violence.

One of Wilson's most dazzling displays of international law scholarship came in her dissenting judgment in *Re Ownership of the Bed of the Strait of Georgia*,[69] heard over three days in October 1982 and at almost the same time as the final session of the United Nations Conference on the Law of the Sea. Both British Columbia and Canada had laid claim to the ownership of the waters and the underlying land between Vancouver Island and the mainland. The majority of the Supreme Court agreed with the decision of the British Columbia Court of Appeal, which had determined that the territory in question had been in the possession of the province at the time of Confederation in 1871 and therefore remained the property of British Columbia.

Wilson dissented. In her view, the potentially lucrative sea bed belonged to Canada. After she had prepared an initial draft of her reasons, clerk Philip Bryden supplied her with a lengthy memo concerning the issue of what constituted an inland water at common law in 1871 and how ownership of the submerged lands could be established.

Wilson's analysis in her reasons begins with a warning salvo: 'This is one of those cases where the resolution of a very contemporary problem depends upon the application of very ancient principles of law. I propose to consider these principles first and then move to their application to the instant case.'[70]

Given the wealth of research material with which she was supplied, Wilson exercised considerable restraint in devoting only twenty pages of her judgment to a survey of the common law doctrine of the low-water mark, the very ambiguous distinction in common law between ownership of and jurisdiction over submerged land, and the very imprecise common law definition of inland waters 'inter fauces terrae' (between the jaws of the headland). On this last point, Wilson cited a 1926 case questioning whether the metaphor refers to the 'open mouth of a man or of a crocodile'; and later in her reasons, she found the judgment in an obscure 1859 case regrettably short because it failed to expand upon the traditional visual tests for determining whether or not a body of water was 'between the jaws,' which depended upon what one could see gazing across to the headlands.

One cannot help but feel in reading this judgment that Wilson was working hard but she was also having fun. She drew on international law treaties, English, Australian, and Canadian statutes, and case law going back as early as 1315. Her conclusion on the applicable principles of law was that British Columbia could establish ownership of the submerged lands only if its boundaries as a colony had been expressly extended beyond the low-water mark as an assertion of effective ownership (not mere jurisdiction) or if that territory had been treated as inland waters at common law at the time of Confederation. There was absolutely no evidence that the low-water mark had ever been extended. Her examination of the 1846 Oregon Treaty between Great Britain and the United States persuaded her that the mid-channel boundary which it established was intended only to guarantee navigational rights and not to negate the common law rule of low-water mark ownership. As Wilson herself acknowledged, the tremendous amount of research in this case meant she 'probably spent far more time than was justified considering the complement of cases that we had to deal with.' But as she said, cases like this 'were the ones I was most awfully interested in and found the most difficult [and] I loved doing it, so it was no burden.'

If Wilson's application of international law principles reached its apotheosis early in *Straits of Georgia*, nevertheless she also drew upon similar analysis in a series of Supreme Court extradition judgments. This is legal territory located almost literally at the boundary crossing between Canadian domestic legislation and the relevant treaties between Canada and the state requesting the extradition of the person accused or convicted of committing a crime within its jurisdiction. Conflicts in criminal law doctrines also frequently required scrutiny. But in the post-Charter era, constitutional issues frequently came into play as well; and it is predictable that Wilson consistently argued for an expansive reading of Charter rights in extradition proceedings.

Three such cases were heard consecutively in December 1985, with the decisions released simultaneously in May 1987. Helen Susan

Schmidt[71] was a Canadian citizen acquitted in the United States of a federal charge of kidnapping who fled to Canada prior to trial on a state charge of child stealing arising out of the same incident. Mrs Schmidt argued that her section 7 right to liberty and her section 11(h) right not to be tried twice for the same offence would be infringed by extradition proceedings. But by the time the case reached the Supreme Court, these arguments had been rejected by the extradition judge, the reviewing judge who considered the application of *habeas corpus* doctrine, and the Ontario Court of Appeal. The Court held that the appeal should be dismissed, that Charter protections had no extra-territorial reach, and that the Court should be extremely cautious not to interfere in decisions that implicate the good faith and the honour of the country in its sovereign relationship with other states.

What made a separate diverging concurrence essential for Wilson was her desire to stress the absolute necessity of Charter application to any adjudicative activity which takes place within Canada:

> If the Court refuses to commit the appellant to prison for extradition in the discretion of the Executive because to do so would violate the appellant's Charter rights, the Charter is not being given extraterritorial effect. The effect is right here in Canada, in the Canadian proceedings, although it will, of course, have repercussions abroad. But there is nothing wrong with this. We would not permit a Canadian citizen to be extradited for torture in a foreign land on the basis that to refuse to permit it would be to give the Charter extraterritorial effect ... If the participation of a Canadian court or the Canadian government is required in order to facilitate extradition so that suspected criminals may be brought to justice in other countries, it seems to me that we must face up to the question whether such persons have the benefit of the Charter or not in the Canadian proceedings. We must, in other words, decide whether Canada's treaty obligations override Charter rights in respect of the Canadian proceedings or whether Charter rights must be recognized in those proceedings whether or not similar rights are available to the person in the foreign proceedings for which he or she may be ordered extradited.[72]

Mellino,[73] one of the companion cases, turned on the applicability of the guarantee of the right to trial within a reasonable time; disagreeing with the majority, Wilson insisted that the Charter did apply, although in this instance the disposition was not changed given that the delay was caused by the failure of the Republic of Argentina to produce the necessary documentation to proceed with the trial. And in *Allard*,[74] the third case of the trilogy, where it was the American government causing the delay of some five years, Wilson was still able to concur with the majority disposition which upheld the appeal although again she asserted the applicability of the Charter to extradition hearings generally and to unreasonable delays in particular when such delays are caused by Canadian authorities.

Cotroni[75] was the extradition case in which Wilson was finally pressed into out and out dissent because the Court still had to deal with the issue unresolved in *Schmidt* of whether extradition is a reasonable limit on the section 6(1) guarantee of the right to remain in Canada. This was a distinctly unsavoury criminal case involving Canadian citizens well known to the police for their underworld associations; as we have seen repeatedly, for Wilson scrupulous protection of the rights of such unpopular people was of particular importance. Cotroni and El Zein in this instance were alleged to have participated in a conspiracy to import and to distribute heroin in the United States. The crimes had been committed in Canada, neither accused had ever left Canada, and their actions meant that they could have been charged in Canada with the appropriate violations of our Criminal Code and our Narcotic Control Act. The majority of the Court held that although the Charter right was infringed, under the section 1 *Oakes* test the concern of the governments to investigate, prosecute and suppress crime in order to maintain peace and public order was sufficiently pressing and substantial to justify the extradition and because the goal required transnational cooperation this was not too intrusive a means for achieving the desired end. The committals for extradition were reinstated.

Wilson certainly agreed that the section 6(1) mobility right had been infringed by the extradition orders, but she rejected strenuously the relaxed application of the section 1 test in circumstances when the acts for which extradition was requested had been committed in Canada:

> Since it was not necessary to my decision in *Schmidt* I did not express an opinion as to the soundness of the proposition ... that extradition was *per se* a reasonable limit justified under section 1 because I was not sure that it should not be subject to qualification in some circumstances. In other words, it seemed to me unwise and unnecessary to state this as a bald and absolute proposition and preferable, while acknowledging that in general extradition is a reasonable limit, to deal with particular circumstances on a case by case basis.[76]

And this was just such a case: the accused were Canadian citizens whose alleged wrongful conduct took place in Canada and who could be prosecuted here, and the *Oakes* test ought to be applied in the particular factual context in which it arises. There is that tone of personal moral indignation which we encounter only rarely in Wilson judgments, fully merited in this instance because Wilson was displeased at the suggestion that prosecution in the United States would entail only a 'peripheral violation' of the section 6(1) guarantee.

Wilson was offended by the lack of propriety implicit in the majority judgment, a too-apparent eagerness to curry favour in a situation of implicit inequality of bargaining power by issuing a decision that Canada assumed had the greater incentive to sustain its amiable relationship with the United States through compromise. The decision, holding once again that *Oakes* ought not to be applied in an overly rigid and mechanistic fashion, produced a fragmented doctrine of comity crumbling into little more than expediency. It contrasts sharply with Wilson's principled contextuality and her robust common-sense comity which moves beyond the traditional dichotomy between the splendid isolation of absolute modernist sovereignty, on the one hand, and a deference amounting to abdication of nationhood, on the other.

Wilson travelled widely during her years on the Supreme Court, both within Canada and internationally. This was part of her judicial responsibility and also part of her education, shaping the broadly national and international perspective she contributed to the Supreme Court. And beyond the judgments she wrote, Wilson participated in many other activities during her Supreme Court years which helped establish the Court's reputation both nationally and internationally during these challenging Charter years. Her life involved a great deal of work, but there was also time for some play. Before we leave the Supreme Court altogether to survey her post-judicial career, then, we will consider briefly the multiplicity of other ventures which were also engaging Bertha Wilson's heart and mind and which contributed to the integration of her life with the law.

12

Outside the Court

Supreme Court justices are routinely called upon to fill in when the governor general must be absent. But because no woman had yet been appointed governor general of Canada[1] and because Wilson herself was the first woman Supreme Court justice, March 1982 was the first occasion in Canada when a woman had taken on the vice-regal duties and was required to give royal assent to three bills. Press scrutiny was heightened accordingly. Several newspapers reported the event, with photographs showing the pinch-hitting governor general in a black long-sleeved dress with a crisp white collar and a serious expression receiving the required documentation. It was a function she was to perform again from time to time during her years on the bench.

And for Bertha Wilson, who has been heard to refer somewhat airily to the role of deputy governor general as requiring that one 'learn how to nod in both official languages,' these extra-judicial tasks never did become routine or second nature to her. Even in February 1991, at the end of her career on the bench, Wilson remembered that she had had a certain level of anxiety about carrying out the job properly with due respect for the majesty of the crown. More guidance would have been appreciated as to what was required; typically, as she was leaving the Court she offered a few notes to make things easier for successor judges slated for first-time deputy governor general duties.[2]

Life as a Supreme Court judge did offer undeniable glamour and buzz. To be appointed is to be plugged into the very highest levels of official Ottawa society as it presents its international face to the world. The Wilsons never took themselves seriously but they did understand that the job encompassed certain duties of hospitality meant to be carried out with propriety and grace. There were receptions, gala performances, musical evenings and state dinners hosted by chief justices and governors general and prime ministers; they were held in private houses and at Rideau Hall or at various hotel ballrooms or the National Arts Centre; and they honoured ambassadors or government leaders or visiting jurists or scholars from all over Canada and many international origins.

The Wilsons also enjoyed hosting their fair share of such entertainments. They invited each of the law clerks in turn to attend at a ballet or symphony as their guests in their private box. There was a hugely successful reunion of all the clerks able to attend in January 1989, with arrangements initiated the previous year by Jim Phillips and Allan Donovan; Wilson's notes make it clear that she had gone to a lot of trouble to find out about current partners and new babies and job situations in advance of the dinner, which was held in the Supreme Court judges' dining room. The Wilsons entertained visiting academics and former colleagues and friends and gave small dinner parties at a favourite restaurant or at home, for example, to welcome a new judge. What was memorable for many of the people who attended these events was the distinctively Wilsonian spontaneous humour which leavened many such formal moments.

When Beverley McLachlin was appointed to the Supreme Court in 1989, she went to Ottawa with an enormous respect for Bertha Wilson. In 1982 McLachlin, who had never met Wilson and was then just one year into her time on the British Columbia bench, sent her a heartfelt note of congratulations on the occasion of Wilson's own appointment. But if McLachlin was at first a little awestruck, she immediately found Wilson wonderfully welcoming. As McLachlin lined up with Claire L'Heureux-Dubé so that photographers could take a picture marking this historic occasion which made the Supreme Court fully one-third female, she recalls Bertha Wilson leaning over to say mischievously just before the shutter snapped, 'Three down, six to go!'.

John Wilson was inevitably included in many of these social invitations and, especially in the early years, was often the only non-wife spouse present.[3] This did not bother him a bit; he took epicurean pleasure in the entertainments on offer, enormous pride in his wife's accomplishments which had occasioned the invitations, and a certain sardonic delight in setting things straight when mistakes were made (as they sometimes were) about which of the two of them was the judge.

Of course, there was an initial round of champagne receptions on Wilson's appointment to the Supreme Court – for a period she likes to say with a little hyperbole, this seemed to be the sole beverage she was offered anywhere she went. And then there was a steady stream of convocations and honourary degrees and other recognitions throughout her years at the Court and continuing well after retirement before ill health made it necessary to decline further honours. The doctoral hoods in dazzling silks, customarily given to the recipient at the convocation ceremony, have been carefully folded away in storage. For each of these degrees Wilson kept a file detailing all the arrangements, from the initial invitation through the arrangements for transportation and hotel accommodation to the sizes needed for the borrowed academic gown and required academic headwear[4] to her final letter of appreciation. On almost every one of these occasions Wilson delivered a speech, some very short if that was requested and others quite substantial if she were delivering the convocation address; the texts of these speeches reveal that she put a great deal of thought and warmth into all of them.[5]

The Dalhousie LL.D., the first much-appreciated recognition from her own law school, had come in 1980 while she was still at the Court of Appeal; there were two more (from Queen's and Calgary) in 1983, three in 1984, two in 1985, one each in 1986 and 1988, and then a particularly cherished doctorate in 1989 from her first alma mater, the University of Aberdeen. On this occasion the citation was in Wilson's opinion embarrassingly long, 'a complete review of my life from day one,' and she noted that so much detail could only have been produced by canvassing all her friends and relatives still readily to hand in her home town.[6] Her brief remarks at the ceremony included commendation for the acts of heroism of Chinese youth at Tiananmen Square the previous month; she received a standing ovation, with the substantial contingent of Chinese students studying engineering at University of Aberdeen first on their feet.

Whenever the demands of her 'day job' permitted her to do so, Wilson was happy to deliver multiple speeches to different audiences in any given locality; if she were going to be in Vancouver or Saskatoon or Calgary or Windsor there might be a speech to the student body at the law school and then another just for the first-year class with perhaps a question-and-answer session for the upper-year classes, and additional addresses to a local service club and the provincial law society and the local bar association. It was not unusual for her to deliver a total of four or five speeches within a couple of days;[7] typically, even when she was attending high-level international conferences in Australia or Scotland or New Zealand she would willingly take on subsidiary speaking engagements before smaller local audiences on the way to and from the primary presentation.

On the way home from that Aberdeen convocation in 1989, Wilson stopped in England to attend the Canadian Institute for Advanced Legal Studies at Cambridge. There she delivered a major speech, 'Law and Policy in a Court of Last Resort,'[8] and participated in a panel discussion with American Supreme Court justice Sandra Day O'Connor and Lord Ackner of the British House of Lords.

The speech presented Wilson's somewhat contentious position (as it relates to her understanding of Charter-mandated judicial obligation) that policy considerations had always been an aspect of judicial decision-making. But it was a feather-ruffling incident during the panel discussion, not widely publicized at the time, which is most revealing of Bertha Wilson's personality bridging the more conventional divide between the public and the private.

Robert Sharpe (now on the Ontario Court of Appeal) was then serving as executive legal officer at the Supreme Court of Canada. Sharpe was present at Cambridge in 1989 as a participant and in his personal capacity as a legal scholar; he was responsible for chairing the panel which was to take place after a private lunch. Over friendly conversation during that lunch, the topic of the appointment of women judges came up. There were, after all, two women judges present in the room from North America but no woman has ever been appointed to the House of Lords. Wilson asked Lord Ackner why this was the case and he replied that in the British system – which requires a particular path for appointment from barrister to QC to trial judge to appellate judge to the House of Lords – no woman had ever been qualified. It would not have been possible to be appointed, as Wilson herself had been, directly from solicitor's practice to the appellate level.

The topic of appointment of women to the House of Lords came up publicly during the panel discussion. Someone in the audience directed a question to Wilson on the issue. She replied matter of factly and without any particular heat, 'Well, we discussed this at lunch and I asked Lord Ackner why there were no women on the House of Lords and his answer was ...' And at that point, Lord Ackner exploded, saying 'That was a privileged discussion, privileged circumstances.' But Wilson would not be shut up and she went on, damn the torpedoes, to report what he had said: no woman had been appointed because no woman was qualified. Lord Ackner was very upset, feeling, as Sharpe put it, 'that somehow his answer to her at lunch was some deep dark secret that she wasn't allowed to reveal to the public at large.'

The reaction in the room was mixed, with some of those present agreeing with Lord Ackner that the conversation had been a private one and others siding with Wilson that an important public issue deserved open discussion. Sharpe himself considered that the incident illustrated Wilson's fearlessness:

> I think she knew that he would not like what she was doing. She is also scrupulously fair and honest, she knew that there was absolutely no reason why she shouldn't say what he had said and so she said it. And that is typical of why she is such an important figure in our legal and judicial history, she tells it like it is whether we like it or whether we don't ... Even with close associates and people who she knows it is going to annoy, if she feels that it has to be said, she will say it and that is something that I enormously admire about her.

In 1988, through the Department of External Affairs, Wilson took an active role in organizing a trip to Canada of Soviet justice officials.[9] There was considerable interest in considering what aspects of the Canadian legal system might be transferable to the massive judicial and legal reforms then under way in the Gorbachev era of glasnost and perestroika.

Wilson had helped arrange preparation of scholarly background research papers to assist the Court in welcoming their Soviet counterparts to Ottawa, and had set up a panel presentation on the role of the Canadian Supreme Court. There were significant seminars on various aspects of law and opportunities to observe sittings at provincial, district, or Supreme Court of Ontario. The visitors received an introduction to Canadian legal education with a demonstration of cross-examination by York University law students and they were welcomed to a Toronto law firm. There were various official social events, including a dinner at the Supreme Court, a meeting with Ontario Lieutenant-Governor Lincoln Alexander, and a dinner at Osgoode Hall hosted by Ontario Chief Justice William Howland, as well as more typically tourist-oriented

activities. What most astonished the visiting judges was the independence of the judiciary and the law profession, and of legal education
from party control and the apparatus of the state.

Wilson had arranged for interpreters and photographers and all of the
small gracious touches which make such a trip successful on a human
level. Because her court attendant, Jean Plourde, had had so much experience dealing with international dignitaries in his previous United
Nations posting, she could rely upon him implicitly. And after he had
driven the Wilsons to Mirabel for the visiting dignitaries' departure to
Moscow, he was particularly proud that she asked him, instead of someone at a more senior management level, to arrange preparation of com-
memorative albums of pictures of their Canadian tour for each of the
distinguished Soviet guests. Plourde went off to Zellers, bought the
albums, and set them all up in his tidy manner to show to his judge. She
had to tell him gently, 'That is not quality enough.' But Wilson knew
exactly where to get the right kind of albums to mark a state visit and
it was a simple matter to transfer his work to the more appropriate
bindings.

In September of 1989 Sharpe accompanied Chief Justice Dickson and
Wilson, with their spouses on a reciprocal visit. It was one of the high-
lights of Wilson's career on the bench. The party visited a trial court, a
military court, and the Soviet Supreme Court of final appeal with its
chairman and three deputies and twenty-six judges. The system was
very different, relying heavily on advisory boards comprised of legal
academics and judges to study upcoming cases in an attempt to coordinate different rulings in the separate republics; the Supreme Court itself
heard only five or six of the highest profile cases a year in a trial capacity.

Wilson, who prepared a detailed report on the visit,[10] was fascinated
by the relatively low status of the legal profession and especially the
judiciary; at that time, control was overwhelmingly centralized in the
office of the Procurator General, which was responsible for legislative
drafting, human rights, diplomacy, and every legally oriented aspect of
Soviet society. But her report indicates that she was also very interested
in the economic circumstances facing ordinary citizens not privy to the
red-carpet treatment they were enjoying, with their fleet of limousines
whisking them swiftly through the streets of Moscow to the Kremlin.
She did not fail to notice or to ask about the perpetual queuing, the
shortage of food, the lack of housing and all the social problems resulting from overcrowding; and there was a quite remarkable openness
from Moscow officials in their replies.

And there were also certain sidetrips which created lasting memories. Despite the persistent poverty of the people, incongruously in Leningrad the lavish summer palace of the czars had been completely restored at great expense. The Canadians were taken to a performance of the ballet. They would have very much enjoyed the opportunity of an extended visit to the Hermitage, which had among its collection some magnificent Impressionist paintings, but unfortunately their hosts were more intent on having them view various objects rendered in gold and jewels representing the treasures of the historic past. But at Leningrad they did visit the monument to the victims of the siege; Dickson, wounded during the Second World War, was deeply moved by the suffering it commemorated, as were the Wilsons. The entire party was reduced to tears.

What Wilson took away from this trip primarily was an immense gratitude for the Western concept of the rule of law. When their hosts asked what was meant by this axiom, as Wilson said at a convocation address the following spring, this was the most difficult question of all to answer because 'we took it for granted like the air we breathe'; we are confident that no one is above the law and that the law applies to all no matter what position they hold in society.[11] But in the Soviet Union, where this was a very new idea, one had the feeling of being present at history in the making, she said. In the event, of course, the history being made turned to be rather different than what was then anticipated.

One of the most memorable and enjoyable of Bertha Wilson's extra-judicial jaunts was the September 1990 'Pilgrimage to Paisley' following the annual meeting of the Canadian Bar Association which was that year held in London. First, however, came a preliminary cavalcade – several chartered motor coaches with a total of 106 prominent Canadian lawyers, legal academics, and judges who had signed up to attend 'Tea with Lord and Lady Denning' at their home in Whitchurch, Hampshire, about two hours southwest of London. The legendary Lord Denning, whose creative and often iconoclastic judgments are read with delight by every law student in the common law world, was ninety-one that year; Lady Denning was ninety. There was an opportunity to enjoy the gardens by the river and to tour the house itself with its large collection of legal memorabilia in the library; tea was catered by local ladies and the Dennings circulated among their guests, welcoming each of them individually.

Chief Justice Lamer was unable to attend, so Bertha Wilson had been appointed to head up the Canadian contingent and bring greetings from the Court. And Wilson, who was within months of announcing her own retirement and had long been considered something of a Canadian Denning herself, paid Denning the highest tribute in her brief remarks. She was thoroughly thrilled and did not mind at all sounding just as starstruck as she genuinely was:

> Like a great many lawyers and judges in Canada, my library contains a Denning shelf the beginning of which dates back to my student days at Dalhousie Law School. The wall is also adorned with a framed copy in colour of your cartoon portrait by David Langdon in Punch. I remember as a young lawyer too junior in the firm to be financed to attend the Canadian Bar Convention stealing a day off specially to travel to Montreal to stand at the back of the auditorium as a non-paying guest and listen to your address at the annual dinner.
>
> You can imagine then the feelings which this visit engenders and I know they are shared by all who are assembled here this afternoon. This gathering of enthusiastic and admiring Canadians carries with it some of the earmarks of a pilgrimage to pay tribute to one who had become a living legend in his own time. You, Sir, are one of those few 'larger than life' figures whom time has never wearied and who possess that pristine vigour of speaking your mind and 'damn the torpedoes.'

A few days later Lord Denning wrote on the red-crested cream House of Lords stationery in his scrawling handwriting a personal letter thanking the chief justice for the visit and the gift (a polar bear sculpture) in which he mentioned in particular 'your good Bertha Wilson who made a charming speech.' In all of the excitement, in fact, the presentation of the gift had been forgotten and the parcel was presented on a follow-up visit several days later.[12]

The Pilgrimage to Paisley itself was billed as a Tribute to *Donoghue* v. *Stevenson*, the legendary torts case involving the snail in the bottle of ginger beer which had given birth to modern negligence law some fifty-eight years earlier. The historic and newly renovated Paisley Town Hall was chosen as the venue for the celebration because it was in the Wellmeadow Café at Paisley that Mrs May Donoghue had drunk the ginger beer manufactured in the bottling plant owned by the hapless David Stevenson. An ambitious three-day program offered presentations on tort law by distinguished scholars drawn from throughout the common law world, including Mr Justice Allen Linden, Bertha

Wilson's good friend who had helped seal her appointment to the Supreme Court.

Although the event was solidly learned, it is clear that a thoroughly good time was had by all. Local citizenry lined a parade route of the conference participants led by pipers from the Town Hall to the café. There was a buffet boat cruise on the Clyde, dedication of a memorial in Wellmeadow Park, a learned interdenominational service with a rousing sermon on the 'Good Neighbour' theme, and even golf for those so inclined. According to contemporary newspaper accounts, this was the first gathering ever of the Canadian and Scottish legal communities. Once again it was completely fitting that Wilson was designated to bring greetings from the chief justice of Canada. Bertha had come home and she had brought a good part of the Canadian legal community with her.

TIME TO MOVE ON

I have been increasingly conscious over the last year of diminishing energy, yet the workload of the Court continues to mount ... One is either able to discharge one's full share of the burden or should move over for those at the height of their powers. The job deserves no less.

So wrote Bertha Wilson to Justice Minister Kim Campbell in a letter dated 21 November 1990 announcing her resignation from the Court.

Beverley McLachlin, for one, will have none of that. Wilson, she says, was always impeccably prepared and informed and always functioned at the highest intellectual and professional level. Most of us, McLachlin believes (and she modestly includes herself in this group), have good days and not so good days but in her opinion, Wilson was 'always on top of her game.'[13] Nevertheless, in 1990 Wilson was sixty-seven, she had been enduring ill health (including progressively more debilitating arthritis which required powerful medications to alleviate the pain) for many years, and she had been contemplating retirement since 1974 when she had first talked with Hal Mockridge at Oslers about stepping down from partnership.

Like the good Humean she is, Wilson is unable to point to a specific cause or event underlying her decision that her Supreme Court days were over. The converging factors were multiple and complex. In part and very pragmatically she had completed the fifteen years necessary to make her eligible for her judicial pension; it is ironic that it was not until two years past the conventional mandatory retirement age that this judge who had dissented in *McKinney* was herself able to retire without significant financial penalty.

Chief Justice Dickson had retired the previous June. Even within five months, Wilson realized how much she missed his leadership. None of Wilson's attempts to establish memo-based decision-making protocols or to initiate some awareness of leave to appeal as a juridical tool or to ensure reforms in the leave to intervene procedure to provide the kind of legislative fact necessary to ensure a stringent application of section 1 had met with much success. Change seemed, if anything, less likely with Dickson gone.

With the escalating work load eating into their weekends and heavier traffic between Ottawa and Bobcaygeon increasing travel time to four or five hours, the Wilsons had had to give up their beloved boat house. Membership in the Five Lakes Club, which offered cottage-like accommodations in the Gatineau Hills closer to home, proved to be no real substitute, and the casual shared times with the extended Wernham family no longer had the same focus which had meant so much to both Bertha and John.

Travel with John was high on Bertha's list of priorities. He had been waiting a long time for her to retire. The two of them very much wanted to return to the program of reading and thinking and talking about subjects other than law which they had always enjoyed during the Oslers and Court of Appeal years. Bertha regretted that while she was on the Supreme Court she had fallen behind with developments in literature and films and painting and theology, and lost touch with cultural life to such an extent that she felt no longer capable of conversation with some of the friends with whom she had shared many deep interests. We may think of Wilson primarily as a Supreme Court judge, the first woman on the Supreme Court in the historic early Charter era. While justifiably proud of that epoch in her life, Wilson thinks of herself as a person who has done many things and prefers a multiplicity of roles. What in her own estimation was her most important work was still to come, although she resigned from the Court without knowing what that would be.

The swearing-out ceremony was on 4 December 1990. Frank Iacobucci was delighted to be among the invited members in the audience in the court room that day. He says it was completely typical of Wilson that she had made sure Micheline Barette, the secretary who worked with her for her last several months at the Court, and Jean-Marie Plourde, her long-standing and loyal court attendant, were given prime seating, and as it happened Iacobucci was placed between them. Of course, neither Wilson nor Iacobucci had any idea at the time that he would be succeeding her on the Supreme Court in 1991 and inheriting her staff, just as she had acquired Martland's when she had been appointed.

For a ceremonial occasion this was an unusually emotional send-off. Chief Justice Antonio Lamer paid her special tribute for the inhuman burden of work she had assumed on the Court, noting that her signature had gone on 161 crucial decisions, of which fifty-one were major decisions under the Charter of Rights and Freedoms. He mentioned that while on the Court the sixty or more major speeches she had delivered illustrated how multi-faceted her abilities were; he made specific reference to her lengthy paper on the Scottish Enlightenment which (he humorously assured his audience) she had demonstrated through her own scholarly analysis was 'far from being a contradiction in terms.' And Lamer, who was photographed kissing her soundly at the end of his speech, says he is quite sure this was the first occasion on which a chief justice embraced a retiring Supreme Court justice in quite that way. But even more telling, perhaps, were the quiet comments of an assistant court registrar who had worked in the building for some twenty-nine years: 'I feel sad for the Court. Anyone who has met her will never forget her.'[14]

As soon as the retirement was made public, there had been a huge outpouring of stories in the popular and professional press which continued for some time. More privately, there was a flood of letters,[15] some from public figures and former colleagues at Oslers or on the bench, but also a touching number from judges or lawyers and law clerks whom she had never met and even from citizens not connected with the profession in any way. The letters on the occasion of her appointment had imposed such unrealistic expectations about what she would be able to accomplish for women and such an optimistic timetable about how quickly these changes could be effected that Wilson had not wanted to keep many of them; this retirement correspondence has been carefully filed away.

Most of the letters express congratulations and gratitude for all she had done, mixed in some instances with regret that she was taking early retirement. Her jurisprudence professor William Lederman, still teaching at Queen's, wrote addressing her for the first time as Bertha and inviting her to call him Bill; his letter praises her for her 'splendid contribution to Canadian jurisprudence' and in particular her 'sheer rational force and wisdom' on Charter cases such as *McKinney*. There was another from a provincial chief justice acclaiming her as among the top ten of the best judges ever produced in this country with an affectionate aside in brackets, 'in addition you are nice to be with.' A woman in Greeley, Ontario, wrote simply, 'You have given a very important gift to the citizens of Canada. Thank you.'

And there was also a good deal of personal mourning among her colleagues, particularly the other two women judges. Beverley McLachlin says that she was profoundly disappointed when she left. Claire L'Heureux-Dubé wept, as she had done when Dickson left the Court, because in her opinion the two of them had created a breathing space for everyone and because she knew that an era was coming to an end.

First came the six-month period during which retired Supreme Court justices write those judgments for which they have volunteered that are still in reserve; Wilson, 'demoted to an office on the Federal Court floor,'[16] was confident that she could be completely wrapped up by June of 1991. And at the same time came a surge of retirement honours, with five new LL.D.s in 1991 alone and more speaking engagements and more celebrations. Within days the dean of law at Dalhousie had written to invite her to consider a teaching position on any terms she cared to propose; Wilson replied with a promise to visit but said she intended to continue living in Ottawa, at least in the short run.[17]

The law clerks immediately rallied around to stage a second retirement reunion, scheduled for late April of 1991 and held once again in the Supreme Court judges' dining room. This was a particularly jovial occasion which almost everyone attended, most with spouses or partners. Several also had their kids in town to meet their judge before or after the dinner. A collection had been taken up and an Inuit lithograph representing a hunting scene was given to the Wilsons, with hilarious comments about which of the figures chasing across the snowy tundra represented which of her various colleagues from the Supreme Court; it now hangs in the Wilsons' dining room. The clerks hired a photographer to take a posed group shot and informal pictures of the festivities. After the event these photos were pulled together into an album which was presented to the Wilsons – and it was not a Zellers album.

There was a witty speech about Wilson's contributions to the preservation of the 'comma law'; many a clerk had drafted a judgment or a speech only to get it back with Wilson's busy pencil having excised commas throughout.[18] And although most of the clerks were already on excellent terms (just a few met each other for the first time) there was also a certain amount of restrained jockeying for attention and musical chairs, as is typical of social occasions in almost any extended family.

Typically, Wilson had selected the sumptuous menu (crabmeat and avocado, veal marsala, strawberry mousse) and the wines and then picked up the costs herself. The warm and affectionate letters of thanks which came in afterwards indicated that this was an absolute surprise and very much appreciated. Clerk after clerk invited her to visit with them at home when next she happened to be visiting in their cities; clerk after clerk mentioned how grateful they had been to work with her during their year at the Supreme Court and that in retrospect the gruelling workload they helped shoulder had offered them the experience of a life time.

In May, Bertha and John Wilson were invited house guests of the Lord High Commissioner to the General Assembly of the Church of Scotland at Holyroodhouse in Edinburgh. Holyroodhouse is now ordinarily a tourist attraction when the royal family is not in residence and for the one week a year when the Lord High Commissioner is attending the Scottish General Assembly it functions again as a working household with banquets and pipers and a garden party. This week is used as an opportunity to honour a small group of distinguished visitors drawn from throughout the Commonwealth with all possible pageantry and ceremonial grandeur. The Wilsons' invitation had been received on 4 December 1990, the very day of the swearing-out ceremony. They accepted for the evening of 20 May 1991 and were among the dozen guests shown to private rooms for an overnight stay. The following morning, after prayers in the Morning Drawing Room, the Wilsons attended at General Assembly with the Lord High Commissioner. If serving as deputy governor general had been an incredible experience, then it is hard to imagine an honour of greater significance or historical interest to Bertha and John Wilson than this gala stay at Holyroodhouse.

A week later and back in Ottawa, Wilson participated in a three-day seminar on the functioning of government at which she delivered a substantial paper, 'Human Rights and the Courts'; her co-presenter was Max Yalden, chairman of the Human Rights Commission and father of law clerk Rob Yalden.[19] In June the Wilsons were in Hong Kong attending the Bill of Rights Conference where Bertha Wilson presented her paper, 'Women, the Family and the Constitutional Protection of Privacy.'

This Hong Kong trip was another red-carpet affair with a reception hosted by the attorney general, the film premiere of *Bethune*, and numerous state dinners, including one hosted by Chief Justice Lamer to honour the chief justice of the Supreme Court of Hong Kong. Hong Kong was seeking international commentary on its new human rights legislation from a comparative perspective and accordingly the lineup of speakers drew from the highest calibre of international constitutional scholars.[20]

There was a sense of history being made, in an atmosphere of apprehension pending the transfer of Hong Kong to China slated for 1997, which had already triggered the mass exodus of about a third of the legal profession. For John Wilson, of course, it was also an opportunity to revisit and to share with Bertha some of the places he had first seen while on leave during the Korean War.

During the first six months right after Wilson's retirement the Department of External Affairs had been aggressively campaigning through all possible diplomatic channels for her election as jurist on the Inter-American Court of Human Rights. Wilson was intensely interested in many aspects of international law from her earliest law school years. Had she been elected the Wilsons were both quite ready to move for part of the year to Costa Rica, the site of the court. But on the secret ballot held that year in Santiago, Chile, Canada missed out by a single vote. Wilson was disappointed but was primarily concerned to express appreciation for all the work on her behalf by those in the diplomatic service, who were even more disappointed.

Once this announcement had been made, Bertha Wilson accepted a position as scholar-in-residence at University of Ottawa in the common law section; this, she knew, would not be a demanding post, requiring only that she meet with students from time to time and perhaps give the occasional address, but it did offer her some office space and clerical support.

New honours were still being created and conferred upon her. Oslers had established a visiting professorship which rotated among Dalhousie, University of Toronto, and York University. A 'Wilson Moot' was established to bring together Canadian law students to hone their skills in advocacy. That September a special workshop on Changing Laws and Aspects of Law Reform at the University of Toronto was organized by Rosalie Abella under the auspices the Ontario Law Reform Commission to honour Bertha Wilson.[21]

But the culminating celebration of the retirement year was undoubt-edly the Democratic Intellect conference held in Halifax over three days in early October and intended (as the letter proposing the event to Wilson billed it) as 'a serious academic symposium focusing on your contributions to Canadian law.'[22] Dalhousie had on faculty its own former Wilson clerk, Moira McConnell, who took on the formidable task of chairing the Wilson Symposium Committee.

The symposium opened with the presentation of the theme that had been developed by legal historian and the acting dean, Philip Girard. It was intended to unify all the symposium presentations in consideration of the various contributions of the Scottish Enlightenment philosophy imported to Canada in the nineteenth century and embedded in its egalitarian culture as its social institutions were developed by Scottish immigrants. The theme also offered the opportunity of looking at Wilson's contemporary contributions as a Scottish immigrant to the modification of democratic traditions which were required with the advent of the Charter.[23] Former Chief Justice Brian Dickson delivered the 1991 Horace Read lecture at the law school. Even although he was not feeling particularly well, his tribute to Wilson was strong and scholarly and deeply felt, and she most sincerely appreciated that he was there.

A formal dinner was held the following evening attended by about four hundred of Bertha Wilson's colleagues and friends who had come to Halifax to honour her from across the country. There were a number of short and affectionate reminiscences by people who had known John and Bertha Wilson during the Dalhousie days. A group called Swallow's Tale offered the premiere performance of 'The Flowers of Fife,' a special piece of Celtic music commissioned in her honour[24] and arranged for voice and harp and dulcimer and synthesizer. Wilson made a few appreciative and rather humble comments and proposed a toast to Dalhousie Law School to bring the event to a close. The next day Pat Fownes Harris had organized a reunion at her own home for all of Wilson's law school classmates and their spouses, which turned out to be a much more relaxed and rollicking affair.

At this stage, it looked as if Wilson's retirement had offered anything but repose and relaxation; there had been lots of official travel but very little opportunity for the personal jaunts or the reading and conversation she and John had had in mind. And even before the schedule for the Dalhousie symposium had been firmly established, Wilson found herself enmeshed simultaneously in two massive endeavours: the Canadian Bar Association Gender Equality study, and the Royal Commission on Aboriginal People. By early 1992, when Wilson was sixty-eight years old, she was travelling from one end of the country to the other and working even harder than she had ever done at the Supreme Court of Canada. As she told CBA president Wayne Chapman, 'I guess I'm not quite ready to sip Campari on the Riviera yet.'

PART THREE

Life after Judging

13

The Gender Equality Study

It is 26 August 1992 at the Canadian Bar Association's annual meeting in Halifax. The schedule of events has drawn the largest registration ever in CBA history and one thousand members are in attendance. Bertha Wilson, retired justice of the Supreme Court of Canada and voluntary chair of the Canadian Bar Association Task Force on Women in the Legal Profession, is back in the city where Dean Horace Read had told her almost forty years earlier to take up crocheting.

Bertha Wilson has a few telling comments to make. Existing research confirms what her own experience of working in a large law firm taught her – many male lawyers over the age of forty find it hard to respond to women in the work place professionally instead of sexually. But most of Wilson's contribution takes the form of questions:

> *The profession was shocked that so many women were leaving the practice and moving into other fields ... Why do they find the climate of the large law firm so inhospitable? ... Must women practitioners accommodate to the 'maleness' of their environment? Must they change some basic aspects of their nature in order to fit in? Or should the structure of the large law firm itself be re-examined? Do some of the values it reflects impose a tyranny of their own that even men are beginning to chafe at? ... Do we need to inject a new humanity into our profession and, if so, are we capable of meeting the challenge?*

Wilson has a particular reason for wondering if the profession is capable of meeting this challenge. In April of 1991 she had first told CBA President Wayne Chapman she would head up the two-year Gender Equality study. She had anticipated getting down to business right away in the fall. But a full year later Wilson has an interim report to present which is very discouraging indeed.

The truth is that once the announcement had been made, the task force had been given almost no support, either financial or clerical. Its work is floundering and in imminent danger of collapse. Wilson does not mince words:

> When I was asked to chair the Task Force I was assured that it was a top priority of the Association and that funding would not be a problem since the project had the enthusiastic support of the Minister of Justice, women's organizations across the country, and the legal profession as a whole ...
>
> However, your Task Force has been afflicted with major funding problems ... We are currently limping along on a shoestring and we are now half-way through our mandate. The CBA's goal was to raise $250,000 to fund our two-year mandate. When I checked last week at the head office we had $54,000 in commitments ...
>
> The gender equality project is probably different from any other project the CBA has undertaken in that it calls for substantial empirical research on a Canada-wide basis. I don't need to tell you what it costs to bring people together to meetings. We are no longer able to meet as a Task Force: we rely on conference calls instead. We have no money to fund the provincial and territorial working groups we set up in order to do the required research for us at the local level. They have had to try to raise their own funds ...
>
> All of us who are working on this project view the Canadian Bar Association as having a special responsibility to provide leadership in this very sensitive area of gender equality. It is an ethical as well as a legal issue of fundamental importance to our society ... Will our profession be the protagonist in the drama of women's advancement or merely a Greek chorus?[1]

Wilson's remarks create a sensation; when she leaves the stage she is immediately besieged by reporters.

And when the meeting reconvenes after a coffee break, Joan MacDonald from Hamilton is on her feet to speak. A former legal secretary and law clerk, MacDonald had applied three times for admission to law school before she was accepted at the age of forty. A single mother whose long-term marriage had disintegrated by the end of her first year commuting to Western, she is helping support her daughter and her own mother. In 1992 she has been in practice only four years and is still coming to terms with a massive debt load left over from law school. Returning as a lawyer to the law firm where she had worked as a clerk, she found that the pressure of billable hour quotas was fundamentally incompatible with her other responsibilities. Now she has set up as a sole practitioner, trying to build her career and her income through legal aid representation of young offenders and support-seeking wives and mental health patients.

Even attending at the Halifax annual meeting has been a very significant financial sacrifice for MacDonald. She knows that Bertha Wilson is heading this task force for people like her. Although pressed for money herself, in her opinion imposing upon Wilson the necessity of coming cap in hand to the profession is a public indignity.

MacDonald cannot stand to see the task force fail, confirming the opinion of many that gender inequality does not exist in the profession or that not enough people care even if it does.

A year ago, we brought Justice Wilson out of retirement because we need to know what is happening and why we are losing women in the first three years of practice. I am one of the oddities in the legal profession who does not fit the mould and this study is something so crucial that we have to find the money. It would be unfair not to do so when we have enlisted Madame Justice Wilson in our cause. I pledge $1,000 to the funding of this report.

And then MacDonald turns to face everyone in the audience, eyeball to eyeball, as she adds: 'I challenge the rest of the legal profession in Canada to do the same.'

There is a deafening silence. No one else seems prepared to put a hand into a personal pocket or to write a cheque. But by the evening session various lawyers have called their firms. The commitments began to come in, at first in small amounts and then over the next several months in quantities sufficient to get the project back on track.[2]

FINDING THE FUNDING: COSTLY CONSULATIONS

Bertha Wilson had never met Joan MacDonald and was not even in the room when she issued her challenge to the profession; but Wilson gives MacDonald the entire credit for getting the ball rolling at an absolutely crucial point in the task force's mandate. There is no question that this was a defining moment for Joan MacDonald, who has gone on to perform distinguished service to her profession and to her community, but who believes she has also reaped certain repercussions from her identification as a feminist.[3]

Why was it so difficult to garner support for this study? Wilson suggested quite straightforwardly to reporters after her Halifax speech that part of the problem was the old boys' network undercutting the task force's efforts because they did not consider gender equality to be a top priority issue. But although the legal profession is a wealthy profession,[4] as Wilson also pointed out, lawyers and law firms were feeling a certain financial pinch during the recession of the early nineties which had plunged many Canadians into economic conditions not seen since the Depression.

It had also been anticipated by the CBA that substantially more funding would be forthcoming from the federal government and from provincial law foundations than in fact was available; the recession had resulted in sharp cutbacks in these traditional sources of grants as well. The Department of Justice, for example, had provided only $25,000 in 1991 instead of the anticipated $100,000 and that had come with no guarantees of further funding; there had been $25,000 from the Ontario branch of the Canadian Bar Association, $25,000 from the Law for the Future Fund, and a few more thousands from the Law Foundations of Yukon and Prince Edward Island, but not all of this committed money was at hand. The Gender Equality study was by far the most ambitious project that the CBA had ever undertaken and in the end cost about $425,000 instead of the $250,000 originally estimated.[5] The association had obviously not budgeted enough resources; but in its defence, it never expected it would be necessary for its task force to go out and beat the bushes to find its own funding.

Most costly were the massive consultations mandated by the study's terms of reference. The task force was to inquire into and make recommendations for improvement of the status of women within the legal profession by looking at CBA's constitution and by-laws and rules and internal operating procedures and by considering such issues as parental leave policies, flex-time and job sharing, promotion of upward mobility, and mentoring. But it was also to serve as a 'conduit for collection and distribution of information regarding initiatives on gender equality' by consulting fourteen different groups across Canada and by establishing a nation-wide working group with appropriate representation across the country drawn from CBA's provincial branches and national sections. All this was to be done and the final report tabled within two years; by August 1992 half the time allocated had evaporated but the consultation process had barely begun.

And the CBA had also grossly underestimated the amount of administrative resources required to coordinate these tasks. It had assigned only one staff person to work on the project half-time, a recently called lawyer named Melina Buckley. But Buckley, who was herself juggling work responsibilities with the demands of a young family and thoroughly sympathetic to the purposes and objectives of the task force, was certainly too junior to call her time her own. She had been assigned long hours assisting on various other CBA projects.

Certainly there was tremendous interest in the project from the profession as soon as Bertha Wilson had lent her name to it. Over two hundred people offered their services to the task force; the five initially selected as members were intended to provide 'broad representation in geographic regions, areas of practice, size of law firm and personal experience.' Sophie Bourque, called in 1984, was active in the Young Bar of Montreal, where she had helped create daycare facilities and spoken on balancing professional and family responsibilities; Daphne Dumont, from Prince Edward Island, was a founder of LEAF and active in family law reform; John Hagan, a professor of Law and Sociology at University of Toronto, had written extensively on law and gender issues; Patricia Blocksom practised family law and mediation, was active in the Calgary Association of Women and the Law, and taught family law at University of Calgary; and Alec Robertson was senior corporate counsel at Davis & Company in Vancouver, had been president of CBA-BC and had also taught at the University of British Columbia and Victoria.

The first meeting of the new task force had been held right after the 1991 CBA convention. A deliberately moderate approach was selected; all were agreed that it was best to avoid high-profile radical feminists for the provincial committees, that the approach to large law firms should be through policy-makers not managing partners, and that the aim was seeking co-operation and assistance not confrontation, given that the task force was operating on the premise that inequality exists and focusing on possible solutions.[6]

From the beginning, there was some disagreement over the need to provide opportunity for victims of discrimination to submit their experiences to the task force, and it was decided to seek out such victims' statements 'not so much to establish discrimination but to express their views as to what the proper solution would have been.' Even if the personal experience statements were useful (and Wilson, for one, wondered if the task force needed this material at all) there was a further concern about how it would be possible to guarantee confidentiality. As it turned out, Wilson's worry on this point was prophetic.

Wilson came to the first meeting with a clear idea about the methodology necessary to fulfil the task force mandate. Particular members were assigned primary responsibility for the various areas of consultation required: John Hagan, for example, was to cover academia from the perspective of both law students and faculty members; Pat Blocksom, corporate counsel; Daphne Dumont, government lawyers and administrative tribunals; Sophie Bourke, the small firms and professional associations; Alec Robertson, the large law firms; and it was agreed by everyone that only Bertha Wilson herself could ensure the confidentiality necessary for women in the judiciary to feel comfortable disclosing any incidents of discrimination they might be experiencing. In early October of 1991 the various CBA section chairs (who headed up practice areas such as family law and administrative law and wills and estates practice) had been asked for their input. By the end of that month the manual and guidelines had been drafted for the provincial working groups and work was under way to establish various questionnaires to facilitate the sectoral analysis.

But despite this initial progress, it had become obvious to Bertha Wilson and to Alec Robertson as early as November 1991 that the task force was in serious trouble; both of them had contacted J.J. Camp with urgent requests for assistance with funding and administrative support.[7] In desperation, Wilson had already hired a part-time coordinator who was working out of the University of Ottawa.[8] But when J.J. Camp sat in on the task force meeting in January 1992, he had to report that his attempts to shake loose more funding commitments from provincial bar associations and law foundations and private foundations and governments had been relatively unsuccessful.

It was already apparent that there was either very little or absolutely no data available in a number of key areas; John Hagan, for example, had found nothing on the shelf relating to issues of gender equality in Canadian legal academia. It was also apparent that a full-time paid director was needed to field phone calls and collate data and respond to correspondence – preferably a lawyer with excellent research and writing skills, an upbeat personality, and sufficient seniority to cement relationships among the consultative groups. The market salary for such a person was estimated even in 1991 at $75,000. Such a person would need secretarial assistance and office space.

There simply was not enough money to pay salaries or rent. There was not even enough money to bring the task force members together for the meetings it had planned on calling every three months; most of the time, they realized, they would have to make do with conference calls. How could they acquire a director and secretary at no cost? Various options were considered, including secondment from a female-friendly law firm or from a university law faculty. But there was considerable discomfort among task force members that improving the status of women in the profession should be achieved by pressing someone (more likely than not a woman) into assuming these tasks at low pay or no pay at all. And certainly Wilson, whose own health was not good and who was fully occupied with the gruelling travel required for the hearings of the Royal Commission on Aboriginal People, could not possibly take on any more than she was already handling.

In January of 1992 Melina Buckley, realizing that the project was spiralling out of control, presented to the task force a List of Critical Dates. Intelligence, willingness to work hard even when assigned menial tasks, and above all the ability to get along with people: these were the qualities which Wilson prized. On meeting the 'tremendously capable' Buckley (Wilson's own assessment) it is apparent she possesses all these qualities plus a wry sense of humour which must have been life-saving. This CBA job was her first and she was in a very difficult position.

On the one hand, it would be no exaggeration to say that she absolutely reveres Wilson as a judge and as a person and she was overjoyed – even overawed – at the opportunity of working with her. On the other hand, there were thoroughly uncomfortable moments when this junior lawyer with big responsibilities but no real authority had to position herself at cross purposes with Wilson. Wilson was dismayed that the consultation process was necessarily truncated for reasons of time and funding. Moreover, Wilson is enormously skilled at writing and enjoys it; Buckley is sure that she would have wished to write considerably more of the report than she had either time or energy to take on. But it was up to Buckley to orchestrate the multiple contributors in order to meet the interim and final deadlines so that the report could be released at the 1993 CBA annual meeting scheduled for Quebec. And as a result it was Buckley who ended up writing vast portions of the report.[9] Even though writing the report was clearly a full-time job, Buckley was still only on 50 per cent loan to the task force, which never did get its full-time director. As a result she readily acknowledges that the organization and the writing is a little rough in places.

Before the writing could begin, of course, those limited consultations which were possible had to be carried out. Each of the provincial working groups had only $2,000 in funding but nevertheless, with the valiant efforts of the provincial chairs, all of them managed to pull together a report and submit it on time. Fundraising was ongoing and cheques came in slowly. After the Halifax interim report, for example, the CBAO held a series of fundraising dinners at $100 a ticket. Wilson attended the one in Ottawa where she gave a barn-burner of a speech and prepared a video for the other centres. The task force managed to commission six scholarly papers by distinguished feminist academics on various aspects of gender equality[10] (which helped augment data in areas where it was most scanty) and then to pull together a three-day continuing legal education conference for 150 participants in October of 1992 where these thematic papers were presented and discussed. A consultation meeting was held in Toronto in January 1993 with representatives of twelve women's organizations; there was another consultation with law school representatives in April 1993 and more informal regional consultations with women of colour and aboriginal women and lesbian women.

It had not been until a motion from the floor at the October 1992 CLE conference that a decision was made to expand the task force by adding two more women who could contribute perspectives of multiple discrimination: Sharon McIvor to represent aboriginal women and Madam Justice Corrinne Sparks to represent women of colour. Sparks was selected also because she was able to contribute substantial leadership in developing a more generally inclusive stance with respect to minority women. There was considerable embarrassment at the lack of earlier recognition that the task force (which Wilson had insisted from the beginning in the interests of credibility had to include two men) ought not to have been all-white. But if this recognition came late, nevertheless Alec Robertson considers the expansion to have been a defining moment in the study; it demonstrated to the task force that it was able to change directions and incorporate multiplicity without losing momentum.

In the end, after the completion of all the draft sections of the report in late June of 1993 and its translation into French in July, there was still a short fall of some $6,000 to pay for publication and binding. Joan Mac-Donald swiftly organized a 'Rock and Roll' for the Hamilton bar – a completely nonthreatening, nonfeminist evening of rock music and bowling – and she twisted arms to sell tickets until this final sum had been raised. Melina Buckley had written non-stop for two months. She was completely exhausted but thrilled and relieved that she was able to meet her final deadline in time for the August annual meeting.

BILLABLE HOUR QUOTAS AND THE DUTY
TO ACCOMMODATE

The report was as much of a bombshell as Wilson's 1990 'Will Women Judges Really Make a Difference?' speech. And given the starvation diet on which it had been nourished, the finished report was remarkably robust. In five parts, it begins with a conceptual framework for achieving gender equality looking at demographics, discrimination law, and the duties imposed by self-regulation. Part 2 investigates those issues that create barriers for women seeking to enter the profession and proposes solutions, such as part-time articles. Part 3 reviews discrimination in employment opportunities, career development, accommodation of families, and sexual harassment, while Part 4 focuses on gender inequality in professional organizations. The conclusion provides a summary of all the task force's recommendations. In addition to the report, the task force had also generated an action plan linking the recommendations to the various bodies charged with the duty of carrying them out, and fourteen appendices which include model policies on accommodation and harassment, the various reports prepared by the provincial working groups and the sectoral analysis project, reports from the continuing legal education conference and consultation process, and the annotated bibliography.

To a certain degree, however, some of these solid accomplishments got lost in the debate which followed the report's release. Within the report itself there were two particularly challenging topics which sparked especially vociferous criticism in the professional and popular press. And Wilson was directly responsible for both of them.

The first had to do with the controversial issue of the legal duty to accommodate women with childcare responsibilities and the recommendations that billable hour quotas be adjusted to reflect this legal duty to accommodate.[11] Buckley recalls that Wilson had arrived at one of the regular meetings of the task force with her own hand-written notes spelling out in no uncertain terms her conviction that law firms which failed in this duty to accommodate were breaking the law. Illegality was a theme with variations that Wilson repeated skilfully throughout her introduction, concluding in a forceful crescendo:

It would be ironic indeed if the legal profession were using its self-governing status not for the public protection but for its own. It would be unthinkable if it were using its monopoly to violate the law which it is dedicated to uphold ...

Will the reforms the task force advocates in this Report be implemented as a free and dignified act of justice? Is the profession ready for equality of opportunity for all women – white women, Women of Colour, Aboriginal women, women with disabilities, lesbian women? Or will their male colleagues make them wait another fifty years until time will have robbed their consent of its graciousness and tainted it with the meanness and cowardice of expediency?[12]

But it was one thing for law firms to consider, for example, voluntary enactment of maternity leave policies (knowing that in any event the work culture made it impossible for women to take advantage of them). It was another for them to be told that they were in breach of their special duty as a self-regulating profession to adhere to the rule of law with the utmost punctiliousness – especially when compliance might demand economic sacrifice from males when it came time for setting of associate salaries or distribution of partnership drawings. For the firms which had finally provided some funding for the task force in particular – and Oslers, Wilson's own firm, had been the most generous, giving $25,000 – this was a little too much like biting the hand that feeds you.

Wilson's position on the issue ought not to have come as any surprise. It was completely congruent with her doctrine of duty to accommodate up to the point of undue hardship. The report insisted that reduced billable hour quotas ought not to delay accession of women associates to partnership and that law firms ought to develop alternate methods of weighing lawyers' contributions which focus on the quality rather than the quantity of time expended.

Nevertheless, the profession did not readily accept this judgment.[13] Even before the official August publication date of the report, lawyer Karen Selick had written an indignant column for the Toronto *Globe and Mail* which expressed what many lawyers were thinking. Law firms, she argued, are entitled to adopt whatever billable hour policies they believe will best achieve their goals. Women lawyers should weigh for themselves the costs in loss of income and prestige against whatever benefits they perceive result from what is an essentially private decision to have children, but they should never be able to require that their legal colleagues compensate them for their losses.[14] Selick clearly did not subscribe to the *Brooks*[15] doctrine in which Chief Justice Dickson had determined that pregnancy is a benefit to society as a whole and concluded that imposing its costs exclusively on women was sexual discrimination contrary to section 15 of the Charter.

The CBA was also slow to accept these recommendations and there was considerable internal foot-dragging and behind-the-scenes negotiation. Bertha Wilson herself refused to be bitter that the profession was unwilling to accept these obligations on principle. She indicated in an interview when the report was first released that it was not necessary for law firms to oppose discrimination out of principle, at least in the first instance. Lacking genuine altruism, simple propriety and an Adam Smith-style self-interest might be sufficient to evoke an appropriate behaviour:

> If we can't touch any streak of idealism in you, let's talk your language ... We're saying that if we cannot persuade you that you have an obligation in this area then let us persuade you that it's in your own best interests to change. You are not going to get the best young lawyers in your firm if you stick to the traditional model.
>
> More and more women are coming out of law school and bar ad courses and, by and large, if you look at the statistics they're in the top group in almost every law school in the country. If you want those people, the best minds, then maybe you have to show them that you have sexual harassment policies, employment equity policies, that you try to accommodate women who are raising children. You're going to have to have these things as a matter of enlightened self interest.[16]

With the advent of the Charter, the Supreme Court's increased workload had meant that the law profession had had to be educated on the leave to appeal procedure; to effect long-term change it was possible that the profession simply required more education about discrimination. A November 1993 internal draft resolution of the CBA shows it opting only to recognize the existence of inequalities in the legal profession and to receive, rather than adopt, the report as a whole.[17] But this language masks the controversy, since to an unprecedented degree the debate at council had been both ugly and personal.[18]

A Blue Ribbon Working Group was struck to work on implementation. Professor Sheilah Martin (who had prepared the task force study on balancing work and family in the legal profession) wrote a follow-up paper on the duty to accommodate to clarify the law for members of the profession; Melina Buckley spent the better part of a year on the road speaking to provincial branches and local bar associations on this issue; and the incoming president, Cecilia Johnstone, was also an extremely outspoken advocate of the report.

Nevertheless, it is telling that at the February 1994 CBA winter meeting in Jasper, where the task force report was a major item for discussion on the agenda and many of the less controversial recommendations were adopted, only belatedly did the organizers come to the recognition that a co-ed toga party might not be an appropriate form of entertainment. In fact, the key duty to accommodate resolutions were not adopted either then or at the August 1994 CBA annual meeting in Toronto.

This was a full year after the report's release but the controversy had not abated much. James F. Hutchinson, a lawyer from Woodstock, Ontario, wished he was a member of the CBA just so that he could resign in disgust over these recommendations, which he characterized as providing that 'female lawyers should be paid equally even while they are producing children whom the world doesn't need.' And Norma Priday, then a recent University of Toronto law graduate, suggested that it was risky to measure the work of women lawyers raising children differently from the work of other lawyers because it would encourage law firms to adopt preferential hiring policies for male candidates and exclude women from opportunities altogether.[19]

Such objectors (and there were many more) drew overwhelmingly on uninflected laissez-faire economics. There seemed to be little consideration of Adam Smith's doctrine that ethics and economics can be integrated, especially in closely knit social groups. The practical recommendations proposed by the task force to mitigate the hardship of the duty to accommodate for individual law firms seem not to have been explored with any degree of commitment.

WOMEN IN THE JUDICIARY

For Bertha Wilson it was the second area of controversy – discrimination against women in the judiciary – which caused her the greatest personal grief. She designed a questionnaire asking women judges what sort of discrimination they had encountered and took responsibility for its distribution to the two hundred women who in 1991 had received either provincial or federal appointments to the bench; all the replies (some in writing, some in person, some by telephone) came to her directly. To ensure confidentiality the raw data were not revealed to any other member of the task force and Wilson made absolutely sure it was destroyed as soon as it had been collated and summarized.

However, in January of 1992 and in her role as scholar in residence at University of Ottawa she had presented a video prepared by the Western Judicial Centre (an institution for judicial education) on gender bias in the courts. Not only was this video misinterpreted by a small group of students as an indication that the CBA task force considered racial discrimination to be separable from and of less importance than issues of gender bias, the press also picked up the story in a manner which was potentially very damaging. Wilson, it was alleged, was revealing information received from the CBA survey of women judges before release of the report and in direct breach of her commitment to confidentiality.[20]

Wilson was horrified that her own ethical standards were impugned. Moreover, at that point she had heard from only about sixty of the two hundred judges surveyed and she knew that if she was not quick to correct this misinformation it was unlikely she would hear from anyone else. Immediately she sent out a memo to all the women judges assuring them that 'none of your letters have been seen by anyone except myself nor will they' and reiterating her promise not to disclose their contents or the source of any information she received.[21]

Collating the information she had received, Wilson began her analysis of discrimination in the judiciary by looking at the figures. Whether as a percentage of the population in general or as a percentage within the legal profession, women were under-represented on almost every court in Canada; moreover, by drawing on Ontario statistics she demonstrated that there was no longer any lack of women qualified for appointment to excuse such under-representation. This was a situation which could be alleviated through development and publication of objective criteria for judicial appointment together with an affirmative action policy.

In her opinion, there could be no conflict between judicial independence and compulsory race and gender sensitivity courses as an element of judges' training. Moreover, she suggested, the training could be provided exclusively by judges themselves. Recalling, perhaps, her own early judicial education in Colorado, Wilson added with unimpeachable logic: 'I must say, however, that I have never heard judges resist instruction in judgment-writing on the ground that it was delivered by those non-judges especially schooled in the art of the English language.'[22]

Wilson's chapter dealt with the discriminatory behaviour inflicted by some male judges upon female counsel, something she characterized forthrightly as an abuse of judicial power. Women lawyers disliked being made fun of by male judges in court or in chambers, especially in front of their clients; they resented male judges tolerating (and even enjoying) derogatory comments made by opposing male counsel; they simply wanted to be treated with the same courtesy and respect generally afforded male counsel.

Wilson described the inequality in judicial appointment deriving from the apparently neutral and justifiable practice of choosing those who had been most active in professional organizations; biological timing means that many women lawyers are preoccupied with child care during their early careers and have less time for such activities. She questioned the tenure requirement specifying that candidates are not eligible for the bench until they have practised law for at least ten years; again for biological reasons, more women than men enter the profession late. However, they bring to it a wider range of pre-law life experiences which ought to be valued in the judicial appointment process. And she considered the issue of judicial discipline, calling for a much more transparent process comparable to the disciplinary process in place for lawyers. Judges, lawyers, and members of the public ought to participate, she concluded after the consultative process; judicial independence is not incompatible with the enhancement of public confidence which could be achieved by opening the door to disciplinary hearings.

But the core of the controversy derived from Wilson's revelation that women in the judiciary, once appointed, were compelled to endure many instances of both professional and personal discrimination. Of the 132 responses received, '58 reported having personally experienced discrimination in one form or another while on the bench.'[23]

Sexual harassment of provincial court judges was not widespread but serious. Women judges also reported significant discrimination in the allocation of work. Chief justices and chief judges, many of whom considered that their responsibility was to assign a particular case to the judge best qualified by training and experience to handle it, were not taking into account the importance of providing opportunities and mentoring for new female judges; moreover, it was perceived that new male judges with similar gaps in their preparation for the bench were not channelled away from unfamiliar areas of the law.

As a result, women judges were too often denied the opportunity of handling complex trials and high-profile criminal matters. Instead and regardless of their prior experience they were expected to pick up more than their fair share of the family law docket to relieve their male colleagues of this demeaning 'women's work.' And women judges, especially when there were few female appointments to their courts, had signalled that they felt lonely on the bench. They had no real sense of belonging. There was not necessarily any deliberate malice in their exclusion from the informal discussions which went on among their male colleagues, and yet because of judicial confidentiality the women judges had no one else with whom they could discuss their problems.

It was a depressing enough litany, but the report offered solid recommendations for improving the situation.[24] Chief Justice Lamer, however, was extremely upset; 'I can think of few worse allegations than to say judges have been discriminated against by other judges so as to interfere with the full discharge of their judicial responsibilities,' he said.

Lamer put enormous pressure on Wilson to disclose which judges were complaining and which judges were offending.[25] She refused to do so. Of course she could not break her promise of confidentiality to the women who had confided in her only on condition that they not be identified; moreover, she believed it would be damaging to the Canadian Bar Association if she revealed any of the sources of her information. And Wilson was sharply criticized for keeping silent; the assumption (much more palatable than facing up to the fact of the discrimination in the judiciary which she had reported) was that if she could produce no evidence, the discrimination did not really exist.

Stymied by Wilson's principled stubbornness, Lamer attempted an independent investigation of his own. He wrote directly to every federally appointed judge and invited them to tell him about any 'bias or unequal treatment at the hands of judges.' He got no response.

If asked, Wilson will say that she personally encountered only isolated instances of discrimination instigated by particular individuals during all her years in the legal profession. When she became involved in the task force she was surprised and even shocked by the extent of the problems experienced by other women because her own career did not illustrate persistent or systemic discrimination. For Wilson the whole experience became enormously painful. Her work on the Gender Equality study was in her own estimation, ironically, her first unequivocal and deeply personal experience of gender discrimination. She and Lamer had been good friends, but for a time this incident created an unhappy rift in their relationship. But neither of them is the kind of person to hold a grudge for long. Wilson came to the conclusion that Lamer's intervention was kindly meant and that he wanted only to protect the impressive reputation she had established on the bench.

Chief Justice McEachern of British Columbia was particularly unhappy that the report had not specified (as he believed he had been promised it would) that British Columbia was free of all discrimination against women judges. Cecilia Johnstone met with him in Vancouver to discuss the issue. Johnstone tried to explain that, given how few women had been appointed in some regions, any breakdown province by province would have had the effect of disclosing confidences.[26] At some point after that meeting between McEachern and Johnstone, a letter was written by a female member of the British Columbia bench asserting that women judges were consistently well treated in that province.[27]

Apparently another letter was written by a group of women judges who reaffirmed that the information on discrimination in the judiciary had indeed been supplied by them to Bertha Wilson just as she had reported it.[28] Wilson certainly had never expected anyone to speak out in her defence; she understood full well that the women judges had confided in her only because they trusted her and moreover that many of them were sincerely afraid of repercussions. Even task force member Pat Blocksom felt treated differently after the report was published and the hostility was such that she worried her participation would damage her career.[29] And when several provinces set up 'safe counsel' programs to advocate, investigate, and set equity targets, very little use was made of them out of fear of reprisal.[30]

Wilson certainly knew about the response from the women on the British Columbia bench. But it is too bad that until the information turned up in the course of researching this biography Wilson had never been informed that another group of women judges had written a letter endorsing the report and supporting her in the face of the very public criticisms she experienced. It would have meant a great deal to her to see the letter, particularly at the time the controversy erupted, or even seven years later. Unfortunately, repeated requests for access to the CBA archival materials were denied.[31]

At the CBA annual meeting in 1994 Cecilia Johnstone, who considers her attempts to implement the task force recommendations the most painful and rewarding experience of her life, had the great pleasure of presenting Wilson, with the St Laurent Award. And Wilson was able without any reservations whatsoever to congratulate members of council for their 'diligent work in moving forward the recommendations in the report.'[32] Not everything had been achieved because everything could not be achieved once and for all; there was room for optimism and the courage to be satisfied.

In her postscript to the report Wilson had quoted from her own hero, Lord Denning, citing one of her favourite judgments: 'It is all very well to paint justice blind, but she does better without a bandage around her eyes. She should be blind indeed to favour or prejudice, but clear to see which way lies truth: and the less dust there is about the better.'[33]

What worried her most of all was the loss of power in the profession and the despair and resignation experienced by too many lawyers, both male and female. The report had been meant to offer an alternative vision of the profession, a series of touchstones or practical tests to measure the process of reform over time. Despite the difficulties she had experienced raising funds and staffing the task force, and despite the rather humiliating and public repudiation of her own findings of discrimination in the judiciary, Wilson was reasonably content with the pace of that reform. It was enough if the bandage preventing clarity of vision about discrimination in the legal profession had been stripped away and if the task force has helped to remove some of the dust.

14

The Royal Commission on
Aboriginal Peoples

Bertha Wilson, travelling with the Royal Commission on Aboriginal Peoples, is in a hall in an aboriginal community. Each of the commissioners has an Indian partner. To honour their guests the Indians are dressed in traditional fringed doeskin robes decorated with geometric bead motifs. The commissioners have been welcomed into the inner ring and are participating in a traditional circle dance.

Bertha Wilson's partner is a tall teenaged Indian girl with a wide beaded hairband. The two of them are stepping in lively fashion around the circle. Wilson's cheeks are pink and a delighted smile lights up her face as the singers' ululations float free form over the beat of the drums. She and her partner swing their joined hands and stomp their feet in time to the music. Wilson looks thoroughly at home.[1]

According to Commissioner Viola Robinson, a Micmac and past president of the Native Council of Canada, this kind of experience was repeated over and over again as the commissioners travelled to remote aboriginal settlements throughout Canada:

You would go into a community, they would have a feast ... you would go in there and they would entertain us with their cultural activities, their dances and ceremonies, and talking circles, whatever it was, we were all invited to share and we all did. And that is one thing, you know, about Bertha, she would just, she would be right in there, you know, whatever it was that was happening, she was just so eager, just to understand and learn.

Bertha Wilson is in a penitentiary sitting with the other commissioners and listening intently as an aboriginal inmate speaks. A sturdy young man with an earnest expression, the speaker explains in a calm but intense voice what he had experienced before the justice system had put him into a series of violent and abusive foster homes, all white, where he lived in a state of perpetual fear.

When he was six his angry foster father had broken his arm in two places. The small boy was not taken to hospital until the broken bones had set themselves in a goose-neck shape. And then when his arm had had to be rebroken and reset his foster father told him to tell the doctor that he had fallen down the stairs.

Georges Erasmus, one of the co-chairs of the commission, asks how many of the inmates had spent their childhoods in foster or group homes. Almost every hand is raised. The video camera recording the expression on Wilson's face reveals her profound horror, indignation, and compassion. 'One could almost say that they were criminals because of defects in the system,' she is thinking and an observer can see her thinking it. But Wilson says nothing and keeps on listening.

As Viola Robinson and Bertha Wilson both understood it, the essential task of the commissioners was to absorb as much information as possible and to help native peoples claim ownership of the solutions which they themselves could generate during the process.

Bertha Wilson is in a large meeting in a northern Quebec community. She has noticed a number of aboriginal women in the back of the hall who have not spoken. A male trapper is very angrily describing the hydro developments which denuded the forests and caused the animals to leave or to die, plunging his people into poverty and despair.

In part to encourage the women to participate if they wish to do so Wilson says to the speaker, 'One of the things that has interested me as we have criss-crossed the country is the important role that the aboriginal women have played in many communities. They seem to occupy a leadership role.'

The trapper is furious. He spits back at her, 'Don't speak to me about leadership roles. Do you have any idea what a man feels like when he can't put bread on the table for his family? That is the situation for many of us.'

Wilson feels shattered. This is the first time that any aboriginal person has torn a strip off her for something she has said. But when she thinks about it, it is perfectly understandable.

The trapper is not prepared to have her contrast the leadership abilities of the women with the men. Women had always been powerful in aboriginal cultures within their own spheres but the balance of power has been tilted. The men's whole means of livelihood had been trapping; that power is gone. When they are no longer able to trap they cannot show leadership nor can they be expected to feel comfortable that the power of their women has not been similarly extinguished.

There is no question that Wilson did her very best to get inside the skin of the aboriginal peoples during the five years she spent working on the Royal Commission for Aboriginal Peoples. Her husband John teased her that she had gone completely native and (at least in some photographs) even come to look like an aboriginal person. And as Bertha jovially admits, 'My sole topic of conversation was about the commission, about our trips, about our sessions and so on, so he must have thought that it was very much a single theme I was living for.'

But on a more serious note, Wilson was enormously moved by the communal reverence of the aboriginal people in which she had the opportunity to participate during her years on the royal commission:

> What has impressed me most about aboriginal people is their deep-seated spirituality, their close attachment to the land, Mother Earth, and their profound sense of God the Creator. This exposure to native spirituality has for me been a very humbling experience. I am awed by the natural serenity of their prayers and their sense of being completely at home in the universe.

Within the aboriginal world she no longer felt the fragmentation of the immigrant, neither Scots nor Canadian, but with one foot in each of two cultures. Her immersion in aboriginal spirituality integrated these two worlds, she said; it 'completed my baptism into the Canadian society and in a strange way ... made me whole.' If there can be little question that Bertha Wilson had already given a great deal to Canada, then the royal commission was the assignment where she gave the most and also in her own estimation where she was given the most in return.

GETTING UNDER WAY: MANDATE AND METHODOLOGY

Chief Justice Brian Dickson had retired from the Supreme Court in June 1990. A month later came the armed stand-off at Oka with the Mohawks of Kanesatake rebelling against municipal plans to build a golf course over their sacred burial grounds. For many Canadians, aboriginal and non-native alike, the scenes of the violent clashes between the provincial police and the Mohawk peoples were frightening and profoundly disturbing; the barricades were stormed to let the bulldozers through and in the cross-fire a corporal was killed. It was difficult for non-natives to acknowledge that racially oriented violations of fundamental human rights, so shamefully at odds with Canada's proud international reputation, were routinely occurring within our own country; it was especially difficult to acknowledge that we are complicit in keeping these problems out of sight and mind on impoverished reserves.

But Oka made clear to Prime Minister Mulroney that a full exploration of aboriginal issues was long overdue.[2] In April 1991 he announced the establishment of a royal commission intended to 'work with Canada's aboriginal peoples so that they can control their own lives, can contribute to Canadian prosperity and can share fully in it'; by May he had appointed Dickson as special representative, charged with the duty of establishing the commission's terms of reference.

Dickson was an excellent choice. He had taken a leading role in cases such as *Guérin* and *Simon* and *Sparrow* which had established key principles of treaty interpretation and key doctrines of fiduciary duty; he was keenly interested in aboriginal issues and deeply knowledgeable about them. Dickson wanted to do what he could both to alleviate the near-universal frustration and alienation experienced by Indians, Inuit, and Métis in Canada and to 'educate the non-native public about aboriginal history, culture and aspirations.'[3] Before preparing the terms of reference, Dickson met with hundreds of individuals and groups and received hundreds of written submissions. His optimistic report on these preliminary investigations stressed that the commission had an opportunity to make a difference at a crucial crossroads in Canadian society; he pointed out that despite the deep despair many had expressed to him, the vast majority of 'Canadian natives are remarkably decent, fair, tolerant and compassionate people' possessed of a 'palpable integrity' and, in his opinion, their leaders possessed 'dedication, eloquence and common sense.'

Dickson presented the commission with an extraordinarily detailed and complex task. It was charged with investigating every aspect of aboriginal life in Canada: natives' historical relationships with non-native governments; the potential for aboriginal self-government; techniques for negotiating and resolving land claims; the impact of the constitution and the need for constitutional reform; the legal status of both reserve and off-reserve Indians and Métis; the validity of existing treaties and the development of new ones; the role of the Indian Act and the Department of Indian Affairs; a multiplicity of justice issues; the effect of northern factors, including isolation and climate, on aboriginal communities; an enormous range of social issues, including health and unemployment and suicide on and off reserves; economic issues and the development of economic self-sufficiency; cultural issues including preservation and restoration of traditional language and family structures; and special concerns relating to the role of elders, women, and youth. The commissioners, faced with this daunting job, joked that it would have been much easier to list what they were not required to investigate and at their first meeting proposed a prize for the commissioner who could come up with a topic Dickson had left out; no one qualified.

Dickson was also responsible for recommending appointment of the commissioners. Bertha Wilson had, of course, worked closely with him on the aboriginal cases at the Supreme Court. When he asked her to take on the royal commission, she simply could not refuse him. Allan Blakeney, the former premier of Saskatchewan, was, like Wilson, noted for his sympathy with aboriginal issues; there were those who thought this alone should have disqualified both of them from participation.[4] René Dussault, a justice of the Quebec Court of Appeal, was named by Mulroney one of the co-chairs.

But of the seven commissioners, the majority were themselves aboriginals, selected to be representative of all First Nations constituencies in Canada. Viola Robinson, a Nova Scotia Micmac, was joined by Paul Chartrand, a Métis who headed up the Department of Native Studies at University of Manitoba, Mary Sillett, a social worker from Labrador who had served as president of the Inuit Women's Association and vice-president of the Inuit Tapirisat, and Georges Erasmus, the other co-chair, a Dene from the Northwest Territories and a former national chief of the Assembly of First Nations.

Dickson also listed a number of matters for the commission to consider in deciding what approaches it might choose to take; almost all his suggestions were followed. Extensive travel to native communities was key; some hearings, he thought could be more cost-effective and more efficient if conducted by panels of two or three members; the release of interim reports would be of assistance in the ongoing development of policy and reform processes; elders, highly respected in aboriginal communities, were recommended as a valuable resource; and the report's greatest potential for achieving change would result from a focus not on documentation of problems but rather on identification of solutions to problems.

The government, Dickson warned, needed to ensure adequate funding so that individuals and groups could afford to appear before the commission. Moreover, given the number of previous studies which had gathered dust, it was equally important that the government prepare well in advance so that the commission's final report, when released, could be considered, adopted, and implemented without undue delay.

When Dickson recruited Viola Robinson, he told her that he expected that the whole process would take eighteen months to two years. The commissioners themselves, once they had met and reviewed the terms of reference, estimated it would take three years. But in the event, the commissioners worked together for a little more than five years and the final report was not ready for release until November 1996.

HEARING STORIES, SEEKING SOLUTIONS

There were four separate rounds of hearings, some in the most remote aboriginal communities where few outsiders had ever ventured before and others in Canada's largest cities where substantial communities of aboriginal peoples so often live in equally abject poverty. Beginning in June of 1992, this was a process which kept the commissioners on the road almost constantly for twelve months and then continued more sporadically for a further two years. Before the hearings were finished the commission had been to over one hundred communities and heard from well over one thousand presenters.

Bertha Wilson found the hearings a traumatic experience, revealing a degree of human misery and injustice she could not have imagined and would never have believed Canadians willing to ignore had she not seen it for herself. Much as she sympathized with the plight of women in the legal profession, Wilson was keenly aware that the CBA Gender Equality study surveyed a very privileged sector in Canadian society; at the same time with the royal commission she was looking at perhaps the most underprivileged.

Over and over again what had struck her about the aboriginal cases which she had helped to decide on the Supreme Court was how pathetic the petty injustices were that gave rise to the legal battle – the size of mesh in a fishing net, the selling of a grizzly pelt – and how enormous the ramifications radiating out from these particular human situations. There is no question that she felt a personal sense of outrage about Canada's treatment of its First Nations; she was fiercely committed to redressing these wrongs. Earlier in their marriage during the Korean War the Wilsons had endured a year's separation; the commissioners travelled without their spouses and it was out of a similar sense of commitment that Bertha, in total, spent more than a year on the road away from her husband.

In order to put everyone appearing before them on the same basis the commissioners made a point of not staying in the native peoples' own homes. But of course they visited many communities where there had never been any tourists and there were no hotels. The aboriginal communities did their best to accommodate them but in some instances commissioners had to bunk down in schools or community halls. Wilson, who had turned seventy before the hearings phase was completed, found the travel almost unbearably gruelling at times. With her advanced arthritis she suffered from the intense cold in some of the northern communities which the commission visited in the very depths of winter. The pace was cruel and it took a considerable toll on her health.

These visits involved more than participation in the feasts and dancing and hunting rituals and sweat lodges and sweet grass smudges. However, wherever they were, first of all came the religious ceremonies of thanks to the Creator and greetings to each other. In the aboriginal tradition the commission took time to create an atmosphere of harmony and peace, relying upon the Spirit of the Creator to unite minds and hearts and to make the participants conscious of their connection with all the living things in the universe.

Because aboriginal children retained an optimism and cheerful confidence about their futures, the commissioners tried to arrange school visits whenever they could. But the adult institutions were often far less pleasant; in addition to penitentiaries and community centres they also visited band council offices; friendship centres; hockey rinks; aboriginal hospitals; old folks' homes; women's groups; sentencing circles; and (particularly painful) the site of a former residential school, then closed scarcely a decade, where former students taken far from their families described in wrenching terms the treatment they had endured.

By the end of the first round it was obvious that listening alone would not be successful in generating solutions. The commission was viewed by some aboriginals as 'government' to be blamed for creating all the problems. Viola Robinson found that attitude especially upsetting but she knew that the non-aboriginal commissioners were in no position to challenge it; from time to time, she considered it necessary to deliver a speech along these lines: 'We are not the government here, we have been sent to listen to what you have to say ... You are whining about what has already been done. You said yourself you have been studied to death ... Now we have got to go on. What would you like to see done?' She may have had some initial doubts about her abilities to make a contribution, but the other commissioners considered Robinson invaluable for her ability to 'puncture sacred balloons'[5] without offending either hearings participants or the aboriginal commission staff. With her grandmotherly persona and fifteen years of experience at the national level in native governance, Robinson provided a refreshing frankness when it was most needed.

In time the commission developed an appropriate protocol to make the hearings more productive. What seemed to work best was sending out, prior to the visit, a small team of individuals carefully selected for their people skills. It helped if they were familiar with the particular community so they could find out what issues were of most pressing concern and who were likely to be the spokespersons. The reconnaissance team prepared memos so that the commissioners knew what to expect. It was helpful, too, if they could identify in advance an elder of the community who would sit with the commissioners and chair the session, calling upon those who wished to make a presentation and introducing them by name and position.

During the actual meeting the scouts would circulate around the room to take note of those who seemed to be bursting to speak and prepare a list of names so that the commissioners could call upon the shy or intimidated individually and encourage them to say what was on their minds. The commission also began posing its own questions of the hearing participants to focus the discussion on finding solutions. It might ask, 'If you could have self-government tomorrow,' or 'If you could write a policy on this issue, what would you do?' This more active intervention, when it worked, had the effect of jolting the participants out of despair and cynicism. The difference between this study and all the previous studies, the commissioners tried to explain, was that the government was finally acknowledging that what had been done was wrong. It was finally committed to consultation with aboriginal people (not the white bureaucrats in the Department of Indian Affairs) in order to correct the errors of the past.

Of course there were some issues – in particular, wife battering and sexual abuse – which aboriginal women could not bring themselves to speak about in public. Although Georges Erasmus was initially reluctant, Wilson, with the support of Mary Sillett and Viola Robinson, was successful in persuading him that it would be necessary to set up some women's-only sessions if they were to hear from this important constituency. For the women commissioners these closed sessions were among the most disturbing of all. A full day of listening was totally exhausting and overwhelming.

Overviews of the hearings were prepared and published,[6] but in addition there were a number of Round Table discussions focusing on particularly urgent issues. The Round Tables resulted in the writing and release of intermittent reports when, in the opinion of the commissioners, further delay would have been unconscionable. These interim reports were, by and large, generated by the commission's own in-house staff. The process of their production was frequently a difficult one where Wilson's skills at mediation and conciliation were absolutely vital.

STAFFING THE COMMISSION: THE INTERIM REPORTS

Even before the hearings had begun, an initial six months were spent scrutinizing the mandate, establishing systems, and dealing with staffing concerns. The commission had taken offices in a highrise office tower on Albert Street in Ottawa; at any given time there might be anywhere between eighty and 120 employees, almost all hired on contract and the majority young people drawn from various aboriginal communities across Canada. Wilson in particular was deeply committed to the concept of a substantially aboriginal staff and the notion that, whenever it was possible to find an aboriginal person to do a particular job, that person should be hired.

Almost from the beginning, the commissioners had an executive director to handle administrative matters. They hired Jean Fournier for eighteen months to set up the academic research teams and also the logistical systems. The royal commission was the first commission with a majority of aboriginal commissioners and aboriginal staff and also the first to make extensive use of computer technology. When Fournier left in 1993 the commission hired Tony Reynolds as executive director. The gentle and congenial Reynolds[7] brought extensive expertise in trade and economic issues, sensitivity to cross-cultural communication, and a depth of experience in policy development ideally suited to the upcoming phases of the commission's work.

Nevertheless, much of the day-to-work of managing the young aboriginal staff fell on Wilson's shoulders – perhaps because of her experience in working with young law clerks at the Supreme Court. Many of the staff members found their participation in the commission's work extremely difficult. A significant number had never been off their reserves before, and for quite a few this was also their first time living in a big city. Moreover, most of the staff members had no previous experience working with aboriginal peoples of different groups – Inuit with Indian or Métis – and they turned out to have rather less in common than Wilson had assumed they would. A few staff members experienced overwhelming stress, but the great majority were happy and productive and grateful for the opportunity to contribute to this historic achievement. And fortunately a deep well of spirituality underlying all the disparate aboriginal cultures could be drawn upon when the inevitable clashes and conflicts became too hurtful.

Every month or so there was a healing circle for the staff. Sometimes the commissioners and various non-aboriginal consultants attended as well. The participants would spend three or four hours in prayer, experiencing the unifying and cleansing power of the smoke ceremony. Then one at a time people would grasp the eagle feather to speak truth – an aboriginal truth with the implicit commitment not to hurt others – about what was in their hearts. Very often there were tears; on one occasion, a crusty non-native economist who had attended in a mood of considerable cynicism sobbed most of all and his attitude, said Tony Reynolds with a certain impish satisfaction, forever afterwards transcended mere number crunching. The commissioners also opened their own private meetings with prayers – Jewish or Christian sometimes, but most often aboriginal prayers.

The sessions themselves were like the best kind of classroom seminar with the commissioners sitting around the table fully engaged in the issues before them and sometimes arguing heatedly. No matter how opposing their opinions, however, they shared a sense of high purpose expressed as a determination to 'approach the day with a good mind, to speak clearly and honestly with one other, and to listen carefully to what was being said.'[8] This was the kind of shared engagement where Wilson thrived best and which she had craved on the Supreme Court; the royal commission provided it to her.

However, Wilson had been very frank in telling the staff that they

were not the only people with adjustment difficulties. Just as the CBA
Gender Equality task force was reluctant to inveigle a woman into taking on the executive director's job for low pay, the royal commission
was committed to carrying out its mandate of enhancing respect for
aboriginal spiritual values by enacting them. 'Things are never rushed:
we take time,' Wilson had said about the pace.[9] It was important to walk
the talk.

Commissioner Allan Blakeney found that he could not modify his
expectations of efficiency and speed to this consensual process fundamental to the aboriginal ethos. Accustomed to his status as Saskatchewan
premier and a certain hierarchy inherent in the political process, he
wanted things to be done in a particular way to a particular timetable and
if necessary to be redone within the same time frame when work did not
meet with his satisfaction. As a result, and despite his long-established
reputation as a defender and promoter of aboriginal justice, Blakeney
found himself out of sympathy with the flexible adjudicative and
research-based approaches which the commission had evolved. Well-
liked and well-respected by his colleagues, he had nevertheless lost faith
that the commission was on the right path. Although members of the
commission approached him independently to try to persuade him to
continue, by April 1993 Blakeney had decided it was in everyone's best
interests for him to leave.

Peter Meekison, who had been Alberta's deputy minister of Intergovernmental Affairs in the Lougheed administration, replaced him. Meekison brought to the commission solid experience in aboriginal issues and
very strong skills in negotiation and conciliation. As it happened, the
vacant place around the table was next to Wilson and the two of them
quickly struck up a conversation and then a firm friendship. Meekison
made frequent trips to the urn to provide Wilson with the coffee she
required in copious amounts; he got her laughing when he took personal exception to one of her favourite expressions about 'things peter-
ing out'; when he came in for meetings from Alberta he brought the
special Vitamin E enhanced eggs with their bright yellow yolks not then
available in Ottawa.

Factions shifted constantly but never crystallized. It might be possible
to anticipate what a particular commissioner might say about any given
topic but there was no predicting which commissioners might form an
alliance on any given issue; in no circumstance that Peter Meekison
could recall was there opposition between aboriginal and non-aboriginal commissioners. Despite inevitable conflicts, over the five years they

worked together the commissioners grew as close as family members. Their work was a profoundly transformative experience for all of them.[10]

Aboriginal staff members were hired for specific aspects of the report. When their work was done their contracts came to an end; as a result there was a fairly continuous rotation of staff members through commission headquarters. Although this meant that the process of orientation for new staff and farewells for departing staff was ongoing, the arrangement had distinct benefits for the commission in terms of expertise and commitment. It was also an arrangement which could give rise to intense anguish. Certain groups perceived that disproportionate resources were being allocated to issues other than their own primary concerns. There was some worry, moreover, that the commissioners might weaken the impact of their research in their final report after contracts expired and certain staff groups had left. Despite a best effort to raise above petty factionalism, there was inevitably a certain tension between individual agendas and the big picture.

The first interim study completed by the royal commission in 1992 was 'Bridging the Cultural Divide,' a report on aboriginal people and criminal justice[11] which recommended recognition and establishment of separate aboriginal justice systems. With her background as a Supreme Court judge, it is not surprising that Wilson took a very active role in preparation of this interim report:

> We had made a point when we visited the communities of visiting the prisons and hearing from the prisoners and hearing from them the strong sense of injustice that they felt about the way they were being treated in the courts. And that was also a bit of a revelation and of course of particular interest to me and I then started reading around the subject of the possibility of a separate aboriginal justice system in Canada because it became pretty clear to me that just making minor changes here and there in the way that we were dispensing justice to Canadians wasn't good enough, the system was fundamentally unsuited to the way aboriginal people thought ... The adversarial nature of the whole system was the antithesis of the way that aboriginal people thought.

Already in place in a number of cities and reserves were diversion programs building upon aboriginal sentencing circles and concepts of community healing. However, these alternatives were offered for persons who had already been convicted in the regular justice system. Aboriginal ideologies of justice focus less on the sequential steps of proving the offence, conviction, and punishment of the accused and are more integrative with their focus on healing the victim and reconciling the offender within the community.

The commission's interim justice report compiled evidence establishing that aboriginals were more likely than whites to be refused bail, that they waited longer in pre-trial detention, that they were more often charged with multiple offences, and that they were more than twice as likely to spend time in prison as non-native Canadians. Wilson had no hesitation in characterizing these injustices as discrimination, adding that Canada's record of treatment of First Nations peoples 'casts a long shadow over Canada's claim to be a just society.'[12]

The recommendation that aboriginal communities be permitted to develop their own trial procedures, offering aboriginal offenders the opportunity of choosing whether to be tried under aboriginal systems or the existing non-native legal system, generated many subsidiary issues; for example, the applicability of the Charter of Rights and the Criminal Code under aboriginal systems was one of the most controversial subjects among the commissioners. Some considered the availability of such optional systems impossible within a Canadian federation; others, including Wilson, believed with equal fervour that there could be no justice acceptable and acknowledged as justice by aboriginals until and unless these separate statutes and systems were put in place. Moreover Wilson believed that the aboriginal focus on reconciliation rather than punishment was sounder than that offered by the Canadian justice system.

The justice report had clear constitutional implications for the issue of aboriginal self-government. Having held back during the delicate Charlottetown negotiations that would have entrenched that right, the commission forged ahead after the accord's collapse in October 1992. By 1993 it had produced a second interim study, *Partners in Confederation*[13] dealing with precisely these questions. However the report met with only qualified approval within the academic community and was rejected outright by some aboriginal leaders. This report recommended negotiation of individual agreements with aboriginal groups across Canada to give them control over education, health, social services, and enforcement of local aboriginal laws. It proposed retaining provincial and federal control over gaming, fisheries management, environmental protection, immigration, defence, and monetary policy while continuing to assert the supremacy of the Charter over all aboriginal legal constructs. Concepts from the international law of comity between sovereign nations are clearly applicable in this 'nation of nations' framework; as a legal subject within the international community, Canada itself is bound to honour aboriginal rights to self-government and the separate justice system self-government entails because we are signatories to various international instruments committed to this principle.[14] Some aboriginal spokespersons held that self-government on the terms developed by the commission fell far short of the true self-government which aboriginals had never relinquished and which they contended successive Canadian governments had promised to recognize.[15]

Because of Meekison's prior experience in his intergovernmental affairs post, and because he was fresh on the job when his new colleagues were exhausted from the rigours of travel, he was drafted to attend at the presentation of the *Partners in Confederation* report to the federal government. Despite all his political experience and savvy, Meekison was stunned and disappointed to hear the reaction. The report, he heard, went too far. Some of the same government officials who had been present at the 1987 Charlottetown round and again in 1992, where they had endorsed the inherent aboriginal right to self-government, were now hedging on the issue when it was no longer politically necessary to achieve constitutional amendment. They might agree to it, they said with collective and convenient amnesia, if they only knew what it meant. Meekison reported back to the commission accordingly and the others took note but, somewhat jaded, were considerably less surprised.

Prior to the royal commission hearings held in 1993 and publication of its report, little had been known about the forced relocation of Inuit peoples from Inukjuak on Hudson Bay and Pond Inlet on Baffin Island to the High Arctic which had taken place during the early 1950s. The story came to light during a routine hearing at Inukjuak; the relocation had not been singled out in the original terms of reference for specific analysis but Bertha Wilson, persuaded that a terrible wrong had been done which had to be righted, insisted that further hearings be held and a third interim report was written on the topic.[16]

There was a certain well-meant but (in retrospect) misguided paternalism in the establishment of the aboriginal residential school system which took aboriginal children at the age of five or six away from their families and communities. Intended, in accordance with the ethnocentrism of a different era, to provide youngsters with the skills necessary for integration within contemporary Canadian society, this coerced integration amounted to assimilation. The government had no policy of protecting language or culture or family structures – indeed, assimilation was considered a good thing and there was no awareness that such protection was even desirable – but neither was it anticipated that this ill-conceived plan would result in the legacy of physical and sexual abuse suffered by many aboriginals.

However, there was not even a pretence of concern for aboriginal peoples to justify the High Arctic relocation scheme. The federal government, through the agency of the Royal Canadian Mounted police, transported seventeen Inuit families from their familiar fertile hunting grounds and plunked them without food or shelter into a barren landscape of ice and gravel some 1600 kilometres further north. They were left at Grise Fiord and Resolute Bay with the promise that they would be brought back at the end of two years; white bureaucrats were provided with ample supplies and equipment but it was assumed that the Inuit could survive without any such amenities. They were essentially abandoned for thirty years.

Traditional ways of life were lost with disastrous results as inevitably the Inuit were compelled to turn to welfare and dependency on whites; the Inuit word *illira* is used to describe the paralysis of awe and intimidation they experienced. This forced relocation (and the Inuit were never informed of the reason for their involuntary conscription) was intended simply to ensure Canada's sovereignty over the High Arctic. 'Inhumane and illegal' were the forthright words used by the royal commission to describe these incidents in Canadian history; it called upon the federal government for apology and restitution.

Wilson was more involved in all of these issues and their associated interim reports[17] than any other commissioner, with the possible exception of the co-chairs. Nevertheless it was the fourth special report on suicide[18] which was probably most painful for her. This report required all Wilson's skills in dealing with the aboriginal staff; she was key in salvaging the commission's cohesion but she paid a lasting price in terms of her own health.

Suicide in aboriginal communities then occurred (and even a number of years after the commission finished its work was still occurring) at seven times the average national rate. This was considered by the commissioners and staff to be a situation of such urgency that it could not wait for the final report. Work on *Choosing Life*, the interim report title, had begun right away in 1993. Because of the urgency, however, some of the writing was assigned to non-aboriginal persons. Although it was accomplished with considerable skill and imagination, there were muttered accusations from the staff that permitting any outside participation constituted an 'appropriation of voice' they considered particularly offensive given the sensitivity and seriousness of the situation.[19]

Moreover, some of the aboriginal staff members were persuaded that the report's tone was too mild. They wanted a more radical stance going behind symptoms and cures to demonstrate how colonial attitudes generally – and in particular the residential school system – had broken down family structures and given rise to this disturbing culture of suicide; their research supported the causation theory and they wanted this interpretation put forward with vigour. Polarization was such that the ongoing viability of the aboriginal staffing decision was called into question. Wilson, herself sympathetic to the staff position, knew that conciliation and resolution of the internal dispute was even more important. The commission could not be permitted, in effect, to commit suicide over it. She went well beyond her role as a commissioner in an attempt to resolve this stormy situation.

In response to their critique and with Wilson's support, the report was partially rewritten with more aboriginal input but the staff was still not satisfied it was strong enough. At one meeting a staff member expressed his passionate conviction that the commission was in danger of losing its soul; another resigned in protest. But Georges Erasmus, like Wilson enormously skilled in dealing with people, spoke on the larger role of the royal commission and how vital it was to pull together. The tone of all their publications, he stressed, had to be suitable for multiple audiences. An excessively polemical stance would only make it more likely their report would be rejected, working against the larger interests to which everyone was committed. The crisis passed and the meeting broke up without bitterness.

Shortly after this emotional crisis, Wilson's health broke down. She developed shingles and an intensely painful post-herpetic neuralgia; for a time she was unable to attend at the commission offices. Even stronger medications than she was already taking for the ongoing arthritis were prescribed. The neuralgia sapped her strength, the medications increased her fatigue, and she has never fully regained her health since that time.

For a couple of months briefing materials were couriered to her home for her review. Meekison called her every day to review with her the main points in the policy as it was evolving. Adding to her worries John, who had a number of health problems of his own, was also ill and hospitalized from time to time in 1993 and 1994.[20] The work of the commission was taking a good deal longer than expected and was eating up their keenly anticipated retirement years together; they both knew that by the time the final report was prepared it was possible that neither of them would be well enough to enjoy the extensive travel they had planned. Nevertheless, they had agreed on the commitment. Bertha Wilson kept on working.

WRITING THE FINAL REPORT

After the interim reports were drafted and ongoing simultaneously with the documentation and editing they required before publication, came the complex and challenging process of writing the final report. It involved blending 20,000 pages of transcripts from the hearings and distilling them with a considerable body of academic research papers prepared at the behest of the commission into some 3,500 pages divided among five volumes which had to be edited, documented, and translated. The task was truly overwhelming.

Wilson, who has always loved to write, was actively involved in the process. Although the draft chapters were written in big blocks by teams of writers, she thought it important to attempt a certain uniformity of tone. And indeed the final report sustains a distinctively poetic, even a lyrical quality; it speaks in the voice of the aboriginal spirituality which imbued and sustained the entire project in a manner which is in itself deeply moving.

Wilson's writing skills were well recognized and respected by her colleagues. As Viola Robinson recalls, 'When we were reviewing the drafts she would say, "Well, this should be said differently" and she would start to say, "I would say it this way." And then somebody would say, "Well then, write it." So she would always end up having to do that.'

Rewriting was frustrating. The commissioners and staff were tired. Moreover, the problems were not just with style or research gaps; the process shone a spotlight on residual differences of opinion which turned out sometimes to be quite substantive. The commissioners all realized, however, that compromise was necessary to achieve consensus and consensus was vital if the report was to be taken seriously and implemented by successive governments.

Peter Meekison considers Wilson a gifted writer whose facility was very valuable, especially in writing the most difficult and controversial sections. When the commissioners would hit a snag she would offer to help and take it home. Back would come two of three paragraphs, all handwritten in pencil, the agreed-upon meaning intact but expressed with new elegance and clarity of expression.

Some sections she wrote almost in their entirety – 'The Role of the Courts,'[21] for example, and the brief introduction, 'Opening the Door,' which Meekison recalls went through thirteen or fourteen drafts with each one getting better. The 'Rekindling the Fire' chapter[22] towards the end of the first volume, drawing together all the common themes in aboriginal spirituality and the relationship of the people to the land which had moved her so deeply during the hearings, was also her idea. 'Rekindling the Fire,' which was written entirely by the aboriginal staff, is considered by Meekison to be the most important chapter in the entire report. When people ask him what to read out of the total 3,500 pages, this is what he always recommends.[23]

Nevertheless, included among the vast volume of Wilson's personal papers from the royal commission was a photocopied cartoon signed 'Mrs. W. from Peter M.' which shows a small girl annotating a slogan: 'The strongest drive is not Love or Hate. It is one person's need to change another's copy.' 'Change' has been crossed out and replaced variously with 'modify,' 'amend,' 'correct,' 'alter,' 'fix,' 'chop to pieces,' 'edit,' and 'improve'!

The five volumes are organized in accordance with specific topic areas. Volume I (*Looking Forward, Looking Back*) outlines the history of the aboriginal peoples and their relationships with successive waves of government intervention. No one, of course, could write a definitive history of the aboriginal peoples in Canada and for that reason the commission opted for a fragmented vignettes style. This volume includes demographic information and chapters on the Indian Act, residential schools, and relocation of aboriginal communities, but the focus is strongly prospective. It concludes by setting out four principles to establish a renewed relationship: recognition, respect, sharing, and responsibility.

Volume 2, *Restructuring the Relationship*, picks up this theme and moves directly into the meat of the matter. Published in two parts, it provides detailed information concerning treaties, governance, land claims, and economic development. There is a strong focus on education not limited to job training for aboriginals; education must be directed equally towards the non-aboriginal population to ensure recognition that a renewed relationship requires respectful acknowledgment of shared responsibility.

Volume 3, as its title suggests, is all about *Gathering Strength*, drawing on the rich resources of aboriginal cultures to renew family structures, regain health, address intolerable living conditions, ensure appropriate educational opportunities, and sustain cultural heritage through language, publication, visual and performing arts. There is a sensitivity to the balance between social policy as government initiative and leaving space for aboriginal initiative so that both approaches are integrated.

Volume 4, *Perspective and Realities*, offers multiplicity and even contradiction which (paradoxically, perhaps, given the ancient traditions described) is truly postmodern in its impact. We hear from women, elders, youth, and Métis; from the isolated far North and from urban aboriginals. A number of issues already considered in the earlier volumes are revisited here in these more specific contexts: for example, women's historical roles in aboriginal communities; health concerns of aboriginal youth; Métis land claims; and housing for urban aboriginals.

And finally, in Volume 5, the commission presented *Renewal: A Twenty-Year Commitment*. The considerable cost of sustaining the status quo, with the quantifiable and ongoing remedial costs resulting from inadequate health care and housing and economic development, is delineated forcefully; here indeed is one of the pragmatic appeals to enlightened self-interest which we have seen so often before in projects where Bertha Wilson has been involved. This volume speaks to the commission's strategy as a good investment over the decades to come. It returns to the issue of public education to change social consensus. And it emphasizes the necessity of constitutional amendment to require aboriginal representation in such institutions as the Supreme Court;[24] to permit creation of new aboriginal provinces; and to ensure the aboriginal right of self-government, probably the single most radical recommendation generated. The commission proposed creation within Canada (through independent treaty commissions) of between sixty to eighty aboriginal nations, each based on a collective sense of national identity and with natives enjoying dual citizenship. The proposal amounts to a third order of government and perhaps was not intended by the 1982 Constitutional amendments;[25] but in Canada, of course, we are not bound by framers' intent.

About half of this final volume consists of various appendices to the report as a whole. One of these summarizes the 440 recommendations which the commission had generated throughout the preceding volumes. The Queen and Parliament should issue a royal proclamation which acknowledges the mistakes of the past and commits the government to a more just relationship with aboriginal peoples. The old Department of Indian and Northern Affairs had outlived its purpose and should be replaced with an aboriginal relations department. An aboriginal parliament, to be called a House of First Peoples, should serve in an advisory capacity to the House of Commons on all aboriginal issues. There should be a public inquiry into the long-term effects of the residential school system on aboriginal cultures. The Canadian Human Rights Commission should instigate further investiga-tion of the effects of relocation of aboriginal communities. Resolution of land claims, assistance to aboriginal entrepreneurs, and establishment of an aboriginal university were all necessary to ensure economic self-sufficiency of aboriginal peoples. Support for special training of aboriginal professionals in health and social services, allocation of federal resources to remedy the appalling shortage of aboriginal housing and establishment of an aboriginal arts council to protect and foster aboriginal language and literature and culture were all essential to redress past wrongs.

The first drafts of this final report were completed in 1995. As the work was coming to an end in those final months, and before aboriginal staff members drifted away upon expiry of their contracts, it was decided to hold a 'lifting of the burden' ceremony. There were speeches, of course, but also singing and dancing and tears and hugs as everyone moved around the circle saying goodbye to one another. Expectations had been heightened and yet it was clear that the people who had worked for so many months in Ottawa could not themselves implement the changes which the commission had recommended. When one has accomplished all one can, a 'lifting of the burden' gives respite from toil and release from responsibility. And it is in some ways a shifting of the burden to those entrusted to carry out the next phase of the task within aboriginal communities and government circles, a passing of the torch.

Editing and translation and publication remained to be done. The commissioners were very grateful that René Dusssault (who reviewed the French translation, completed by twenty-two different translators, for consistency) also volunteered to prepare the footnotes, meticulously cross-referencing the report to all of the hearings transcripts and research papers; it was this painstaking endeavour which made the commission's work so invaluable a resource for future scholars and policy writers. Wilson's own work was by no means done. She stayed on for another year to edit the interim justice report and to assist in the final polishing.

After working for five years deeply engaged in the complex legal issues affecting aboriginal peoples, it was obvious to all of the commissioners that Viola Robinson had become entranced by the law. She was considering going to law school. Chartrand, Dussault, and Bertha Wilson were lawyers; Robinson had come to the conclusion that the study of law would be the best way of further serving her people. In the spring of 1995, on a trip home to Nova Scotia, she had dropped around to Dalhousie to see if they might admit her and was told to apply. Then Viola (who was in her sixties and had never pursued post-secondary education before) broached the subject rather tentatively with Bertha. 'She was so, "Do it, do it, go." She said, "Yes. Go, go, go." I said, "But maybe I am too set in my ways, I don't think I can study any more, I don't know how to study, I wouldn't know how to write." She said, "You go."'

Wilson wrote the letter of recommendation; she loaned Viola her own law school notes and some of her texts; she consoled and coached her by telephone through the brutal experience of first-year law; and she took enormous pride when Viola Robinson graduated in 1998, having particularly distinguished herself in jurisprudence and constitutional law.

The final report was formally released on 21 November 1996 at a dawn ceremony which began on the banks of the Ottawa River beside the Museum of Civilization designed by aboriginal architect Douglas Cardinal. The ceremony moved inside to the Great Hall with its soaring totem poles for dancing and drumming and singing. After that Peter Meekison went to the House of Commons for the official tabling by the then-minister of Indian affairs, Ron Irwin. It was a distinct anticlimax; Irwin said, 'I table the report' and sat down. And Meekison went home.

But Wilson was not there. She and John, who had postponed their fiftieth wedding anniversary celebrations for a year, were somewhere off the coast of Peru on a cruise around South America. Photographs from a special dinner party on board the ship show the exhaustion on her face. Nevertheless, the two of them are elegant in their formal attire and Bertha is relaxed and beaming with the pleasure of finally having time to be with her husband. When the reaction to the report began, this was a location very remote from demanding reporters seeking sound bites.

RESPONSE TO THE REPORT

The Royal Commission report was two years late. Dickson had warned that timeliness would be important and certainly this delay was an issue seized upon in the immediate reaction. Cost was another issue, and the newspaper articles published the day after the report's release predictably zeroed in on the commission's unprecedented cost of $58 million.[26] They noted also that the commission's recommendations would require an increase in federal and provincial spending on aboriginal peoples by $2 billion a year for at least fifteen and perhaps twenty years. What more needed to be said? Despite Georges Erasmus' best efforts, scant attention was paid to the cost of doing nothing: $7.5 billion a year drained out of the economy in lost productivity, lost income, and lost taxes.

According to Ron Irwin the $2 billion figure would have doubled his annual departmental budget and justified dismissing the report out of hand. 'It's just not realistic,' was his reaction. Of course, even before the report had been released Irwin had expressed the opinion that it would have been better to forget the commission and just spend $50 million on building one thousand houses on reserves.

In his terms of reference Dickson had also advised the government to initiate preparations during the commission's tenure in order that its report could be implemented quickly. Although one might think that the delay in the report's release provided ample time for any necessary planning – and the interim reports offered advance notice of what needed to happen – it was clear that this had not been done.

Mulroney's Tory government had initiated the study in 1991. By 1996 the political atmosphere had changed. The public mood was mean and aboriginal issues no longer seemed so urgent. Chrétien's Liberal government was now in power, and less than enthusiastic about evoking public censure by incurring the huge politically unpopular expenditures demanded by this orphan study from the previous administration.[27] Even so it was only a year after the Quebec secession referendum had been narrowly defeated; the courageous stance of Grand Chief Matthew Coon Come, who had said that if Quebec separated from Canada then the Crees would separate their massive northern territory from Quebec, had been of immeasurable assistance to the Canadian government in preventing a resurgence of sovereigntist power in Quebec and one might have thought it would have been feeling grateful.

The final volume, *Renewal*, is subtitled *A Twenty-Year Commitment*, but the commissioners really knew they were looking at a fifty-year horizon for implementation. However some aboriginal leaders wanted a swift response. By February of 1997 three hundred band chiefs, led by National Chief of the Assembly of First Nations Ovide Mercredi, had converged on Parliament Hill and announced that they were organizing a further day of protest to signal their displeasure with the government's inaction. And even although they accepted that their report's recommendations could be realized only bit by bit, the commissioners had certainly not anticipated that after the initial flurry of reaction their work would be met with complete silence.[28]

On 7 January 1998, when Jane Stewart had become minister of Indian affairs and Phil Fontaine had replaced Mercredi as national chief of the Assembly of First Nations, the federal government made its official response to the royal commission's report – just a few weeks after the first anniversary of the report's release. In a ceremony held on Parliament Hill complete with drumming and chanting, Stewart, delivered a Statement of Reconciliation to Canada's aboriginal peoples. All of the commissioners with the exception of Peter Meekison attended and it was a moving occasion. Stewart, dressed for the occasion in a jacket with aboriginal motifs and holding a feather, acknowledged the 'contributions made by all aboriginal peoples to Canada's development' and she added: 'The government of Canada today formally expresses to all aboriginal people in Canada our profound regret for past actions of the federal government which have contributed to these difficult pages in the history of our relationship together.'

It was generally agreed that Stewart did her best, but the commission had wanted the Queen to issue such a statement – as she had done, clad in a traditional Maori cloak of kiwi feathers, on behalf of the New Zealand government with respect to its treatment of the Maori peoples in 1995 – and it had been looking for a full apology, not merely a statement of reconciliation. The commissioners had also hoped for a new Royal Proclamation to replace the Proclamation of 1763 upon which so much aboriginal jurisprudence still must rely. Moreover, Prime Minister Chrétien, who many considered would have been the appropriate spokesperson in the absence of the Queen, was not in attendance.

In her statement Stewart made specific mention of the government's role in the development and administration of residential schools and she acknowledged the 'legacies of personal pain and distress that continue to reverberate in aboriginal communities to this day' from those misguided policies. And Phil Fontaine, himself a victim of physical and sexual abuse in one of these schools, did not worry about niceties of the wording or who was delivering the message. Choking back tears, he welcomed Stewart's initiative without reservation, saying simply, 'It is a great honour for me to accept the apology of the government.'[29]

Together with the statement of reconciliation came an action plan: $350 million to help victims of abuse in residential schools to get the counselling and assistance they needed; a commitment of $250 million in additional funding to assist with housing and water and sewage treatment facilities on reserves; and an Aboriginal Health Institute and an Aboriginal Head Start program for preschoolers. There were the predictable naysayers who considered it too little and too late; $600 million over four years fell considerably short of the $2 billion a year the commission had said was required, but it was a start.

A full history of the Royal Commission on Aboriginal Peoples and a full explication of what its massive report contained are both, of course, well beyond the scope of this biography of Bertha Wilson. Nevertheless, it is interesting to consider some of the visible results of the commission's work. Key to the economic self-sufficiency implicit in self-government is resolution of aboriginal land claims and in 1997 the historic *Delgamuukw*[30] decision signalled clearly that the Supreme Court had gone to school on the royal commission's work. The majority of the Court reaffirmed that aboriginal title to land is *sui generis*, held communally and inalienable except to the crown. Title includes a right to occupy and possess which is not frozen in accordance with traditional customs and practices but encompasses present-day needs so long as modern uses do not destroy the unique value of the land to its community. *Delgamuukw* stands for the proposition that the economic well-being of all Canadians and the aboriginal peoples' legal rights to occupy and possess land must be evaluated in order to allocate resources in a respectful manner after meaningful consultation; in each instance, the test will be a highly contextual one.[31]

Oral evidence[32] and native law and tradition are to be given significant weight in determining the exclusive and continuous occupation at the time of crown sovereignty necessary to an assertion of aboriginal title; in this instance, for example, the Gitksan oral tradition encompassed in the *adaawk* describing their ancestors and histories and territories and the Wet'suwet'en's *kungax* (a spiritual song and dance binding them to their land) were deemed admissible and probative. The *Delgamuukw* decision, establishing that aboriginal occupancy is determinative of the land claims process and that oral history is admissible to prove exclusive and continuous occupancy, makes it easier for natives to secure title to lands and immediately gave fresh impetus to innumerable negotiations between Indian bands and provincial governments across the country.

Political controversy dogged the negotiations every inch of the way, but the process the royal commission set out was successful in achieving the Nisga'a Treaty.[33] It was signed 5 August 1998, ratified by the House of Commons and the Senate (despite a presentation by former Supreme Court Justice Willard Estey who questioned its consitutionality), and came into force 8 May 2000. As it happened, Alec Robertson, one of the CBA Gender Equality task force members, served a three-year term as chief executive officer of the British Columbia Treaty Commission and he was actively involved in implementing these royal commision recommendations actions. But less than a week after the treaty was in effect the Liberal party in British Columbia initiated a court action challenging its constitutionality which is likely to end up at the Supreme Court and may delay full implementation for four or five more years.

While the Nisga'a process was under way another significant step towards aboriginal self-government was achieved; the largely Inuit territory of Nunavut came into being on 1 April 1999, carved out of the eastern portion of the Northwest Territories. With its eleven ridings and twenty-two members, this legislature embodies a consensus-based government compatible with Inuit values; there are no political parties and election of cabinet and the premier is done by the representatives themselves.

Delgamuukw, the Nisga'a Treaty, and Nunavut illustrate some fairly dramatic increases in national non-aboriginal consciousness about aboriginal issues; a number of smaller and subtler changes also give reason for optimism. Some provinces have instituted or are in the process of establishing aboriginal family and child services.[34] The detailed study which the royal commission recommended be undertaken of the residential school system has been written[35] (although not as a result of a public inquiry process); there have been some successfully litigated cases and some acknowledgment of responsibility and apology for residential school abuses on the part of the church. And some steps have been taken by the federal government to set up the independent and binding tribunal recommended by the commission to resolve native land claims.

Generating the political will to implement more of the royal commission's recommendations probably depends upon persuading the politicians that in Canada we are experiencing a profound shift in social consensus on the issue of justice for aboriginal people. Bertha Wilson had said in her 1983 paper, 'Law in Society: The Principle of Sexual Equality,' that 'you can legislate equality all you want, but you cannot make people *think* it and *live* it.'[36] Law, as Adam Smith well knew, sometimes leads and sometimes follows social consensus in a revolving evolution.

And there are some encouraging indicators that social consensus will lead the legislators on this issue. Perhaps a majority of non-native Canadians now *think* equality and want to *live* in equality with aboriginal citizens. In April 2000 the *Toronto Star* ran a series of three articles[37] about the conditions endured by 12,200 native people living on twenty-four remote reserves in the Sioux Lookout District, Indian Affairs Minister Bob Nault's home riding. There were over one thousand responses on the *Star*'s hotline or by fax and e-mail; the reiterated message was that appropriate aid to aboriginals should take precedence over the 2008 Olympic bid or foreign aid and that conditions of economic prosperity make further delays inexcusable and unconscionable.[38] Particularly outrageous was the revelation that of $58 million promised by the federal government in 1998 to combat diabetes (which has reached epidemic proportions in several aboriginal communities) only $2 million had actually been released: 'Certainly if it was a white community this wouldn't be happening. Two-tiered health care is alive and well in Canada, unfortunately. It's only for those who are white and rich.' And a Mohawk journalist wrote: 'We are an endangered species living in endangered spaces. We're First Nations people living in Third World conditions.'

Two weeks later the letters were still coming in. As the *Toronto Star* editorial accompanying these articles had said: 'Natives still are not on Ottawa's political radar screen. One reasons for this is the absence of public pressure. If Canadians want the situation to change, they will have to demand that Ottawa make native issues a priority.'[39] And that is what seems to be happening; moreover, there is even some evidence that in the absence of action on the part of our own government, our citizens will seek intervention and external sanctions from other nations.

From all over the country, Canadians are expressing the same deep moral indignation and the same sense of shame which motivated Bertha Wilson to persist with the work of the royal commission. It took six years before its report was finally released, but it is a report which crowns her long and distinguished career of public service. It would be her hope that when Canada does justice and restores its disparate aboriginal peoples to their proper, distinct, and self-governing places within the vibrant multiplicity of our postmodern society, all of us will experience the same profound spiritual healing which has been her personal legacy from this final phase of her work.

15

Portrait of a Judge

Outside the offices of the justices on the second floor of the Supreme Court building hang individual portraits of all the Chief Justices clad in their ceremonial scarlet robes with the white mink trim.

In April 2000 no women are among these portraits. Chief Justice Beverley McLachlin, the first woman ever to hold that office, was sworn in only a few months earlier on 17 January and her portrait has not yet been painted. Nevertheless there is a portrait of a woman judge well worth seeking out just one floor up. On the half-landing outside the library where architect Cormier's two flights of stairs meet is a magnificent portrait of Bertha Wilson, clad in her black working silks.

The artist, Mary Lennox Hourd, has chosen a three-quarter figure pose. It is the expression on the face which is most immediately arresting. From whatever angle a viewer approaches this portrait, the blue eyes gaze back steadily. Hourd has painted eyes which have seen everything, faced it all unflinchingly, and remain without cynicism. In those eyes alone she manages to convey a complex and contradictory personality, warmly connecting with the individual viewer while remaining reserved, abstracted, thinking.

The hands are exceptionally beautiful. Wilson's right hand lightly grasps her eyeglasses and rests on two volumes of the Supreme Court Law Review. Hourd creates a still-life of Wilson's profession with realism which contributes to the painterly composition, the shapes and hues repeating the swooping wave of Wilson's hair and her fresh colouring. On Wilson's left hand is the ring given her by her husband fifty-five years earlier, two matched diamonds spar-

kling in the light. Partially concealed by the cuff of the white court shirt is her large watch with its wide metal bracelet, heavy as the demands on her private time of all the public obligations she has willingly undertaken.

All this is immediately accessible, but what is going on in the background? Hourd's brushwork is looser and more suggestive here, inviting the viewer's own interpretation. There is a small passage to the left behind the head rendered in feminine touches of blue and cream and rose and grey, evoking sky and clouds as amorphous as speculation itself. But for the most part Hourd's background brushwork is contained within precise geometric shapes. Luminous with transferred colour, these incisive planes extend right through the figure to be repeated in the sharp folds of the robes and the translucent rectangular tabs and the triangular lines which boundary the mouth. Hourd firmly embeds the figure in its context through broad cubic facetting and through small details. Now we notice the angle of the right eyebrow characteristically lifted: sceptical, challenging. And we are engaged once again by the forthright gaze of the eyes.

In the fall of 1998, long before Lamer had announced his retirement and it had become obvious that she would succeed him, Beverley McLachlin spoke with her colleagues about commissioning a portrait of Bertha Wilson for the Supreme Court. At that point Wilson had been retired from the Court for almost eight years but certainly not forgotten. It is not just that her judgments continue to be cited or that many of her concurrences and even her dissents were working their way into the mainstream. Moreover, it was not simply that Wilson had been the first woman on the Court.

Wilson had done more than most Supreme Court judges, male or female, at a crucial time in Canadian legal history. Her contributions to the development of Charter jurisprudence deserved to be commemorated both to honour her as an individual and to record her image in the minds of all Canadians.

With the enthusiastic support of all the Supreme Court judges, McLachlin contacted Wilson's old law firm. Oslers, grateful for every opportunity to acknowledge their most famous alumna, offered to pick up the tab and also to assist the Wilsons in selecting the right portrait artist to carry out the commission.

Oslers has the finest corporate collection of contemporary Canadian art in the country and lawyer Stephen B. Smart deserves the credit for selecting it.[1] Called to the bar in 1970, Smart joined the firm in 1974, just before Wilson left for the Court of Appeal. Nevertheless, as a young litigation lawyer he remembers sitting in on a number of meetings concerned with a massive intellectual property case for an important American corporation. Wilson provided a legal opinion on behalf of Oslers to the corporation's senior executives; they accepted her advice, Smart recalls, with great respect.[2]

Over the years Smart had become leading counsel in the Osler Arts, Entertainment and Media Law Group,[3] one of a very small number of lawyers in Canada who has developed such expertise in the visual arts that he can devote a considerable portion of his professional life to commercial acquisition of art for corporate clients. As a result, Smart has developed strong connections with many Canadian artists. He invited a number of leading portrait painters to pull together portfolios of their work which he forwarded to the Wilsons for their review. One of these was his neighbour and good friend, Mary Lennox Hourd; Smart wanted the Wilsons to make their own independent choice and so he handed over this folder among the others without drawing any particular attention to it.

The Supreme Court judges were committed to the project and Oslers was eager to get things under way. But at first Bertha Wilson was not sure that she wanted to have her portrait painted. She has always hated to have her photograph taken and thought that the process of working with an artist over many months could only prolong and exacerbate the agony. Instinctively, however, she and John concluded that if the portrait was to be painted Hourd was the right artist; they considered Hourd's portraits of male subjects excellent but it mattered more that she was one of the few who seemed able to paint women sympathetically.

Mary Hourd has thirty years of experience in commissioned portrait painting. She had studied at Beal Tech in London, Ontario, and at Ontario College of Art. Smart had told her a little about Bertha Wilson and her reputation, both professional and personal. Despite all her previous successes, this was a commission Hourd was absolutely thrilled to receive; when she learned Bertha Wilson had agreed to go ahead and had chosen her, she wrote Wilson a 'letter from the heart,' mailed it, and then (unable to wait for a response) immediately picked up the telephone and called her. Believing as she does that to create a good portrait it is essential for the artist to make a deep connection with the sitter, Hourd was just as anxious as Wilson herself; as soon as she heard Wilson's voice, she knew all would go well.

Mary's husband, Cam, drove her to Ottawa with a car full of camera and lighting equipment. They met first at the Wilsons' apartment. Mary took a number of informal photographs of Bertha in various settings on her home turf – in front of her bookshelves, in a favourite chair. She listened to the Wilsons' stories about various artifacts, learning more about both of them while Bertha became accustomed to the camera. Next Bertha and Mary met at the Supreme Court with Beverley McLachlin to consider where the finished portrait might hang; site was an important consideration in determining the right size for the portrait, and the availability of natural lighting needed to be thought through as well.

Meanwhile Cam Hourd – every bit as proud and supportive of Mary as John Wilson is of Bertha – was busily setting up an impromptu photography studio at the Four Seasons Sheraton. In the hotel lobby Mary caught sight of a perfect circular table with a smooth curve of auburn mahogany; the staff, discreetly excited by the project and charmed by Mary's enthusiasm, was happy to have her commandeer it. And then Mary began clicking the shutter, adjusting the lighting, taking innumerable photographs from every possible angle while eliciting from Bertha every possible facial expression. Several of the photographs capture Bertha's quintessentially characteristic 'thinking face,' the expression John Wilson loves most of all.

These photographs document the early stages of what evolved over eight subsequent sittings into a very close bond between artist and subject. Mary, a small and elegant woman in her fifties with white-blonde hair drawn back simply from a serenely youthful face, has a calm and reassuring personality; in Wilson's own words, 'her perceptive eye was matched by her understanding ear.'[4] The minister's wife had listened to her parishioners; the lawyer had listened to her clients; the judge had listened to counsel; the Gender Equality chair had listened to other women judges; and the royal commissioner had listened to aboriginal peoples from one end of the country to another. Now someone who shares many of her religious and spiritual values was listening to her speak about her work, her philosophy, and her general outlook on life itself. The finished portrait speaks volumes about the connection between subject and artist. Bertha Wilson herself believes that Mary Hourd's ability to achieve such a rapport is just as significant to her achievements as an artist as is her obvious technical facility .

After the final sitting – held this time in Toronto in Mary's studio on the third floor of the Hourds' Rosedale home[5] – the Hourds and the Wilsons went out together to look for the perfect frame. It had to be something not too grandiose, not too ornate, but suitable to the formality of the pose and the ceremonial nature of the commission. The simple wood frame they chose is ornamented only with four stylized metal waves. They stretch the rectangle to pour out of the corners as though Wilson's life force could not have been contained within any arbitrary boundary.

The commission called for a portrait of a judge in judicial robes and that is what the artist produced. Yet Mary Lennox Hourd has been able to suggest that judging was only one aspect of Wilson's life. The reason she takes a multitude of photographs before beginning a new portrait, Hourd told me, is because a successful portrait must be the constellation of the many, often contradictory, facets within a single personality. Some of these are more dominant, others less so, but the artist wants to convey them all. Hourd identified modesty, shyness, privacy, femininity, grace, keen intelligence, and especially strength as qualities she sought to convey. And Wilson, who certainly had never heard that flattering list, says only that she no longer believes a camera lens produces a truly unbiased and accurate picture; instead, she recommends, 'if you really wish a true likeness of yourself, have your portrait painted.'[6]

Never before had Hourd rendered a background in neocubist facets. In this instance the subtle disjunction in style between foreground and background evolved spontaneously out of the underpainting. And this background treatment contributes a great deal to the complexity and ambiguity of the finished work. Most literally, the background can be read as an abstraction of a high mountain top and an allusion to the long perspective which Allan Beattie, among others, considers to be one of Bertha Wilson's most salient traits. It functions equally as a prism, describing the formidable concentration powers noted by many who worked with Wilson over the years. By embedding the figure within its facetting, the background illustrates that assertion of contextuality as a principle of legal analysis which many consider Bertha Wilson's strongest and most lasting contribution to Supreme Court jurisprudence. And through its gently explosive force – the extension outwards beyond the confines of its boundaries underscored by the ornamental corner brackets – these cubist facets also suggest the innovation and sheer energy which Wilson brought both to her life in the law and her life beyond the law.

'Law as Large as Life' was the title of a lecture on legal education which Wilson delivered to first-year students at Queen's University in September 1990. The Charter, she told them, had 'put law into the kind of perspective in which I have always seen it – as large as life itself – not a narrow legalistic discipline in which inflexible rules are applied regardless of the justice of the result, but a set of values that we, as a civilized and cultured people, endorse as the right of all our citizens.'[7] She used the same phrase at her retirement ceremony on 4 December of that year and this time she acknowledged, a little shyly, that it had been her own aim on the bench to comply with the mandate of the Charter by making law as large as life.

James MacPherson said at the Dalhousie retirement symposium a year later that Bertha Wilson was a perfect judge for her time. And why is that so?

It is in large part because of Wilson's tireless efforts, both on the bench and afterwards, that Canadian society evolved as expansively and generously and optimistically as it has. We now aspire to include and to recognize as citizens a multiplicity of persons possessing an enormous diversity of characteristics; we routinely admit into evidence legislative facts derived from many sources and perspectives; we sustain respect for the principles of fundamental fairness while according due deference to a multiplicity of adjudicative tribunals, including aboriginal sentencing circles; and soon, it is to be hoped, we will learn how to welcome within our nation of nations new self-governing sovereign entities in accordance with pragmatically revised principles of international comity which nevertheless sustain respect for the supremacy of our law.

A multiplicity of legal subjects, legal facts, legal venues, even legal states; a blurring of boundaries between the professional and the personal, the public and the private; a rolling evolution of law and society in which perpetual change is not feared but confidently accepted; a conviction that principle is not eroded but sustained when we pay vigilant attention to contextual fluctuations: the origins of these powerful ideas are all contained within the neo-Aristotelian approaches of the great Scottish Enlightenment philosophers and are all discernible today within the distinctively postmodern society which Canada is perpetually in the process of becoming.

Bertha Wilson's story is an unusual and deeply human one. It needs to be told because it is part of all that is the very best in the story of Canada itself.

Adjunct Interviews

Arnup, John. The Honourable John Arnup invited me to his Fenelon Falls cottage on 9 July 1999, for a taped interview. Arnup, who took carriage for Oslers in the famous *Texas Gulf Sulphur* case and was later a colleague at the Ontario Court of Appeal, provided me with valuable anecdotal materials about both these aspects of Wilson's career.

Beattie, Allan. Beattie had been managing partner at Wilson's law firm, Osler, Hoskin & Harcourt. We met on 28 June 1999 for a taped interview at the CTV offices in Toronto.

Bhadauria, Pushpa. Mrs Bhadauria answered my questions about her attempts to establish a tort of discrimination in her long-standing lawsuit against Seneca College; Wilson had found in her favour at the Ontario Court of Appeal.

Blair, D. Gordon. The Honourable D. Gordon Blair spoke with me on the telephone in January 2000 and provided additional information by mail; he had been appointed to the Ontario Court of Appeal at the same time as Bertha Wilson.

Bryden, Philip. Phil Bryden, now a professor of administrative law at University of British Columbia, served an extended clerkship with Wilson between 1982 and 1984 when the first Charter cases were going up to the Supreme Court. He met with me in his office at UBC in February 2000 for a taped interview and generously mailed to me a thick stack of bench memos and other documentation; Bryden had assisted with key speeches delivered by Wilson and prepared one of the papers for the 1991 Dalhousie Symposium after her retirement.

Bryden, William. Retired partner and former Wilson colleague at Osler Hoskin & Harcourt. Informal conversation 28 June 1999 on the occasion of the unveiling of the Mary Lennox Hourd portrait at Oslers.

Buckley, Melina. Buckley served as the coordinator of the Canadian Bar Association's Gender Equality study chaired by Wilson after her retirement from the Supreme Court. She consented to a taped interview in February 2000 in her Vancouver home and subsequently provided further clarification by telephone.

Cheetham, Clare and Alfred. Clare Cheetham (née Greig) was Bertha Wilson's closest friend in Aberdeen and accompanied her through high school, university, and teacher's college. She knew Bertha's parents and brothers well. Clare and Alfred welcomed me and my husband to their home in Bieldside, Aberdeen on 10 August 1999. They shared pictures and detailed notes they had prepared recording memories of both John and Bertha. Since then they have kept in regular touch with me, supplying new information as it has come to light.

Clarke, Lorne. The Honourable Lorne Clarke, former Chief Justice of Nova Scotia, had taught Bertha Wilson at Dalhousie and arranged for her to article with Fred Bissett, QC. He spoke with me at length by telephone in Halifax in November 1999.

Coombs, Maurice. Maurice Coombs, the first person Wilson hired to work for her in the Osler research department, spoke to me in Ottawa at the Supreme Court unveiling of the Mary Lennox Hourd portrait and granted a detailed untaped telephone interview in January 2000 during which he provided helpful information about the organization of Wilson's legal department.

Cory, Peter. The Honourable Peter Cory served with Bertha Wilson at both the Ontario Court of Appeal and the Supreme Court of Canada. Now retired and engaged in consulting through the Oslers ADR Centre, Cory met with me in April 2000 for a taped interview.

Gonthier, Charles. Mr Justice Charles Gonthier of the Supreme Court of Canada spoke about Wilson's contributions to the development of Canadian judicial analysis during an untaped telephone interview in March 2000.

Harris, Patricia Fownes. Pat Harris met with me at her club in Halifax in November 1999 to talk about the experience of the women enrolled at Dalhousie with Bertha Wilson.

Hourd, Mary Lennox. The artist who was commissioned by Oslers to paint Wilson's portrait which hangs in the Supreme Court building in Ottawa, Hourd invited me to her Toronto studio for lunch and a lengthy untaped conversation about the process of creating this work. Mary Hourd has graciously consented to the use of this portrait for the cover of the biography.

Iacobucci, Frank. The friendship between the Iacobuccis and the Wilsons dates back to Wilson's years at Oslers. Mr Justice Frank Iacobucci of the Supreme Court of Canada took Wilson's place on the Court when she retired and occupies the office where she spent most of her Supreme Court years; he met with me there and reminisced warmly during a taped interview in April 2000.

Innes, Elsa. A Macduff parishioner of the Reverend John Wilson, Ms Innes invited me and my husband to meet with her in her home in August 1999. She regaled us with reminiscences of both the Wilsons and mailed me additional useful clippings and documents from that era.

Johnstone, Cecilia. Madam Justice Cecilia Johnstone of the Alberta Court of Queen's Bench served as president of the CBA and worked to implement recommendations contained within the Gender Equality study chaired by Wilson; in March 2000 she spoke with me about her association with Wilson from her Alberta office during an untaped interview.

Kennish, Tim. Chairman at Osler, Hoskin & Harcourt. Informal conversation in June 1999 on the occasion of the unveiling of the Mary Lennox Hourd portrait at Oslers and again in December at the Supreme Court unveiling. Kennish arranged with Oslers archivist Frank Clifford to supply me with a copy of his speech notes, other memorabilia from the Oslers archives, and a personal copy of Curtis Cole's *Osler, Hoskin & Harcourt, Portrait of a Partnership*.

Krever, Horace. The Honourable Horace Krever very kindly agreed to an impromptu meeting in his office in November 1999 on his retirement from the Ontario Court of Appeal. Krever also arranged for commissionaire Robert Matthews to show me Wilson's former office and the judges' dining room.

LaForest, Gerald. The Honourable Gerald LaForest, former Wilson colleague on the Supreme Court of Canada, spent considerable time in an untaped telephone interview in May 2000 discussing the intellectual affinities and the points of departure in their respective approaches to judgment.

Lamer, Antonio. The Honourable Antonio Lamer, former chief justice of Canada, provided helpful comments about Wilson's work on the Supreme Court and afterwards during a taped interview in April 2000 at his Ottawa law office.

Lane, Dennis. Mr Justice Dennis Lane of the Ontario Superior Court was one of Wilson's colleagues at Oslers and leading counsel on the *Texas Gulf Sulphur* case; he met with me in February 2000 for a taped interview.

Langlois, Gerald E. Mr Langlois represented Rosa Becker in the famous *Becker v. Pettkus* case Langlois granted me a lengthy untaped telephone interview in October 1999.

Lessard, Hester. Professor Lessard, now of the University of Victoria Faculty of Law, clerked with Wilson in 1985–6 at the Supreme Court. She met with me at UBC in February 2000 and was particularly helpful in describing Wilson's interactions with her clerks as she worked towards her decisions.

L'Heureux-Dubé, Claire. Madam Justice Claire L'Heureux-Dubé of the Supreme Court of Canada granted me a lengthy untaped telephone interview in March 2000. She commented on the notes I prepared during that interview and followed up with candid conversation in April in her Supreme Court office (formerly Wilson's office).

Linden, Allen. I met with Mr Justice Linden in May 1999 for a taped interview at his office at the Federal Court of Appeal in Ottawa. Linden is a good friend and colleague whom Wilson came to know at Osgoode Hall when she was on the Ontario Court of Appeal and he was serving on the trial division bench.

MacDonald, Joan. Joan MacDonald is the Hamilton lawyer who was instrumental in getting funding for the CBA's gender equality study. She met with me at her Hamilton office in April 2000 for a taped interview.

McConnell, Moira. Professor McConnell had served as one of Wilson's

Supreme Court clerks in 1984–5. She spoke with me in November 1999 at Dalhousie's Faculty of Law about the effect this experience has had on her subsequent career, and also about the 1991 Dalhousie symposium.

McIntyre, William. The Honourable William McIntyre permitted me to tape my interview with him in February 2000 in his Vancouver law office about his work on the Supreme Court with Bertha Wilson. Mr McIntyre had also prepared notes on a number of the cases they decided together which he generously supplied to me.

McLachlin, Beverley. Chief Justice Beverley McLachlin of the Supreme Court of Canada met with me in chambers in April 2000 during a taped interview. It was McLachlin who had initiated the project to have Wilson's portrait painted for the Supreme Court.

McNeil, Kathleen. Daughter of the organist who assisted Reverend John Wilson with the music at what was then Doune Church in Macduff, Ms McNeil welcomed me and my husband to her home in 1999 to speak about the Wilsons.

Meekison, Peter. Peter Meekison, who served with Wilson on the Royal Commission on Aboriginal Peoples, offered astute political analysis and anecdotal insights during a lengthy untaped telephone interview in April 2000.

Orgill, Norma and Herb. The Orgills rented their Bobcaygeon boathouse to the Wilsons for some twenty-seven summers. They welcomed me for a tour, lunch, and conversation in April 2000.

Orkin, Andy. Andy Orkin is a Hamilton lawyer specializing in aboriginal treaty issues who met with me in April 2000 in Hamilton and provided helpful background information about the work of the Royal Commission on Aboriginal Peoples.

Phillips, Jim. Professor Jim Phillips, legal historian at the University of Toronto Faculty of Law, clerked for Madame Justice Wilson in 1987–8. We met in his office in July 1999 for a formal taped interview concerning specific cases decided during his clerkship.

Plourde, Jean-Marie. Wilson's attendant at the Supreme Court of Canada, Plourde welcomed me to his home in Ottawa in May 1999 for a taped interview during which he spoke about his work for Madam Justice Wilson and his warm friendship with both the Wilsons.

Pugsley, Ronald. Mr Justice Ronald Pugsley, then of the Nova Scotia Court of Appeal, had been a classmate of Bertha Wilson's at Dalhousie Law School and spoke to me about their friendship in a taped interview in November 1999 at his Halifax office.

Randall, Reverend David. The present minister of what is now called Macduff Parish Church, in August 1999 Reverend Randall offered me and my husband a tour of the manse of Doune where the Wilsons lived after their marriage.

Reynolds, Tony. Reynolds, former executive director for the Royal Commission on Aboriginal Peoples, invited me to his home at Courtenay, British Columbia for a morning of taped conversation about his association with Wilson and the aftermath to that report.

Robertson, Alec. Robertson, a senior partner in a Vancouver law firm, served with Wilson on the CBA Gender Equality Study and is deeply knowledgeable about aboriginal law issues in British Columbia; he met with me in his office for a taped interview in March 2000.

Robinson, Viola. Viola Robinson, a Micmac elder, served with Bertha Wilson on the Royal Commission on Aboriginal Peoples between 1991 and 1996; she herself was inspired by Wilson to enrol in the Dalhousie Faculty of Law. She consented to a taped interview in November 1999 in Halifax.

Russell, Dawn. Dean Dawn Russell of the Faculty of Law at Dalhousie University spoke to me about Wilson's lingering legacy at Dalhousie in November 1999 and was helpful in arranging for access to archival materials concerning Wilson's law school record together with relevant copies of the law school's ANSUL magazine.

Saunders, Edward. The Honourable Edward Saunders, a former colleague of Wilson's from Oslers, now retired from the Ontario Superior Court and working again at Oslers in its Alternate Dispute Resolution department, in February 2000 granted me an untaped telephone interview concerning the law firm culture Wilson helped to shape.

Sharpe, Robert. Mr Justice Robert Sharpe of the Ontario Court of Appeal met with me at his Osgoode Hall chambers in September 1999 for a taped interview. Sharpe had been executive legal officer at the Supreme Court during Wilson's tenure and told me a good deal about this role. He also described the session of the Canadian Institute for

Advanced Legal Studies in Cambridge when Wilson took issue with Lord Ackner about the failure to appoint women judges to the House of Lords.

Smart, Stephen. Informal conversation in June 1999 on the occasion of the unveiling of the Mary Lennox Hourd portrait at Oslers and again in Ottawa at the Supreme Court unveiling.

Wernham, Christopher. I spoke to Chris Wernham, Wilson's nephew, in June 1999 at the Osler unveiling and followed up with an untaped telephone interview.

Yalden, Robert. Yalden clerked for Madame Justice Wilson at the Supreme Court of Canada in 1989–90 and now practises law at Oslers. We met there in June 1999 and again in October 1999. He helped me understand the process of decision-making for the cases on which he had assisted and illuminated more generally Wilson's approach to management of her chambers.

Archival Resources

In early July 1999 the University of Ottawa made me welcome for a full weekend while I sorted through numerous filing cabinets of materials accumulated by Bertha Wilson while she had worked on the CBA gender equity and Royal Commission on Aboriginal Peoples projects during her post-judicial career.

My thanks to Rachel Charnock and the archives staff of the University of Aberdeen where in August 1999 I was permitted to review academic records and other materials relating to the studies of Bertha Wernham, her two brothers, Archie and Jim, and her future husband, John Wilson.

For a week in October 1999 Dr Marianne McLean, Lucie Paquet, and Ross MacKay welcomed me and Bertha Wilson to the National Archives in Ottawa where they had arranged for the materials deposited by Wilson after her retirement from the Supreme Court to be made available for our review. Subsequently, the National Archives staff boxed and shipped four large cartons of materials to my Stroud law office for my use over eighteen months of research, writing, and preparation for publication.

Professor Moira McConnell and Dean Dawn Russell at Dalhousie University helped me obtain academic records from Wilson's law school years, back issues of ANSUL magazine which included historic reminiscences from the Wilson and earlier eras, videotape from the 1991 Dalhousie Symposium, and audiotape of the special music commissioned in Wilson's honour for that symposium.

Susan Lewthwaite of the Law Society of Upper Canada Archives and her colleague Paul Leatherdale assisted me in retrieving materials relating to Bertha Wilson's Law Society membership file and other documents relating to her career as a lawyer. Christine Kates, the professional oral historian who has conducted most of the interviews completed by the Osgoode Society for Canadian Legal History, provided me with a package of instructions and suggestions and some helpful telephone coaching.

Above all, my thanks to John Wilson who for years has kept boxes of clippings relating to Madame Justice Bertha Wilson's career and to major events of interest in Canadian legal history. All of these boxes he turned over to me for my use and they have been of inestimable assistance, particularly in gauging contemporary popular reaction to some of the more controversial Wilson judgments.

Notes

PREFACE

1 Bertha Wilson, 'Will Women Judges Really Make a Difference?' *Osgoode Hall Law Journal* 28, no.3 (1990), 507
2 Barbara Betcherman was herself associated with the feminist movement at Osgoode Hall Law School. She died in a car accident in 1983 and the lecture series was established in her honour.
3 Bertha Wilson, 'Will Women Judges Really Make a Difference?,' 507.
4 Bertha Wilson, 'Law in Society: The Principle of Sexual Equality,' *Manitoba Law Journal* 13, no.2 (1983), 225. The section 15 equality provisions in the Charter did not come into effect until 1985.

CHAPTER 1

1 This account of Bertha Wilson's early life is taken mainly from the interview of 3 August 1998. Before this interview she had spoken or written only rarely about her personal background. See also Sandra Gwyn, 'Sense and Sensibility,' *Saturday Night* (July 1985) and the Susan Lightstone interview, 'Bertha Wilson, a personal view of women and the law' *National* (August-September 1993)
2 I am indebted to Mr and Mrs Cheetham who went to great trouble to obtain documents and photographs for me and also prepared copious notes recording their memories of Bertha and John Wilson. The account in

this chapter is based on those notes and records and our lengthy conversation.

3 Bertha Wilson, 'Aspects of Equality-Rendering Justice.' This is an unpublished speech delivered at Hull, Quebec, on 19 November 1995.

4 Bertha Wilson, 'Remarks Made during Morning Service at Westminster United Church,' (October 1992). This was the first occasion she had even spoken in church during a service and rather than offering a traditional sermon, she recounted a simple personal memory from the SCM retreat she had attended at the age of eighteen.

5 It is, for example, the repository of the manuscripts of common sense philosopher Thomas Reid (1710–1796). Reid had succeeded Adam Smith to the chair of Moral Philosophy at University of Glasgow and did he best to refute what he conceived to be the moral anarchy entailed by the agnosticism of David Hume's *Treatise of Human Nature*, published in 1739. Reid considered common sense to be both a mental ability and a kind of knowledge or set of beliefs generally held by persons in the aggregate. He drew on sense perception to argue that it was intuitively self-evident to everyone that the external world exists as a material phenomenon. Alternatively, one can only believe that nothing is perceived except what is fleetingly present in the mind. That would mean that objects cease to exist as soon as one ceases to be conscious of them, which in Reid's view was incompatible with common sense. The circularity of this reasoning is self-evident, but had an enormous appeal since in the alternative there can be (as Hume acknowledged cheerfully enough) certainty about nothing, including even the possibility of virtue.

6 Bertha Wilson has herself provided a convenient synopsis of the history of the Scottish Enlightenment in 'The Scottish Enlightenment: The Third Shumiatcher Lecture in "The Law as Literature,"' *Saskatchewan Law Review* 51, no. 2 (1987), 258. The Act of Union of 1707 between Scotland and England is a matter of pride for Wilson, since it was the only occasion in history when two sovereign nations united peaceably by means of a treaty. Perversely, as she recognizes, the very spirit of independence among those who opposed the union led to a 'remarkable outburst of intellectual brilliance among the Scots.' The literati sought to display their superiority to the English through their achievements in history, philosophy, science, literature, and literary criticism which constitute the Scottish Enlightenment and led to the mid-eighteenth-century description of Edinburgh as the Athens of the North.

7 Bertha Wilson, ibid. James Burnett, Lord Monboddo (1714–99) was called to the bar in 1737. He knew David Hume well through the Select Society, an Edinburgh gentlemen's club. His academic studies reveal the interdiscipli-

nary and amateur zeal characteristic of the Scottish Enlightenment; he wrote a six-volume treatise on the relationship between linguistic development and political science and another six-volume study of the relationship between human and animal behaviour. Henry Homes, Lord Kames (1696–1782) was a lawyer admitted to practice in 1723 and a Lord of the Judiciary after 1763. He also was a member of the Select Society and a patron of Adam Smith. He published a number of works in law together with studies in anthropology, the theory of language, the origins of poetry, and even works in flax husbandry and other aspects of farming. These scholars exhibit the blurring academic disciplines and the pragmatic application of academic studies in projects intend-ed to improve Scottish civil society which are characteristic of the Scottish Enlightenment.

CHAPTER 2

1 'Macduff New Minister: Welcome to Rev. John Wilson,' no source or date noted. I am grateful to John Wilson who maintained a comprehensive clipping collection of news stories and photographs throughout the Wilsons' married life and generously shared them with me. This collection has been a rich archive which I have made use of throughout the book.
2 Rev. David J. Randall, 'History of Macduff Parish Church,' in *Church Festival Souvenir Programmes*, July 1996. The window was installed in 1929.
3 In recent years John Wilson has returned to his love of children's stories by writing several of his own, including a charming tale called *The Blue Poodle*.
4 Wilson described her life at Macduff in 'Address to the Ottawa Women's Canadian Club,' (Ottawa, 1982) which is included in the collected *Speeches Delivered by the Honourable Bertha Wilson 1976–1991* (Ottawa: Supreme Court of Canada 1992); (hereafter cited as *Speeches*).
5 This can be roughly translated as: 'Get out amongst my turnips you town's dirt. It's not what you eat, it's what you spoil.'
6 'One Woman's Way to the Supreme Court,' *Speeches*, 4. In an interview with Sandra Gwyn, Wilson added: 'Most of us are locked up tight inside ourselves, much of the time, pretending to be something we are not. And from where I sit on the bench today, it is just as important to know about people as it is to know about the law.' 'Sense and Sensibility,' *Saturday Night* (July 1985), 16.
7 The Renfrew congregation was itself comprised of second and third generation Scottish immigrants and had sought out a Scottish minister direct from the old country for their new church because of a somewhat sentimental cult

of 'pro-Scotticism' still prevalent in much of Canada at mid-century. According to Bertha, 'in 1949 when we arrived in Renfrew, Ontario, I recall the Burns supper held in our first January in Canada. Mr. Max MacOdrum, then president of Carleton University in Ottawa, proposed the toast to the immortal memory of Robbie Burns quoting poignantly from his love songs, tears pouring unrestrained down his cheeks. We had haggis and bag pipes and all that! And I felt the country to which I had come was more Scottish than the one I had left behind!'

8 Much of the information about the relationship between John and Bertha Wilson and her brother's family in Canada is derived from conversations with Chris Wernham.

9 'First female Supreme Court justice lived in Renfrew,' undated. This short article from the Wilsons' own clipping files provides reminiscences of members of the Renfrew Presbyterian Church. One young bride wanted a Scottish minister and a Scottish bridesmaid; she recalls that Bertha Wilson was willing to accommodate her. Another young mother decided to name her newborn daughter Heather and recalls the Wilsons sending back to Scotland for a sprig of real heather which was presented at the baptism service. There are happy memories of measuring up the windows in the new manse for curtains. Everyone agreed that Bertha Wilson was 'of course very intelligent but caring and understanding.'

10 'Bertha Wilson, 'Aspects of Equality-Rendering Justice,' unpublished speech, given at Hull, Quebec, 19 November 1995.

11 Bertha Wilson, 'One Woman's Way to the Supreme Court,' *Speeches*, 130.

CHAPTER 3

1 Ian Donaldson, 'Six Women Among Dal Law Graduates,' no date. This article is illustrated with a picture of Mrs Lilias Toward, Miss Enid Land, Miss Patricia Fownes, Miss Justine O'Brien, Miss Yvonne Walters, and Miss [sic] Bertha Wilson. This was at the time the largest group of women to have been admitted to Dalhousie.

2 Bertha Wilson, 'Reminiscences of my years at Dalhousie Law School,' *Ansul* (1977).

3 Christie Blatchford, 'Accident launched career that took her to top court,' *Toronto Star*, 3 March, 1982, A4.

4 Ronald C. Stevenson, 'Reminiscences,' *Ansul* (December 1977), 53.

5 See, for example, Bertha Wilson, 'Remarks to the First Year Class College of Law, University of Saskatchewan,' in *Speeches*, 299–300.

6 This account of her relationship with Professor Lederman is derived partly

from Bertha Wilson, 'The Ideal Teacher,' a tribute prepared for the symposium held at Queen's University honouring the life of William Lederman,
Friday 22 October, 1993.

7 W. Lederman, 'Thoughts on Reform of the Supreme Court of Canada,'
   Alberta Law Review (1970), 1.

8 W.R. Lederman, 'Reminiscences,' *Ansul* (December 1977), 76.

9 Blatchford, 'Accident launched career,' A4. Bertha Wilson was viewed by her
   classmates as sustaining a certain residual primness appropriate to her role
   as a minister's wife.

10 See, for example, the description of the prevailing atmosphere at Dalhousie
   when he joined the faculty in 1957 offered by Professor G.V.V. Nicholls in his
   'Reminiscences,' in *Ansul* (December 1977), 68: 'Most of my new colleagues
   in 1957 were native Nova Scotians. At this distance of time, I hope no one
   will be greatly offended if I confess that at first I found the prevailing atmosphere in the Law School a bit "old boy." After all, the great majority of my
   new colleagues were old Nova Scotians. It is not that they were unkind to the
   new boy, on the contrary, they were as amiable as I knew Nova Scotians can
   be. It was just that now and again something would happen to make me feel
   like substituting "local boy" for "old boy".'

11 See F.W. Bissett, 'Reminiscences,' *Ansul* (January 1976), 19, who considered
   Halifax a delightful place to practise because the lawyers were all friendly
   and all of them kept their word and their commitments.

12 John Willis give full tribute to the downtowners in his 'Reminiscences,' *Ansul*
   (January 1976), 63. They were offered $2 a lecture to attend at the campus at
   5:00 p.m. but were fully expected to donate that stipend back to the law school
   and to attend faculty meetings gratis. On the other hand D.A. Soberman, who
   graduated from Dalhousie in 1951 and returned to join the staff in 1955 before
   heading for the faculty at Queen's, considered that Dalhousie's reliance on
   busy practitioners subtracted from the school's academic quality because they
   tended to teach from stale notes and were seldom available to meet with students between classes; 'Reminiscences,' in *Ansul* (December 1977), 52.

13 Bertha Wilson, unpublished and expanded version of 'Reminiscences of my
   Years at Dalhousie Law School,' (January 1977), special issue of *Ansul*.

14 Heather Hill, 'Supreme Court's first woman may give it a more liberal look,'
   Montreal Gazette, March 1982, B4.

15 Ibid.

16 She was seventh out of seventy in first year; fourth out of fifty-seven in second year; and seventh out of fifty-eight in third year.

17 Sandra Gwyn, 'Sense and Sensibility,' *Saturday Night* (July 1985), 16–17. See
   also George Inrig, 'Reminiscences,' in *Ansul* (December 1977), 64.

18 Bertha Wilson, 'Law as Large as Life,' *Speeches*, 686.
19 Bertha Wilson, 'Address to Special Convocation of the Law Society of Upper Canada,' ibid., 728–9. Bertha Wilson did not reveal in that speech which standard course it was she had not studied during law school, preferring not 'to undermine public confidence in my judgments.'
    At Macduff, the Wilsons had considered it very important to supplement the young peoples' theoretical and academic education with practical information about bank accounts and makeup and the role of policemen, expressing some regret at the failure of the Scottish educational system to adopt a more pragmatic role. And in 'Reflections at the End of One Year on the Bench,' included in *Speeches*, 2, Wilson stated that she could not understand why there was so much public confidence in the institution of the courts when both counsel and judges lacked specific training to carry out their respective roles. The issue of the relationship between theoretical and practical training in law is one to which Wilson has devoted considerable thought throughout her career without arriving at any definitive conclusions.
20 Bertha Wilson, 'Remarks to the First Year Class College of Law, University of Saskatchewan,' in *Speeches*, 297.
21 Donaldson, 'Six Women Among Dal Law Graduates.'
22 Ibid. It is possible Wilson would have had greater opportunities for an academic career in Scotland where Archie Wernham was well established.
23 See, for example, the account of F.W. Bissett's defence of Viola Desmond, a Black woman ejected from the Roseland Theatre in New Glasgow, Nova Scotia, in 1946 because she had had the temerity to sit in the main floor seating then restricted for whites only, described in Constance Backhouse, *Colour-Coded, A Legal History of Racism in Canada, 1900–1950* (Toronto: The Osgoode Society for Canadian Legal History/University of Toronto Press, 1999), chapter 7. Bissett lost at the trial and on appeal; he refused to bill his client and his fee, which had been raised through donations, was used to help establish the Nova Scotia Association for the Advancement of Coloured People.

CHAPTER 4

1 Bertha Wilson, 'Equity and the Tenant for Life,' *Canadian Bar Journal* (1960), 117, Bertha Wilson, 'A Choice of Values,' *Canadian Bar Journal* (1961), 448.
2 Bertha Wilson, 'The Accountant as Executor,' *The Canadian Chartered Accountant*, 357. Wilson moves beyond the usual tangible assets of house, cottage, furniture, car, stocks and bonds, bank accounts, cash and personal belongings to contemplate property in intangibles such as future interests under

another will or trust and potential proceeds from a cause of action in contract, tort or breach of trust. It was written two years before publication of what is often considered the groundbreaking discussion of this issue: Charles Reich, 'The New Property,' *Yale Law Journal* 73, no.5 (1964).

3 Interview with Maurice Coombs, the Osler partner currently responsible for the research department. A good deal of the information relating to the functioning of the research department is derived from that interview.

4 Curtis Cole, *Osler, Hoskin & Harcourt: Portrait of a Partnership* (Toronto: McGraw-Hill Ryerson, 1995), provides a detailed account of the transition in firm culture at Osler, Hoskin & Harcourt during this era.

5 Law firms in Ontario were not then or now permitted to incorporate; not until 1999 did the Law Society of Upper Canada even permit law firms to be structured as limited partnerships. But the corporate mentality became entrenched in the major Bay Street law firms which drew most of their business from corporate clients in the mid-1970s, and Bertha Wilson was active in promulgating the principle that Oslers ought never to lose sight of its higher obligations to society as an association of professionals.

6 Bertha Wilson, 'Tribute to Allan Leslie Beattie, Chairman of the Executive Committee and Managing Partner of Osler, Hoskin & Harcourt on his Move to Become Vice President of Eaton's Canada Ltd,' in *Speeches*, 434.

7 This concept is Humean, but she borrows the phrase here from the novelist and philosopher Iris Murdoch, whose work was much admired by the Wilsons.

8 Cole, in *Portrait of a Partnership*, 126–36, devotes considerable space to a discussion of Crawford. He began in labour law, moved to securities and then to corporate law, but gained his greatest power in the firm for his ability to attract lucrative new clients. Allan Beattie graduated from Osgoode Hall in 1951 and joined the firm, making partner relatively early in 1955. It is interesting that none of these three stayed on at Oslers until retirement age; Beattie went to long-time Oslers' client, Eaton's, in 1987; Crawford went to another Olsers' client, Imasco, in 1975 but has returned to Oslers' ADR department; and Wilson had left in 1975 for the Ontario Court of Appeal.

9 See ibid., 118. Stuart Thom fully subscribed to this philosophy of tax law.

10 On one such occasion, Beattie recalls, a client's son called to speak to Wilson about her progress on a tricky trust problem and she was furious, telling him in no uncertain terms that it was unethical to make inquiries and to attempt to mislead her as to his identity.

11 See Arthur B.C. Drache, 'The English Charity Commission Concept in the Canadian Context,' *Philanthropist* 14, no. 1 (1997), 11, in which Drache traces the history of charitable statutes in the United Kingdom back to the Charita-

ble Trusts Acts of 1853 and 1860. In the same issue Bertha Wilson, in 'By Way of Introduction,' describes the history of those acts.

12 Allan Beattie says that the lawyers asking Wilson for research assistance would frequently have wished her to assist them with the documentation and even pressured her to do so, but Wilson resisted such requests which would have taken time away from the pure research role.

13 Bertha Wilson had a great fondness and respect for Stuart Thom, in part because he managed to balance what is an extremely technical and somewhat dry legal speciality, tax law, with an intense interest in literature and painting sustained throughout his life. And Wilson was fascinated by the complexity and contradiction within his character, questioning his purported cynicism and agnosticism and fully recognizing the price he paid for his perfectionism in a manner which sheds light on her own character; see Bertha Wilson, 'Tribute to Stuart Thom,' in *Speeches*, 765.

14 The 'sameness feminists,' assumed that a restructuring of the work force and a reallocation of gendered domestic labour was achievable. Social change would make it possible for women to function exactly like men, without any need to take into account women's differing ethical or social identities evolving out of their biological and emotional commitments to childcare responsibilities. Early work in 'sameness feminism' as applied to the legal profession was still some years away; see, for example, Cynthia Fuchs Epstein, *Women in Law* (New York: Basic Books, 1981).

15 *Leitch Gold Mines Ltd. et al. v. Texas Gulf Sulphur Co. (Incorporated) et al.* (1968) 1 OR 469. This account is based on conversations with Bill Bryden, John Arnup, and Dennis Lane. See also the account of this case in Cole, *Portrait of a Partnership*, 44ff.

16 In fact, no one with whom I have spoken remembers what the new argument discovered by Bertha Wilson and requiring amendment of the statement of defence actually was.

17 Bertha Wilson, 'The Unappealable Judgment: After Dinner Speech to the Seminar for New Federally-Appointed Trial Judges,' in *Speeches*, 270.

18 Bertha Wilson, 'Tribute to Mr. Justice John D. Arnup 35,' *Speeches*, 267.

19 See John Arnup, *Middleton: The Beloved Judge* (Toronto: McClelland & Stewart, 1988), the touching tribute he wrote to Middleton after his own retirement from the court. Like his hero, Arnup kept his own notebook of cases from the start of his practice to track precedents; he believes that a prodigious memory was not a gift of heredity but created deliberately by training. Arnup also believes that kindness and liking people are the most important attributes of a good judge, and that 'no judge can achieve the first rank unless he does' (p.136). To courtesy and humanity he adds com-

mon sense and a sense of humour as the essential attributes of a good judge.

20 This account is derived in part from Cole's *Portrait of a Partnership*, and from my interview with Bertha Wilson, 25 May 1999.

21 In Toronto during the late 1960s Legal Aid was still in its infancy and very informal in its organization. The sheriff opened his office one night a week and welcomed people with legal problems but no means of paying legal fees. Lawyers willing to help (including a number of Oslers' lawyers) would drop around and offer their services on a pro bono basis. It was about this time that Bertha Wilson was invited to attend a Legal Aid dinner by one of these Oslers' lawyers. During the early 1970s Brian Bellmore, Peter Dey, and Ron Ellis were all released from their duties at Oslers for up to half a day a week to participate in the Parkdale Community Legal Services Clinic. See Cole, *Portrait of a Partnership*, 171.

22 This notion that the nexus of moral sentiment is eroded with increased social distance in the absence of appropriate governance is one which can be traced back to the philosophy of Francis Hutcheson, the founder of Scottish Enlightenment common sense doctrines.

23 For a classic example of the persistence of these sameness feminist approaches to labour and delivery lingering on for more than a decade, see Lorraine Weinrib, 'Women in the Legal Profession: Old Issues: Current Problems,' *Law Society of Upper Canada Gazette* 24 (1990), 73.

24 Although Maurice Coombs worked closely with her and was aware of her occasional absence for doctors' appointments, he had no knowledge of the extent of Wilson's ill health. Occasionally he thought she seemed weary but nothing was permitted to interfere with her sense of responsibility for getting through the work.

25 *Report of the Royal Commission on the Status of Women in Canada* (Toronto: Queen's Printer, 1970), vii.

26 See Bertha Wilson, 'Law in Society: The Principle of Sexual Equality,' *Manitoba Law Journal* 13, no.2 (1983), 222, for a summary account of the work of this group, including establishment of the Canadian Advisory Council on the Status of Women created in 1973.

27 In 1993, however, the Westminister Institute announced a three-year initiative to examine issues of ethics in the legal profession. Bertha Wilson contributed a solid and scholarly paper to this project; see 'Pressing Ethical Questions Facing the Legal Profession,' *Westminster Affairs* 6 (1993), 8.

28 *The United Church of Canada Report of the Commission on Abortion to the Twenty-Eighth General Council* (11 February 1980); Allan Beattie, 'Introduction of the

Report of the Commission on Abortion to the 28th General Council of the United Church of Canada' (18 August 1980).
29 The house had been architecturally designed for a retired couple, its first owners. No children had been born to Bertha and John Wilson, a matter of sad happenstance rather than choice. That the Wilsons loved their house on Moore Avenue is clear from the licence plate on their current and aging Toyota which still combines the Moore Avenue number with their initials.
30 They hired a community college student for this job and were later delighted to encounter him working at the governor-general's residence in Ottawa.

CHAPTER 5

1 Conversation with Mr Justice Horace Krever and with Osgoode Hall commissionaire Robert Matthews. Mr Matthews showed me Wilson's initial office which has now been converted into a small boardroom.
2 '1st woman named to Court of Appeal,' *Toronto Star*, 20 December 1995.
3 B.J. MacKinnon, 'Speech given on the occasion of Bertha Wilson's appointment to the Supreme Court of Canada,' undated. The notes for this witty, warm and affectionate speech were among the Wilsons' personal papers; MacKinnon considered himself an 'emotional Scot' and included Bertha Wilson in that category. MacKinnon pointed out that when Wilson went to the Court of Appeal neither Gale nor Martin had had any intention of give up their private quarters; he humorously noted that they 'were living by that ancient British maxim, "what we have, we hold," or, to mix a metaphor, they were standing on their squatters rights.'
4 Interview with John Arnup.
5 Bertha Wilson, 'My Years in the Court of Appeal, 1975–1982,' unpublished (*circa* 1997).
6 D. Gordon Blair, for example, frankly admits that he also had little experience in criminal law when he joined the court but he sat on his fair share of criminal panels and relied upon the expertise of G. Arthur Martin until he had become more familiar with that area of the law. Mr Justice MacKinnon, in his speech on the occasion of Wilson's appointment to the Supreme Court, also noted her unusual openness in acknowledging any deficiencies she might have in knowledge of the law.
7 John Arnup had a deliberate policy of making very few speeches while he was on the bench although he did participate in various prayer breakfasts as part of his commitment to the United Church.
8 This was an idea which particularly intrigued Wilson and she referred to it a number of times when speaking to classes of law students: see, for example,

'Evidence under the Charter of Rights,' in *Speeches*, 289. It is an idea which also has particular affinities with the postmodern notion that truths in some instances may be multiple and mutable. And it further suggests that the job of an advocate, who is obliged by the rules of professional responsibility and the rules of civil or criminal procedure to be candid with the court and to provide full disclosure even of facts or precedents inimical to his client's case, is nevertheless to argue persuasively that the proofs he presents to support those truths which protect his client's interests are the proofs to which the court should accord greater weight.

9 Bertha Wilson, 'Sitting in Judgment,' 12–13. This speech was delivered to the Women's Auxiliary at Timothy Eaton Memorial Church in 1977.

10 Bertha Wilson, 'Reflections at the End of One Year on the Bench,' remarks made at the Christmas party of the Women's Law Association of Ontario (December 1976), in *Speeches*, 6.

11 *R. v. Olbey* (1978), 37 CCC (2d) 390 (Ont. CA). The case was heard on 1 December 1977; Dubin concurred with Martin. Throughout my discussion of case law at both the Ontario Court of Appeal and the Supreme Court of Canada, I have focused on Wilson's judgments in the context of judging and her own writings. The scope of this biography has not permitted thorough review of the voluminous body of Wilson case analysis by other academics readily available to students of law. Accordingly there is only occasional mention of this body of work.

12 For further discussion of Wilson's contribution to contextualism, see Shalin M. Suganasiri, 'Contextualism: The Supreme Court's New Standard of Judicial Analysis and Accountability,' *Dalhousie Law Journal* 1 (1999), 129 ff.

13 *R. v. Thibert* [1996] 1 SCR 37.

14 Bertha Wilson, 'My Years in the Court of Appeal 1975–1982,' 3–4.

15 *Dominion Chain Co. Ltd. v. Eastern Construction Co. Ltd.* (1976), 12 OR (2d) at 201.

16 *Dabous v. Zuliani* (1976), 12 OR (2d) at 239.

17 The 'neighbour' doctrine was first expressed in *Donoghue v. Stevenson* (1932) AC 572 per Lord Atkin. In this case a manufacturer of ginger beer was held liable for the harm arising from his negligence to ensure that his produce was snail-free. Even through the manufacturer did not know who the particular consumer of the snail-infested ginger-beer would be, it was held that he had a duty to protect that consumer by taking reasonable care just as we all have a duty not to harm a 'neighbour' by taking reasonable care. The case, which had gone up to the House of Lords from the Scottish town of Paisley, is completely congruent with the Scottish Enlightenment doctrine relating moral sympathy to law. David Hume, for example, argued that rational

reflection (inference) is essential to ensure consistency in benevolent behaviours among citizens in a social relationship, and that this consistency is most likely to occur when encoded in law.

18 A 'tortfeasor' is a person who has committed a tort – that is, an act or omission which causes harm to another person, whether intentionally or not, if he or she ought reasonably to have anticipated that the victim might be hurt by the action or omission; this is, however, only a simple definition and the permutations in the common law are considerably more complex.

19 *Dominion Chain* at 224.

20 Nine years after *Dominion Chain*, Wilson participated in the *Central Trust* v. *Rafuse* case which resolved the issue in accordance with this approach. The Supreme Court found that there are instances in which there can be concurrent liability in contract and tort because what is at issue for tort liability is the relationship of proximity between the plaintiff and the defendant, regardless of whether or not that proximity has arisen in the context of a contract. See *Central Trust Co.* v. *Rafuse* [1986] 2 SCR 147.

21 This doctrine is at the heart of the English case, *Hedley Byrne & Co. Ltd.* v. *Heller & Partners Ltd.* [1964] AC 465, but Wilson's judgments in *Fine Flowers Ltd.* v. *General Accident Assurance Co.* (1977), 17 OR (2d) 529 (CA) and in *Carman Construction Ltd.* v. *Canadian Pacific Railway Co.* (1981), 33 OR (2d) 472 (CA) imported the doctrine into the Canadian context.

22 The Wilson partial dissent in *Lister* v. *Dunlop Canada Ltd.* (1979), 27 OR (2d) at 168; rev. (1982), 135 DLR 1 SCC is one instance of such reasoning.

23 *Chomedy Aluminum Co. Ltd.* v. *Belcourt Construction (Ottawa) Ltd.* (1979), 24 OR (2d) 1 (CA); aff'd *sub nom Beaufort Realties (1964) Inc.* v. *Chomedy Aluminum Co. Ltd.* (1980), 116 DLR (3d) 193 (SCC).

24 *Re: Downing and Graydon* (1978), 21 OR (2d) at 292.

25 Madam Justice Rosalie Abella, Royal Commission on Equality in Employment, *Equality in Employment* (Ottawa: Supply and Services Canada, 1984).

26 See Louise Brown, 'Women's pay appeal upheld: court orders province to tell why her complaint rejected,' *Toronto Star*, 26 October 1978, D10; nevertheless the law still did not contemplate equal pay for work of equal value. Another undated clipping was headed, 'Equal pay hearing wasn't fair, court decides.'

27 Bertha Wilson, 'Sitting in Judgment,' 13.

28 RSO 1980, c. 152. The 1978 Ontario Family Law Reform Act required sharing of family assets but permitted the titled spouse to retain non-family assets; the act was subsequently overhauled and a new policy of deferred community of economic assets acquired during the course of the marriage was introduced in 1986.

29 *Becker* v. *Pettkus* (1978), 20 OR 105 (Ont. CA).
30 Ibid., at 106.
31 Ibid., at 108.
32 *Murdoch* v. *Murdoch* (1973), 41 DLR (3d) 367 (SCC). Irene Murdoch was married for twenty-five years to an Alberta farmer who spent a good part of the year engaged in forestry while she operated the cattle ranch; she was awarded only $200 a month support. Wilson also referred to Dickson's judgment in *Rathwell* v. *Rathwell* (1978), R.F.L. (2d) 1, quoting with approval Laskin's dissent from *Murdoch* in which he had stated that the principle of resulting and constructive trust is not confined to the matrimonial home alone but applicable to all property jointly acquired.
33 *Pettkus* v. *Becker* (1980), RFL (2d) 165 (SCC).
34 John P. Maclean, 'Common-law wife to learn her worth,' *Toronto Star,* 17 December 1980; 'Need more women judges to end bias,' ibid., 19 December 1980, A4; Patricia Bluch and John F. Maclean, 'Common-law wife gets half, flood of claims now predicted,' ibid; and 'Fair shares,' *Globe and Mail,* 27 December 1980.
35 I am indebted to Mr Langlois for discussing this case with me and providing additional details beyond those available in the judgments and in contemporary news reports.
36 *Leatherdale* v. *Leatherdale* [1982] 2 SCR 743.
37 This paper was subsequently selected for publication in a collection, *Family Law: Dimensions of Justice* (Toronto: Butterworth's, 1983).
38 *Welsh* v. *Welsh* (1980), 28 OR (2d) 255.
39 The relevant words then were, 'as the court thinks reasonable, having regard to the means and needs of each of them.'
40 *Cure* v. *Cure* (1982), 36 OR (2d) 345.
41 Bertha Wilson, Memo re 'The Variation of Support Orders' to All Judges of the Court of Appeal, 1 September 1981 (emphasis in original).
42 Bertha Wilson, 'Sitting in Judgment,' 13–14.
43 Bertha Wilson, 'Children: The Casualties of a Failed Marriage,' *UBC Law Review* 19 (1983), 245.
44 *Kruger* v. *Kruger* (1979), 25 OR 673 (Ont. CA).
45 Ibid. at 694.
46 *Baker* v. *Baker* (1979), 23 OR (2d) 392 (Ont. CA), rev. 3 RFL (2d) at 193.
47 *Kruger,* at 676.
48 See, for example, *Anson* v. *Anson* (1987), 10 DCLR (2d) at 357 which made an order of joint guardianship and joint custody; *Heyman* v. *Heyman* (1990), 24 RFL (3d) at 402 (BCSC), in which the court held that one parent should not be able to deprive the child of the benefit of both parents' guidance ; *Stewart* v.

Stewart (1994), 2 RFL (4th) 53 (BCCA), in which a joint custody order was successfully appealed because the parents had not been able to cooperate without hostility damaging to the best interests of the child; *Massan v. Klotild-Houser* [1999] BCJ No. 196 (BCSC), in which the court awarded sole custody to the father because it found on the evidence that to do so was in best interests of the child; and *Fawcett v. Fawcett* [1999] BCJ No. 506 (BCSC) which awarded joint custody and joint guardianship of the child on the grounds that it was in his best interests to do so and because the history of his parents' relationship with them showed that they could cooperate in decisions concerning his care.

49 *Ishaky v. Ishaky* (1978), RFL (2d) 138 (Ont. CA).
50 Ibid., at 139.
51 *Bezaire v. Bezair*, 20 RFL (2d) 358 (Ont. CA).
52 *Re. K* (1995), 23 OR (3d) 679 (Ont. Ct. Prov. Div.) Per Nevins J.; in this case, the court found in favour of four lesbian couples which had each applied to adopt a child or children of whom one partner was the natural parent.
53 Ibid., at 365–6. The evidence available to the trial judge showed that Mrs Bezaire had had a series of short-lived lesbian relationships, moved her children seven times in four years, and uprooted them from their schools without reference to their need for continuity.
54 *Cooney v. Cooney* (1982), 36 OR (2d) at 137.
55 Ibid., at 141. This excerpt represents about half of the fulminations of Cory on this subject.
56 Bertha Wilson, 'Notes for Speech to Women's Canadian Club' (Ottawa, February 1979).
57 *Re Cummings and Ontario Minor Hockey Association* (1979), 26 OR (2d) 7.
58 *Re Ontario Human Rights Commission and Ontario Rural Softball Association* (1979), 26 OR (2d) at 134.
59 Ibid., at 143.
60 'Human Rights Code should be clarified,' *Brantford Expositor*, 1 September 1979; 'Girl-haters,' *Toronto Sun*, 10 September 1979; 'If this is the law then change it,' *Globe and Mail*, 4 September, 1979.
61 Ontario Human Rights Code, SO, 1981, c. 53, s. 19 (2).
62 *Re Blainey and Ontario Hockey Association* (1986), 54 OR (2d) 514.
63 *Bhadauria v. Board of Governors of Seneca College of Applied Arts and Technology* (1979), 27 OR (2d) at 142.
64 Vianney Carriere, 'Court allows damages suit based on racial discrimination,' *Globe and Mail*, 13 December 1979.
65 (1981), 124 DLR (3d) 193 (SCC).
66 Teaching certificates have never been required for teaching in Ontario's community colleges.

67 This account is derived from a telephone interview with Pushpa Bhadauria, 28 October 1999. She was delighted to hear that Wilson was still living and that a biography was being prepared; she wanted to know if Wilson had married, whether or not she had children and other details to fill out the vivid impression she had retained of Wilson as a human being. In fact, these details were of far greater interest to Pushpa Bhadauria than the developments in the common law which are slowly eroding the *Bhadauria* exclusive jurisdiction doctrine arising out of the Laskin reversal.

68 This account is derived from an interview with the Honourable Mr Justice Allen Linden (now of the Federal Court of Appeal). I had first met Mr Linden when he was on leave from the court and enrolled in a class in administrative law at the University of Toronto in 1994–5; we had several conversations in which he discussed his friendship with Bertha Wilson and the role he had played in her appointment to the Supreme Court.

69 William Monopol, 'Exclusive interview with Chief Justice Bora Laskin,' quoting Laskin, *Financial Post*, 20 September 1980, 21.

70 Bertha Wilson, 'My Years in the Court of Appeal.'

71 B.J. MacKinnon, 'Speech delivered on the occasion of Wilson's appointment to the Supreme Court of Canada.'

72 Bertha Wilson, 'Tribute to Chief Justice Howland on the Occasion of His Retirement,' 23 February 1990, in *Speeches*, 635.

73 Susan Lightstone, 'Bertha Wilson, A personal view of women and the law,' *National* (August-September 1993), 14.

74 Chief Justice Bora Laskin, reported in 'The Honourable Madam Justice Bertha Wilson,' *Law Society of Upper Canada Gazette* 16 (1982), 173.

75 Ibid., 175; although Laskin had not enjoyed much collegiality when he was appointed as the first Jew on the Supreme Court of Canada, he had been noted for his own innovative and frequently dissenting judgments during his early days on the Court.

76 Ibid., 176.

77 Ibid., 179.

1 James MacPherson, 'Canadian Constitutional Law and Madam Justice Bertha Wilson,' *Dalhousie Law Journal* 15, no. 1 (1992) 220–1.

2 Allan L. Beattie, 'Notes of a tribute to the Honourable Madame Justice Bertha Wilson,' 14 May 1982, unpublished.

3 See, for example, Bertha Wilson, 'Remarks Made at Queen's University Convocation Upon Acceptance of an Honourary Degree of Doctor of Laws,' in *Speeches*, 98.

4 Bertha Wilson, 'Methods of Appointment and Pluralism,' speech prepared for Lederman Symposium 23 October 1993 at Queen's University, Kingston.

5 See, for example, Annette C. Baier, 'Hume, The Woman's Moral Theorist?' in *Women and Moral Theory*, Eva Feder Kittay and Diana T. Meyers, eds. (Savage, Maryland: Rowman & Littlefield, 1987) and also *A Progress of Sentiments, Reflections of Hume's* Treatis (Cambridge, Mass.: Harvard University Press, 1991); Martha Nussbaum, *Poetic Justice, The Literary Imagination and Public Life* (Boston: Beacon Press, 1995), xvi, 72ff; Barbara Hernstein Smith, *Contingencies of Value, Alternative Perspectives for Critical Theory* (Cambridge, Mass.: Harvard University Press, 1991), 56–73, and *Belief and Resistance, Dynamics of Contemporary Intellectual Controversy* (Cambridge, Mass.: Harvard University Press, 1997), 73ff; Charles Taylor, *Sources of the Self, the Making of the Modern Identity* (Cambridge University Press, 1989), 259 and 343ff, and 'The Politics of Recognition' in *Multiculturalism; Examining the Politics of Recognition*, Amy Guttman ed. (Princeton University Press, 1994), 28; and Mark Kingwell, 'Politics and the Polite Society in the Scottish Enlightenment,' *Historical Reflection/Reflexions Historiques* 19, no.3 (1993), 363. I have discussed these connections at greater length in 'Enlightened Postmodernism: Scottish Influences on Canada's Legal Pluralism.'

6 A useful account in provided in Jane Rendall, *The Origins of the Scottish Enlightenment, 1707–1776* (St Martin's Press: New York, 1978); Rendell's study is one of the sources Wilson drew on for her speech, 'The Scottish Enlightenment: The Third Shumiatcher Lecture in 'The Law as Literature,' *Saskatchewan Law Review* 51, no. 2 (1987).

7 Joan Tronto, *Moral Boundaries* (Routledge: New York and London, 1993). Tronto mentions that misreading of Carol Gilligan's *In a Different Voice; Psychological Theory and Women's Development* (Cambridge, Mass.: Harvard University Press, 1982) is one source of the conflation between feminism and an ethics of care; Wilson also cites Gilligan in her 1990 'Will Women Judges Really Make a Difference?' speech.

8 See, for example, Charles Taylor, 'Justice after Virtue,' paper presented at University of Toronto Law School Legal Theory Workshop, 23 October 1987.

9 See Hans Bertens, 'The Postmodern Weltanschauung and its Relation to Modernism: An Introductory Survey' in *Approaching Postmodernism*, Douwe Fokkema & Hans Bertens, eds. (Amsterdam/Philadelphia: John Benjamins Co., 1986), 9. Canadian postmodernism, says Bertens (and he looks to works by Marshall McLuhan and Northrop Frye to support this thesis) is typically ironic and concerned with deflation of modernist intellectual pretentiousness.

10 There are many sources of this identification. See generally Richard Gwyn's

Nationalism without Walls; The Unbearable Lightness of Being Canadian (Toronto: McClelland & Stewart, 1995), particularly at p. 243 where he writes: 'Wilfrid Laurier got it wrong when he said that the 20th century might belong to Canada. Instead, Canada belongs to the 21st century. We are the world's first postmodern state.' Gwyn believes that Canadian society is moving in the wrong direction and that it would be possible and desirable to choose not to do so. Nevertheless he provides a useful overview of the evolution of the idea that Canada is becoming a postmodern state. Linda Hutcheon is Canada's leading postmodern scholar. She is the author of over seventy published articles and a dozen or more books on postmodernism. See, for example, *The Canadian Postmodern: A Study in Contemporary English Canadian Fiction* (Toronto: Oxford University Press, 1988).

11 In architecture there is a distinctly Canadian postmodernism, characterized by buildings such as Toronto Eaton Centre (Eberhard Zeidler, 1977) or the National Art Gallery (Moshe Safdie, 1990) with their functional atrium spaces which work well in our extreme climate.

12 That Canada has produced a distinctive postmodern literature, employing strategies of multiple narration, irony and ambiguity, is well documented; see, for example, Linda Hutcheon, *A Poetics of Postmodernism: History, Theory, Fiction* (New York and London: Routledge, 1988). Exemplars of Canadian postmodern literature include such writers as Margaret Laurence, Carol Shields, and Michael Ondaatje. Northrop Frye and Margaret Atwood have been particularly conscious of wilderness and winter as formative influences on the Canadian collective consciousness.

13 John Ralson Saul, *Reflections of a Siamese Twin: Canada at the End of the Twentieth Century* (Toronto: Viking, 1997), 9.

14 See, for example, R.E. Hawkins and R. Martin, 'Democracy, Judging and Bertha Wilson,' *McGill Law Journal* 41, no.1 (1995), 58, a lengthy study of Wilson's judgments which derides her for her lack of judicial objectivity.

15 Precedent has moral weight as a universal yardstick justifying its modernist role in the incremental development of the common law because, if Kant is right, the autonomous agent obeys self-generated laws which, since rational, are also universal.

16 Bertha Wilson, undated notes prepared in response to interview questions presented in 1991 after her appointment to the common law section as scholar in residence within the Faculty of Law at University of Ottawa.

17 In 1999 University of Toronto Faculty of Law could engage in celebrating its fifty years of modern legal education without a hint of irony or any apparent awareness of the anachronism this represented in a postmodern era. A brief note on the relationship between modernism and legal formalism may be

useful here. Legal formalism is grounded in Platonic and Kantian doctrines of rationality which preceded modernism but gained strength from the modernist establishment of the study of law as a science. The term modernism reflects the notion that the coherence and unity of law make it amenable to rational study as a science, and this is the idea which spread from Harvard under Dean Langdell in the 1870s throughout North American law schools but was not firmly established in Canada until it was adopted at University of Toronto in 1949.

Legal positivism began to nudge out formalism as the mainstream approach to legal analysis during the 1950s. Positivism acknowledges in a limited way the plurality of law associated with Critical Legal Studies and postmodernism in so far as the positivists believe that law may embody goals extrinsic to itself, such as the wealth maximization of the law and economics school. Positivists distinguish between the law which exists and which the judge must apply, and the law that ought to exist. Owen Fiss and Ronald Dworkin (with his formalist ideal of law as a seamless web) are probably the pre-eminent scholars in this field now.

18   Brian Dickson, 'Madame Justice Wilson: Trailblazer for Justice,' *Dalhousie Law Journal* 15, no.1 (1992), 18.
19   Charles Jencks, *What Is Post-Modernism?* (London: St Martin's Press, 1986).
20   This phrase was used by Lord Sankey, British jurist in *Edward* v. *The Attorney-General of Canada* [1930] AC 124 (PC), the famous 'Persons case' in which the Privy Council overruled the Canadian Supreme Court to find that women are indeed persons and as such eligible to be appointed to the Canadian Senate. And this is a horticultural metaphor which Wilson herself expands upon in 'The Making of a Constitution,' a speech which she delivered first at the ninth annual conference of the National Association of Women Judges held in Seattle, Washington, 11 October 1987 and again at the University of Edinburgh conference on the Constitutional Protection of Hugh Rights in May 1988. See *Speeches*, 521, where she wrote, citing Lord Sankey: the courts, he urged, should not 'cut down the provisions of the Act by a narrow and technical construction, but rather give it a large and liberal interpretation.' And so Canada's constitution was to be a living tree. The judges would supervise and tend its growth; they were to be judicial gardeners to the nation. Changes in approach were to be seen as new branches, new leaves and new roots.
21   Bertha Wilson, 'The Scottish Enlightenment: The Third Shumiatcher Lecture in "The Law as Literature",' *Saskatchewan Law Review* 51, no.2 (1987), 252.
22   I have borrowed these ideas and some of the language which expresses them

from Kenneth McRoberts, *Misconceiving Canada: The Struggle for Canadian Unity* (Toronto: Oxford University Press, 1997).

23 Bertha Wilson, 'Law in Society: The Principle of Sexual Equality,' *Manitoba Law Journal* 13, no. 2 (1983), 224.

24 I am drawing here on the legislative history outlined in Wilson, 'Law in Society,' and also 'Human Rights Legislation in Canada: Its Origin, Development and Interpretation,' *University of Western Ontario Law Review* 15, (1973), 21.

25 Schedule B to the Canada Act (U.K.), 1982, c.11, came into force on 17 April 1982.

26 There has been very little scholarly writing on the history of legal theory or the history of legal ideology in Canada. Some Canadian legal historians who have raised the issue include: R.C.B. Risk, 'Prospectus for Canadian Legal History,' *Dalhousie Law Journal* 1 (1973), 228; Graham Parker, 'The Masochism of the Legal Historian,' *University of Toronto Law Journal* 24 (1974), 300,306; Barry Wright, 'The Ideological Dimensions of Law in Upper Canada,' *Papers Presented at the Canadian Law in History Conference* (Ottawa: Carleton University, 1987), 373; Louis A. Knafla and Susan W.S. Binnie, 'Beyond the State: Law and Legal Pluralism in the Making of Modern Societies,' in *Law, Society and the States*, Knafla and Binnie, eds. (Toronto: University of Toronto Press, 1995).

27 Shalin M. Sugunasiri, 'Contextualism: The Supreme Court's New Standards of Judicial Analysis and Accountability,' *Dalhousie Law Journal* 1 (1999), 128.

CHAPTER 7

1 Some of the information in this account is derived from a pamphlet, *The Supreme Court of Canada* (Ottawa: Supply and Services Canada, 1980) included among Bertha Wilson's personal papers. Information directly relating to the swearing-in ceremony and her first hearing is in part derived from 'New person on Supreme Court grateful for job of her dreams,' Ottawa *Citizen*, 31 March 1982. As John Wilson pointed out, the news report got it wrong; it was no dream of Bertha Wilson's to go to the Supreme Court although it may well have been a dream fulfilled for the women's groups who had lobbied so vigorously for the appointment.

2 Included among the Wilson clipping collection is a cartoon from the Ottawa *Citizen* by Rusins dated 6 March 1982 showing Bertha Wilson sitting in a spotlight on the far right (as one faces the bench) with several of the judges conferring towards the centre of the bench. The cutline reads, 'Who's going to tell her it's always been the junior member's job to fetch the coffee?'

3 *Shell Oil Company* v. *Commissioner of Patents* [1982] 2 SCR 536.

4 Lamer made these comments on the occasion of the unveiling of the portrait of Bertha Wilson on 9 December 1999.

5 Wilson has provided a rare account of this process. See Bertha Wilson, 'Decision-making in the Supreme Court,' *University of Toronto Law Journal* 36 (1986), 227 generally and especially 236. The speech was initially delivered at the University of Toronto as the David B. Goodman Lectures; Wilson says, in fact, that it is the single piece of her academic writing in greatest demand in the academic community.

So unusual was it for a judge to open a window on these internal procedures that Wilson was criticized for doing so in a report of the lectures written by Peter Calamai and published in the Ottawa *Citizen* on November 27 and 30; see 'Justice Bertha Wilson: odd judge out in the Supreme Court.' Calamai characterized her as a rebel judge exposing a serious split and an intellectual donnybrook on the Court. Wilson, stung, wrote a sharply worded rebuke which was published in the *Citizen* several days later in which she asserted her intention to provide a rational and objective description of the decision-making process. She wrote, 'I am not a "rebel" judge nor do I aspire to be one; that is not how legitimate dissent is characterized on a collegial court where differing views are accepted with courtesy and respect.'

For my account of the process by which the Supreme Court judges formulated their decisions during Wilson's years on the court, I rely also upon Bertha Wilson's 'Remarks to Visitors to our Courts,' an unpublished informal speech probably delivered in 1990. I also interviewed a number of Wilson's colleagues on the Supreme Court. Although it is clear from these interviews that Wilson's colleagues did not always agree with her approaches, what was also evident was the esteem and respect in which she is uniformly held; equally apparent is the palpable decency and high principle of all the individuals who occupy these positions.

6 Wilson had believed that all of the bench books were discarded at the time she stepped down from the Supreme Court of Canada in late 1990; however, on deposit in the National Archives of Canada in the Bertha Wilson papers (MG 35 B8, not yet catalogued or assigned permanent numbered storage boxes) was discovered an almost complete set. I am grateful to Dr Marianne McLean, Lucie Paquet, and Ross McKay of the National Archives for their cooperation in permitting me to make extensive use of this material.

7 Bertha Wilson, 'Remarks to Visitors to our Court.'

8 David Vienneau, '"Conservative" judge quits Supreme Court,' *Toronto Star*, December 1988.

9 That is Wilson's recollection, but according to McIntyre, he had bet Bora Laskin a bottle of Scotch that Wilson would be appointed and won.

10 In a telephone conversation Gerald LaForest said of Wilson, 'We admired each other and improved each other's judgments by fighting over them.'

11 Collegiality and congeniality are, in Wilson's own mind, two very different matters. On the one hand, it ought to be possible to have congenial (or friendly) relationships without affecting mutual respect for the collegial duty of independent decision-making. And this also implies that an inability to agree is consistent with collegiality and ought not to affect the atmosphere of congeniality on the Court. Gerald LaForest was a great admirer of Brian Dickson because he maintained a happy court by holding many meetings where everything was on the table; in LaForest's opinion, Dickson achieved efficiency by permitting none of the inevitable misunderstandings about small things to fester.

12 According to Wilson, 'the trouble with the kind of congeniality of the like relating to like because they played the same sports, was that ... tended to carry over and you had the group approach to discussing the judgments, the same people would get together to discuss and those who weren't part of that didn't have the benefit of that private intimate discussion and exchange of views.'

13 In fact, as Peter McCormick points out, Laskin led the Supreme Court to its lowest rate of dissents since the Second World War and the rate of dissents continued to decline under Dickson: see Peter McCormick, *Canada's Courts* (Toronto: James Lorimer, 1994), 95–9, where McCormick also takes into consideration the decline in case load and the increase in panel size, which are more usually correlated with the increase in the number of dissenting judgments.

14 In an article by Bindman, Cory was quoted as saying: 'There's a conscious desire now to try and achieve greater consensus. We're hoping to try, with the conscience of everybody. There's a recognition that this is a very real problem and something should be done about it' (Stephen Bindman, 'Decision-making in the Inner Sanctum,' *Ottawa Citizen*, 12 April 1992).

15 McLachlin has been quoted as saying that excessive pressure to unanimity would interfere with judicial independence and that there should be no pressure to eliminate necessary differences serving good purposes since, 'it's not so important where you stand as where you're going' – an opinion which is similar to Wilson's position concerning the value of dissents and concurrences to the future development of the common law. See Stephen Bindman, 'S.C.C. is trying to reduce number of concurring decisions,' *Lawyers Weekly*, 23 August 1991, 2.

16 Iacobucci has always been of the view that the Court as an institution is far more important than any individual judge who is sitting on it. In his opinion,

the Court has moved substantially to more reconferencing in order to build consensus.

17 Ritchie was seventy-two and close to the mandatory judicial retirement age of seventy-five. Chouinard had been ill for some time before he stepped down shortly before he died in 1987. Estey was absent for an extended period of time heading up the Estey Commission before he left in April 1988. Beetz, also suffering from cancer, stepped down in November 1988. LeDain, appointed in 1984 after Laskin's retirement, was hospitalized from time to time; ultimately his health compelled him to resign in November 1988. McIntyre left a month later at the age of seventy. At that point only Dickson (by then seventy-two, wounded during the war and frequently struggling to cope with his pain) and Lamer, then fifty-five, remained on the Court from the original 1982 complement.

Jean-Marie Plourde, Wilson's court attendant, pointed out that between 1982 and 1990–1 there was not a single year that a judge was not missing at the Court through sickness, death, or special commissions.

18 Jean-Marie Plourde, who served as court attendant to Wilson from 1983 until the end of her career on the bench, came to the Supreme Court after a career as a chief warrant officer in the Ministry of National Defence; he was shocked at how little support staff was accorded a Supreme Court justice in comparison with the staffing routinely supplied to senior officers in the military.

19 The relationship between the court administration and the secretaries seems not to have been particularly pleasant. The secretaries worked long hours and were provided with few amenities. There was, for example, a small common room allocated to the secretaries but no place to lie down. When they sought the use of a sofa which had been discarded from one of the judges' offices and was languishing in storage in the basement, they were peremptorily refused. Their request for a microwave oven to heat up a meal when they were detained over the dinner hour was also denied out of hand. Wilson was enraged by this pettiness; she took it upon herself to price a suitable microwave, and, having divided the cost by nine, set out to raise the funds among the judges. She went first of all into Dickson's office and he had already written his cheque for his donation before he fully understood the situation. No further donations were required; Dickson made one phone call and the microwave was quickly obtained out of the administrative budget.

20 Wilson's Supreme Court clerks included: 1982, Patricia Rowbottom; 1982–3, Hugh Verrier and Philip Bryden; 1982–4, Philip Bryden, Stephen Perry, and Diane Teeple; 1984–5, Ed Morgan and Moira McConnell; 1985–6, Hester Lessard and David Loukidelis; 1986–7, Tanya Lee and David Stratas; 1987–8, Alan Donovan and Jim Phillips; 1988–9, Ed Holt and Kent Roach; 1989–90

(the first year that each judge was assigned three clerks) Audrey Macklin, Karen Thompson, and Robert Yalden; 1990, Douglas Alderson, Colin Baxter, and Mary Eaton; and 1991 (continuing to assist Wilson after her resignation with the six months' period during which judges complete work on judgments arising out of their final cases), Mary Eaton. Wilson expresses immense appreciation for all of the assistance her law clerks gave over the years; and yet, if the Supreme Court justices tended to be of an age at which ill health could interfere with their abilities to function, the law clerks were of an age where problems concerning personal relationships (strained by absences, given that law clerks were also uprooted and flown into Ottawa from every corner of the country) sometimes presented difficulties for them in focusing fully on the tasks at hand.

21 Plourde's account of that memorable conversation, which he recounted to me during my interview with him, is very similar to Wilson's.

22 Plourde was touched when the Wilsons tucked a generous gift into a bon voyage card to help defray expenses on a trip to Africa to visit his doctor son; and he was very moved when Bertha would greet him after his vacations with an affectionate hug and a sigh of relief that he was back on the job. Never once during all of her years on the Supreme Court did Plourde see Wilson raise her voice or lose her temper, he reports, no matter what the provocation.

Plourde became seriously ill in 1995, compelling his retirement. He assisted the Wilson with their 1997 move from their house to the apartment, carrying boxes, scrubbing out the hearth in their new fireplace, and helping them arrange for quantities of bookshelving to be installed.

23 At first, according to Jim Phillips, the deadline was 5:00 p.m. Fridays. Later, by 1989 when Yalden was one of her clerks, it had been moved back to noon in order that she might take a few hours for personal chores. She was sixty-six that year and Yalden was astonished at the pace of work that Wilson and the other judges past the conventional age for retirement were expected to keep up. It was obvious to him that she was often totally exhausted by the end of the week.

24 I derived this account from the interviews with Plourde, Jim Phillips, and Moira McConnell.

25 There are two large corner offices, one for the chief justice and the other for the senior puisne judge. For most of her years on the Court Wilson was assigned the relatively small office adjacent to the senior puisne office. The office had been inhabited by Dickson before he was appointed chief justice in 1984 and when she moved in, Wilson had considerable additional bookshelving installed.

26 Rob Yalden was one clerk who not only made a point of arriving early in the morning, when he knew Wilson would be in her chambers, but also tried quite deliberately to adopt Wilson's characteristic vocabulary in writing his memos so that she would find it easier to assimilate the arguments he was making.

27 Bertha Wilson, 'Remarks Made to Law Clerks on the Occasion of Their Orientation Program,' (emphasis added).

28 Wilson's special judgment-writing ability was recognized by her colleagues. LaForest, for example, commended her simple, clear, and beautiful style which in his opinion was particularly suited to the conviction with which she expressed her opinions.

29 Claire Bernstein, 'Behind the scenes with judges who rule Canada's highest court,' *Toronto Star*, 22 May 1990, A17.

30 This account is distilled from interviews with a number of the Supreme Court judges; some unattributed comments were made for background information only.

31 See Stephen Bindman, 'Decision-making in the inner sanctum.' Sopinka is quoted as saying: 'When someone has announced they will be writing a dissent it's a courtesy that nobody concurs with the majority judgment until they've read the dissent, again to give the dissenter a chance to persuade the court that they're right.' Sopinka added that one of the greatest challenges of the job is 'to write not only the judgment that you think is the right result but one that will also persuade your colleagues because they are all really strong-minded individuals with their own views and they're bound to have their own way of expressing something.'

32 Hester Lessard was one clerk aware that Wilson was frequently excluded from informal conferencing among her colleagues, that support she had expected to be forthcoming had evaporated when her opinion was circulated because of private discussions in which she had not been included, and that consequently she was compelled to rely upon her clerks for information.

33 Chief Justice Dickson tried to create the collegial court which had evolved out of the social interactions around the lunch table and in the continuing legal education seminars at the Ontario Court of Appeal, but was unable to do so. McLachlin acknowledges that there is a very human tendency to want to be on the winning team; that is why she considers 'know thyself' to be an important adage for a judge and memos useful in the decision-making process.

34 Wilson did prepare a five-page memo to put the issue on the agenda for the Judges' Retreat held shortly after her retirement while she was still completing her final judgments. In it she makes reference to a July 1990 memo to Lamer on the same issue, specifying that tackling the lobbying issue was in

her view of utmost importance in the functioning of the court and should supersede concerns about the management role.

CHAPTER 8

1 Bertha Wilson, 'The Making of a Constitution: Approaches to Judicial Interpretation,' in *Speeches*, 523. Wilson acknowledged that judges, in scrutinizing the legislation, have a particular duty to scrutinize at the same time their own assumptions and ideologies as these might affect their interpretations of the legislation and their understandings of anti-majoritarian rights:

> As Canadian judges we are appointed, not elected, officials. There would be something deeply illegitimate about our forays into judicial review of legislation if all there was to them was a desire to substitute our own personal values for those of our duly elected representatives. We cannot placidly assume that by some mysterious process we, the judges, have been given access to the true answers to fundamental social and political dilemmas, ... While things are slowly changing, it cannot be said that judges on this continent are broadly representative of the general public. There is, therefore, no plausible justification for us to substitute *our* personal values and *our* moral choices for those of the elected legislature.

2 See Bertha Wilson, 'Women, the Family and the Constitutional Protection of Privacy,' *Queen's Law Journal* 17 (1992), 11: 'Taking a contextual approach to constitutional adjudication, as I believe the Supreme Court has done, helps us to see that inequality defies doctrinal categorization and that all constitutional guarantees must be expounded in a way that is responsive to contemporary reality ... Respect for precedent is not, in my view, sufficient reason to adhere to tradition if the result is to perpetuate inequalities.'

3 Wilson confirmed that it was always important to her and to Dickson to tie any new variation in the law to an existing principle. But the principle that the courts must interpret the Charter to strike a balance between flexibility and certainty is one which was established by Justice Estey in the very first Supreme Court Charter case, *Law Society of Upper Canada* v. *Skapinker* [1984] 1 SCR 357 at 365–6 and reiterated by Chief Justice Dickson in the first section 8 search and seizure case, *Hunter* v. *Southam* [1984] 2 SCR 145 at 155.

4 Charles Taylor, 'The Politics of Recognition,' in Amy Guttman, ed., *Multiculturalism: Examining the Politics of Recognition* (Princeton: Princeton University Press, 1994), esp. 33–4, 52, and 60.

5 Nitya Iyer, 'Categorical Denials: Equality Rights and the Shaping of Social Identity,' *Queen's Law Journal* 19 (1994), 179.

6 See, for example, Cornel West, 'Black Culture and Postmodernism,' in Barbara Kruger and Phil Mariania, eds., *Remaking History* (Bay Press: 1989).

7 In *McKinney* v. *University of Guelph* [1990] 3 SCR 229, Wilson outlines how the Charter became part of Canadian life:

Canadians recognize that government has traditionally had and continues to have an important role to play in the creation and preservation of a just Canadian society. The state has been looked to and has responded to demands that Canadians be guaranteed adequate health care, access to education and a minimum level of financial security to name but a few examples. It is, in my view, untenable to suggest that freedom is co-extensive with the absence of government. Experience shows the contrary, that freedom has often required the intervention and protection of government against private action.

This passage in its entirety is one of the most philosophical to be found in any of Wilson's judgments; Professor Lederman wrote from Queen's to congratulate her upon it.

8 *Bhinder* v. *CNR* [1985] 2 SCR 561. The case was heard in early 1985 and came up through the courts before the section 15 equality provisions of the Charter became law.

9 *Ontario Human Rights Commission and O'Malley* v. *Simpsons-Sears Ltd.* [1985] 2 SCR 536.

10 *Alberta Human Rights Commission* v. *Central Alberta Dairy Pool* [1990] 2 SCR 489.

11 *O'Malley*, at 555.

12 *Re Singh and Minister of Employment and Immigration* (1985), 17 DLR (4th), 422. I have also reviewed a series of memos concerning the issue of procedural difficulties involved in the leave to appeal in this matter deposited at the National Archives together with the bench memo prepared for Wilson by one of her clerks.

13 Ann Silversides, 'Oral hearings for refugee claims urged in report,' *Globe and Mail*, 5 June 1984, 14.

14 Everyone has the right to life, liberty, and security of the person and the right not to be deprived thereof except in accordance with the principles of fundamental justice.

15 Bertha Wilson, 'Constitutional Law – Section 7,' in *Speeches*, 451–2.

16 A few months after *Singh*, in the *Motor Vehicle Reference Case* [1985] 2 SCR 486, the Court established that the section 7 principles of fundamental justice required strict scrutiny to determine whether substantive rights had also been infringed by an impugned statute. Nevertheless, Wilson found herself unable to read economic rights into section 7 analysis when she had the

opportunity to do so in the prostitution cases that came before the courts during her tenure; however, the concept of psychological integrity as an aspect of security of the person suggested in *Singh* was over a decade later explicitly endorsed and incorporated into a Supreme Court child welfare case which may yet lead to that interpretation.

17 Victor Malarek, 'Court ruling on refugees wins praise,' *Globe and Mail*, 5 April 1985.

18 See Theresa Boyle, 'Refugee funding demanded,' *Toronto Star*, 11 February 2000, A10; for example, costs in 2000 arising from the settlement of the 12,000 refugees who make claims in Ontario were estimated at $20 million for social assistance, $6.8 million for legal aid, $4.5 million for housing, and over $100 million to assume responsibility for defaulting sponsors.

19 *R. v. Big M Drug Mart Ltd.* [1985] 1 SCR 360 was the first significant post-Charter freedom of religion case to go up to the Supreme Court. It challenged the federal Lord's Day Act which by forbidding the sale of goods on a Sunday was held to infringe the section 2 (a) guarantee in a manner not justifiable under the balancing provisions set out in section 1. Wilson agreed with the reasoning of the Court and accepted Dickson's definition of freedom of religion, which includes the right to entertain chosen religious beliefs, to declare those beliefs openly without fear of reprisal, and the right to manifest religious beliefs openly through worship, practice, teaching and dissemination.

20 *Edwards Books and Art Ltd.* v. *The Queen* [1986] 2 SCR 713.

21 Ibid. Wilson's comments here go to the definition of freedom of religion and its intersection with other Charter rights guarantees such as freedom of association.

22 In a memo dated 18 September 1986 addressed to the chief justice and copied to members of the Court, Wilson indicated that she agreed with the legislative purpose of a common pause day but took issue only with the disparate impacts of a uniform legislative pause day; she commented, 'there was no actual inference with the complainants' own religious practices, simply a price tag attached to them,' which she considered at that point to be more of an interference with section 7 liberty rights than section 2 (a) freedom of religion rights.

23 'Sunday shopping: not yet,' *Ottawa Citizen*,19 December 1986, A8; 'The Sunday laws,' *Globe and Mail*, 19 December 1986, A6; and 'A valid law but a bad one,' *Toronto Star*, 19 December 1986, A22.

24 *Bardal* v. *Globe and Mail Ltd.* (1960), 24 DLR (2d) 140 is the leading case defining these factors.

25 *Vorvis* v. *Insurance Corporation of British Columbia* [1989] 1 SCR 1085.

26 Ibid., at 1129, 1127.

27 Ibid., at 1130.
28 *Wallace* v. *United Grain Growers* [1997] SCJ No. 94.
29 *Andrews* v. *Law Society of British Columbia* [1989] 1 SCR 143.
30 This is the provision which limits the absoluteness of rights by providing for some balancing of social policy concerns. The case of *R.* v. *Oakes* [1986] 1 SCR 103 had established the test for application of section 1. The *Oakes* test provides that the onus of proving any limitation on a Charter right is reasonable and demonstrably justified in a free and democratic society rests upon the party which is seeking to uphold that limitation. First, the objective of the limitation must be pressing and substantial and relate to social concerns important enough to justify overriding a Charter right. Second, a proportionality test must be met: the means must be reasonable and justified in proportion to the importance of the objective. Proportionality is measured against three further subtests: the measure must be fair and not arbitrary, tailored to meet the legislative objective and rationally connected to that objective; the means must impair the Charter right as little as possible; and there must be proportionality between the effects of the limiting measure and the objective. Wilson frequently found herself in the minority at the Supreme Court because she believed it essential to apply the *Oakes* test with utmost stringency.
31 *Andrews*, at 152–3. It was Justice Stone of the American Supreme Court who had coined the phrase, 'discrete and insular minority,' in *United States* v. *Carolene Products Co.* 304 US 144 (1938).
32 *McKinney* v. *University of Guelph* [1990] 2 SCR 229 was decided at the same time as *Harrison* v. *University of British Columbia* [1990] 3 SCR 451; *Stoffman* v. *Vancouver General Hospital* [1990] 3 SCR 483; and *Douglas/Kwantlen Faculty Association* v. *Douglas College* [1990] 3 SCR 570.
33 Bertha Wilson, 'Women and the Canadian Charter of Rights and Freedoms,' address to the Tenth Biennial Conference of the National Association of Women and the Law, Vancouver, February 1993, 6.
34 Cited in *McKinney*, at 322; emphasis added by Wilson.
35 Ibid., at 370. Of the other justices on the panel, Cory adopted these tests most enthusiastically. According to Rob Yalden, who was clerking with Bertha Wilson that year, Wilson believed very strongly 'that it was incumbent on the court to try to articulate clear tests; she was very sensitive to the fact that people have to work with these judgments and that you therefore need to try to be clear and set out approaches as best you could.'
36 Ibid., at 415–16. Wilson's analysis is consistent throughout all of these associated cases but most thoroughly developed in *McKinney*.
37 *Sociéte des Acadiens du Nouveau-Brunswick* v. *Association for Parents for Fairness in Education* [1986] 1 SCR 549.
38 Ibid., at 627.

39 Ibid., at 620.

40 Ibid., at 644.

41 See, for example, 'Not all disappointing,' *Montreal Gazette*, 3 May 1986, B2; and 'Shrinking the fabric of Canada,' Ottawa *Citizen*, 2 May 1986, A8.

42 As Wilson concluded her 1993 speech, 'Women and the Canadian Charter of Rights and Freedoms,' 'I remain an eternal optimist about the Charter, ... We just have to learn how to make more effective use of it. In today's society change is occurring so rapidly and radically that the law and the courts cannot keep up with it. But we must! The challenge of change is the watchword of our time; to march to the beat of its drum is to keep pace with no less than the tempo of history itself.'

43 *Martin v. Chapman* [1983] 1 SCR 365.

44 Wilson wrote for Ritchie, Dickson, and Beetz; dissenting were Estey, McIntyre, and Lamer.

45 *Racine v. Woods* [1983] 2 SCR 173.

46 It was, however, heard by the minimum quorum of five judges; Ritchie, Dickson, Estey, McIntyre, and Wilson.

47 *Guérin v. The Queen* [1984] 2 SCR 335.

48 Ibid., at 354.

49 *R. v. Sparrow* [1990] 1 SCR 1075 (SCC).

50 *R. v. Sioui* [1990] 1 SCR 1025.

51 *Mitchell v. Peguis Indian Band* [1990] 2 SCR 85.

52 *Nowegijick v. The Queen* [1983] 1 SCR 29.

53 LaForest and Wilson were concerned that if it is impossible to collect for a debt on a private contract with an Indian, aboriginal economic development would be stunted because lenders would understandably be reluctant to loan money. As LaForest recalls, Wilson considered that Dickson had simply gone too far in this instance.

54 *R. v. Horseman* [1990] 1 SCR 901.

55 Yalden came to work for Wilson with considerably more background experience in the role of the civil servant than most clerks. He had had summer jobs working in the Speaker's Office and with the Privy Council Office during the Trudeau years. He studied law first at Oxford and later at University of Toronto. It was Toronto administrative law professor Hudson Janisch (Yalden's chief mentor) who had written the letter of recommendation supporting Yalden's application to clerk at the Supreme Court. When Wilson called Janisch to check his references, however, she cut past Yalden's sterling academic record to ask the question which matter to her most: 'But Hudson, will he do?' What she wanted to know was not whether he was bright and hardworking but 'Will he do whatever is necessary, will he get along with the other clerks?' Yalden was comfortable with Wilson's own attitude that to

work is to be formal, professional, and of service to others. Nevertheless, on a point of principle such as *Horseman* raised, he was as incapable of keeping completely silent as Wilson herself would have been.

56 *Horseman*, at 919.

CHAPTER 9

1 Bertha Wilson's male colleagues have all been eager to draw attention to John Wilson's remarkable character. At the same time there has been a scarcely concealed tone of incredulity that John (whose intellectual abilities are fully apparent to anyone who meets him) had been willing to reduce what was a more typical entitlement to male privilege that most men his contemporaries took for granted within marriage.

2 Bertha Wilson, 'Will Women Judges Really Make a Difference?,' *Osgoode Hall Law Journal* 28, no.3 (1990), 515.

3 *New Brunswick (Minister of Health and Community Services)* v. *G. (J.)*, [1999] SCJ No. 47.

4 Mary Jane Mossman, ' "The Family" in the Work of Madame Justice Wilson,' *Dalhousie Law Journal* 15, no.1 (1992), 142. Mossman is critical of this stance which she seems to find merely naive and romanticized, but it is very much in accordance with the philosophy of eighteenth-century Scotland which grounded the potential for social improvement in the advances of scientific knowledge and the duty of improving oneself in order to benefit society as a whole. In this instance, of course, Wilson was relying upon the psychological assessments which indicated that the parents were capable of cooperating in the best interests of their children.

5 Bertha Wilson, 'A Choice of Values,' *Canadian Bar Journal* 448 (1961), 448, 455. This notion that framing can be a determinative step in skewing judgment is related to the Aristotelian notion of rhetoric as an integral element of phronesis. Certainly framing of the cause of action was the determinative factor in the *Pelech* trilogy decisions for which Wilson was so heartily criticized by her feminist supporters.

6 Bertha Wilson, 'State Intervention in the Family,' in R.S. Abella and Melvin L. Rothman, eds., *Justice Beyond Orwell* (Montreal: Edition Y. Blais, 1985), 355 ff. Wilson discusses Lord Devlin's Maccabaean Lecture in Jurisprudence of 1959, 'The Enforcement of Morals,' and the reply by Professor H.L.A. Hart in which Hart pointed out that conventional moralities change over time often without damage to their originating societies.

7 Ibid., at 357 (emphasis in original).

8 Bertha Wilson, 'Respecting the Law and Our Democratic Institutions,' Jackson Lecture 1985, The Ontario Institute for Studies in Education, 10–11.

9 Wilson ended the speech with a ringing call to action:

> The plea I am making this evening is that while remaining ever vigilant
> we should not allow ourselves to be infected by an insidious cynicism or
> be frightened into despair and darkness. John Ruskin's thunder on the
> horizon, you will remember, presaged as well the dawn. Let us respect
> the democratic heritage which is ours to hand on to future generations.
> As the Queen said, "In this age of rapid change, the continuity of our
> institutions becomes of profound importance." And I maintain that it is
> up to each one of us in our place and station to cherish and guard and
> defend these bastions of democratic freedom, for the fabric of civilized
> society is a very fragile thing. What can one person do, you may ask.
> Edward Everett Hale gave the only answer:
>> I am only one man, but I am one man. I cannot do everything, but I
>> can do something. And what I can do, I ought to do. And what I ought
>> to do by the grace of God, I will do.

10 Note in Wilson's handwriting initialled 'BW' and attached to 'Memo to the
Court from Estey J. re Leave Application – *Pelech* v. *Pelech*, dated 24 May 1985.
11 Bertha Wilson, 'The Variation of Support Orders,' in R.S. Abella and C.
L'Heureux-Dubé, eds., *Family Law: Dimensions of Justice* (Toronto: Butterworth, 1983), 38, 42.
12 Ibid., at 50 (emphasis added).
13 Mossman, ' "The Family",' 181.
14 *Ross* v. *Ross* (1984), 39 RFL (2d) 51 per Matas J.A.
15 *Pelech* v. *Pelech* [1987] 1 SCR, 849–51.
16 *Richardson* v. *Richardson* [1987] 1 SCR 857, 871–2.
17 *Caron* v. *Caron* [1987] 1 SCR 892.
18 Ibid., at 903.
19 *Moge* v. *Moge* [1993] 1 WWR 481 (SCC).
20 *Bracklow* v. *Bracklow* [1999] 1 SCR 420; [1999] SCJ No. 14.
21 Bertha Wilson, 'Children: The Casualties of a Failed Marriage,' *UBC Law
Review* 19, no. 2 (1985), 245–70.
22 *Frame* v. *Smith* [1987] 2 SCR 99; the bench notes for this case together with
several memos prepared by clerk David Loukidelis have survived among
the materials deposited at the National Archives.
23 Ibid., at 136:

> (i) The fiduciary has scope for the exercise of some discretion or
> power.
> (ii) The fiduciary can unilaterally exercise that power or discretion so
> as to affect the beneficiary's legal or practical interests.

(iii) The beneficiary is peculiarly vulnerable to or at the mercy of the fiduciary holding the discretion or power.

24 Wilson disagreed strongly that reversing the custody decision could ever be a proper solution to the problem of blocked access.

25 *Re Beson* v. *Director of Child Welfare (Nfld)* [1982] 2 SCR 715 at 716.

26 This was another case with a bare quorum of five judges sitting. Wilson considered 'the attitude of my colleagues was really strange because, you know, it was as if they didn't realize that these cases dealing with the future lives of children were probably the most important things that we could deal with.'

27 *R.* v. *Lavallée* [1990] 1 SCR 852.

28 Ibid., 871–2.

29 Sopinka concurred in the result (that the appeal should be allowed), wishing only to establish that expert opinion based in part upon suspect information and in part upon admitted facts or facts sought to be proved ought to be admitted with the lack of independent proof going only to the weight to be given such evidence. In this instance, however, Sopinka agreed that the trial judge had not erred in admitting the evidence and that he had properly instructed the jury as to the weighing of that evidence.

30 Bertha Wilson, 'Women and the Canadian Charter of Righters and Freedoms,' address to the National Association of Women and the Law, Vancouver, February 1993, 10–11.

31 Bertha Wilson, 'Family Violence,' *Canadian Journal of Women and the Law*, 5, 1 (1992), 140–1.

32 *R.* v. *Hill*, 25 CCC (3d) 322 SCC.

33 Bertha Wilson, 'The Making of a Constitution: Approaches to Judicial Interpretation,' in *Speeches*, 381.

34 *Reference Re Criminal Code* (Man.) [1990] 1 SCR 1123, in which a question was asked about the constitutionality of Criminal Code provisions aimed at controlling prostitution; *R.* v. *Stagnitta* [1990] 1 SCR 1226, in which Charter guarantees were examined in the light of a charge against a prostitute who had communicated for the purposes of selling her sexual services in public; and *R.* v. *Skinner* [1990] 1 SCR 1235, the john's case in which a person seeking to purchase sexual services was charged with communicating for the purposes of prostitution.

35 *Reference Re Criminal Code*, at 1204.

36 Ibid., at 1214 (emphasis in original).

37 *Reference Re Public Service Employee Relations Act (Alta.)* [1987] 1 SCR 313.

38 *Skinner*, at 1249.

39 'The court and the soliciting law,' *Globe and Mail*, 6 June 1990, A6.

40 *R. v. Morgentaler* [1988] 1 SCR 30.

41 Bertha Wilson, 'Women, the Family, and the Constitutional Protection of Privacy,' paper given at Hong Kong Bill of Rights Conference, June 1991.

42 See Lynda Hurst, 'Reverend's abortion stand a humane one,' *Toronto Star*, 26 February 1985, B1. Timothy Eaton was Allan Beattie's church (and very much the church of the Toronto establishment); Bertha Wilson had spoken there, and Stan Lucyk was a good friend to both the Wilsons.

43 It was Professor DeLloyd Guth of the University of Manitoba who approached Chief Justice Dickson and then spoke to the Supreme Court judges (too late for preservation of most of the *Morgentaler* correspondence) about retaining their documents as resource materials for legal and social historians.

44 *Morgentaler*, at 161–2.

45 Ibid., at 171. Some women believed that Wilson, although a woman, lacked the experience qualifying her to comment on this issue. There was an unattributed newsclipping among the Wilsons' personal papers of a letter to the editor from a member of REAL women condemning the *Morgantaler* decision and slamming Wilson by pointing out that she had never had any children of her own.

46 In an interview I asked: 'It seems to me that at the very ending of this judgment you leave the door open, that if there were further scientific information about the viability of a child that you might revise, or would have wished to revise your opinion? She replied, 'Yes, I think so, because there was a lot of new knowledge at that time, even. About, you know, how early a foetus could be thought viable. It is kind of a fluid situation from a physical point of view.' I followed up, 'If new scientific information rolled back the time of the viability of the foetus to the first couple of weeks and that fertilized embryo could be harvested without much intrusion, ... do you think you might revise your opinion?' She replied, 'I don't know. I am not sure. I am sure that my opinion would in fact change.'

47 Michele Landsberg, for example, wrote, 'At a stroke, the Supreme Court of Canada has wiped out one of our country's meanest injustices. The abortion law, a shabby and cringing deal made among men who rule, and made at the expense of women, has been named for what it is: painful, arbitrary and unfair.' See Michele Landsberg, 'Jubilation: the shabby abortion law has been struck down,' *Globe and Mail*, 30 January 1988.

Morgentaler himself made a number of intemperate remarks in which he referred to anti-abortionists as stupid and ignorant and compared them to ayatollahs and fascists: See Mark Kennedy, 'Morgentaler calls opponents stupid,' Ottawa *Citizen*, 29 January 1988, A3.

48 Henry Morgentaler to Bertha Wilson, 14 April 1993; from the Wilsons' personal papers; Bertha Wilson to Henry Morgentaler, 3 May 1993.

CHAPTER 10

1 See Mary Gooderham, 'Law out of reach of many, Supreme Court judge says,'*Globe and Mail*, 16 April 1985; on this occasion, Wilson was responding to questions from the audience after she had delivered the Jackson lecture, 'Respecting the Law and Our Democratic Institutions,' at the Ontario Institute for Studies in Education in 1985.
2 Mr Justice Dennis Lane of the Superior Court of Justice of Ontario (who himself had spent five years on the *Texas Gulf Sulphur* case and was thoroughly familiar with Wilson's work at Oslers) commented fondly on this pragmatic element of Wilson's character.
3 Maureen Maloney, 'Economic Actors in the Work of Madame Justice Wilson,' Dalhousie *Law Journal* 15 (1991), 197.
4 Bertha Wilson, 'Leave to Appeal to the Supreme Court of Canada,' *Advocates Quarterly* 4, no.1 (1983), 1; the paper was originally presented in a speech delivered at the Lawyers' Club in Toronto on 6 January 1983.
5 Philip Bryden, now a distinguished scholar in administrative and constitutional law at University of British Columbia, had at that time practised law in a New York practice specializing in anti-trust litigation and then worked as a political aide in Ottawa to Gerald Regan during his stints as minister of labour and secretary of state; when he was taken on as a clerk in Wilson's chambers in January 1983 his skills and experience were particularly suited to this task.
6 Here Wilson is borrowing the language of Chief Justice Bora Laskin in his response to the 1975 Bill, 'The Role and Functions of Final Appellate Courts: The Supreme Court of Canada,' *Canadian Bar Review* 53 (1975), 469.
7 Bertha Wilson, 'Leave to Appeal,' 5.
8 Bertha Wilson, 'Remarks to the Civil Litigation Section of the British Columbia Bar,' in *Speeches*, 244; Bertha Wilson, 'Remarks to the Saskatoon Bar Association,' ibid., at 302.
9 The deficiency in commercial law development has been ameliorated in part as various provinces (notably Ontario, still home to the primary Canadian business community) have developed highly specialized commercial courts at the trial division level.
10 *Kamloops (City)* v. *Nielsen* [1984] 2 SCR 2; the case was heard on 22 November 1982, and the decision released on 26 July 1984.
11 McIntyre and Estey dissented.

12 *Crocker* v. *Sundance Northwest Resorts Ltd.* (1988) 51 DLR (4th) 321.

13 *V.K. Mason Construction* v. *Bank of Nova Scotia* [1985] 1 SCR 271.

14 *Hunter Engineering Co. Inc.* v. *Syncrude Canada* (1989), 57 DLR (4th) 321 (SCC).

15 Ibid., at 381.

16 *The Queen in Right of British Columbia* v. *Tener* (1985), 17 DLR (4th) 1.

17 Stroud's *Judicial Dictionary* defines *profit a prendre* as a right vested in one man of entering upon the land of another and taking therefrom a profit of the soil.

18 *LAC Minerals Ltd.* v. *International Corona Resources Ltd.* (1989) 61 DLR (4th) 14.

19 Susan Lightstone, 'Bertha Wilson, a personal view on women and the law,' *National* 12 (August-September 1993), 12.

20 *Stubart Investments Ltd.* v. *The Queen* [1984] 1 SCR 536.

21 This dictum derives from Lord Tomlin's judgment in *Inland Revenue Commissioners* v. *Duke of Westminster* [1936] AC 1 at 9.

22 *R.* v. *Eldorado Nuclear Ltd.*, *R.* v. *Uranium Canada Ltd.* [1983] 2 SCR 551.

23 Ibid. (emphasis is in the original).

24 *Molchan* v. *Omega Oil and Gas Ltd.* [1988] 1 SCR 348.

25 Ibid., at 379.

26 *Constitution Insurance Co. of Canada* v. *Kosmopoulos* (1987), 34 DLR (4th) 208.

27 Ibid., at 210.

28 The principle was first formulated in *Macaura* v. *Northern Assurance Co. Ltd.* [1975] AC 619 (HL). Macaura owned Killymoon Estate in Northern Ireland and took out five insurance policies in his own name on the estate's standing timber, which was owned by the Irish-Canadian Saw Mills Ltd. Macaura was the sole shareholder and the sole creditor. The timber was destroyed by fire, the case originally went to arbitration on a question of fraud which was not upheld, but the House of Lords subsequently held that Macaura had no insurable interest and so could not collect on his politicies.

29 *Reference Re Public Service Relations Act* [1987] 1 SCR 313; *Public Service Alliance of Canada* v. *Canada* [1987] 1 SCR 424, and *R.W.D.S.U.* v. *Saskatchewan* [1987] 1 SCR 460. Wilson wrote four memos on these cases: one to file summarizing her own thoughts, 11 October 1985; one to Chief Justice Dickson, which was also copied to members of the Court, 4 June 1986; and two more to Chief Justice Dickson, 29 July 1986.

30 Wilson cites H.W. Arthurs, 'Public Interest Labor Disputes in Canada: A Legislative Perspective,' *Buffalo Law Review* 17 (1967), 39, and 'Free Collective Bargaining in a Regulated Society,' in *The Direction of Labour Policy in Canada* (Montreal: McGill University Industrial Relations Centre, 1977).

31 *BCGEU* v. *British Columbia (Attorney General)* [1982] 2 SCR 214.

32 An injunction under certain circumstances of urgency is obtainable *ex parte,* meaning without hearing from the opposing side.

33 *Sobey's Stores* v. *Yeomans and Labour Standards Tribunal* [1989] 1 SCR 238.

34 *Re Residential Tenancies Act, 1979* [1981] 1 SCR 714. The case concerned testing the constitutional validity of residential tenancy legislation in relation to the allocation of powers to the provinces pursuant to section 96 of the Constitutional Act 1867.

35 Again, this was an instance of Wilson fortuitously having to hand a clerk with exactly the kind of expertise in historical research she required. Phillips had completed an MA in history at the University of Edinburgh and then a PhD in history at Dalhousie where he subsequently enrolled as a student in the Faculty of Law and came second in each of his three years.

36 *Lavigne* v. *OPSEU* (1991), 81 DLR (4th) 545 (SCC).

37 *Thomson Newspapers* v. *Canada* [1990] 1 SCR 425.

38 *R.* v. *McKinlay Transport* [1990] 1 SCR 627.

39 Maloney, 'Economic Actors.'

40 *Thomson,* at 457.

41 Ibid., at 460–1.

42 This provision, frequently invoked in criminal trials where there has been some error in police procedure, provides that evidence will not be admitted when it will bring the administration of justice into disrepute.

43 *Edmonton Journal* v. *Alberta (A.G.)* [1989] 2 SCR 1326.

44 See Shalin M. Sugunasiri, 'Contextualism: The Supreme Court's New Standard of Judicial Analysis and Accountability,' *Dalhousie Law Journal* 1 (1991). This article provides an outstanding account of the development which he traces back to *Edmonton Journal.*

45 *Edmonton Journal,* at 1355–6.

46 Ibid., at 1353–4.

47 *Irwin Toy* v. *Quebec (Attorney General)* [1989] 1 SCR 927.

48 *R.* v. *Keegstra* [1990] 3 SCR 697. This case concerned the constitutionality of section 319 (2) of the Criminal Code which prohibits wilful promotion of hatred against identifiable groups, allowing a defence of truth to be established by the accused on a balance of probabilities. An Alberta high-school teacher had made anti-semitic comments to his students. Dickson wrote the majority judgment, concurred in by Wilson, L'Heureux Dubé, and Gonthier, in which he held that section 319 (2) did infringe freedom of expression, given that all non-violent forms of expression are protected by section 2 (b). Nevertheless, the provision was justified on section 1 analysis because of the substantial and pressing objective of the legislation to prevent the harm caused by hate propaganda. But the Court split 4:3 with LaForest, Sopinka,

and McLachlin dissenting. Two years later, after Wilson's retirement in *R. v. Zundel* [1992] 2 SCR 731, the Court revisited the issue and split again 4:3. This time it upheld freedom of expression in the context of Criminal Code section 181 which provides for sanctions against the wilful spreading of false news likely to cause injury or mischief to the public interest. Zundel had published tracts challenging historical accounts of the Nazi holocaust under the title, 'Did Six Million Really Die?' The majority per McLachlin (including LaForest, L'Heureux-Dubé, and Sopinka) allowed the appeal on the grounds that the original purpose of the impugned legislation had not been the control of hate propaganda but rather protection of nobles from slander; that there was no social problem justifying its contemporary existence; and that the means were not proportional. Gonthier, Cory, and Iacobucci dissented, reasoning that false speech still affects community security.

CHAPTER 11

1 Mr Justice Charles Gonthier indicated that the need for a schedule to encourage prompt release of judgments was in large part obviated once the Court was at full complement; in any case, it is his opinion that both the cases and the judges' responses differ so much from context to context that any 'first in, first out' protocol could not be implemented successfully. Gonthier had spent fourteen years at the Quebec Superior Court and then a brief period at the Quebec Court of Appeal before his appointment to the Supreme Court in February 1989; based on this experience he expressed the view that one of the main differences between the task of the trial judge and the appellate judge is the interdependency on work product and the loss of the luxury of focusing on one case at a time at the appellate levels.

2 Bertha Wilson, 'Guaranteed Freedoms in a Free and Democratic Society, A New Role for the Courts,' in *Speeches*, 161.

3 *Edmonton Journal* v. *Alberta AG* [1989] 2 SCR 1326.

4 Interview with Claire L'Heureux-Dubé. The two had first met in the late 1970s when L'Heureux-Dubé helped host social evenings for the French-language seminars held every winter in Quebec that the Wilsons enjoyed attending. L'Heureux-Dubé found that the Supreme Court was still pretty much a boys' club; she took Wilson's advice and resigned herself to the necessity (despite her six years as a trial judge and eight years as an appellate judge) of proving herself all over again.

5 Lamer, who announced his resignation from the Supreme Court in August 1999, has been outspoken about the effects of judge-bashing on the fragility of the judiciary. He believes that the court system may devolve into chaos if

some greater measure of propriety is not exercised by those who have engaged in excessively harsh criticisms, especially of the Court's Charter decisions.

6 Bertha Wilson, 'Guaranteed Freedoms in a Free and Democratic Society,' *Speeches*, 102.

7 Ibid.

8 Bertha Wilson, 'Decision-Making in the Supreme Court,' *University of Toronto Law Journal* 36 (1986), 238, 240.

9 Bertha Wilson, 'Remarks Made at the Superior Court Judges' Seminar,' Vancouver, August 1987 in *Speeches*, 503–4.

10 Bertha Wilson, 'The Making of a Constitution,' in *Speeches*, 512.

11 Ibid. (emphasis added). Although I am in agreement with this contextual methodology, it seems to me that Wilson was not entirely successful in applying it in *Edmonton Journal* and this passage helps to illuminate the problem. Her approach to the issue of publication of pleadings in matrimonial causes in my opinion did not sufficiently accord with the 'general purpose of having rights,' which is 'the protection of the individual from the overbearing collectivity.' In that instance, what was at issue was a limitation of the protection of individual privacy in the context of the contesting value of the freedom of expression of the press or even the public interest in an open court process, both overwhelming collectivities. Freedom of expression of the press, however, is of value not in and of itself but because the core of its purpose is to sustain freedom of expression for individuals; in this instance, the party putting forward the unproven allegations in the pleadings gets a free ride and perhaps the advantage of a chilling effect out of the newspaper coverage.

12 The development of the law must be both principled and flexible, sufficiently connected to precedent to satisfy peoples' longing for certainty and yet productive of justice in new situations. It is because Wilson holds this principle so dear that she enjoyed my somewhat audacious transformation of Lord Sankey's living tree into the strawberry patch of enlightened postmodernism, spreading its new plantlets on runners into more friable soil like new legal principles firmly attached to the precedents of common law or their originating statutes but rooted in new social circumstances.

13 Interviews with Antonio Lamer and William McIntyre.

14 *Perka v. The Queen* [1984] 2 SCR 232.

15 Ibid., at 269.

16 *Perka* has been cited many times since 1984 but so far the defence of necessity based on justification seems not to have clearly applied. If justification can never be a successful defence in instances where a life is sacrificed, it is diffi-

cult to see how the defence of necessity through justification could have applicability in instances of mercy killing such as R. v. Latimer [2001] SCC 1 File No. 26980, the case of the Saskatchewan farmer who euthanized his severely disabled daughter when she was facing yet another painful operation. And in fact the Supreme Court judgment dismissing Latimer's appeal against conviction and sentencing in 2001 considered only the Dickson defence of necessity based on involuntariness in situations of imminent peril.

17 R. v. Bernard [1988] 2 SCR 833.

18 Leary v. The Queen [1978] 1 SCR 29.

19 R. v. Daviault [1994] 3 SCR 63; the case concerned a sexual assault on a sixty-five-year-old woman partially paralysed in a wheelchair, the appellant (a chronic alcoholic) testifying that he had no recollection of the event. The Court held that expert evidence of intoxication amounting to automatism must go to the trier of fact and the onus is on the appellant to establish on a balance of probabilities that he lacked the necessary intention to perform the act. These cases are rare: implicit in Wilson's judgment is the common sense recognition that in most instances of drunkenness amounting to automatism the accused will be incapable of sexual performance. The Criminal Code was amended in 1995 to preclude this controversial drunkenness defence when intoxication is self-induced.

20 R. v. Chaulk [1990] 3 SCR 1303.

21 Lamer wrote the majority reasons for Dickson, LaForest, Sopinka, and Cory; L'Heureux-Dubé, Gonthier, and McLachlin dissented on this issue, finding that the presumption of sanity refers not to an actual state of mind but a capacity for criminal responsibility. Because it is neither an element of the offence, nor a defence, the presumption of sanity does not infringe the presumption of innocence.

22 Chaulk, 1372, 1373 (emphasis in the original).

23 Bertha Wilson, 'Constitutional Advocacy,' Ottawa Bar Review 24 (1992), 269.

24 See R. v. Butler [1992] 1 SCR 452, a very important case for the definition of pornography under section 163 of the Criminal Code. Using the relaxed analysis under section 1, the law prohibiting pornography survived a freedom of expression challenge. The pornography in question corrupted morals not because it was explicitly sexual material but because it was deemed so degrading and dehumanizing that it could cause harm to women and children by evoking violence. The decision drew on then-current feminist anti-pornography theory which has since 1992 been challenged and significantly revised in the light of new scientific evidence; it was lauded as a victory for feminists at the time. Since Butler's challenge, the law has been used primarily to harass distributors of gay/lesbian erotic literature.

25 The constitutional exemption was invoked by the British Columbia Court of Appeal in *R. v. Chief* (1989), 39 BCLR (2d) 358, when a native person who had assaulted his wife with a rifle was sentenced to twenty-one days' imprisonment and two years' probation but did not lose use of his firearms for the five-year period mandated by the Criminal Code because his hunting and trapping activities were deemed essential to the support of his family.

26 *R. v. Gamble* [1988] 2 SCR 595.

27 *Operation Dismantle v. The Queen* [1985] 1 SCR 441.

28 Ibid., at 472.

29 Ibid., at 488–9.

30 *Osborne v. Canada* [1991] SCJ No. 45.

31 Ibid., at 69.

32 *R. v. Hébert* [1990] 2 SCR 151.

33 *R. v. Wong* [1990] 3 SCR 36.

34 Bertha Wilson, 'Making of a Constitution,' 517–18.

35 *Ford v. Attorney General Quebec* [1988] 2 SCR 712; 54 DLR (4th) 577.

36 This key point is not well understood by F.L. Morton and Rainer Knopff in *The Charter Revolution and the Court Party* (Peterborough: Broadview Press, 2000). The book renews criticism of the Supreme Court as a political censor, laying particular blame on law clerks whom, they say, have taken over more and more of the judicial function and are excessively influenced by the activist biases of their university law school professors.

37 Bertha Wilson, 'We Didn't Volunteer,' *Policy Options* 20 (April 1999), 10.

38 Ibid., 11.

39 The classic example of this is the omission in the Criminal Code since *Morgentaler* of any provisions governing abortion, which Wilson herself considers the best possible outcome under the circumstances.

40 Bertha Wilson, 'Evidence under the Charter of Rights,' Lecture to Upper Year Class, College of Law, University of Saskatchewan, November 1984, in *Speeches*, 289.

41 Memorandum for Members of the Court from 'B.D.' dated 8 February 1985.

42 The list of appellants includes Canadian Union of Public Employees, Canadian Union of Postal Workers, National Union of Provincial Government Employees, Ontario Federation of Labour, Arts for Peace, Canadian Peace Research and Education Association, World Federalists of Canada, and many more. There were also five named respondents, all again with full party status: the Queen, the Prime Minister, the Attorney General of Canada, the Secretary of State for External Affairs and the Minister of Defence. Although Wilson concurred in the majority decision to dismiss the appeal,

she referred in the opening words of her judgment to the sheer numbers of citizens involved in this case, which she clearly considered significant.

43 Bertha Wilson, 'Decision-Making in the Supreme Court,' 243. Not only was this session open to the press but the speeches were subsequently published and have been widely reprinted.

44 *Daigle* v. *Tremblay* [1989] 2 SCR 530.

45 Some of the detail provided here is derived from D'Arcy Jennish, 'Abortion on Trial,' *Macleans* magazine, 31 July, 1989.

46 Reasons in writing were released 16 November 1989. As Chief Justice McLachlin recalls, there were some members of the Court who had felt initially that Daigle, because she had already obtained the abortion, had abused the process of the Court which accordingly ought not to consider the case further. However, McLachlin herself understood it was necessary as a judge to put yourself in her shoes because Daigle was in an extremely difficult position and that was the view which prevailed: interview with Chief Justice McLachlin, 18 April 2000.

47 In an interview on 11 May 1999 Wilson was prepared to say that she 'worked very hard on that to get the judgment by the Court,' and that she 'was happy with the way that one worked out in the end.'

48 Bertha Wilson, 'Statutory Interpretation: The Use of Extrinsic Evidence Pre and Post Charter,' paper delivered at the Commonwealth Law Conference New Zealand, April 1990, in *Speeches*, 640.

49 Ibid., at 653. 'Grounded contextuality' is, of course, what I am calling 'enlightened postmodernism' and connecting this variant of postmodern theory with Scottish Enlightenment philosophy.

50 Bertha Wilson, 'Judicial Reasoning: Myths and mysteries,' The Butterworth Lectures, *New Zealand Law Journal* (October 1990), 357–8.

51 See Luiza Chwialkowska, 'Rein in lobby groups, senior judges suggest,' *National Post*, April 2000, A1–2; on the intervention issue McLachlin told me she had been misquoted but agreed that all three judges deny the Court has been highjacked by the clerks.

52 *R.* v. *Askov* (1990), 74 DLR (4th) 355. The Court was astonished at the sheer number of stays which resulted from the *Askov* decision because a proper evidentiary base had not been supplied by the crown.

53 *Operation Dismantle*, at 475–6, 478.

54 *Hunt* v. *Carey Canada Inc.* [1990] 2 SCR 959.

55 Ibid., at 990.

56 Bertha Wilson, 'A Choice of Values,' *Canadian Bar Journal* 448 (1961), 456. This phrase was coined by Lord Hewart of Bury in an early study of the

emergence of post-industrial regulatory regimes: see *The New Despotism* (London: Benn, 1945).

57 See, for example, *Re Proctor* (1979), 24 OR (2d) 715, and *Re Downing* (1978), 21 OR (2d) 292. See also *Re Milstein and Ontario College of Pharmacy* (1978), 20 OR (2d) 283, a case involving a decision of the Ontario College of Pharmacy to suspend the licence of a pharmacist as a disciplinary sanction for alleged unprofessional conduct because he had failed to adhere to a fee schedule for municipal welfare recipients established by a municipal welfare department.

58 Bertha Wilson, 'Respecting the Law and Our Democratic Institutions,' the Jackson Lecture at the Ontario Institute for Studies in Education, 1985.

59 The 'patently unreasonable' test had been formulated three years before Wilson went to the Supreme Court by Dickson in *Canadian Union of Public Employees, Local 963* v. *New Brunswick Liqour Corporation* [1979] 2 SCR 277. This was a landmark case for the shift in judicial attitude towards the authority of administrative tribunals, specifically on the issue of statutory interpretation. Dickson had held that in an instance in which a provision of the enabling legislation is sufficiently ambiguous that there can be no obvious consensus about its meaning, the court ought to defer to the expertise of the tribunal because it will have greater familiarity with the context in which the statute customarily functions, except in those rare instances when the tribunal's decision can be shown to be patently unreasonable.

60 William Eskridge and Gary Peller, 'The New Public Law Movement: Moderation as a Postmodern Cultural Form,' *Michigan Law Review* 89 (1991), 709. Eskridge and Peller believe that four broad strategies have repositioned postmodernism from polarized anarchy to centrist moderation: first, that if enough facts can be gathered a 'functionally normative resolution' to a social problem will evolve; second, that there can be coherence between law and 'nonformalistically identified social values,' which Wilson attempts to achieve through linking purposive analysis of legislation to the specific facts in a case; third, 'simple empathy with the "other",' a stance which we have traced back to Scottish Enlightenment doctrines of moral sympathy; and finally, good faith conviction that a decision-maker with confidence in its authority will take responsibility for the outcome of a social conflict, a concept entirely compatible with curial deference to expert administrative tribunals.

61 *CAIMAW [Canadian Association of Industrial, Mechanical and Allied Workers, Local 14]* v. *Paccar of Canada Ltd.* [1989] 2 SCR 983.

62 *National Corn Growers* v. *Canadian Import Tribunal* [1990] 2 SCR 1324. This was a case involving multiple appellants, respondents, and intervenors and accordingly the trial record supplied to the Court was particularly rich and detailed. Included in the lengthy list of academic writers who were critical of

the courts' record on curial deference which were cited by Wilson are H.W. Arthurs, J.M. Evans and Brian Langille.

63 Ibid., at 1347–8 (emphasis in the original).
64 *Lester* v. *UAJAPPI, Local 740* [1990] 3 SCR 644.
65 *Cuddy Chicks Ltd.* v. *Ontario (Labour Relations Board)* [1991] 2 SCR 5.
66 *Morguard Investments Ltd.* v. *De Savoye* [1990] 3 SCR 1077. The case concerned a mortgage which went into default on a property in Alberta after the mortgagor had moved to British Columbia. There was no clause in the mortgage establishing that Alberta law applied, no steps taken to defend, and no attornment to the jurisdiction. Judgment was obtained in Alberta and an action commenced in British Columbia to enforce the Alberta judgment; the issue was whether the foreign Alberta judgment ought to be recognized in the British Columbia court. The Court held that the rules of private international law ought to be adapted to the federal structure of Canada, given that modern states cannot live in splendid isolation if there is to be an orderly flow of wealth and skills and money across borders. The content of comity itself required adjustment in the light of a changing world order.
67 See *Hunt* v. *Carey Canada* [1993] SCJ No. 125, concerning a conflict of laws and drawing together private international law doctrines with constitutional law. When permitted to proceed with his novel tort of conspiracy, Hunt required evidence to make out his claim. He invoked the Rules of Court of British Columbia to obtain disclosure of certain business documents located at the respondent's place of business in Quebec and received no reply from the respondent which would have signalled attornment to B.C. jurisdiction. On appeal, the respondent pleaded the Quebec Business Concerns Records Act, a blocking statute preventing removal of documents of business concern from the province, which it argued provided a lawful excuse for its failure to comply with disclosure. The Court held that the Quebec Act was *ultra vires* because the province's legislation purported to exert extraterritorial control over matters relating to out-of-province concerns. The appointment of federal judges spoke to the essential unitary nature of the Canadian court system and this unitary nature was further confirmed by the supervisory jurisdiction of the Supreme Court and its power to take judicial notice of all the laws prevailing in every province.
68 For example, in 'The Making of a Constitution,' Wilson suggested that Canadian lawyers and judges can best understand the limitations on the guaranteed rights contained within our Charter by looking to international experience in the protection of human rights.
69 *Re Ownership of the Bed of the Strait of Georgia* [1984] 1 SCR 388.
70 Ibid., at 427.

71 *Canada* v. *Schmidt* [1987] 1 SCR 500.
72 Ibid., at 532–3.
73 *Argentina* v. *Mellino* [1987] 1 SCR 536. There had been a delay of seventeen months and the extradition judge dismissed the application; the Court allowed the appeal and the matter was remitted to the extradition judge to continue the proceedings.
74 *United States* v. *Allard* [1987] 1 SCR 564.
75 *United States* v. *Cotroni* [1989] 1 SCR 1469.
76 Ibid., at 1509.

CHAPTER 12

1 Jeanne Sauvé became the first woman governor general, appointed in 1984 by Trudeau and serving until 1990.
2 Memo to Madam Roland, 22 February 1991; Roland, of the Supreme Court administrative staff, had the responsibility of pulling together a Judges' Information Manual.
3 Bill Bryden hosted a Supreme Court retirement party at the Albany Club in 1991 at which Allan Beattie gave a wonderful tribute to John because he felt he deserved explicit recognition for the role he had played in supporting Bertha Wilson's remarkable career. 'John is truly one of the most widely read persons I have known,' Beattie said, speculating that he 'must have been an invaluable resource researching, editing and providing informed commentary, especially in non-legal aspects of the job,' when no one else on the Supreme Court had that kind of help so readily and cheerfully available. Both Beattie and Frank Clifford, the Osler archivist, provided me with copies of this unpublished speech.
4 John Wilson roared with laughter when I pointed out that after the first dozen or so doctorates his wife had begun to request a medium-sized instead of a small mortarboard; conversation, 9 May 1999.
5 The texts of these speeches are included among the Wilsons' personal papers. It is unfortunate that so few have been published for more general readership. What is notable about them in the aggregate is the effort Wilson put into mentioning items of current interest to her fellow graduates based upon their courses of study, offering words of unabashed optimism and inspiration leavened by humour and personal anecdote, and then wishing them well as they embarked upon their chosen careers.
6 Bertha Wilson to Professor R. St J. Macdonald, 20 March 1990.
7 The table of contents for *Speeches Delivered by the Honourable Bertha Wilson*, shows that she thriftily followed this pattern on a number of occasions

between 1983 and 1990. For Wilson, this was genuinely one of the most enjoyable aspects of her work, not just an obligation. Many of her colleagues also made it a point to accept as many speaking engagements as possible. Chief Justice Lamer, for example, always preferred to schedule presentations within the profession back-to-back, with at least one presentation to a local service club or other public venue whenever he was travelling outside Ottawa.

8 This speech was subsequently published in the Cambridge Lectures of 1989.

9 The Soviet delegation had included Gvido Zemribo, chairman of Latvia's Supreme Court, Vladimir Terebilov, the Supreme Court chairman and top justice official, and Robert Tikhomirnow, criminal division chairman.

10 Bertha Wilson, 'Report on the Exchange Visit to the Soviet Union,' a memo in Wilson's file on the Soviet exchanges.

11 Bertha Wilson, 'Remarks Made at Chatham College upon Acceptance of an Honourary Degree,' in *Speeches*.

12 All the information relating to this event, Wilson's speech notes, and the original letter of thanks dated 28 September 1990 and signed Tom Denning, have survived among the Wilson's personal papers.

13 McLachlin's choice of metaphor, given Wilson's distress over the sports-affiliated lobbying which may have influenced the decision-making process during her time on the bench, is an unconsciously ironic one. Gonthier concurred in McLachlin's evaluation; in an affectionate note dated 16 November 1990 he expressed his sorrow and great loss over Wilson's approaching retirement and assured her that, 'to the very last you are contributing in the fullest measure not only to the work of the Court but also quite selflessly to its administration.'

14 Eddy Bison, quoted in Shi-Lain Chan, 'Charter Must Continue to Play Major Role in Shaping Society, Justice Wilson Tells Retirement Ceremony,' *Law Times* 42 (10–16 December 1990), 4.

15 Reading these letters in the aggregate one cannot help but find the tributes extremely moving. Two general impressions may be worth noting. First, the handwritten notes from law students and law clerks and legal secretaries and housewives, many on flowered drugstore stationery or even notebook paper, have been filed away in order of receipt and just as carefully as the official letters on crested stationery from the governor general, Supreme Court justices, university presidents and law school deans, and distinguished authors. Secondly, it is notable how many of the writers who had met Bertha Wilson even peripherally when they sat in audiences where she had spoken or appeared before her in motions court recall some personal kindness or some incident of good humour which made her

stand out in their memories as a great and good person and not just a great judge.

16 This move was, of course, not at all a demotion but customary; Wilson used this self-deprecating phrase in her reply to Lederman, 20 February 1991.

17 Innis Christie to Bertha Wilson, 3 December 1990; Bertha Wilson to Innis Christie, 18 December 1990.

18 A number of the clerks whom I interviewed described this occasion to me; I am particularly grateful to Rob Yalden and Jim Phillips. Having been warned about the 'minimal commas' propensity in advance, as I prepared draft chapters for review by the Wilsons I attempted to eliminate them whenever possible and on occasion was rewarded for this vigilance when one or other of the Wilsons actually inserted a comma not proposed by me. The transcripts of the taped interviews with the Wilsons prepared by Marilyn MacFarlane of the Osgoode Society for Canadian Legal History are, on the other hand, replete with commas since both Wilsons tend to speak rather slowly and thoughtfully with regular pauses to collect their thoughts.

19 The Yaldens had invited the Wilsons to dinner together with their son some months after Rob had gone to the Supreme Court; they wanted to meet the woman who was having such a remarkable influence on him and also to share with John their extensive selection of fine single malt whiskies for which, they had been correctly informed, he has a particular fondness.

20 See Yash Ghai and Johannes Chan, eds., *The Hong Kong Bill of Rights: A Comparative Approach* (London: Butterworths, 1992).

21 Participants in the workshop included Allan Hutchinson, Roderick Macdonald, John McCamus, and Robert Pritchard; Brian Dickson, Antonio Lamer, Bob Sharpe, Charles Dubin, and Jim MacPherson were all invited to the dinner. And Wilson delivered a short, pithy speech which reviewed her life and her great good fortune in the appointment to the Supreme Court coinciding with the entrenchment of the Charter.

22 Innis Christie to Bertha Wilson, 9 January 1991. The first of these events had been held in Winnipeg in late 1990 to honour retiring Chief Justice Brian Dickson, and since that time they have become something of a tradition.

23 In the event, Girard's suggested theme was not much adhered to by the speakers; however, it is one which helped spark my attempt to sketch out connections between the Scottish Enlightenment philosophies with which Wilson was deeply familiar and contemporary legal postmodernisms.

24 Moira McConnell knew of the Wilsons' devotion to the arts and was confident that they would prefer this tribute in lieu of any more material gift; the cost of the commission was defrayed by assistance from the Nova Scotia

Department of Tourism and Culture and the composition was subsequently broadcast over CBC.

CHAPTER 13

1 Bertha Wilson, 'Interim Report: Task Force on Gender Equality,' August 1992. Wilson's original notes for this speech were, in July 1999, still in a filing cabinet at the University of Ottawa. There are numerous crossings-out and additions indicating that Wilson struggled over what she was prepared to say publicly. She had been a member of CBA and active in its committees at both a provincial and national level since her earliest years at Oslers. She took on the project because she believed that the CBA had given her a great deal over the years and that she really could not refuse; accordingly, she was reluctant to reveal the frustrations and obfuscations with which she had been dealing. Yet she knew without funding it would be impossible to meet the expectations of women in the profession which had been raised when she agreed to serve.

2 Joan MacDonald was given a total of $130 by various lawyers; a large Toronto law firm promised $10,000; outgoing CBA president J.J. Camp announced that his law firm, Ladner Downs of Vancouver, intended to give $2,500.

3 Joan MacDonald helped found the Ontario Trial Lawyers' Association, chaired its Women's Caucus and served as its first woman governor. She has been active in the Canadian Bar Association Councils at both provincial and executive levels. She was the first Canadian elected to chair the Women Trial Lawyers Caucus of ATLA; it was at ATLA, she says, that she first encountered a distinctively American commitment to personal philanthropy (with members customarily leaping to their feet in meetings to pledge support for various projects that otherwise might very well never get off the ground) and her actions in Halifax were inspired by that experience.

4 'Old Boys' Network Hinders Task Force Fundraising: Wilson': clipping from the Wilsons' files, undated and unattributed. These comments, which are attributed directly to Wilson, were not included in the Interim Report but must have been provided to the reporters who thronged around her after her speech.

5 Interview with Melina Buckley, 28 February 2000; I was not able to confirm these figures because I was not granted access to the CBA archives concerned with this project.

6 Bertha Wilson, handwritten notes, 'Matters discussed at Calgary meeting,' Wilson's personal papers.

7 Alec Robertson to Bertha Wilson, 8 November 1991, reporting a meeting

with J.J. Camp. Bertha Wilson to J.J. Camp, 11 November 1991. Her annotation reads 'not sent' – meeting with J.J. instead'; the tone of this letter makes
it unmistakable that Wilson was very upset. Robertson and Wilson worked
closely on the Gender Equality report; they came from similar corporate law
backgrounds and Robertson served as Wilson's closest confidant. Because of
his seniority in the profession, Robertson served as the other heavyweight on
the task force. He acknowledges that he felt able to take the risk of participating in this controversial study and realized his presence would add credibility: interviews with Melinda Buckley and Alec Robertson.

8 The handwritten notes and records from the Wilsons' personal papers reveal
the extreme shortage of clerical help; it is obvious that John Wilson was
pitching in to help, even preparing printed drafts of speeches that were subsequently annotated and revised by Wilson.

9 Buckley reports that Pat Blocksom and Daphne Dumont also assisted with
drafting certain sections dealing with their assigned subject areas. See also,
Melina Buckley to Bertha Wilson, 12 May 1993. She wrote tactfully:

> Over the past year, there has been discussion about you writing the
> first part of the report. At the April meeting, the other committee mem-
> bers thought that this might be too onerous as the first part as currently
> envisioned is quite substantial. The suggestion was that you might want
> to write an introduction to the report and that I write the first draft of the
> rest of the report with full opportunity for revisions by all members of
> the Task Force. Please advise me on how you would like to proceed.

10 Professor Lynn Smith, 'Gender Equality – Professional and Ethical Issues';
Professor Sheilah Martin, 'The Dynamics of Exclusion: Women in the Le-
gal Profession'; Professor Mary Jane Mossman, 'Work and Family in the
Legal Profession: Re-thinking the Questions'; Professor Marie-France
Bich, 'De L'art de passer à travers les mailles du filet – prolégomènes et
polemique,' and Professor Carrie Menkel-Meadow, 'Change in the Legal
Profession: Is the Glass Ceiling Half Full or Half Empty?'

11 *Touchstones for Change: Equality, Diversity and Accountability*. Report of the
Canadian Bar Association Task Force on Gender Equality in the Legal Profession (Ottawa: August 1993). The recommendations read:

> 5:18 That law firms set realistic targets of billable hours for women
> with child rearing responsibilities pursuant to their legal duty to
> accommodate.
>
> 5:19 That, as part of the same legal duty to accommodate, the reduced
> target of billable hours should not delay or affect eligibility for
> partnership nor affect normal compensation.

5:20   That law firms evaluate lawyers on a basis that gives due weight to the quality of time expended rather than exclusively to the quantity of time expended.

12 Bertha Wilson, 'Introduction from the Chair,' in ibid., 4–5.
13 In retrospect, Alec Robertson considers that one of the weaknesses of the report is that it was too much written as a judgment; he believes that a more graphic and visual presentation focusing on the threshold issue of what discrimination is might have evoked less antagonism within the profession.
14 Karen Selick, 'Why should law firms subsidize moms?' *Globe and Mail*, 19 July 1993.
15 *Brooks* v. *Canada Safeway Ltd.* [1989] 1 SCR 1219.
16 Susan Lightstone, 'Bertha Wilson, A personal view on women and the law,' *National* 12 (August–September 1993), 16.
17 Canadian Bar Association Standing Committee on Gender issues, third draft resolution, 16 November 1993.
18 Interview with Madam Justice Cecilia Johnstone, 28 March 2000.
19 James F. Hutchinson, in *Lawyers Weekly* 14, 30 September 1994; Norma Priday, 'Special status for lawyers raising children? Objection.' *Globe and Mail*, 28 September 1994, A22.
20 Claire Hoy, 'Wilson Should Identify Judges Who Exhibit Sex Discrimination,' *Law Times*, 10–16 February 1992; the Hoy article makes reference to a similar article in the *Lawyers Weekly*.
21 'Memo to All Women Judges' from Bertha Wilson dated 14 February 1992; Wilson explained in this memo that a woman student was freelancing at the private session as a reporter for the *Lawyers Weekly* and had not disclosed her role to Wilson.
22 *Touchstones for Change*, 191.
23 Ibid., 192.
24 In total Wilson set out fifteen recommendations designed to alleviate discrimination against women in the judiciary: these include compulsory courses in gender and racial sensitivity for all judges (not just recent appointments); funding conferences for women judges; providing early-career mentoring for new women judges; and establishing that those judges discriminating against other judges or counsel would be made subject to judicial discipline.
25 David Vienneau, 'One on one with Bertha Wilson,' *Law Times*, 21–27 March 1994, 11.
26 Johnstone had not, of course, seen any of the raw data and this comment is not intended to confirm or to deny that Wilson had received any information regarding discrimination against the judiciary in British Columbia. Never-

theless, considering the extent of systemic gender bias revealed in the Law Society of British Columbia 1992 reports it seems highly unlikely that women in the judiciary were completely exempt from this problem.

27 There is no question that extraordinary efforts had been made to accommodate women in the judiciary in British Columbia. Chief Justice Beverley McLachlin gave Chief Justice McEachern full credit for the support and sensitivity he had shown when she was first appointed to the bench in British Columbia; realizing that she had a young child, for example, McEachern had voluntarily arranged her schedule to minimize travel time out of Vancouver.

28 The existence of both these letters was independently recalled to me by several persons whom I interviewed who remembered copies of both letters being received at the CBA office in Ottawa; however, I have seen neither of them. The existence of substantial response to Wilson's survey on discrimination in the judiciary was also independently confirmed on several occasions during the course of the research for this biography.

29 David Vienneau, 'Biases on agenda as lawyers review contentious study,' *Toronto Star*, 20 February 1994, A4.

30 Sean Fine, '"Safe counsel" efforts fall short,' *Globe and Mail* 12 August 1997, B31. The safe counsel service was to be set up by the law societies so that women could speak out in safety about harassment and discrimination without fear of reprisal.

31 See note 5 above.

32 The CBA established a Bertha Wilson Touchstones Award which was presented to Cecilia Johnstone by Bertha Wilson in 1997 for her steadfast efforts to implement the report's recommendations, an experience which Johnstone also found deeply moving. At a press conference held after the report was tabled in 1993, Cecilia Johnstone was asked rather cynically by a reporter whether this was an effort which would sit on a shelf for ten years until someone came along and blew the dust off it. Johnstone replied, 'Not so long as I'm alive and breathing.'

33 *Touchstones for Change*, at 273.

CHAPTER 14

1 'Framing the Issues,' 15–minute video produced by the Royal Commission on Aboriginal Peoples, October 1992, in conjunction with Discussion Paper 1, *Framing the Issues*. Despite her obvious pleasure, Wilson said in 1998 'I must say that I found the dancing very hard with my arthritis but you had to participate because I don't think they would have appreciated anybody sitting out.' This account of the royal commission is based on the 'Framing the

Issues' video and another video, 'No Turning Back,' together with discussion of the work of the commission, during interviews with Bertha Wilson, Viola Robinson, Tony Reynolds, and Peter Meekison. Although it was not possible to interview every commissioner, it was obvious that all of them and their staff worked extremely hard on the research and the writing of the interim and final reports.

2 For a capsule history of the relationship between the Canadian government and aboriginal peoples underlying the Oka flare-up, see Sue Bailey, 'What next for Canada's aboriginals?' *Toronto Star*, 29 December 1999, A7. For a general account of the systemic racism faced by aboriginals in the Canadian justice system, see Public Inquiry into the Administration of Justice and Aboriginal People, *The Justice System and Aboriginal People* (Winnipeg: Queen's Printer, 1991).

3 Report of the Special Representative respecting the Royal Commission on Aboriginal Peoples, 2 August 1991 in *Mandate*, Background Documents of the Royal Commission on Aboriginal Peoples, 3.

4 See Jeffrey Simpson, 'The telling nature of the new Royal Commission on Aboriginal Affairs, *Globe and Mail*, 30 August 1991, A14. See also Melvin H. Smith, *Our Home or Native Land?* (Altona, Manitoba: Friesen Printers, 1995); Smith is sharply critical of the aboriginal land claim settlement process in general and the royal commission in particular. He questions the impartiality of the commission based on its composition, noting that four of the seven commissioners were drawn from the aboriginal community although only 3 per cent of the nation's population is aboriginal.

5 Interview with Tony Reynolds. Reynolds was appointed the second executive director of the royal commission in 1993.

6 See, for example, the overviews of the four rounds of meetings, prepared by Michael Cassidy for Ginger Group Consultants for the Royal Commission on Aboriginal Peoples (Ottawa: 1992, 1993, 1994).

7 Princeton-trained in Chinese history, Ottawa-based and approaching retirement, Reynolds had spent many years as a journalist and volunteer in Asia and had held a variety of academic and civil service jobs.

8 Report of the Royal Commission on Aboriginal Peoples, Vol. I, *Looking Forward, Looking Back* (Ottawa: Canada Communications Group, 1996), Preface.

9 Bertha Wilson, 'Address on Native Spirituality,' address given at Westminster United Church, Winnipeg, 25 October 1992. She was speaking here of the hearings protocol but this stance (an element of aboriginal spirituality deeply implicated in the harmony and peace essential for all meaningful dialogue) was equally vital to the internal work of the commission.

10 Tony Reynolds, Peter Meekison, and Bertha Wilson all retired from public life at the end of the commission and all of them considered it the most significant achievement of their careers. Viola Robinson, who has continued to be very active in the aboriginal community, agrees that work with the commission fundamentally changed her life.

11 Royal Commission on Aboriginal Peoples, *Bridging the Cultural Divide*, co-chairs R. Dussault, and Georges Erasmus (Ottawa: Canada Communications Group, 1992), the report was not edited, translated, and published, however, until 1996.

12 Tim Harper, 'Let natives enforce own set of laws panel urges,' *Toronto Star*, 24 February 1996, A3, in which Wilson cites the figures for aboriginal inmates in federal penitentiaries in Manitoba (47%) and in Saskatchewan (72%), concluding bluntly, 'This is not equality. This is discrimination.'

13 Royal Commission on Aboriginal Peoples, *Partners in Confederation: Aboriginal Peoples, Self-Government and the Constitution*, co-chair R. Dussault, and Georges Erasmus (Ottawa: Canada Communications Group, 1993).

14 See Delia Opekokew, *First Nations: Indian Government and the Canadian Confederation*, Appendix A, 'the Indigenous People of Saskatchewan' (Saskatoon: Federation of Saskatchewan Indians, 1980) for a thorough overview of international conventions and covenants related to the issue of aboriginal self-government preceding entrenchment of the Charter.

15 Phil Fontaine of the Assembly of Manitoba Chiefs pointed out that a previous agreement with Ottawa had acknowledged the right of Manitoba chiefs to establish their own economic, political, judicial affairs. Fontaine subsequently replaced Ovide Mercredi as leader of the Assembly of First Nations.

16 See Royal Commission on Aboriginal Peoples, *The High Arctic relocation: A Report on the 1953–1955 relocation*, co-chairs R. Dussault and Georges Erasmus (Ottawa: Canada Communications Group, 1994); see also *The High Arctic relocation; summary and supporting information*, in two volumes, 1994.

17 See, for example, Royal Commission on Aboriginal Peoples, *National Round Table on Aboriginal Urban Issues* (Edmonton, 1992); *National Round Table on Aboriginal Health and Social Issues* (Vancouver, 1993); *National Round Table on Aboriginal Economic Development and Resources* (Ottawa, 1993); *Treaty Making in the Spirit of Co-existence* (1995); *Canada's Fiduciary Obligation to Aboriginal Peoples in the Context of Accession to Sovereignty of Quebec* (1995).

18 Royal Commission on Aboriginal Peoples, *Choosing Life: Special Report on Suicide among Aboriginal Peoples*, co-chairs R. Dussault and G. Erasmus (Ottawa: Canadian Communications Group, 1995.

19 My account of this incident is derived from the interviews with Tony Reynolds and Peter Meekison; Reynolds indicated that Marlene Brant

Castellano, a Mohawk and Trent University professor, also participated actively in the writing of this key report.

20 John Wilson himself does not consider that his health was ever seriously impaired. Nevertheless, a number of those working with Bertha Wilson mentioned that she was noticeably concerned about him.

21 *Looking Forward, Looking Back*, chapter 7, 'Stage-Four: Negotiation and Renewal,' 216–28.

22 Ibid., chapter 15, 615–73.

23 The idea of this chapter was to provide non-aboriginal people some means of comprehending the fundamentally spiritual focus permeating aboriginal cultures, says Meekison. It was the most difficult chapter to write.

24 Meekison wrote much of this last chapter and he himself would have preferred an aboriginal advisory committee for the Supreme Court of Canada, but (ever conscious of judicial impartiality) Wilson indignantly refused this suggestion.

25 The section 37 provision contemplates a constitutional conference with participation of aboriginal peoples to identify and to resolve issues directly affecting them – and nothing affects them more than the inherent right to self-government with its implicit commitment to resolution of land claims.

26 Peter Meekison points out that every newspaper account mentions the $58 million figure, which is not accurate. Some $8 million of this had gone to David Crombie, chairman of the Intervenor Participation Program. Another $20 million had been spent on the research program; costly computer technologies also had to be developed but were essential to the future usefulness of the date compiled. Translation and printing increased the budget, too; the report was not only the longest ever produced by a royal commission, it was published all at one time. And the expense of travel by the commissioners and their staff for the hearings undertaken in so many and such remote locations was a significant factor increasing overall costs. For typical newspaper reactions focusing on these financial issues see, for example, Dan Smith, 'New deal urged for First Nations,' *Toronto Star*, 22 November 1996; and Rudy Platiel, 'Vast changes sought to aid natives,' *Globe and Mail*, 22 November 1996, A1 and A8.

27 Chrétien had been minister of Indian affairs in 1969 when his white paper proposed scrapping the Indian Act and disbanding the Department of Indian Affairs. There had been calls for his resignation and he was forced to retract them. From this perspective, the failure of the Chrétien administration to implement many of the royal commission's recommendations becomes more understandable.

A recently published book by University of Calgary political scientist and former Reform Party advisor Tom Flanagan attempts to resurrect the long-discredited doctrine that assimilation is in the best interests of aboriginal peoples as well as Canadians more generally; see Tom Flanagan, *First Nations? Second Thoughts* (Montreal: McGill-Queen's University Press, 2000). And from a more liberal perspective, Alan C. Cairns has also been willing to re-examine the notion of integration so long as it is initiated by aboriginal peoples themselves as an alternative to the commission model of sovereign self-governing nations, arguing that although particular aboriginal peoples are different from other Canadians (and from each other) there are significant areas of overlap; see Alan Cairns, *Citizens Plus: Aboriginal Peoples and the Canadian State* (Vancouver: UBC Press, 2000).

28　For news stories commenting upon the lack of substantive response by the government see, for example, Rudy Platiel, 'Irwin seeks discussion of proposals for natives,' *Globe and Mail*, 23 November 1996, A1 and Scott Feschuk, 'Natives call for PM's reaction to report,' ibid., 6 December 1996, A4. Even this kind of coverage, however, seems to have disappeared within days of the report's release. For news stories expressing the view that the commission's recommendations deserved silence because they were essentially unimplementable, see, for example, Jeffrey Simpson, 'A view of life that harkens to a golden age for aboriginal peoples,' ibid., 26 February, 1997, A16, and 'Just what is a nation and how can it work like a province?' ibid., 27 February 1997, A18.

29　'On the right path for native people,' *Toronto Star*, 9 January 1998, A20.

30　*Delgamuukw* v. *British Columbia* [1997] 3 SCR 1010.

31　Ibid., para 201 and 204.

32　The decision to admit oral evidence in aboriginal land claim cases was fully congruent with earlier developments in Canadian jurisprudence (in *R.* v. *Khan* [1990] 2 SCR 531, for example) relating to the admissibility of hearsay based on criteria of necessity and reliability. However, for a contrary point of view particularly popular with residents of British Columbia, see Gordon Gibson, 'The land-claims ruling is a breathtaking mistake,' *Globe and Mail*, 16 December 1997, A 21.

33　The treaty between the Nisga's and the British Columbia government provides for aboriginal ownership of 1,930 square kilometres of land in the ancestral Nass valley northwest of Vancouver, self-government powers comparable to that of a municipality but including courts, correctional services, citizenship, language, culture, property rights, justice, social services, employment and traffic; resource rights; $300 million in cash; and the relinquishment of tax exempt status together with any future treaty claims.

34　Manitoba, for example, announced such a scheme in early April 2000.

35 See John Milloy, *A National Crime* (1999). Dr Milloy was the researcher hired by the royal commission and his study, 'Suffer the Little Children – A History of the Residential School System,' formed the basis of chapter 10 in Volume 1 of the commission's report. *A National Crime* draws upon research compiled in 1989 by the Native Women's Association of the Northwest Territories. It points out that as early as 1908 official inspectors had found 75 per cent of these schools to be in deplorable condition, and nothing was done. Very disturbing is the discovery that many of those who experienced sexual abuse in the residential schools inflicted such abuse upon their own children when they returned to their aboriginal communities.

36 Bertha Wilson, 'Law in Society: The Principle of Sexual Equality,' *Manitoba Law Journal 13* (1983), 225.

37 See Louise Elliott and Sonia Verma, 'The Lost People,' *Toronto Star* 29, 30 April, and 1 May 2000.

38 See Louise Elliott and Sonia Verma, 'Natives' plight sparks outrage,' *Toronto Star* 1 May 2000, A1 and A6–7.

39 'Our silence hurts native people,' *Toronto Star*, 30 April 2000, A12. The *Star* followed up on 23–24 May 2000 with a two-part series by Kelly Toughill, 'Labrador's Innu: Quest for survival,' pointing to the problems created because these Indian bands are not governed by the Indian Act.

CHAPTER 15

1 Smart says there are three purposes served by a corporate collection: 'to enhance the work environment, help mould the corporate identity and support the arts in Canada,' quoted in Thomas Hirschmann, 'The making of a corporate collection,' *National Post* 15 January 2000. Smart takes enormous personal pleasure in the art works displayed throughout Osler's Toronto offices and is eager to show them to visitors. For several months before the official unveiling at the Supreme Court, the Wilson portrait hung in the main reception area at Oslers; there was regret expressed by lawyers and staff alike when it was removed.

2 Stephen Smart, 'Remarks of Stephen Smart on the Unofficial Toronto Unveiling of the Portrait of Bertha Wilson at the Office of Osler, Hoskin & Harcourt,' 28 June 1999.

3 Oslers had thirty-one lawyers in this practice group with some counsel drawn from intersecting areas of intellectual property, tax, corporate, and other practice areas as necessary.

4 See Bertha Wilson, 'Reflections of a Sitter,' unpublished notes prepared for Mary Lennox Hourd, summer 1999.

5 Through one of those quirks of fortuity which the Wilsons enjoy so much, the Hourds' former red-brick neo-Georgian house where the portrait was painted was originally built in 1931 for the Tory family which founded another of the great Toronto law firms, and the Hourds purchased it from John Tory in 1992.

6 Wilson, 'Reflections of a Sitter.'

7 Bertha Wilson, 'Law as Large as Life,' in *Speeches*, 684.

8 James MacPherson, 'Canadian Constitutional Law and Madame Justice Bertha Wilson – Patriot, Visionary and Heretic,' *Dalhousie Law Journal* 15, no.1 (1992), 239. The written text fails to convey the dynamic energy and spontaneity with which MacPherson delivered this speech.

Select Bibliography

The original thesis upon which this biography is based ran to over one thousand manuscript pages, a quarter of which were single-spaced notes. In the course of editing the manuscript for publication, some of the detailed case analysis had to be cut and the notes drastically reduced. What follows is a listing of a few of the key texts used during the research for this biography. For those readers who want a more complete discussion of these sources, the three volumes of the original thesis are available at the Bora Laskin Law Library, University of Toronto, and may be borrowed with the written permission of the author by contacting that library.

Anderson, Ellen Mary. 'Enlightened Postmodernism: Scottish Influences on Canada's Legal Pluralism.' LL.M. dissertation, Graduate Department of Law, University of Toronto, 1998.
Andrews, Allen. *The Scottish Canadians*. Toronto: Van Nostrand Reinhold, 1981.
Aristotle. *Rhetoric*, trans. and ed. by W.F. Ross, *The Works of Aristotle*, vol. 2. Oxford: Clarendon Press, 1924.
– *The Nicomachean Ethics*, trans. and with introduction by David Ross. Oxford and New York: Oxford University Press, 1980.
Baar, Carl, and Perry S. Millar. *Judicial Administration in Canada*. Toronto: Institute of Public Administration of Canada, 1981.
Baier, Annette C. 'Hume, the Women's Moral Theorist?,' in Eva Feder Kittay and Diane T. Meyers, eds., *Women and Moral Theory*. Savage, MD: Rowan and Littlefield, 1987.

– *A Progress of Sentiments: Reflections on Hume's Treatise*. Cambridge, Mass.: Harvard University Press, 1991.

Beattie, David. *Talking Heads and the Supremes*. Toronto: Carswell, 1990.

Beiner, Ronald. *Political Judgment*. Chicago: University of Chicago Press, 1983

Bertens Hans. 'The Postmodern Weltanschauung and its Relation to Modernism: An Introductory Survey,' in Douwe Fokkema and Hans Bertens, eds., *Approaching Postmodernism*. Philadelphia: John Benjamins Co., 1984.

Cairns, Alan C. *Citizens Plus: Aboriginal Peoples and the Canadian State*. Vancouver: University of British Columbia Press, 2000.

Campbell, Wilfred, *The Scotsman in Canada*, vol. 2. London: Musson Book Co., n.d., *ca*. 1880, 1981.

Cole, Curtis. *Osler, Hoskin & Harcourt: Portrait of a Partnership*. Toronto: McGraw-Hill Ryerson, 1995.

Cornell, Drucilla. *Beyond Accommodation: Ethical Feminism, Deconstruction, and the Law*. New York and London: Routledge, 1991.

Daiches, David, Peter Jones, and Jean Jones, eds. *A Hotbed of Genius, The Scottish Enlightenment, 1730–1970*. Edinburgh: Edinburgh University Press, 1986.

Davie, George Elder. *The Democratic Intellect: Scotland and the Universities in the Nineteenth Century*. Edinburgh: Edinburgh University Press, 1961.

– *A Passion for Ideas: Essays on the Scottish Enlightenment*. Edinburgh: Polygon Press, 1994.

Derrida, Jacques. *The Languages of Criticism and the Sciences of Man: The Structuralist Controversy*. Baltimore, MD: Johns Hopkins University Press, 1970.

Fish, Stanley. *Doing What Comes Naturally*. Durham, NC, and London: Duke University Press, 1989.

Flanagan, Tom. *First Nations? Second Thoughts*. Montreal and Kingston: McGill-Queen's University Press, 2000.

Frug, Mary Jo. 'Postmodern Legal Feminism.' *Harvard Law Review* 105 (1992).

Fulford, Robert. *The Triumph of Narrative: Storytelling in the Age of Mass Culture*. Toronto, Anansi, 1999.

Gilligan, Carol. *In a Different Voice: Psychological Theory and Women's Development*. Cambridge, Mass.: Harvard University Press, 1982.

Gwyn, Richard. *Nationalism without Walls: The Unbearable Lightness of Being Canadian*. Toronto: McClelland and Stewart, 1995.

Hont, Istvan, and Michael Ignatieff. eds. *Wealth and Virtue, The Shaping of Political Economy in the Scottish Enlightenment*. Cambridge: Cambridge University Press, 1983.

Hume, David. *A Treatise of Human Nature*. Oxford: Oxford University Press, 1978.

Hutcheon, Linda. *A Poetics of Postmodernism: History, Theory, Fiction.* New York and London: Routledge, 1988.

– *The Politics of Postmodernism.* New York and London: Routledge, 1989.

Hutchinson, Allan C. *Waiting for Coraf.* Toronto: University of Toronto Press, 1995.

Johnstone, Ian. 'Treaty Interpretation: The Authority of Interpretive Communities.' *Michigan Journal of International Law* 12 (1991).

Ignatieff, Michael. *The Rights Revolution.* Toronto: Anansi, 2000.

Kingwell, Mark. 'Politics and the Polite Society in the Scottish Enlightenment.' *Historical Reflections / Reflexions Historiques* 19, no.3 (1993).

– *A Civil Tongue: Justice, Dialogue and the Politics of Pluralism.* University Park, Penn.: Penn State University Press, 1995.

– *Better Living: In Pursuit of Happiness from Plato to Prozac.* Toronto: Penguin Books, 1998.

– *The World We Want: Virtue, Vice and the Good Citizen.* Toronto: Viking, 2000.

Knafla, Louis A., and Susan W.S. Binnie. 'Beyond the State: Law and Legal Pluralism in the Making of Modern Societies,' in Knafla and Binnie, eds., *Law, Society, and the State.* Toronto: University of Toronto Press, 1995.

Lyotard, Jean-François. *The Postmodern Condition: A Report on Knowledge,* trans. Geoff Bennington and Brian Massumi. Minneapolis: University of Minnesota Press, 1979.

Malloy, Robin Paul, and Jerry Evensky. *Adam Smith and the Philosophy of Law and Economics.* Dordrecht: Kluwer Academic Publishers, 1994.

McCormick, Peter. *Canada's Courts.* Toronto: James Lorimer, 1994.

McKay, Ian. *The Quest of the Folk, Antimodernism and Cultural Selection in Twentieth-Century Nova Scotia.* Montreal and Kingston: McGill-Queen's University Press, 1994.

McKillop, A.B. *A Disciplined Intelligence: Critical Inquiry and Canadian Thought in the Victorian Era.* Toronto: University of Toronto Press, 1987.

Moore, Christopher. *The Law Society of Upper Canada and Ontario's Lawyers, 1797–1997.* Toronto: University of Toronto Press, 1997.

Morton, F.L., and Rainer Knopff. *Charter Politics.* Toronto: Nelson Press, 1992.

– *The Charter Revolution and the Court Party.* Peterborough, Ontario: Broadview Press, 2000.

Posner, Richard. *Economic Analysis of Law.* Boston: Little Brown, 1972.

Rattray, W.J. *The Scot in North America,* vol. 4. Toronto: Maclear & Co., 1880.

Reid, W. Stanford. *The Scottish Tradition in Canada.* Toronto: McClelland and Stewart, 1976.

Rendall, Jane. *The Origins of the Scottish Enlightenment, 1707–1776.* New York: St.Martin's Press, 1978.

Rhode, Deborah. *Justice and Gender*. Cambridge, Mass.: Harvard University Press, 1989,

Rorty Richard. 'Human Rights, Rationality and Sentimentality,' in Stephen Shute and Susan Hurley, eds., *On Human Rights: The Oxford Amnesty Lectures*. New York: Basic Books, 1993.

Saul, John Ralston. *The Unconscious Civilization*. Toronto: House and Anansi Press, 1995.

- *Reflections of a Siamese Twin: Canada at the End of the Twentieth Century*. Toronto: Viking, 1997.

Scales, Ann. 'The Emergence of Feminist Jurisprudence: An Essay.' *Yale Law Journal* 95 (1986).

Smart, Stephen, and Michael Coyle, eds. *Aboriginal Issues Today*. North Vancouver: Self-Counsel Press, 1996.

Smith, Adam. *The Theory of Moral Sentiment*. Glasgow Edition of the Works and Correspondence of Adam Smith. Oxford: Oxford University Press, 1976.

- *Lectures on Jurisprudence* (1766), ed. by R.L. Meek, D.D. Raphael, and P.G. Stein. Oxford: Oxford University Press, 1978.

- *An Inquiry into the Nature and Causes of Wealth*. 2 vols. Indianapolis: Liberty Press, 1981.

Smith, Barbara Herrnstein. *Contingencies of Value: Alternative Perspectives for Critical Theory*. Cambridge, Mass.: Harvard University Press, 1991.

- *Belief and Resistance: Dynamics of Contemporary Intellectual Controversy*. Cambridge, Mass.: Harvard University Press, 1997.

Smith, Melvin H. *Our Home or Native Land*. Altona, Man: Friesen Printers, 1995.

Smith, T.B. *British Justice: The Scottish Contribution*. London: Stevens and Sons, 1961.

Taylor, Charles. *Sources of the Self: The Making of the Modern Identity*. Cambridge: Cambridge University Press, [need date]

- 'The Politics of Recognition,' in Any Guttman, ed., *Multiculturalism: Examining the Politics of Recognition*. Princeton: Princeton University Press, 1994.

Trebilcock, Michael J. *The Limits of Freedom of Contract*. Cambridge, Mass.: Harvard University Press, 1993.

Tronto, Joan. *Moral Boundaries*. New York and London: Routledge, 1993.

Walker, Lenore W. *The Battered Woman Syndrome*. New York: Harper & Row, 1979.

Index

1995   David Williams, *Just Lawyers: Seven Portraits*
       Hamar Foster and John McLaren, eds., *Essays in the History of Canadian Law: Volume VI – British Columbia and the Yukon*
       W.H. Morrow, ed., *Northern Justice: The Memoirs of Mr Justice William G. Morrow*
       Beverley Boissery, *A Deep Sense of Wrong: The Treason Trials and Transportation to New South Wales of Lower Canadian Rebels after the 1838 Rebellion*
1996   Carol Wilton, ed., *Essays in the History of Canadian Law: Volume VII – Inside the Law: Canadian Law Firms in Historical Perspective*
       William Kaplan, *Bad Judgment: The Case of Mr Justice Leo A. Landreville*
       F. Murray Greenwood and Barry Wright, eds., *Canadian State Trials: Volume I – Law, Politics, and Security Measures, 1608–1837*
1997   James W. St.G. Walker, *'Race,' Rights, and the Law in the Supreme Court of Canada: Historical Case Studies*
       Lori Chambers, *Married Women and Property Law in Victorian Ontario*
       Patrick Brode, *Casual Slaughters and Accidental Judgments: Canadian War Crimes and Prosecutions, 1944–1948*
       Ian Bushnell, *A History of the Federal Court of Canada, 1875–1992*
1998   Sidney Harring, *White Man's Law: Native People in Nineteenth-Century Canadian Jurisprudence*
       Peter Oliver, *'Terror to Evil-Doers': Prisons and Punishments in Nineteenth-Century Ontario*
1999   Constance Backhouse, *Colour-Coded: A Legal History of Racism in Canada, 1900–1950*
       G. Blaine Baker and Jim Phillips, eds., *Essays in the History of Canadian Law: Volume VIII – In Honour of R.C.B. Risk*
       Richard W. Pound, *Chief Justice W.R. Jackett: By the Law of the Land*
       David Vanek, *Fulfilment: Memoirs of a Criminal Court Judge*
2000   Barry Cahill, *The Thousandth Man: A Biography of James McGregor Stewart*
       A.B. McKillop, *The Spinster and the Prophet: Florence Deeks, H.G. Wells, and the Mystery of the Purloined Past*
       Beverley Boissery and F. Murray Greenwood, *Uncertain Justice: Canadian Women and Capital Punishment*
       Bruce Ziff, *Unforeseen Legacies: Reuben Wells Leonard and the Leonard Foundation Trust*
2001   Ellen Anderson, *Judging Bertha Wilson: Law as Large as Life*
       Judy Fudge and Eric Tucker, *Labour before the Law: The Regulation of Workers' Collective Action in Canada, 1900–1948*
       Laurel Sefton MacDowell, *Renegade Lawyer: The Life of J.L. Cohen*